ULTIMATE GUIDE TO GRILLING

TASTE OF HOME BOOKS • RDA ENTHUSIAST BRANDS, LLC • MILWAUKEE, WI

Taste of Home

EDITORIAL

Editor-in-Chief: Catherine Cassidy
Creative Director: Howard Greenberg
Editorial Operations Director: Kerri Balliet

Managing Editor, Print & Digital Books: Mark Hagen
Associate Creative Director: Edwin Robles Jr.

Editor: Christine Rukavena
Art Director: Raeann Sundholm
Layout Designer: Courtney Lovetere
Editorial Production Manager: Dena Ahlers
Editorial Production Coordinator: Jill Banks
Copy Chief: Deb Warlaumont Mulvey
Copy Editor: Mary-Liz Shaw
Contributing Copy Editors: Kristin Sutter, Valerie Phillips
Editorial Intern: Michael Welch
Business Analyst, Content Tools: Amanda Harmatys
Content Operations Assistant: Shannon Stroud
Editorial Services Administrator: Marie Brannon

Food Editors: Gina Nistico; James Schend; Peggy Woodward, RDN
Recipe Editors: Sue Ryon (lead); Mary King; Irene Yeh

Test Kitchen & Food Styling Manager: Sarah Thompson
Test Cooks: Nicholas Iverson (lead), Matthew Hass, Lauren Knoelke
Food Stylists: Kathryn Conrad (lead), Leah Rekau, Shannon Roum
Prep Cooks: Bethany Van Jacobson (lead), Megumi Garcia, Melissa Hansen
Culinary Team Assistant: Megan Behr

Photography Director: Stephanie Marchese
Photographers: Dan Roberts, Jim Wieland
Photographer/Set Stylist: Grace Natoli Sheldon
Set Stylists: Melissa Franco, Stacey Genaw, Dee Dee Jacq

Editorial Business Manager: Kristy Martin
Editorial Business Associate: Samantha Lea Stoeger

BUSINESS

Vice President, Group Publisher: Kirsten Marchioli
Publisher: Donna Lindskog
General Manager, Taste of Home Cooking School: Erin Puariea

TRUSTED MEDIA BRANDS, INC.

President and Chief Executive Officer: Bonnie Kintzer
Chief Financial Officer/Chief Operating Officer: Howard Halligan
Chief Revenue Officer: Richard Sutton
Chief Marketing Officer: Alec Casey
Chief Digital Officer: Vince Errico
Chief Technology Officer: Aneel Tejwaney
Senior Vice President, Global HR & Communications:
Phyllis E. Gebhardt, SPHR; SHRM-SCP
Vice President, Digital Content & Audience Development: Diane Dragan
Vice President, Business Development: Beth Gorry
Vice President, Financial Planning & Analysis: William Houston
Publishing Director, Books: Debra Polansky
Vice President, Consumer Marketing Planning: Jim Woods

For other Taste of Home books and products, visit us at tasteofhome.com.

International Standard Book Number: 978-1-61765-492-3
Library of Congress Control Number: 2015948970

Pictured on the cover (clockwise from left):
Peppered Ribeye Steaks, p. 289; Barbecued Burgers, p. 124;
Peppers and Zucchini in Foil, p. 39; Chicken & Vegetable Kabobs, p. 178
Pictured on back cover (left to right):
Mushroom Bacon Bites, p. 12; Ultimate Grilled Pork Chop, p. 215;
Cookout Caramel S'mores, p. 263

Printed in China.
1 3 5 7 9 10 8 6 4 2

LIKE US
facebook.com/tasteofhome

TWEET US
@tasteofhome

FOLLOW US
pinterest.com/taste_of_home

SHOP WITH US
shoptasteofhome.com

SHARE A RECIPE
tasteofhome.com/submit

GRILLED FAJITAS,
PAGE 139

CHICKEN & CARAMELIZED
ONION GRILLED CHEESE, PAGE 62

BACON-WRAPPED
CORN, PAGE 41

PEACH-CHIPOTLE BABY
BACK RIBS, PAGE 210

CONTENTS

LIP-SMACKIN' BBQ CHICKEN,
PAGE 181, FIRE BEEF, PAGE 160, AND
ULTIMATE GRILLED PORK CHOP, PAGE 215

Get Ready to Grill!

You just can't beat the satisfaction of a flame-broiled classic. From meaty ribs grilled to perfection and slathered in sauce to juicy cheeseburgers made to order and piled high with toppings, the thrill of the grill never disappoints.

Now you can be the barbecue king you always knew you could be with **Ultimate Guide to Grilling!** Inside you'll find 466 stick-to-your-ribs favorites sure to impress. Whether you're starting up the grill for a fast weeknight dinner or charbroiling an entire menu for a Saturday night party, the fiery ideas found here promise to secure your spot as charbroil master.

GRILLED SEASONED SHRIMP, PAGE 17

SOUTHWEST BURGERS, PAGE 113

HONEY-MUSTARD BRATS, PAGE 108

SOUTHWESTERN CATFISH, PAGE 243

DIG IN!

Inside this incredible collection, you'll find plenty of mouthwatering steaks, juicy burgers, fiery chicken entrees and enough barbecued pork recipes to carry you through grilling season. You'll also discover fast side dishes that make the most of your time at the grill as well as easy appetizers, sweet desserts, and tangy sauces and rubs that will have everyone asking for your secrets.

Scattered throughout the book, the following At-a-Glance Icons point out dishes that grill up quickly and easily.

⑤ INGREDIENTS
Create these specialties with just a few items.

FAST FIX ▷
Fix a memorable meal in 30 minutes or less.

You'll always find time to barbecue with **Ultimate Guide to Grilling.** So what are you waiting for? Fire up a finger-licking favorite today!

> **BONUS CHAPTER**
> *Like to take your thrill of the grill on the road?* Turn to the special section, Tailgate Favorites, on page 284! You'll find more than 40 recipes and tips to make your tailgate the most memorable yet!

**HOT DOG SLIDERS WITH
MANGO-PINEAPPLE SALSA, PAGE 20**

SOUTHWEST HUMMUS, PAGE 14

VERY VEGGIE APPETIZER PIZZAS, PAGE 26

GRILLED WING ZINGERS, PAGE 19

CROWD-PLEASING APPETIZERS

Nothing gets the party started like a **charbroiled bite.** Turn to your grill for some saucy wings, beefy skewers and other **smoky specialties.** Not only are these hearty appetizers sure to impress and satisfy your gang, but they're guaranteed to jump-start the **good times!**

CORN SALSA

CORN SALSA

This colorful salsa is worth the extra time it takes to grill the ears of corn. It's great with chips, but the flavor goes well with barbecued meats, too.
—**NANCY HORSBURGH** EVERETT, ON

PREP: 30 MIN. • **GRILL:** 20 MIN. + COOLING
MAKES: ABOUT 2½ CUPS

- 2 **medium ears sweet corn in husks**
- 2 **medium tomatoes, chopped**
- 1 **small onion, chopped**
- 2 **tablespoons minced fresh cilantro**
- 1 **tablespoon lime juice**
- 1 **tablespoon finely chopped green pepper**
- 1 **tablespoon finely chopped sweet red pepper**
- 1 **teaspoon minced seeded jalapeno pepper**
- ¼ **teaspoon salt**
   Dash pepper
   Tortilla chips

1. Peel back husks of corn but don't remove; remove silk. Replace husks and tie with kitchen string. Place corn in a bowl and cover with water; soak for 20 minutes. Drain. Grill corn, covered, over medium-high heat for 20-35 minutes or until husks are blackened and corn is tender, turning several times. Cool.

2. Remove corn from cobs and place in a bowl. Add tomatoes, onion, cilantro, lime juice, peppers, salt and pepper. Serve with tortilla chips.

NOTE *Wear disposable gloves when cutting hot peppers; the oils can burn skin. Avoid touching your face.*

GRILLED CHEESE & TOMATO FLATBREADS

I discovered this combination of grilled pizza and a cheesy flatbread years ago. It's a great appetizer, side or even a meatless main dish. Yum!

—TINA MIRILOVICH JOHNSTOWN, PA

PREP: 30 MIN. • **GRILL:** 5 MIN.
MAKES: 2 FLATBREADS (12 SERVINGS EACH)

- 1 package (8 ounces) cream cheese, softened
- ⅔ cup grated Parmesan cheese, divided
- 2 tablespoons minced fresh parsley, divided
- 1 tablespoon minced chives
- 2 garlic cloves, minced
- ½ teaspoon minced fresh thyme
- ¼ teaspoon salt
- ¼ teaspoon pepper
- 1 tube (13.8 ounces) refrigerated pizza crust
- 2 tablespoons olive oil
- 3 medium tomatoes, thinly sliced

1. In a small bowl, beat the cream cheese, ⅓ cup Parmesan cheese, 1 tablespoon parsley, chives, garlic, thyme, salt and pepper until blended.

2. Unroll pizza crust and cut in half. On a lightly floured surface, roll out each portion into a 12x6-in. rectangle; brush each side with oil. Grill, covered, over medium heat for 1-2 minutes or until bottoms are lightly browned. Remove from the grill.

3. Spread grilled sides with cheese mixture. Sprinkle with remaining Parmesan cheese; top with tomatoes. Return to the grill. Cover and cook for 2-3 minutes or until crust is lightly browned and cheese is melted, rotating halfway through cooking to ensure an evenly browned crust. Sprinkle with remaining parsley.

SWEET SRIRACHA WINGS

SWEET SRIRACHA WINGS

Serve my fiery hot wings on game day or anytime friends and family get together. If you don't like things very sweet, simply add the honey to taste.

—LOGAN HOLSER CLARKSTON, MI

PREP: 20 MIN. + MARINATING • **GRILL:** 15 MIN.
MAKES: 1 DOZEN

- 12 chicken wings (about 3 pounds)
- 1 tablespoon canola oil
- 2 teaspoons ground coriander
- ½ teaspoon garlic salt
- ¼ teaspoon pepper

SAUCE
- ¼ cup butter, cubed
- ½ cup orange juice
- ⅓ cup Sriracha Asian hot chili sauce
- 3 tablespoons honey
- 2 tablespoons lime juice
- ¼ cup chopped fresh cilantro

1. Place chicken wings in a large bowl. Mix oil, coriander, garlic salt and pepper; add to wings and toss to coat. Refrigerate, covered, 2 hours or overnight.

2. For sauce, in a small saucepan, melt butter. Stir in orange juice, chili sauce, honey and lime juice until blended.

3. Grill wings, covered, over medium heat 15-18 minutes or until juices run clear, turning occasionally; brush with some of the sauce during the last 5 minutes of grilling.

4. Transfer chicken to a large bowl; add remaining sauce and toss to coat. Sprinkle with cilantro.

JALAPENO
CHICKEN WRAPS

JALAPENO CHICKEN WRAPS

These easy appetizers are always a hit at parties! Zesty strips of chicken and bits of onion sit in jalapeno halves that are wrapped in bacon and grilled. Serve them with blue cheese or ranch salad dressing for dipping.

—LESLIE BUENZ TINLEY PARK, IL

PREP: 15 MIN. • **GRILL:** 20 MIN.
MAKES: 2½ DOZEN

- 1 **pound boneless skinless chicken breasts**
- 1 **tablespoon garlic powder**
- 1 **tablespoon onion powder**
- 1 **tablespoon pepper**
- 2 **teaspoons seasoned salt**
- 1 **teaspoon paprika**
- 1 **small onion, cut into strips**
- 15 **jalapeno peppers, halved and seeded**
- 1 **pound sliced bacon, halved widthwise**
  Blue cheese salad dressing

1. Cut chicken into 2x1½-in. strips. In a large resealable plastic bag, combine the garlic powder, onion powder, pepper, seasoned salt and paprika; add chicken and shake to coat. Put a chicken and onion strip in each jalapeno half. Wrap each with a piece of bacon and secure with toothpicks.

2. Grill, uncovered, over indirect medium heat for 18-20 minutes or until chicken is no longer pink and bacon is crisp, turning once. Serve with blue cheese dressing.

NOTE *Wear disposable gloves when cutting hot peppers; the oils can burn skin. Avoid touching your face.*

GREEK SANDWICH BITES

FAST FIX
GREEK SANDWICH BITES

Here's a grilled appetizer that tastes just like traditional spanakopita but much less work to assemble.

—LYNN SCULLY RANCHO SANTA FE, CA

START TO FINISH: 25 MIN.
MAKES: 16 APPETIZERS

- 1 **medium onion, finely chopped**
- 1 **tablespoon olive oil**
- 2 **garlic cloves, minced**
- 1 **pound fresh baby spinach**
- 1 **cup (4 ounces) crumbled feta cheese**
- ¼ **cup pine nuts, toasted**
- ¼ **teaspoon salt**
- ¼ **teaspoon pepper**
- ⅛ **teaspoon ground nutmeg**
- 8 **slices Italian bread (½ inch thick)**
- 4 **teaspoons butter, softened**

1. In a large nonstick skillet, saute onion in oil until tender. Add garlic; cook 1 minute longer. Stir in the spinach; cook and stir until wilted.

Drain. Stir in the feta, pine nuts, salt, pepper and nutmeg.

2. Spread over four bread slices; top with remaining bread. Spread outsides of sandwiches with butter. Grill, uncovered, over medium heat for 3-4 minutes or until bread is browned and cheese is melted, turning once. Cut each sandwich into quarters.

 **GRILL SKILL**

Grilling appetizers is a wonderful way to get summer parties sizzling. Before grilling, however, be sure the foods have reached cool room temperature. Cold foods, particularly those in bite-size portions, may burn on the outside before the interiors are cooked.

TANDOORI CHICKEN KABOBS

When I prepare this recipe it brings back memories of my childhood and rich Indian heritage. The chicken has a nice spice level, but if you like your food on the mild side, then reduce each spice a little.

—**RAVINDER AUJLA** GRIDLEY, CA

PREP: 30 MIN. + MARINATING • **GRILL:** 10 MIN.
MAKES: 6 SERVINGS

- 1¼ cups plain yogurt
- ⅓ cup chopped onion
- 2 tablespoons lemon juice
- 2 garlic cloves, minced
- 2 teaspoons garam masala
- 2 teaspoons minced fresh gingerroot
- 1 teaspoon salt
- 1 teaspoon cayenne pepper
- 3 drops yellow food coloring, optional
- 3 drops red food coloring, optional
- 2 pounds boneless skinless chicken breasts, cut into 1-inch cubes
- 2 teaspoons minced fresh cilantro
- 1 medium lemon, cut into six wedges

1. In a large resealable plastic bag, combine the first 10 ingredients. Add the chicken; seal bag and turn to coat. Refrigerate for at least 8 hours or overnight.

2. Drain and discard marinade. Thread chicken onto six metal or soaked wooden skewers. Moisten a paper towel with cooking oil; using long-handled tongs, lightly coat the grill rack.

3. Grill chicken, covered, over medium heat or broil 4 in. from the heat for 10-15 minutes or until juices run clear, turning occasionally.

4. Sprinkle with cilantro; garnish with lemon wedges.

NOTE *Look for garam masala in the spice aisle.*

MUSHROOM BACON BITES

⑤ INGREDIENTS FAST FIX
MUSHROOM BACON BITES

When we have a big cookout, these tasty bites are always a hit. They're easy to assemble and brush with prepared barbecue sauce.

—**GINA ROESNER** ASHLAND, MO

START TO FINISH: 20 MIN.
MAKES: 2 DOZEN

- 24 medium fresh mushrooms
- 12 bacon strips, halved
- 1 cup barbecue sauce

1. Wrap each mushroom with a piece of bacon; secure with a toothpick. Thread onto metal or soaked wooden skewers; brush with barbecue sauce.

2. Grill, uncovered, over indirect medium heat for 10-15 minutes or until the bacon is crisp and the mushrooms are tender, turning and basting occasionally with remaining barbecue sauce.

⑤ INGREDIENTS FAST FIX
GRILLED PROSCIUTTO ASPARAGUS

After tasting an asparagus appetizer at a lovely restaurant, I created my version of it to enjoy at home.

—**MICHELE MERLINO** EXETER, RI

START TO FINISH: 30 MIN.
MAKES: ABOUT 2 DOZEN

- ½ pound thinly sliced prosciutto
- 1 log (4 ounces) fresh goat cheese
- 1 pound fresh asparagus, trimmed

1. Cut prosciutto slices in half; spread with cheese. Wrap a prosciutto piece around each asparagus spear; secure ends with toothpicks. Using long-handled tongs, moisten a paper towel with cooking oil and lightly coat the grill rack.

2. Grill, covered, over medium heat for 6-8 minutes or until prosciutto is crisp, turning once. Discard toothpicks.

(5) INGREDIENTS FAST FIX ▶

NECTARINE & GOAT CHEESE CROSTINI

At our house, we love the summery taste of sweet grilled nectarines and fresh basil over goat cheese. I can usually find all the ingredients at the farmers market.

—**BRANDY HOLLINGSHEAD** GRASS VALLEY, CA

START TO FINISH: 25 MIN.
MAKES: 1 DOZEN

- ½ cup balsamic vinegar
- 1 tablespoon olive oil
- 12 slices French bread baguette (¼ inch thick)
- 2 medium nectarines, halved
- ¼ cup fresh goat cheese, softened
- ¼ cup loosely packed basil leaves, thinly sliced

1. In a small saucepan, bring vinegar to a boil; cook 10-15 minutes or until liquid is reduced to 3 tablespoons. Remove from heat.
2. Brush oil over both sides of baguette slices. Grill, uncovered, over medium heat until golden brown on both sides. Grill nectarines 45-60 seconds on each side or until tender and lightly browned. Cool slightly.
3. Spread goat cheese over toasts. Cut nectarines into thick slices; arrange over cheese. Drizzle with balsamic syrup; sprinkle with basil. Serve immediately.

NECTARINE & GOAT CHEESE CROSTINI

HAWAIIAN BEEF SLIDERS

Sweet and savory with just a hint of heat, these dynamite burgers are packed with flavor. If you ask me, pineapple and bacon are a perfect match.

—**MARY RELYEA** CANASTOTA, NY

PREP: 30 MIN. + MARINATING • **GRILL:** 10 MIN.
MAKES: 6 SERVINGS

- 1 can (20 ounces) unsweetened crushed pineapple
- 1 teaspoon pepper
- ¼ teaspoon salt
- 1½ pounds lean ground beef (90% lean)
- ¼ cup reduced-sodium soy sauce
- 2 tablespoons ketchup
- 1 tablespoon white vinegar
- 2 garlic cloves, minced
- ¼ teaspoon crushed red pepper flakes
- 18 miniature whole wheat buns
  Baby spinach leaves
- 3 center-cut bacon strips, cooked and crumbled
  Sliced jalapeno peppers, optional

1. Drain pineapple, reserving juice and 1½ cups pineapple (save remaining pineapple for another use). In a large bowl, combine ¾ cup reserved crushed pineapple, pepper and salt. Crumble beef over mixture and mix well. Shape into 18 patties; place in two 11x7-in. dishes.
2. In a small bowl, combine soy sauce, ketchup, vinegar, garlic, pepper flakes and reserved pineapple juice. Pour half of marinade into each dish; cover and refrigerate 1 hour, turning once.
3. Drain and discard marinade. Moisten a paper towel with cooking oil; using long-handled tongs, coat grill rack lightly.
4. Grill patties, covered, over medium heat or broil 4 in. from heat 4-5 minutes on each side or until a thermometer reads 160° and juices run clear.
5. Grill buns, uncovered, 1-2 minutes or until toasted. Serve burgers on buns with spinach, remaining pineapple, bacon and jalapeno peppers if desired.

NOTE *If miniature whole wheat buns are not available in your area, you can also use whole wheat hot dog buns cut into thirds.*

SOUTHWEST HUMMUS

Not your ordinary hummus, this dip is a combination of two things I love—chick peas and Southwestern flavors. You can substitute three-fourths cup frozen corn, thawed, for the grilled corn.
—**CHERAY BUCKALEW** CUMBERLAND, MD

PREP: 15 MIN. • **GRILL:** 20 MIN.
MAKES: 2 CUPS

- 1 **medium ear sweet corn, husk removed**
- 1 **can (15 ounces) garbanzo beans or chickpeas, rinsed and drained**
- 2 **tablespoons minced fresh cilantro**
- 1 **teaspoon ground cumin**
- ½ **teaspoon chili powder**
- ¼ **teaspoon salt**
- ¼ **teaspoon pepper**
- ½ **cup chopped roasted sweet red peppers**
- ¼ **cup canned fire-roasted diced tomatoes**
  Baked pita chips or assorted fresh vegetables

1. Grill corn, covered, over medium heat for 10-12 minutes or until tender, turning occasionally. Meanwhile, in a food processor, combine the beans, cilantro, cumin, chili powder, salt and pepper. Cover and process for 30 seconds or until blended. Transfer to a small bowl. Cover and refrigerate for at least 15 minutes.
2. Cut corn from cob. Add the corn, red peppers and tomatoes to bean mixture; mix well. Serve with pita chips or vegetables.

HONEY MUSTARD BACON-WRAPPED CHICKEN

These sweet-salty dippers go over big with kids and adults alike. Guests at my daughter's 13th birthday party couldn't get enough of the bacon-wrapped chicken and yummy sauce.

—KIM FORNI LACONIA, NH

PREP: 30 MIN. + MARINATING • **GRILL:** 10 MIN.
MAKES: 4 DOZEN (1½ CUPS SAUCE)

- 1 cup chicken broth
- ½ cup honey
- 2 tablespoons ground mustard
- ½ teaspoon salt
- ½ teaspoon dried rosemary, crushed
- ¼ teaspoon pepper
- 1½ pounds boneless skinless chicken breasts, cut into 1-inch cubes (about 48)

SAUCE
- 1 cup Dijon mustard
- ½ cup honey
- 4 teaspoons ground mustard
- ½ teaspoon dried rosemary, crushed

ASSEMBLY
- 16 bacon strips

1. In a small bowl, whisk the first six ingredients. Pour into a large resealable plastic bag. Add chicken; seal bag and turn to coat. Refrigerate 4 hours or overnight.
2. In a small bowl, combine sauce ingredients; set aside. Cut bacon strips crosswise into thirds. In a large skillet, cook bacon over medium heat until partially cooked but not crisp. Remove to paper towels to drain.
3. Drain chicken, discarding marinade. Wrap a bacon piece around each chicken piece; secure with a toothpick.
4. Moisten a paper towel with cooking oil; using long-handled tongs, rub on grill rack to coat lightly. Grill chicken, covered, over medium heat or broil 4 in. from heat 3-4 minutes on each side or until bacon is crisp and chicken is no longer pink. Serve with sauce.

⑤INGREDIENTS FAST FIX
ASIAN BEEF SLIDERS

My family loves orange chicken, but we don't eat it often because of the high sodium, fat and calories. These sliders remind us of our favorite takeout, only they're much healthier.

—MINDIE HILTON SUSANVILLE, CA

START TO FINISH: 30 MIN.
MAKES: 4 SERVINGS

- ½ cup orange marmalade, divided
- 2 teaspoons Thai chili sauce, divided
- 1 pound lean ground beef (90% lean)
- 2 slices reduced-fat Swiss cheese, quartered
- 8 slices whole wheat bread, toasted

1. In a large bowl, combine ¼ cup marmalade and 1 teaspoon chili sauce. Crumble beef over mixture and mix well. Shape into eight patties. Moisten paper towel with cooking oil; using long-handled tongs, coat grill rack.
2. Grill burgers, covered, over medium heat or broil 4 in. from the heat for 4-5 minutes on each side or until a thermometer reads 160° and juices run clear. Top with cheese; grill 1-2 minutes longer or until cheese is melted
3. Meanwhile, with a 2-in. round biscuit cutter, cut 16 circles from toasts. In a small microwave-safe bowl, combine remaining marmalade and chili sauce. Microwave for 20 seconds or until heated through.
4. Place burgers on toasts; top with marmalade mixture and remaining toasts.

⑤INGREDIENTS FAST FIX
GRILLED GREEK CROSTINI TOPPING

I got the idea for this quick and easy appetizer while on a vacation in Greece. It's nice for summer get-togethers and gives you a taste of Mediterranean food right in your own backyard.

—STEPHANIE PROEBSTING BARRINGTON, IL

START TO FINISH: 20 MIN.
MAKES: 8 SERVINGS

- 2 large vine-ripe tomatoes, halved and thinly sliced
- 1 package (8 ounces) feta cheese, halved lengthwise
- 3 teaspoons minced fresh oregano
- 3 teaspoons olive oil
  Ground pepper
  Sliced French bread baguette, toasted

1. Arrange a third of the tomato slices in a single layer on a double thickness of heavy-duty foil (about 12 in. square). Place half of the cheese over tomatoes; sprinkle with 1 teaspoon oregano and drizzle with 1 teaspoon oil. Sprinkle with a dash of pepper. Repeat layers.
2. Top with remaining tomato slices. Drizzle with remaining oil and sprinkle with remaining oregano and a dash of pepper. Fold foil around mixture and seal tightly.
3. Grill, covered, over medium heat for 8-10 minutes or until heated through. Open foil carefully to allow steam to escape. Transfer to a serving platter; serve with toasted baguette.

🍴 HOW-TO PREVENT STICKING

To oil a grill grate to prevent foods from sticking, fold a paper towel into a small pad and moisten it with cooking oil. Holding the pad with long-handled tongs, rub it over the grate.

GRILLED POTATO SKINS

JALAPENO QUAIL APPETIZERS

My husband quail hunts every season, and this recipe has become our favorite way to serve the poultry. The bacon keeps the meat from drying out, and the jalapeno lends a little zip. I sometimes serve these cute bundles as a main dish.

—**DIANA JOHNSTON** KINGSTON, OK

PREP: 15 MIN. + MARINATING • **GRILL:** 20 MIN.
MAKES: 1 DOZEN

- 2 large jalapeno peppers, halved lengthwise and seeded
- 12 boneless quail breasts (about 1 pound)
- 12 bacon strips
- 1 bottle (16 ounces) Italian salad dressing

1. Cut each jalapeno half into three long strips. Place a strip widthwise in the center of each quail breast; roll up from a short side. Wrap each with a bacon strip and secure with toothpicks.
2. Place in a large resealable plastic bag. Add salad dressing; seal bag and turn to coat. Refrigerate for 8 hours or overnight.
3. Drain and discard marinade. Grill appetizers, covered, over indirect medium heat for 16-20 minutes or until quail juices run clear and bacon is crisp, turning occasionally.
NOTE *Wear disposable gloves when cutting hot peppers; the oils can burn skin. Avoid touching your face.*

FAST FIX ▶

GRILLED POTATO SKINS

Everyone just loves these delicious appetizers! They're nice to serve outside when you invite friends over for a grilled meal. They remind me of the potato skins I've enjoyed at casual restaurants.

—**MITZI SENTIFF** ANNAPOLIS, MD

START TO FINISH: 30 MIN.
MAKES: 8 APPETIZERS

- 2 large baking potatoes
- 2 tablespoons butter, melted
- 2 teaspoons minced fresh rosemary or ½ teaspoon dried rosemary, crushed
- ½ teaspoon salt
- ½ teaspoon pepper
- 1 cup (4 ounces) shredded cheddar cheese
- 3 bacon strips, cooked and crumbled
- 2 green onions, chopped
  Sour cream

1. Cut each potato lengthwise into four wedges. Cut away the white portion, leaving ¼ in. on the potato skins. Place skins on a microwave-safe plate. Microwave, uncovered, on high for 8-10 minutes or until tender. Combine the butter, rosemary, salt and pepper; brush over both sides of potato skins.
2. Grill potatoes, skin side up, uncovered, over direct medium heat for 2-3 minutes or until lightly browned. Turn potatoes and position over indirect heat; grill 2 minutes longer. Top with cheese. Cover and grill 2-3 minutes longer or until cheese is melted. Sprinkle with bacon and onions. Serve with sour cream.
NOTE *This recipe was tested in a 1,100-watt microwave.*

GRILLED SEASONED SHRIMP

A marinade using balsamic vinegar, lemon juice and Italian dressing boosts the flavor of these grilled yet tender shrimp. Best of all, you can make them well before the party because they're served chilled.

—DIANE HARRISON MECHANICSBURG, PA

PREP: 10 MIN. • **GRILL:** 5 MIN. + CHILLING
MAKES: 4 SERVINGS

- 1½ **pounds uncooked large shrimp**
- 1 **small red onion, sliced and separated into rings**
- ¼ **cup Italian salad dressing**
- 2 **green onions, chopped**
- 2 **tablespoons lemon juice**
- 2 **tablespoons balsamic vinegar**
- 2 **tablespoons olive oil**
- 3 **garlic cloves, minced**
  Salt and coarsely ground pepper to taste, optional

1. Peel and devein shrimp, leaving tails intact if desired. Coat a grill rack with cooking spray before starting the grill.

2. Grill shrimp, covered, over indirect medium heat for 2-3 minutes on each side or until shrimp turn pink. Cool; cover and refrigerate until chilled.

3. In a large resealable plastic bag, combine the remaining ingredients; add shrimp. Seal bag and turn to coat; refrigerate for at least 2 hours. Serve with a slotted spoon.

GRILLED
SEASONED
SHRIMP

GRILLED WING ZINGERS

GRILLED WING ZINGERS

My husband fine-tuned this recipe, and the results were spectacular! These spicy-hot wings are true party pleasers. You can easily adjust the heat level by altering the amount of chili powder. The wings take a little time, but they're certainly worth it.

—**ANGELA ROSTER** GREENBACKVILLE, VA

PREP: 35 MIN. • **GRILL:** 35 MIN.
MAKES: ABOUT 6½ DOZEN

- 8 **pounds chicken wings**
- 1 **cup packed brown sugar**
- 1 **cup Louisiana-style hot sauce**
- ¼ **cup butter, cubed**
- 1 **tablespoon cider vinegar**
- ⅓ **cup sugar**
- ½ **cup Italian seasoning**
- ¼ **cup dried rosemary, crushed**
- ¼ **cup paprika**
- ¼ **cup chili powder**
- ¼ **cup pepper**
- 2 **tablespoons cayenne pepper**
- 1 **cup blue cheese salad dressing**
- ½ **cup ranch salad dressing**
  Celery sticks

1. Cut chicken wings into three sections; discard wing tip sections. Set wings aside.

2. In a small saucepan, bring brown sugar, hot sauce, butter and vinegar to a boil. Reduce heat; simmer, uncovered, 6-8 minutes or until butter is melted and sauce is heated through. Cool.

3. In a gallon-size resealable plastic bag, combine sugar and seasonings. Add chicken wings in batches; seal bag and toss to coat evenly.

4. Grill, covered, over indirect medium heat 35-45 minutes or until juices run clear, turning and basting occasionally with sauce.

5. In a small bowl, combine blue cheese and ranch salad dressing; serve with chicken wings and celery sticks.

NOTE *Uncooked chicken wing sections (wingettes) may be substituted for whole chicken wings.*

BRUSCHETTA FROM THE GRILL

BRUSCHETTA FROM THE GRILL

Dijon mustard, mayonnaise and oregano make a savory spread for chopped tomatoes, garlic and fresh basil in this fun twist on a favorite appetizer.

—**MARY NAFIS** CHINO, CA

PREP: 15 MIN. + CHILLING • **GRILL:** 5 MIN.
MAKES: 8-10 SERVINGS

- 1 **pound plum tomatoes (about 6), seeded and chopped**
- 1 **cup chopped celery or fennel bulb**
- ¼ **cup minced fresh basil**
- 3 **tablespoons balsamic vinegar**
- 3 **tablespoons olive oil**
- 3 **tablespoons Dijon mustard**
- 2 **garlic cloves, minced**
- ½ **teaspoon salt**

MAYONNAISE SPREAD
- ½ **cup mayonnaise**
- ¼ **cup Dijon mustard**
- 1 **tablespoon finely chopped green onion**
- 1 **garlic clove, minced**
- ¾ **teaspoon dried oregano**
- 1 **loaf (1 pound) French bread, cut into ½-inch slices**

1. In a large bowl, combine the first eight ingredients. Cover and refrigerate for at least 30 minutes. For mayonnaise spread, in a small bowl, combine the mayonnaise, mustard, onion, garlic and oregano; set aside.

2. Grill bread slices, uncovered, over medium-low heat for 1-2 minutes or until lightly toasted. Turn bread; spread with mayonnaise mixture. Grill 1-2 minutes longer or until bottoms are toasted. Drain tomato mixture; spoon over tops.

HOT DOG SLIDERS WITH
MANGO-PINEAPPLE SALSA

FAST FIX

HOT DOG SLIDERS WITH MANGO-PINEAPPLE SALSA

For parties, we shrink down lots of foods to slider size, including these quick hot dogs. Pile on the easy but irresistible fruit salsa for a burst of fresh flavor.

—**CAROLE RESNICK** CLEVELAND, OH

START TO FINISH: 30 MIN.
MAKES: 2 DOZEN (2 CUPS SALSA)

- 3 **tablespoons lime juice**
- 2 **tablespoons honey**
- ¼ **teaspoon salt**
- 1 **cup cubed fresh pineapple (½ inch)**
- 1 **cup cubed peeled mango (½ inch)**
- ¼ **cup finely chopped red onion**
- 2 **tablespoons finely chopped sweet red pepper**
- 12 **hot dogs**
- 12 **hot dog buns, split**

1. In a small bowl, whisk lime juice, honey and salt until blended. Add pineapple, mango, onion and pepper; toss to coat.

2. Grill hot dogs, covered, over medium heat or broil 4 in. from heat 7-9 minutes or until heated through, turning occasionally.

3. Place hot dogs in buns; cut each crosswise in half. Serve with fruit salsa.

 **GRILL SKILL**

To easily determine when the grill is at medium heat, carefully set your hand 4 inches over the heat source. If you can hold your hand above the heat without quickly pulling away for 4 seconds, the coals are at medium heat.

THAI STEAK SKEWERS

You'll feel like you're on an exotic vacation after one bite of these slightly spicy kabobs. Combining peanut butter and coconut milk creates a combination sure to wow everyone. There's no doubt you'll want seconds!

—AMY FRYE GOODYEAR, AZ

PREP: 20 MIN. + MARINATING • **GRILL:** 10 MIN.
MAKES: 16 SKEWERS (1⅓ CUPS SAUCE)

- ¼ cup packed brown sugar
- 2 tablespoons lime juice
- 2 tablespoons reduced-sodium soy sauce
- 1 tablespoon curry powder
- 1 teaspoon lemon juice
- 1 can (13.66 ounces) coconut milk, divided
- 1½ teaspoons crushed red pepper flakes, divided
- 2 pounds beef top sirloin steak, cut into ¼-inch slices
- 2 medium limes, halved and thinly sliced, optional
- ¼ cup creamy peanut butter
- 1 tablespoon chopped salted peanuts

1. In a large resealable plastic bag, combine the brown sugar, lime juice, soy sauce, curry powder, lemon juice, ¼ cup coconut milk and 1 teaspoon pepper flakes; add the steak. Seal bag and turn to coat. Refrigerate for 2-4 hours.
2. Drain and discard marinade. On 16 metal or soaked wooden skewers, alternately thread beef with lime slices if desired. Grill, covered, over medium-hot heat or broil 4-in. from the heat for 6-8 minutes or until meat reaches desired doneness, turning occasionally.
3. Meanwhile, in a small saucepan, combine the peanut butter, remaining coconut milk and pepper flakes. Cook and stir over medium heat until blended. Transfer to a small bowl; sprinkle with peanuts. Serve with steak skewers.

GRILLED LEEK DIP

(5) INGREDIENTS
GRILLED LEEK DIP

Smoky leeks from the grill add punch to this creamy appetizer served with veggies or crackers. If baby Vidalia onions are available, I use those.

—RAMONA PARRIS MARIETTA, GA

PREP: 10 MIN. • **GRILL:** 10 MIN. + CHILLING
MAKES: 1¼ CUPS

- 2 medium leeks
- 2 teaspoons olive oil
- ½ teaspoon salt, divided
- ¼ teaspoon pepper
- 2 cups (16 ounces) reduced-fat sour cream
- 2 tablespoons Worcestershire sauce
  Assorted fresh vegetables

1. Trim and discard dark green portions of leeks. Brush leeks with oil; sprinkle with ¼ teaspoon salt and pepper. Grill leeks, covered, over medium-high heat 8-10 minutes or until lightly charred and tender, turning occasionally. Cool slightly; chop leeks.
2. In a small bowl, combine sour cream, Worcestershire sauce and remaining salt; stir in leeks. Refrigerate, covered, 2 hours before serving. Serve with vegetables.

(5) INGREDIENTS FAST FIX
BLUE CHEESE & BACON STUFFED PEPPERS

Grilling is a huge summer highlight for my family, which is one reason we're such fans of this recipe. Whenever I put out a plate of these cute little appetizers, people come flocking.

—TARA CRUZ KERSEY, CO

START TO FINISH: 20 MIN.
MAKES: 1 DOZEN

- 3 medium sweet yellow, orange or red peppers
- 4 ounces cream cheese, softened
- ½ cup crumbled blue cheese
- 3 bacon strips, cooked and crumbled
- 1 green onion, thinly sliced

1. Cut peppers into quarters. Remove and discard stems and seeds. In a small bowl, mix cream cheese, blue cheese, bacon and green onion until blended.
2. Grill peppers, covered, over medium-high heat or broil 4 in. from heat 2-3 minutes on each side or until slightly charred.
3. Remove peppers from grill; fill each with about 1 tablespoon cheese mixture. Grill 2-3 minutes longer or until cheese is melted.

FAST FIX ▶

CHICKEN, MANGO & BLUE CHEESE TORTILLAS

Tortillas packed with chicken, mango and blue cheese make a light appetizer to welcome the summer season. We double or triple the ingredients for large parties.
—JOSEE LANZI NEW PORT RICHEY, FL

START TO FINISH: 30 MIN.
MAKES: 16 APPEITZERS

- 1 **boneless skinless chicken breast (8 ounces)**
- 1 **teaspoon blackened seasoning**
- ¾ **cup (6 ounces) plain yogurt**
- 1½ **teaspoons grated lime peel**
- 2 **tablespoons lime juice**
- ¼ **teaspoon salt**
- ⅛ **teaspoon pepper**
- 1 **cup finely chopped peeled mango**
- ⅓ **cup finely chopped red onion**
- 4 **flour tortillas (8 inches)**
- ½ **cup crumbled blue cheese**
- 2 **tablespoons minced fresh cilantro**

1. Moisten a paper towel with cooking oil; using long-handled tongs, rub on grill rack to coat lightly. Sprinkle chicken with blackened seasoning. Grill chicken, covered, over medium heat 6-8 minutes on each side or until a thermometer reads 165°.

2. Meanwhile, in a small bowl, mix yogurt, lime peel, lime juice, salt and pepper. Cool chicken slightly; finely chop and transfer to a small bowl. Stir in mango and onion.

3. Grill tortillas, uncovered, over medium heat 2-3 minutes or until puffed. Turn; top with chicken mixture and blue cheese. Grill, covered, 2-3 minutes longer or until bottoms of tortillas are lightly browned.

4. Drizzle with yogurt mixture; sprinkle with cilantro. Cut each tortilla into four wedges.

CHICKEN, MANGO & BLUE CHEESE TORTILLAS

SHRIMP POPS WITH PEANUT SAUCE

Take a trip to the Pacific Rim with these seafood bites. If you like, serve bottled Asian chili-garlic sauce as a second dip.

—**PETER HALFERTY** CORPUS CHRISTI, TX

PREP: 25 MIN. • **GRILL:** 10 MIN.
MAKES: 1 DOZEN (1½ CUPS SAUCE)

- 1 cup coconut milk
- ⅓ cup creamy peanut butter
- 3 tablespoons lime juice
- 1 tablespoon brown sugar
- 1 tablespoon soy sauce
- 1 teaspoon grated lime peel
- 1 teaspoon Sriracha Asian hot chili sauce or ½ teaspoon hot pepper sauce
- ½ teaspoon minced fresh gingerroot

POPS
- 1 pound ground pork
- ¾ pound uncooked large shrimp, peeled and deveined
- ½ cup fresh basil leaves
- ¼ cup panko (Japanese) bread crumbs
- 2 garlic cloves
- 1 tablespoon soy sauce
- ½ teaspoon pepper
- 12 sugar cane or soaked wooden skewers

1. In a small saucepan, combine the first eight ingredients. Bring to a boil; cook and stir for 2-3 minutes or until slightly thickened. Remove from the heat and keep warm.

2. Place the pork, shrimp, basil, bread crumbs, garlic, soy sauce and pepper in a food processor; cover and process until finely chopped. Shape into 12 oval patties; insert a soaked wooden skewer into each patty.

3. Grill, uncovered, over medium heat or broil 3-4 in. from the heat for 3-5 minutes on each side or until a meat thermometer reads 160° and juices run clear. Serve with sauce.

FIRE-ROASTED TOMATO SALSA

I've been making this for a few years now. Chipotle pepper gives it an added smoky kick. The recipe makes a big batch, but the salsa doesn't last a day in our house.

—**PAMELA PAULA** SPRING HILL, FL

PREP: 30 MIN. + CHILLING
MAKES: 4 CUPS

- 2 pounds tomatoes (about 6 medium)
- 1 jalapeno pepper
- ½ cup fresh cilantro leaves
- 2 green onions, cut into 2-inch pieces
- 4 garlic cloves, peeled
- 1 chipotle pepper in adobo sauce
- 1 can (4 ounces) chopped green chilies
- 2 tablespoons lime juice
- 1 tablespoon olive oil
- ¼ teaspoon salt
  Tortilla chips

1. Grill tomatoes and jalapeno, covered, over medium-hot heat for 8-12 minutes or until skins are blistered and blackened, turning occasionally. Immediately place in a large bowl; cover and let stand for 20 minutes.

2. Peel off and discard charred skins. Discard stem and seeds from jalapeno; cut tomatoes into fourths. Set jalapeno and tomatoes aside.

3. Place the cilantro, onions and garlic in a food processor; cover and process until blended. Add the chipotle pepper, tomatoes and jalapeno; cover and pulse until blended.

4. Transfer to a large bowl; stir in the chilies, lime juice, oil and salt. Cover and refrigerate for at least 1 hour. Serve with chips.

NOTE *Wear disposable gloves when cutting hot peppers; the oils can burn skin. Avoid touching your face.*

HONEY-SOY PORK SKEWERS

People can't seem to get enough of these tender hors d'oeuvres that are marinated in a sauce slightly sweetened with honey. The party starters also make a wonderful entree when served over rice.

—**SUSAN LEBRUN** SULPHUR, LA

PREP: 10 MIN. + MARINATING • **GRILL:** 10 MIN.
MAKES: 8 SERVINGS

- 1 pound boneless pork loin roast
- 3 tablespoons reduced-sodium soy sauce
- 3 tablespoons honey
- 1 tablespoon lemon juice
- 1 tablespoon canola oil
- 3 garlic cloves, minced
- ½ teaspoon ground ginger

1. Cut pork into ⅛-in. slices, then cut each slice widthwise in half. In a large resealable plastic bag, combine the remaining ingredients; add pork. Seal bag and turn to coat; refrigerate for 2-4 hours, turning occasionally.

2. Drain and discard marinade. Thread pork onto metal or soaked wooden skewers. Using long-handled tongs, moisten a paper towel with cooking oil and lightly coat the grill rack.

3. Grill, uncovered, over medium heat or broil 4 in. from the heat for 2-3 minutes on each side or until meat is no longer pink.

FAST FIX

ZUCCHINI & CHEESE ROULADES

My husband enjoys this recipe so much that he even helps me roll up the roulades! You can change the filling any way you like. I have used feta instead of Parmesan, or try sun-dried tomatoes instead of olives.
—**APRIL MCKINNEY** MURFREESBORO, TN

START TO FINISH: 25 MIN.
MAKES: 2 DOZEN

- 1 **cup part-skim ricotta cheese**
- ¼ **cup grated Parmesan cheese**
- 2 **tablespoons minced fresh basil or 2 teaspoons dried basil**
- 1 **tablespoon capers, drained**
- 1 **tablespoon chopped Greek olives**
- 1 **teaspoon grated lemon peel**
- 1 **tablespoon lemon juice**
- ⅛ **teaspoon salt**
- ⅛ **teaspoon pepper**
- 4 **medium zucchini**

1. In a small bowl, mix the first nine ingredients.
2. Slice zucchini lengthwise into twenty-four ⅛-in.-thick slices. Moisten a paper towel with cooking oil; using long-handled tongs, rub on grill rack to coat lightly. Grill zucchini slices in batches, covered, over medium heat 2-3 minutes on each side or until tender.
3. Place 1 tablespoon ricotta mixture on the end of each zucchini slice. Roll up and secure each with a toothpick.

ARTICHOKE MUSHROOM CAPS

ARTICHOKE MUSHROOM CAPS

These crumb-topped appetizers never last long at our get-togethers. The rich filling of cream cheese, artichoke hearts and Parmesan cheese is terrific. Green onion adds a nice pop of color.
—**RUTH LEWIS** WEST NEWTON, PA

PREP: 30 MIN. • **GRILL:** 10 MIN.
MAKES: ABOUT 2 DOZEN

- 1 **package (3 ounces) cream cheese, softened**
- ¼ **cup mayonnaise**
- 1 **jar (6½ ounces) marinated artichoke hearts, drained and finely chopped**
- ¼ **cup grated Parmesan cheese**
- 2 **tablespoons finely chopped green onion**
- 20 **to 25 large fresh mushrooms, stems removed**
- ¼ **cup seasoned bread crumbs**
- 2 **teaspoons olive oil**

1. In a large bowl, beat cream cheese and mayonnaise until smooth. Beat in the artichokes, Parmesan cheese and green onion.
2. Lightly spray tops of mushrooms with cooking spray. Spoon cheese mixture into mushroom caps. Combine bread crumbs and oil; sprinkle over mushrooms.
3. Grill, covered, over indirect medium heat for 8-10 minutes or until mushrooms are tender.

FAST FIX▸

JERK CHICKEN WINGS

I've been making this recipe ever since I can remember. It's so simple to fix, doesn't take a lot of ingredients or time, and is always a favorite with my guests. You can change it up for different crowds by varying the seasoning for a mild to extra-spicy kick.

—CAREN ADAMS FONTANA, CA

START TO FINISH: 30 MIN.
MAKES: ABOUT 2 DOZEN

- ½ cup Caribbean jerk seasoning
- 2½ pounds chicken wingettes and drumettes
- 2 cups honey barbecue sauce
- ⅓ cup packed brown sugar
- 2 teaspoons prepared mustard
- 1 teaspoon ground ginger

1. Place jerk seasoning in a large resealable plastic bag; add chicken, a few pieces at a time, and shake to coat. In a small bowl, combine the barbecue sauce, brown sugar, mustard and ginger; set aside.

2. Moisten a paper towel with cooking oil; using long-handled tongs, lightly coat the grill rack. Grill chicken wings, covered, over medium heat or broil 4 in. from the heat for 12-16 minutes, turning occasionally.

3. Brush with sauce mixture. Grill or broil 8-10 minutes longer or until juices run clear, basting and turning several times.

NOTE *Caribbean jerk seasoning may be found in the spice aisle of your grocery store.*

FIRECRACKER SHRIMP WITH CRANPOTLE DIPPING SAUCE

Bacon-wrapped shrimp is always a big hit at my parties. I like to serve mine with a little bit of heat and tang. This recipe is easy to prepare, which makes it an amazing appetizer in my book!

—SUZANNE FORSBERG MANTECA, CA

PREP: 30 MIN. • **GRILL:** 10 MIN.
MAKES: 20 APPETIZERS (1 CUP SAUCE)

- ½ cup whole-berry cranberry sauce
- ¼ cup canola oil
- 3 tablespoons lemon juice
- 1 teaspoon Dijon mustard
- 2 chipotle peppers in adobo sauce, chopped
- 1 garlic clove, minced
- ½ teaspoon crushed red pepper flakes
- ¼ teaspoon cayenne pepper
- 10 bacon strips
- 20 uncooked jumbo shrimp, peeled and deveined (tails on)

1. For sauce, place the first eight ingredients in a blender; cover and blend for 30 seconds or until smooth. Transfer to a small bowl; cover and refrigerate until serving.

2. Cut each bacon strip in half widthwise. In a large skillet, cook bacon over medium heat until partially cooked but not crisp. Remove to paper towels to drain. Wrap a piece of bacon around each shrimp; thread onto metal or soaked wooden skewers.

3. Moisten a paper towel with cooking oil; using long-handled tongs, lightly coat the grill rack. Grill, covered, over medium heat or broil 4 in. from the heat for 3-5 minutes on each side or until shrimp turn pink and bacon is crisp. Serve with dipping sauce.

JERK CHICKEN WINGS

VERY VEGGIE APPETIZER PIZZAS

portions. Press or roll each portion into a 10-in. circle; place each on a piece of greased foil (about 12 in. square). Brush tops with remaining oil; cover with plastic wrap and let rest 10 minutes.

4. For topping, in a 6-qt. stockpot, heat oil over medium-high heat. Add beet greens; cook and stir 3-5 minutes or until tender. Add garlic; cook 30 seconds longer. Remove from heat; stir in vinegar.

5. Moisten a paper towel with cooking oil; using long-handled tongs, rub on grill rack to coat lightly. Carefully invert pizza crusts onto grill rack; remove foil. Grill, covered, over medium heat 3-5 minutes or until bottoms are lightly browned. Turn; grill 1-2 minutes or until second side begins to brown.

6. Remove from grill. Spread with pesto; top with beet greens, cheeses and tomatoes. Return pizzas to grill. Cook, covered, over medium heat 2-4 minutes or until cheese is melted. Sprinkle with chopped basil leaves.

⑤INGREDIENTS FAST FIX

CINNAMON FLAT ROLLS

I shared this recipe when 4-H leaders requested an activity for younger members. The kids had a ball rolling out the dough and enjoying the sweet chewy results made on the grill.

—**ETHEL FARNSWORTH** YUMA, AZ

START TO FINISH: 15 MIN.
MAKES: 1 DOZEN

- 1 **package (16 ounces) frozen bread dough dinner rolls, thawed**
- 5 **tablespoons olive oil**
- ½ **cup sugar**
- 1 **tablespoon ground cinnamon**

On a floured surface, roll each dinner roll into a 5-in. circle. Brush with oil. Grill, uncovered, over medium heat for 1 minute on each side or until golden brown (burst any large bubbles with a fork). Combine sugar and cinnamon; sprinkle over rolls.

VERY VEGGIE APPETIZER PIZZAS

This smoky grilled pizza scores big with me for two reasons. It encourages my husband and son to eat greens, and it showcases fresh produce.

—**SARAH GRAY** ERIE, CO

PREP: 15 MIN. + RISING • **GRILL:** 10 MIN
MAKES: 2 PIZZAS (4 SLICES EACH)

- 1½ **cups all-purpose flour**
- 1½ **cups whole wheat flour**
- 2 **teaspoons kosher salt**
- 1 **teaspoon active dry yeast**
- 3 **tablespoons olive oil, divided**
- 1¼ to 1½ **cups warm water (120° to 130°)**

TOPPING

- 2 **tablespoons olive oil**
- 10 **cups beet greens, coarsely chopped**
- 4 **garlic cloves, minced**
- 2 **tablespoons balsamic vinegar**
- ¾ **cup prepared pesto**
- ¾ **cup shredded Italian cheese blend**
- ½ **cup crumbled feta cheese**
- 2 **medium heirloom tomatoes, thinly sliced**
- ¼ **cup fresh basil leaves, chopped**

1. Place flours, salt and yeast in a food processor; pulse until blended. While processing, add 2 tablespoons oil and enough water in a steady stream until dough forms a ball. Turn dough onto a floured surface; knead until smooth and elastic, about 6-8 minutes.

2. Place in a greased bowl, turning once to grease the top. Cover with plastic wrap and let rise in a warm place until almost doubled, about 1½ hours.

3. Punch down dough. On a lightly floured surface, divide dough into two

TERIYAKI STEAK SKEWERS

When these flavorful skewered steaks are sizzling on the grill, the aroma makes everyone around stop what they're doing and come to see what's cooking. The tasty marinade is easy to make, and these little steaks are quick to cook and fun to eat.

—JERI DOBROWSKI BEACH, ND

PREP: 15 MIN. + MARINATING • **GRILL:** 10 MIN.
MAKES: 6 SERVINGS

- ½ cup reduced-sodium soy sauce
- ¼ cup cider vinegar
- 2 tablespoons brown sugar
- 2 tablespoons finely chopped onion
- 1 tablespoon canola oil
- 1 garlic clove, minced
- ½ teaspoon ground ginger
- ⅛ teaspoon pepper
- 2 pounds beef top sirloin steak

1. In a large resealable plastic bag, combine the first eight ingredients. Trim fat from steak and slice across the grain into ½-in. strips. Add the beef to bag; seal bag and turn to coat. Refrigerate for 2-3 hours.

2. Drain and discard marinade. Loosely thread meat strips onto six metal or soaked wooden skewers. Grill, uncovered, over medium-hot heat for 7-10 minutes or until meat reaches desired doneness, turning often.

 **GRILL SKILL**

If you're using wooden skewers for a grilled appetizer, be sure to soak them in water for a few hours first. Wet skewers don't splinter as easily as dry skewers, which helps when assembling your kabobs. In addition, wet skewers won't burn as easily on the grill.

Consider wooden skewers for bite-sized appetizers as well as delicate items such as shrimp or thinly sliced vegetables.

TERIYAKI STEAK
SKEWERS

**QUICK BARBECUED
BEANS, PAGE 50**

PESTO-CORN GRILLED PEPPERS, PAGE 53

BUTTERY HORSERADISH CORN ON THE COB, PAGE 56

SIZZLING SIDES

Make the most of your grill, and fire up a **side dish** while the entree sizzles. In addition to **potato favorites** and new takes on **buttery corn staples,** you'll learn how to make bread on the grill, prepare rice over hot coals and create other **savory sensations** sure to round out meals!

SAVORY GRILLED POTATOES, PAGE 36

VEGETABLE GRILLING CHART

Grilling up side dishes is easy with a few colorful vegetables. Best of all, grilling truly brings out the earthy flavor in veggies without a lot of work on your part. Follow the guidelines below, being sure to turn the items halfway through the grilling time for even cooking. Always grill vegetables until they are tender.

TYPE	WEIGHT OR THICKNESS	HEAT	APPROXIMATE COOKING TIME (IN MINUTES)
ASPARAGUS	1/2 in. thick	medium/direct	6 to 8
CORN	in husk	medium/direct	25 to 30
	husk removed	medium/direct	10 to 12
EGGPLANT	1/2 in. slices	medium/direct	8 to 10
FENNEL	1/4 in. slices	medium/direct	10 to 12
MUSHROOMS	Button	medium/direct	8 to 10
	Portobello, whole	medium/direct	12 to 15
ONIONS	1/2 in. slices	medium/direct	8 to 12
POTATOES	whole	medium/indirect	45 to 60
SWEET PEPPERS	halved or quartered	medium/direct	8 to 10

GRILL SKILL

Disposable aluminum pans are ideal for grilling vegetables. The pans allow you to cook the veggies without steaming them! Give it a try with this dish, Thyme Grilled Vegetables (page 45).

TRIPLE TOMATO
FLATBREAD

FAST FIX ▶

TRIPLE TOMATO FLATBREAD

Tomatoes are the reason I have a vegetable garden, and I developed this recipe as a way to show off my garden's harvest. It will absolutely impress.
—**RACHEL KIMBROW** PORTLAND, OR

START TO FINISH: 20 MIN.
MAKES: 8 PIECES

- 1 **tube (13.8 ounces) refrigerated pizza crust**
  Cooking spray
- 3 **plum tomatoes, finely chopped (about 2 cups)**
- ½ **cup soft sun-dried tomato halves (not packed in oil), julienned**
- 2 **tablespoons olive oil**
- 1 **tablespoon dried basil**
- ¼ **teaspoon salt**
- ¼ **teaspoon pepper**
- 1 **cup shredded Asiago cheese**
- 2 **cups yellow and/or red cherry tomatoes, halved**

1. Unroll and press dough into a 15x10-in. rectangle. Transfer dough to an 18x12-in. piece of heavy-duty foil coated with cooking spray; spritz dough with cooking spray. In a large bowl, toss plum tomatoes and sun-dried tomatoes with oil and seasonings.

2. Carefully invert dough onto grill rack; remove foil. Grill, covered, over medium heat 2-3 minutes or until bottom is golden brown. Turn; grill 1-2 minutes longer or until second side begins to brown.

3. Remove from grill. Spoon plum tomato mixture over crust; top with cheese and cherry tomatoes. Return flatbread to grill. Grill, covered, 2-4 minutes or until crust is golden brown and cheese is melted.

TO BAKE FLATBREAD *Preheat oven to 425°. Unroll and press dough onto bottom of a 15x10x1-in. baking pan coated with cooking spray. Bake 6-8 minutes or until lightly browned. Assemble flatbread as directed. Bake 8-10 minutes longer or until crust is golden and cheese is melted.*

TRIPLE TOMATO
FLATBREAD

⑤ INGREDIENTS FAST FIX
GRILLED PINEAPPLE

Fresh pineapple makes a fun side dish when grilled, topped with butter and maple syrup and sprinkled with nuts. Try cutting each pineapple quarter into bite-size pieces before serving.
—**POLLY (PAULINE) HEER** CABOT, AR

START TO FINISH: 20 MIN.
MAKES: 4 SERVINGS

- ¼ cup maple syrup
- 3 tablespoons butter, melted
- 1 fresh pineapple
- 2 tablespoons chopped macadamia nuts or hazelnuts, toasted

1. Combine syrup and butter; set aside. Quarter the pineapple lengthwise, leaving top attached.
2. Moisten a paper towel with cooking oil; using long-handled tongs, rub on grill rack to coat lightly. Grill, uncovered, over medium heat for 5 minutes. Turn; brush with maple butter. Grill 5-7 minutes longer or until heated through; brush with maple butter and sprinkle with nuts. Serve with the remaining maple butter.

ZUCCHINI WITH SCALLIONS

GRILLED PINEAPPLE

⑤ INGREDIENTS FAST FIX
ZUCCHINI WITH SCALLIONS

Wondering what to do with all of your garden-grown zucchini? Tired of the same old bread and cupcakes? My grill recipe is a great change of pace with the added bonus of being healthy.
—**ALIA SHUTTLEWORTH** AUBURN, CA

START TO FINISH: 20 MIN.
MAKES: 4 SERVINGS

- 6 small zucchini, halved lengthwise
- 4 teaspoons olive oil, divided
- 2 green onions, thinly sliced
- 2 tablespoons lemon juice
- ½ teaspoon salt
- ⅛ teaspoon crushed red pepper flakes

1. Drizzle zucchini with 2 teaspoons olive oil. Grill, covered, over medium heat for 8-10 minutes or until tender, turning once.
2. Place in a large bowl. Add the green onions, lemon juice, salt, pepper flakes and remaining oil; toss to coat.

**GRILLED VEGGIES WITH
MUSTARD VINAIGRETTE**

GRILLED VEGGIES WITH MUSTARD VINAIGRETTE

I make this healthy and inviting side dish whenever friends come over for a cookout. The honeyed vinaigrette really lets the veggies shine.

—**SHELLY GRAVER** LANSDALE, PA

PREP: 20 MIN. • **GRILL:** 15 MIN.
MAKES: 10 SERVINGS (¾ CUP EACH)

- ¼ **cup red wine vinegar**
- 1 **tablespoon Dijon mustard**
- 1 **tablespoon honey**
- ½ **teaspoon salt**
- ⅛ **teaspoon pepper**
- ¼ **cup canola oil**
- ¼ **cup olive oil**

VEGETABLES

- 2 **large sweet onions**
- 2 **medium zucchini**
- 2 **yellow summer squash**
- 2 **large sweet red peppers, halved and seeded**
- 1 **bunch green onions, trimmed**
   Cooking spray

1. In a small bowl, whisk the first five ingredients. Gradually whisk in oils until blended.

2. Peel and quarter each sweet onion, leaving root ends intact. Cut zucchini and yellow squash lengthwise into ½-in.-thick slices. Lightly spritz onions, zucchini, yellow squash and remaining vegetables with cooking spray, turning to coat all sides.

3. Grill sweet onions, covered, over medium heat 15-20 minutes until tender, turning occasionally. Grill zucchini, squash and peppers, covered, over medium heat 10-15 minutes or until crisp-tender and lightly charred, turning once. Grill green onions, covered, 2-4 minutes or until lightly charred, turning once.

4. Cut vegetables into bite-size pieces; place in a large bowl. Add ½ cup vinaigrette and toss to coat. Serve with remaining vinaigrette.

GRILLED POTATOES WITH RANCH SAUCE

SPICY CORN KABOBS

GRILLED POTATOES WITH RANCH SAUCE

These potatoes are fantastic by themselves, but pairing them with the sauce creates a perfect combination. It's a side dish compatible with any entree.

—**CRAIG CARPENTER** CORAOPOLIS, PA

START TO FINISH: 30 MIN.
MAKES: 5 SERVINGS

- 2 tablespoons olive oil
- 1 tablespoon barbecue seasoning
- 2 garlic cloves, minced
- 2 teaspoons lemon juice
- 1½ pounds small potatoes, quartered

SAUCE
- ⅔ cup ranch salad dressing
- 4 teaspoons bacon bits
- 2 teaspoons minced chives
- Dash hot pepper sauce

1. In a large bowl, combine oil, barbecue seasoning, garlic and lemon juice. Add potatoes; toss to coat. Place on a double thickness of heavy-duty foil (about 28 in. square). Fold foil around potato mixture and seal tightly.
2. Grill, covered, over medium heat 20-25 minutes or until the potatoes are tender.
3. In a small bowl, combine sauce ingredients. Serve with potatoes.
NOTE *This recipe was tested with McCormick Grill Mates Barbecue Seasoning. Look for it in the spice aisle.*

CHEDDAR HERB BREAD

This crunchy, delicious bread is a hit with my husband and children. It's a fun accompaniment to any meal you might make on the grill.

—**ANN JACOBSEN** OAKLAND, MI

START TO FINISH: 25 MIN.
MAKES: 10-12 SERVINGS

- 1 cup (4 ounces) finely shredded cheddar cheese
- ½ cup butter, softened
- ¼ cup minced fresh parsley
- 1 garlic clove, minced
- ½ teaspoon garlic powder
- ½ teaspoon paprika
- 1 loaf (1 pound) French bread, sliced

In a bowl, combine the first six ingredients; beat until smooth. Spread on both sides of each slice of bread; reassemble loaf. Wrap in a large piece of heavy-duty foil (about 28x18 in.); seal tightly. Grill, covered, over medium heat 15-20 minutes or until heated through, turning once.

SPICY CORN KABOBS

Corn transforms from a so-so side dish to a tangy sensation when grilled, dotted with sour cream and cheese, and jazzed up with a splash of lime.

—**LEAH LENZ** LOS ANGELES, CA

PREP: 10 MIN. • **GRILL:** 25 MIN.
MAKES: 6 SERVINGS

- 6 medium ears husked sweet corn, halved
- ¼ cup sour cream
- ¼ cup mayonnaise
- ½ cup grated cotija cheese or Parmesan cheese
- 2 teaspoons chili powder
- ¼ teaspoon cayenne pepper, optional
- 6 lime wedges

1. Insert a metal or soaked wooden skewer into the cut end of each piece of corn. Grill, covered, over medium heat for 25-30 minutes or until tender, turning often.
2. In a small bowl, combine sour cream and mayonnaise; spread over corn. Sprinkle with cheese, chili powder and, if desired, cayenne. Serve with lime wedges.

SAVORY GRILLED POTATOES

These tasty potato packets are so easy to prepare ahead of time and toss on the grill when needed. Plus, they complement just about any main course.

—DARLENE BRENDEN SALEM, OR

PREP: 10 MIN. • **GRILL:** 30 MIN.
MAKES: 2 SERVINGS

- ¼ cup mayonnaise
- 1 tablespoon grated Parmesan cheese
- 1 garlic clove, minced
- ½ teaspoon minced fresh parsley
- ¼ to ½ teaspoon salt
- ¼ teaspoon paprika
- ¼ teaspoon pepper
- 2 medium baking potatoes, cut into ¼-inch slices
- 1 small onion, sliced and separated into rings
- 2 tablespoons butter

In a large bowl, combine the first seven ingredients. Add potatoes and onion; toss gently to coat. Spoon onto a double thickness of greased heavy-duty foil (about 18 in. square). Dot with butter. Fold foil around potato mixture and seal tightly. Grill, covered, over medium heat for 30-35 minutes or until potatoes are tender, turning once.

**SAVORY GRILLED
POTATOES**

(5) INGREDIENTS
GRILLED CORN ON THE COB

I'd never grilled corn until one summer when my sister-in-law served it. What a treat! So simple, yet delicious, grilled corn is now a must for my favorite summer menu. This version offers a lovely burst of herb flavors.

—**ANGELA LEINENBACH** MECHANICSVLLE, VA

PREP: 20 MIN. + SOAKING • **GRILL:** 25 MIN.
MAKES: 8 SERVINGS

- 8 medium ears sweet corn
- ½ cup butter, softened
- 2 tablespoons minced fresh basil
- 2 tablespoons minced fresh parsley
- ½ teaspoon salt

1. Soak sweet corn in cold water for 20 minutes. Meanwhile, in a small bowl, combine the butter, basil, parsley and salt. Carefully peel back corn husks to within 1 in. of bottoms; remove silk. Spread butter mixture over corn.
2. Rewrap corn in husks and secure with kitchen string. Grill corn, covered, over medium heat for 25-30 minutes or until tender, turning occasionally. Cut strings and peel back husks.

🍴 GRILL SKILL

To quickly butter my grilled corn on the cob, I place a few tablespoons of butter in a 13x9-in. baking dish and add the hot corn. Simply roll the corn in the butter and serve in the dish.
DEBBY K. ST. LOUIS, MISSOURI

ITALIAN STUFFED PORTOBELLOS

Golden caramelized onions and creamy roasted garlic are an ideal match for the flavors in this recipe. It's like a quick transport to a ristorante in Rome. For a bit of heat, add red pepper flakes while sauteeing the onions.

—**JEANNE HOLT** MENDOTA HEIGHTS, MN

PREP: 1 HOUR • **BAKE:** 10 MIN.
MAKES: 4 SERVINGS

- 4 ounces sliced pancetta or bacon strips, finely chopped
- 1 tablespoon plus 1 teaspoon olive oil, divided
- 4 cups sliced onions
- 2 tablespoons finely chopped oil-packed sun-dried tomatoes
- ¼ teaspoon salt
- ⅛ teaspoon pepper
- 1 whole garlic bulb
- 3 tablespoons crumbled goat cheese

PIZZAS
- 4 large portobello mushrooms
- 2 tablespoons olive oil
- ⅓ cup shredded part-skim mozzarella cheese
- 3 tablespoons shredded Parmesan cheese
- 1 tablespoon minced fresh basil or 1 teaspoon dried basil

1. In a large skillet over medium heat, cook pancetta in 1 tablespoon oil until crisp. Remove to paper towels with a slotted spoon; set aside.
2. In the same skillet, cook and stir sliced onions until softened. Reduce heat to medium-low; cook, stirring occasionally, 30 minutes or until deep golden brown. Stir in the sun-dried tomatoes, salt, pepper and pancetta. Remove from heat; keep warm.
3. Remove the papery outer skin from the garlic bulb (do not peel or separate cloves). Cut top off garlic bulb. Brush with remaining oil. Wrap the bulb in heavy-duty foil. Bake at 425° for 30-35 minutes or until softened. Cool 10-15 minutes. Squeeze softened garlic

into a small bowl; stir in crumbled goat cheese and onions.
4. Brush mushrooms with oil. Grill, covered, over medium heat or broil 4 in. from heat for 6-8 minutes on each side or until tender. Fill mushrooms with onion mixture. Sprinkle with cheeses.
5. Place on a greased baking sheet. Bake at 375° for 8-10 minutes or until cheese is melted. Sprinkle with basil.

FAST FIX
ITALIAN-STYLE EGGPLANT

What a delicious way to dress up eggplant! Piled high with herbs, cheese and fresh tomatoes, this fail-proof side nicely complements a variety of main dishes.

—**THERESA LASALLE** MIDLOTHIAN, VA

START TO FINISH: 25 MIN.
MAKES: 5 SERVINGS

- ¼ cup shredded Parmesan cheese
- 3 tablespoons lemon juice
- 2 tablespoons minced fresh basil
- 5 teaspoons olive oil
- 3 garlic cloves, minced
- 1 teaspoon minced fresh oregano
- 1 large eggplant, cut into 10 slices
- 10 slices tomato
- ½ cup shredded part-skim mozzarella cheese

1. In a small bowl, combine the first six ingredients.
2. Grill eggplant, covered, over medium heat for 3 minutes. Turn slices; spoon Parmesan mixture onto each. Top with tomato; sprinkle with mozzarella cheese.
3. Grill, covered, 2-3 minutes longer or until cheese is melted.

SHIITAKE SALAD WITH SESAME-GINGER VINAIGRETTE

2. Place shiitake mushrooms in a small bowl; drizzle with olive oil and toss to coat. Transfer to a grill wok or basket. Grill, uncovered, over medium heat for 6-8 minutes or until tender, stirring frequently.

3. In a large bowl, combine the salad greens, onions, radishes, carrots and water chestnuts. Add half of vinaigrette; toss to coat. Divide among four plates; top salad with mushrooms. Drizzle with remaining vinaigrette and sprinkle with sesame seeds.

NOTE *Look for mirin in the Asian condiments section.*

FAST FIX

RICE ON THE GRILL

Believe it or not, you can cook rice on the grill! My husband loves to barbecue, so when it's hot outside, we do entire meals on the grill. Since our kids love rice, we often turn to this tangy rice side dish as part of the menu.

—**SHIRLEY HOPKINS** OLDS, AB

START TO FINISH: 30 MIN.
MAKES: 4 SERVINGS

- 1⅓ cups uncooked instant rice
- ⅓ cup sliced fresh mushrooms
- ¼ cup chopped green pepper
- ¼ cup chopped onion
- ½ cup water
- ½ cup chicken broth
- ⅓ cup ketchup
- 1 tablespoon butter

1. In a 9-in. round disposable foil pan, combine the first seven ingredients. Dot with butter. Cover with heavy-duty foil; seal edges tightly.

2. Grill, covered, over medium heat for 12-15 minutes or until liquid is absorbed. Remove foil carefully to allow steam to escape. Fluff with a fork.

SHIITAKE SALAD WITH SESAME-GINGER VINAIGRETTE

This salad combines my favorite Asian flavors with crisp, colorful veggies and smoky grilled shiitakes. Mirin for the dressing can be found in the Asian section of well-stocked supermarkets.

—**KATHI JONES-DELMONTE** ROCHESTER, NY

PREP: 25 MIN. • **GRILL:** 10 MIN.
MAKES: 4 SERVINGS

- ½ cup mirin (sweet rice wine)
- 6 tablespoons rice vinegar
- 4½ teaspoons reduced-sodium soy sauce
- 1 shallot, minced
- 1 tablespoon minced fresh gingerroot
- 2 teaspoons lemon juice
- 2 teaspoons Sriracha Asian hot chili sauce or 1 teaspoon hot pepper sauce
- 1 teaspoon coarsely ground pepper
- 2 tablespoons olive oil
- 1 tablespoon sesame oil

SALAD
- ½ pound fresh shiitake mushrooms
- 2 teaspoons olive oil
- 4 cups spring mix salad greens
- 4 green onions, chopped
- ⅓ cup thinly sliced radishes
- ⅓ cup thinly sliced fresh carrots
- 1 can (8 ounces) sliced water chestnuts, drained and rinsed
- 2 tablespoons sesame seeds, toasted

1. In a small saucepan, bring mirin to a boil. Reduce heat; simmer, uncovered, for 5-7 minutes or until slightly thickened. Transfer to a small bowl; cool to room temperature. Whisk in the vinegar, soy sauce, shallot, ginger, lemon juice, chili sauce, pepper and oils; set aside.

PEPPERS AND ZUCCHINI IN FOIL

This versatile side dish is so simple and quick that I had to share it. Grilling the colorful veggies in a foil packet means one less dish to wash, but I sometimes stir-fry the mixture on the stovetop, too.

—**KAREN ANDERSON** FAIR OAKS, CA

START TO FINISH: 20 MIN.
MAKES: 4 SERVINGS

- 1 **medium green pepper, julienned**
- 1 **medium sweet red pepper, julienned**
- 2 **medium zucchini, julienned**
- 1 **tablespoon butter**
- 2 **teaspoons soy sauce**

Place the vegetables on a double layer of heavy-duty foil (about 18x15 in.). Dot with butter; drizzle with soy sauce. Fold foil around vegetables and seal tightly. Grill, covered, over medium heat for 5-7 minutes on each side or until vegetables are crisp-tender.

 **HOW-TO BBQ**

Grilling with foil packets allows vegetables to cook using steam the packets capture inside. To create a packet, center the ingredients on a double thickness of heavy foil. Bring sides of foil together and double fold with 1-inch folds. Make sure to leave room for heat circulation at the top. Double fold the ends with 1-inch folds. After grilling, carefully open both ends of the packet to let the steam escape, and then open the top. Serve food out of the packet or spoon into a serving dish.

PEPPERS AND ZUCCHINI IN FOIL

HERBED POTATO PACKS

HERBED POTATO PACKS

Fingerlings are small, waxy and tender, and they are often sold in bags of assorted colors (red, purple and gold). These little potatoes are memorable when grilled in convenient single-serve foil packs.
—*TASTE OF HOME* TEST KITCHEN

START TO FINISH: 25 MIN.
MAKES: 4 SERVINGS

- 2 **pounds fingerling potatoes**
- 2 **tablespoons olive oil**
- 2 **garlic cloves, minced**
- 1 **teaspoon salt**
- 2 **teaspoons minced fresh thyme**
- ½ **teaspoon coarsely ground pepper**

1. Pierce potatoes with a fork. Place in a large microwave-safe dish; cover and microwave for 4-7 minutes or until crisp-tender, stirring halfway. Add the remaining ingredients; toss to coat.
2. Place one-fourth of the potatoes on a double thickness of heavy-duty foil (about 14 x 12 in.). Fold foil around potatoes and seal tightly. Repeat with remaining potatoes.
3. Grill, covered, over medium-high heat for 6-9 minutes on each side or until potatoes are tender. Open foil carefully to allow steam to escape.

ITALIAN GRILLED VEGGIES

Here's a zesty side that will complement any main course. This recipe was an experiment I tried when I had some leftover vegetables in the refrigerator. Now, it's one of our favorites.

—ANNA MARIE SHORT LONEDELL, MO

PREP: 10 MIN. + MARINATING • **GRILL:** 20 MIN.
MAKES: 2 SERVINGS

- ⅓ cup chopped green pepper
- 3 medium fresh mushrooms
- ½ cup fresh broccoli florets
- ½ cup fresh cauliflowerets
- ¼ cup thinly sliced red onion
- ¼ cup Italian salad dressing
- 3 cherry tomatoes, halved

1. Place the green pepper, mushrooms, broccoli, cauliflower and onion in a large resealable plastic bag. Add salad dressing; seal bag and turn to coat. Refrigerate for 1 hour, turning at least one time.

2. Transfer vegetables to a double thickness of heavy-duty foil (about 18x12 in.). Fold foil around vegetables and seal tightly.

3. Grill, covered, over medium heat for 20-25 minutes or until tender. Open foil carefully to allow steam to escape. Spoon vegetables into a serving bowl; stir in tomatoes.

BACON-WRAPPED CORN

(5) INGREDIENTS FAST FIX

BACON-WRAPPED CORN

After one bite of this grilled corn on the cob, you'll never go back to your old way of preparing it. The incredible flavor of roasted corn combined with bacon and chili powder is sure to please your palate and bring rave reviews at your next backyard barbecue.

—LORI BRAMBLE OMAHA, NE

START TO FINISH: 30 MIN.
MAKES: 8 SERVINGS

- 8 large ears sweet corn, husks removed
- 8 bacon strips
- 2 tablespoons chili powder

1. Wrap each ear of corn with a bacon strip; place on a piece of heavy-duty foil. Sprinkle with chili powder. Wrap securely, twisting ends to make handles for turning.

2. Grill corn, covered, over medium heat for 20-25 minutes or until the corn is tender and the bacon is cooked, turning once.

TARRAGON ASPARAGUS

TARRAGON ASPARAGUS

I grow purple asparagus, so I'm always looking for new ways to prepare it. Recently, my husband and I discovered how wonderful any color of asparagus tastes when it's grilled.
—**SUE GRONHOLZ** BEAVER DAM, WI

START TO FINISH: 15 MIN.
MAKES: 8 SERVINGS

- 2 **pounds fresh asparagus, trimmed**
- 2 **tablespoons olive oil**
- 1 **teaspoon salt**
- ½ **teaspoon pepper**
- ¼ **cup honey**
- 2 **to 4 tablespoons minced fresh tarragon**

On a large plate, toss asparagus with oil, salt and pepper. Grill, covered, over medium heat 6-8 minutes or until crisp-tender, turning occasionally and basting frequently with honey during the last 3 minutes. Sprinkle with minced tarragon.

BROCCOLI CAULIFLOWER PACKET

This is a great side to just about any meat. For a variation, add one chopped large baking potato, or mix in asparagus for a veggie extravaganza!
—**TARA DELGADO** WAUSEON, OH

START TO FINISH: 20 MIN.
MAKES: 2 SERVINGS

- 1 **cup fresh broccoli florets**
- 1 **cup fresh cauliflowerets**
- 1 **small onion, cut into wedges**
  Refrigerated butter-flavored spray
- ¼ **teaspoon garlic salt**
- ⅛ **teaspoon paprika**
- ⅛ **teaspoon pepper**

1. In a large bowl, combine the broccoli, cauliflower and onion; spritz with butter-flavored spray. Sprinkle with the garlic salt, paprika and pepper; toss to coat. Place vegetables on a double thickness of heavy-duty foil (about 18x 12 in.); fold foil around vegetables and seal tightly.

2. Grill, covered, over medium heat for 10-15 minutes or until vegetables are tender. Open foil carefully to allow steam to escape.

NO-FUSS SWEET POTATOES

I love trying new recipes, so when my son-in-law suggested we grill sweet potatoes, I quickly agreed! Served with steak, these honey-topped spuds are a great change of pace from traditional baked potatoes. They're attractive, too.
—**LILLIAN NEER** LONG EDDY, NY

PREP: 10 MIN. • **GRILL:** 30 MIN.
MAKES: 4 SERVINGS

- 2 **large sweet potatoes, halved lengthwise**
- 2 **tablespoons butter, softened**
  Garlic salt and pepper to taste
- 2 **teaspoons honey**

Cut two pieces of heavy-duty foil (about 18x12 in.); place a potato half on each. Spread cut side with butter. Sprinkle with garlic salt and pepper. Top each potato with another half. Fold foil over potatoes and seal tightly. Grill, covered, over medium-hot heat for 30 minutes or until tender, turning once. To serve, fluff potatoes with a fork and drizzle with honey.

🍴 GRILL SKILL

Here's an easy way to enjoy sweet potatoes in the summer. Just peel and wash them, then cut into ½ in. slices. Cook them on the grill, brushing each side with butter several times and turning them often until tender.
KERI H. WELLESLEY, MA

SNAPPY PEAS 'N' MUSHROOMS

Seasoned with dill, this versatile side dish can be on the table in mere minutes. Just wrap the fresh vegetables in foil, seal tightly and grill until tender. It's that easy!
—**LAURA MAHAFFEY** ANNAPOLIS, MD

START TO FINISH: 20 MIN.
MAKES: 8-10 SERVINGS

- 1 **pound fresh sugar snap or snow peas**
- ½ **cup sliced fresh mushrooms**
- 2 **tablespoons sliced green onions**
- 1 **tablespoon snipped fresh dill or 1 teaspoon dill weed**
- 2 **tablespoons butter**
  Salt and pepper to taste

1. Place peas and mushrooms on a piece of double-layer heavy-duty foil (about 18 in. square). Sprinkle with onions and dill; dot with butter. Fold foil around the mixture and seal tightly.

2. Grill, covered, over medium-hot heat for 5 minutes. Turn; grill 5-8 minutes longer or until the vegetables are tender. Open foil carefully to allow steam to escape. Season with salt and pepper.

BUTTERY GRILLED ONIONS

Cooking on the grill is a year-round treat in the South. In addition to beef and chicken, we also use our grill for side dishes such as these onions. This recipe usually doesn't require a trip to the grocery store, and you can prepare the onions ahead of time.
—**PENNY MAYS** MEMPHIS, TN

PREP: 15 MIN. • **GRILL:** 30 MIN.
MAKES: 6 SERVINGS

- 6   **medium onions, peeled**
- 6   **tablespoons butter, softened**
- 6   **teaspoons beef bouillon granules**
- ⅛   **teaspoon garlic powder**
- ⅛   **teaspoon coarsely ground pepper**
- 6   **teaspoons sherry, optional**
       Shredded Parmesan cheese

1. Carefully remove a 1x1-in. core from the center of each onion (save removed onion for another use). Place each onion on a double thickness of heavy-duty foil (about 12 in. square).

2. Combine the butter, bouillon, garlic powder and pepper; spoon into onions. Sprinkle with sherry if desired. Fold foil around onions and seal tightly.

3. Grill, covered, over medium heat for 30-40 minutes or until tender.

4. Carefully unwrap foil to allow steam to escape. Sprinkle onions with Parmesan cheese.

 **GRILL SKILL**

Don't toss out the onion cores when making Buttery Grilled Onions. Dice the cores instead and use the onions to top grilled hot dogs, sausages or even burgers.

GRILLED HASH BROWNS

(5) INGREDIENTS FAST FIX

GRILLED HASH BROWNS

Since my husband and I love to barbecue meats, we're always looking for easy side dishes that cook on the grill, too. That's why I created this recipe for hash browns.
—**KELLY CHASTAIN** BEDFORD, IN

START TO FINISH: 20 MIN.
MAKES: 4 SERVINGS

- 3½ **cups frozen cubed hash brown potatoes, thawed**
- 1   **small onion, chopped**
- 1   **tablespoon beef bouillon granules**
-      **Dash seasoned salt**
-      **Dash pepper**
- 1   **tablespoon butter, melted**

1. Place potatoes on a piece of heavy-duty foil (about 20x18 in.) coated with cooking spray. Sprinkle with onion, bouillon, seasoned salt and pepper; drizzle with butter.

2. Fold foil around potatoes and seal tightly. Grill, covered, over indirect medium heat for 10-15 minutes or until potatoes are tender, turning once.

FAST FIX ▸
DILLY GRILLED VEGGIES

Use any combination of vegetables in this versatile dinner accompaniment. I sometimes like to include cauliflower, carrots, green peppers and onions.

—**FRAN SCOTT** BIRMINGHAM, MI

START TO FINISH: 30 MIN.
MAKES: 6 SERVINGS

- 2 **cups sliced fresh mushrooms**
- 2 **cups sliced fresh zucchini**
- 2 **cups fresh broccoli florets**
- ½ **medium sweet red pepper, cut into strips**
- 2 **tablespoons olive oil**
- 2 **tablespoons minced fresh dill or 2 teaspoons dill weed**
- ⅛ **teaspoon garlic salt**
- ⅛ **teaspoon pepper**

1. Place vegetables on a double thickness of heavy-duty foil (about 18 in. square). Drizzle with oil; sprinkle with dill, garlic salt and pepper. Fold foil around vegetables and seal tightly.

2. Grill, covered, over medium heat for 15 minutes or until vegetables are tender. Open foil carefully to allow steam to escape.

DILLY GRILLED VEGGIES

THYME GRILLED VEGETABLES

I love these little garden potatoes made colorful with green, yellow and red pepper strips. It's easy to put the veggies in a foil pan and grill them. Your kitchen won't get hot, and cleanup is a breeze.

—**CHRISTINE WALL** BARTLETT, IL

PREP: 20 MIN. • **GRILL:** 50 MIN.
MAKES: 9 SERVINGS

- 16 **small red potatoes (about 2 pounds), halved**
- ½ **cup chicken broth**
- ¼ **cup olive oil**
- 2 **tablespoons minced fresh thyme or 2 teaspoons dried thyme**
- ½ **teaspoon salt**
- 1 **each large green, sweet red and yellow pepper, julienned**
- 1 **jar (15 ounces) pearl onions, drained**

1. In an ungreased 13x9-in. disposable foil pan, combine the potatoes, broth, oil, thyme and salt. Grill, covered, over medium heat for 25 minutes.

2. Stir in peppers and onions. Grill 25-30 minutes longer or until vegetables are tender.

⑤ INGREDIENTS FAST FIX

EASY GRILLED SQUASH

Great alongside grilled steak or chicken, this is one of the best ways to prepare butternut squash. As a bonus, butternut squash is full of vitamin A.

—**ESTHER HORST** MONTEREY, TN

START TO FINISH: 20 MIN.
MAKES: 4 SERVINGS

- 3 **tablespoons olive oil**
- 2 **garlic cloves, minced**
- ¼ **teaspoon salt**
- ¼ **teaspoon pepper**
- 1 **small butternut squash, peeled and cut lengthwise into ½-inch slices**

1. In a small bowl, combine the oil, garlic, salt and pepper. Brush over squash slices.

2. Grill squash, covered, over medium heat or broil 4 in. from heat 4-5 minutes on each side or until tender.

EASY GRILLED SQUASH

SUMMER VEGETABLE MEDLEY

This is our favorite way to fix summer vegetables. Cleanup is quick and easy, and the veggies only need to be flipped once. This dish goes from the garden to the table in under an hour.

—LORI DANIELS BEVERLY, WV

PREP: 15 MIN. • **GRILL:** 20 MIN.
MAKES: 8 SERVINGS

- ¼ **cup olive oil**
- 1 **teaspoon salt**
- 1 **teaspoon dried parsley flakes**
- 1 **teaspoon dried basil**
- 3 **large ears fresh corn on the cob, cut into 3-inch pieces**
- 2 **medium zucchini, cut into ¼-inch slices**
- 1 **medium yellow summer squash, cut into ¼-inch slices**
- 1 **medium sweet onion, sliced**
- 1 **large green pepper, diced**
- 10 **cherry tomatoes**
- 1 **jar (4½ ounces) whole mushrooms, drained**
- ¼ **cup butter**

1. In a large bowl, combine the oil, salt, parsley and basil. Add vegetables and toss to coat. Place on a double thickness of heavy-duty foil (about 28 x18 in.). Dot with butter. Fold foil around vegetables and seal tightly.

2. Grill, covered, over medium heat for 20-25 minutes or until corn is tender, turning once. Open carefully to allow steam to escape.

GRILL SKILL

Grilled vegetables are fantastic sides for backyard barbecues, but why not add them to other dishes? Charbroil your favorite veggies and serve them on top of a green salad, piled high on a sandwich, scattered over a pizza or even stirred into a pasta entree. Get creative, and you'll find that the smoky flavor of grilled veggies is sure to lend a new twist to your mealtime standbys.

---

⑤ INGREDIENTS FAST FIX

LEMON GARLIC MUSHROOMS

I baste whole mushrooms with a lemony sauce to prepare this simple side dish. Using skewers or a grill basket makes it easy to turn the mushrooms.

—DIANE HIXON NICEVILLE, FL

START TO FINISH: 25 MIN.
MAKES: 4 SERVINGS

- ¼ **cup lemon juice**
- 3 **tablespoons minced fresh parsley**
- 2 **tablespoons olive oil**
- 3 **garlic cloves, minced**
  Pepper to taste
- 1 **pound large fresh mushrooms**

1. In a small bowl, combine the first five ingredients; set aside. Grill the mushrooms, covered, over medium-hot heat for 5 minutes. Brush generously with lemon mixture.

2. Turn the mushrooms; grill for 5-8 minutes longer or until tender. Brush with the remaining lemon mixture before serving.

PARMESAN POTATO FANS

PARMESAN POTATO FANS

Looking for the ultimate grilled potato? These seasoned potato fans are filled with tender onions, roasted garlic cloves and savory Parmesan cheese.

—SHARON CRABTREE GRAHAM, WA

PREP: 20 MIN. • **GRILL:** 35 MIN.
MAKES: 6 SERVINGS

- 6 **medium potatoes**
- 2 **small onions, halved and thinly sliced**
- 6 **tablespoons butter, diced**
- 2 **garlic cloves, minced**
- 6 **tablespoons grated Parmesan cheese**
- 1 **tablespoon minced chives**
- ½ **teaspoon crushed red pepper flakes**
  Dash salt

1. Prepare grill for indirect heat. With a sharp knife, cut each potato into ½-in. slices, leaving slices attached at the bottom. Fan potatoes slightly. Place each potato on a 12-in. square of heavy-duty foil.

2. Insert the onions, butter and garlic between potato slices. Combine the cheese, chives, pepper flakes and salt; sprinkle between slices. Fold foil around potatoes and seal tightly.

3. Grill, covered, over indirect medium heat for 35-45 minutes or until tender. Open foil carefully to allow the steam to escape.

SUMMER SQUASH
VEGGIE PACKS

(5) INGREDIENTS

CAMPFIRE POTATOES

Nothing beats these buttery potatoes grilled in a no-mess foil pack. Try them with your favorite grilled chicken or steak.

—**MICHELLE ISENHOFF** WAYLAND, MI

PREP: 10 MIN. • **GRILL:** 30 MIN.
MAKES: 4 SERVINGS

- 5 **medium potatoes, peeled and sliced**
- ¼ **cup grated Parmesan cheese**
- 2 **teaspoons minced fresh parsley**
- ¾ **teaspoon garlic powder**
- ½ **teaspoon salt**
- ⅛ **teaspoon pepper**
- ¼ **cup butter, cubed**

1. Place half of the potatoes on a large piece of heavy-duty foil. Sprinkle with Parmesan cheese, parsley, garlic powder, salt and pepper; dot with butter. Top with the remaining potatoes. Fold foil over and seal tightly.
2. Grill, covered, over medium heat for 30-35 minutes or until the potatoes are tender.

 **GRILL SKILL**

Summer squash have edible thin skins and soft seeds, making them ideal for grilling. Yellow, zucchini and pattypan are the most common varieties. Look for them at your farmers market. Choose firm summer squash with brightly colored skin that's free of spots and bruises. Generally, the smaller the squash, the more tender it will be. You can refrigerate summer squash in a plastic bag for up to 5 days before grilling.

FAST FIX

SUMMER SQUASH VEGGIE PACKS

Vegetable lovers will truly enjoy this dish, which is a snap to grill. Fresh-picked squash from your garden will make it even better.

—**LISA FINNEGAN** FORKED RIVER, NJ

START TO FINISH: 25 MIN.
MAKES: 4 SERVINGS

- 2 **medium yellow summer squash, sliced**
- 2 **medium sweet red peppers, sliced**
- 1 **large sweet onion, halved and sliced**
- 2 **tablespoons olive oil**
- 2 **garlic cloves, minced**
- 1 **teaspoon sugar**
- ¼ **teaspoon salt**
- ¼ **teaspoon pepper**

1. In a large bowl, combine all eight ingredients. Divide between two double thicknesses of heavy-duty foil (about 18x12 in.). Fold foil around vegetable mixture and seal tightly.
2. Grill, covered, over medium heat for 10-15 minutes or until vegetables are tender. Open foils carefully to allow steam to escape.

GRILLED ROMAINE WITH CHIVE-BUTTERMILK DRESSING

I was grilling steak one night and wanted to make a special side dish. I'd recently seen a grilled Caesar salad recipe and decided to create my own version. This goes well with chicken, too, and it couldn't be easier.

—CRYSTAL SCHLUETER NORTHGLENN, CO

START TO FINISH: 25 MIN.
MAKES: 4 SERVINGS

- 2 **romaine hearts, halved lengthwise**
- 3 **tablespoons olive oil**
- 3 **tablespoons buttermilk**
- 3 **tablespoons reduced-fat plain Greek yogurt**
- 4 **teaspoons minced fresh chives**
- 2 **teaspoons lemon juice**
- ½ **teaspoon minced garlic**
  Dash salt
  Dash pepper
- ¼ **cup shredded Parmesan cheese**
- 4 **bacon strips, cooked and crumbled**

1. Brush romaine halves with oil. Grill romaine, uncovered, over medium-high heat 6-8 minutes or until leaves begin to wilt and color, turning once.

2. Meanwhile, in a small bowl, whisk buttermilk, yogurt, chives, lemon juice, garlic, salt and pepper until blended; drizzle over cut sides of romaine. Top with cheese and bacon.

GRILLED ROMAINE WITH CHIVE-BUTTERMILK DRESSING

QUICK
BARBECUED
BEANS

FAST FIX
QUICK BARBECUED BEANS

Here's a simple, classic recipe. Cooking it on the grill, however, beats the clock and introduces a subtle flavor. Featuring a blend of three types of beans, the side dish comes together quickly, and cleanup is a snap because everything is stirred together, grilled and served in one disposable foil pan.
—**MILLIE VICKERY** LENA, IL

START TO FINISH: 25 MIN.
MAKES: 5 SERVINGS

- 1 **can (16 ounces) kidney beans, rinsed and drained**
- 1 **can (15½ ounces) great northern beans, rinsed and drained**
- 1 **can (15 ounces) pork and beans**
- ½ **cup barbecue sauce**
- 2 **tablespoons brown sugar**
- 2 **teaspoons prepared mustard**

1. In an ungreased 8-in. square disposable foil pan, combine all ingredients.
2. Grill, covered, over medium heat 15-20 minutes or until heated through, stirring occasionally.

GRILLED VEGGIE MIX

This tempting veggie dish is the perfect accompaniment to warm-weather barbecues. To make the recipe even more satisfying, I use my homegrown vegetables and herbs in the mix.
—**JANET BOULGER** BOTWOOD, NL

PREP: 15 MIN. • **GRILL:** 30 MIN.
MAKES: 10 SERVINGS

- 2 **medium zucchini, cut into ½-inch slices**
- 1 **large green pepper, cut into ½-inch squares**
- 1 **large sweet red pepper, cut into ½-inch squares**
- 1 **pound fresh mushrooms, halved**
- 1 **large onion, cubed**
- 6 **medium carrots, cut into ¼-inch slices**
- 2 **cups fresh broccoli florets**
- 2 **cups fresh cauliflowerets**

DRESSING
- ¼ **cup olive oil**
- ¼ **cup butter, melted**
- ¼ **cup minced fresh parsley**
- 2 **garlic cloves, minced**
- 1 **teaspoon dried basil**
- ½ **teaspoon dried oregano**
- ½ **teaspoon salt**

1. Place vegetables in the center of two pieces of double-layered heavy-duty foil (about 18 in. square). Combine dressing ingredients; drizzle over vegetables; toss gently to coat.
2. Fold foil around mixture and seal tightly. Grill, covered, over medium heat for 15 minutes on each side or until vegetables are tender.

CHIPOTLE LIME CORN COBS

CHIPOTLE LIME CORN COBS

In Mexico, grilled corn sometimes comes slathered in mayonnaise, rolled in grated cheese and served with lime and chili powder. This is my family's take on the dish, with our own flavor enhancements.
—**CAROLYN KUMPE** EL DORADO, CA

PREP: 25 MIN. • **GRILL:** 25 MIN.
MAKES: 6 SERVINGS

- 6 **large ears sweet corn in husks**
- ½ **cup mayonnaise**
- 1 **chipotle pepper in adobo sauce, finely chopped**
- 2 **tablespoons minced fresh cilantro**
- 2 **tablespoons lime juice**
- 1½ **teaspoons grated lime peel**
- 1 **garlic clove, minced**
- ½ **cup grated Asiago cheese**

1. Carefully peel back corn husks to within 1 in. of bottoms; remove silk. Rewrap corn in husks and secure with kitchen string. Place in a stockpot; cover with cold water. Soak corn for 20 minutes; drain.
2. Grill corn, covered, over medium heat for 25-30 minutes or until tender, turning often.
3. In a small bowl, combine the mayonnaise, chipotle, cilantro, lime juice, lime peel and garlic; spread one heaping tablespoon over each ear of corn. Sprinkle with Asiago cheese.

PESTO-CORN
GRILLED PEPPERS

FAST FIX
PESTO-CORN GRILLED PEPPERS

We grill almost daily and enjoy using fresh produce from our garden. These pepper halves filled with a basil-seasoned corn mixture are my husband's favorite.

—**RACHAEL MARRIER** STAR PRAIRIE, WI

START TO FINISH: 30 MIN.
MAKES: 8 SERVINGS

- ½ cup plus 2 teaspoons olive oil, divided
- ¾ cup grated Parmesan cheese
- 2 cups packed basil leaves
- 2 tablespoons sunflower kernels or walnuts
- 4 garlic cloves
- ½ cup finely chopped sweet red pepper
- 4 cups fresh or frozen corn, thawed
- 4 medium sweet red, yellow or green peppers
- ¼ cup shredded Parmesan cheese, optional

1. For pesto, combine ½ cup oil, grated cheese, basil, sunflower kernels and garlic in a blender; cover and process until blended.
2. In a large skillet, heat remaining oil over medium-high heat. Add chopped red pepper; cook and stir until tender. Add corn and pesto; heat through.
3. Halve peppers lengthwise; remove seeds. Grill peppers, covered, over medium heat, cut side down, 8 minutes. Turn; fill with corn mixture.
4. Grill 4-6 minutes longer or until tender. If desired, sprinkle with shredded cheese.

GRILLED POTATO ANTIPASTO SALAD

Grilling the potatoes adds a fresh and interesting flavor. With the sweet peppers, cheeses and meat, the salad is not only colorful, but hearty, too. I've served this warm, cold and at room temperature. It's fabulous every way!

—**MARIANNA FALCE** OSCEOLA MILLS, PA

PREP: 20 MIN. • **GRILL:** 20 MIN.
MAKES: 20 SERVINGS (¾ CUP EACH)

- 3 pounds small red potatoes
- ¼ cup olive oil
- ½ teaspoon salt
- ¼ teaspoon pepper
- 1 package (8 ounces) sliced pepperoni
- ½ pound cubed fully cooked ham
- 1 large sweet red pepper, chopped
- 1 large sweet yellow pepper, chopped
- 1 large onion, halved and thinly sliced
- 1 cup chopped cucumber
- 1 cup cubed part-skim mozzarella cheese
- 1 cup cubed cheddar cheese
- 1 cup Italian salad dressing
- 1 can (2¼ ounces) sliced ripe olives, drained

1. Scrub potatoes and cut into wedges. Place in a large bowl. Add the oil, salt and pepper; toss to coat.
2. Transfer potatoes to a grill wok or basket. Grill, covered, over medium heat for 20-25 minutes or until tender, turning occasionally. Transfer to a large bowl.
3. Add the remaining ingredients; toss to coat. Serve warm or cold.

ONION & GARLIC POTATO FANS

Turn everyday baked potatoes into an impressive grilled delight with this simple and flavorful idea.

—**JENNIFER BLACK-ORTIZ** SAN JOSE, CA

PREP: 15 MIN. • **GRILL:** 40 MIN.
MAKES: 2 SERVINGS

- 2 medium baking potatoes
- 1 small onion, halved and thinly sliced
- 2 tablespoons butter, diced
- 1 tablespoon finely chopped celery
- ¼ teaspoon salt
- ¼ teaspoon dried oregano
- ⅛ teaspoon garlic powder
- ⅛ teaspoon pepper

1. With a sharp knife, make cuts ½ in. apart in each potato, leaving slices attached at the bottom. Fan the potatoes slightly. Place each on a piece of heavy-duty foil (about 12 in. square).
2. Insert onion and butter between potato slices. Sprinkle with celery, salt, oregano, garlic powder and pepper. Fold foil around potatoes and seal tightly. Grill, covered, over medium-hot heat for 40-45 minutes or until tender.

(5) INGREDIENTS

BACON CABBAGE WEDGES

My father first fixed these bacon-wrapped cabbage wedges a few years ago. Now I make them for my family when we put steak and potatoes on the grill. Even our three daughters like them.

—DEMI RICE MACKS CREEK, MO

PREP: 10 MIN. • **GRILL:** 40 MIN.
MAKES: 4 SERVINGS

- 1 **medium head cabbage (about 2 pounds)**
- 4 **teaspoons butter, softened**
- 1 **teaspoon salt**
- ½ **teaspoon garlic powder**
- ¼ **teaspoon pepper**
- 2 **tablespoons grated Parmesan cheese**
- 4 **bacon strips**

Cut cabbage into four wedges; place each on a piece of double-layered heavy-duty foil (about 18 in. square). Spread cut sides with butter. Sprinkle with salt, garlic powder, pepper and Parmesan cheese. Wrap a bacon strip around each wedge. Fold foil around cabbage and seal tightly. Grill, covered, over medium heat for 40 minutes or until cabbage is tender, turning twice.

 **GRILL SKILL** _____

When a grilling recipe notes that things should be cooked "covered," it's instructing to close the lid on the grill as the food cooks. A recipe noting that something is cooked "uncovered" simply means the opposite. It has nothing to do with covering or uncovering the food with aluminum foil.

HARVEST
VEGETABLES

HARVEST VEGETABLES

This tasty combination includes so many different vegetables that there's something to please everyone. It's easy, colorful and goes with just about anything.

—LINDA FARNI DURANGO, IA

PREP: 10 MIN. • **GRILL:** 30 MIN.
MAKES: 6 SERVINGS

- 1 **small head cabbage**
- 2 **tablespoons butter, softened**
- ½ **to 1 teaspoon onion salt, optional**
- ⅛ **to ¼ teaspoon pepper**
- 4 **medium carrots, cut into 1-inch pieces**
- 2 **celery ribs, cut into 1-inch pieces**
- 1 **small onion, cut into wedges**
- ½ **pound whole fresh mushrooms**
- 1 **small green pepper, cut into pieces**
- 4 **bacon strips, cooked and crumbled, optional**

1. Cut the cabbage into six wedges; spread butter on cut sides. Place cabbage on a piece of heavy-duty foil (about 24x18 in.). Sprinkle with onion salt, if desired, and pepper.

2. Arrange the carrots, celery, onion, mushrooms and green pepper around cabbage. Sprinkle with bacon if desired. Fold foil over mixture and seal tightly.

3. Grill, covered, over medium-hot heat for 30 minutes or until vegetables are tender, turning occasionally. Open foil carefully to allow steam to escape.

BAKED HARVEST VEGETABLES *Place vegetable packet on a baking sheet. Bake at 400° for 25-30 minutes or until vegetables are tender.*

5 INGREDIENTS FAST FIX
SPICY GRILLED EGGPLANT

This versatile recipe goes well with pasta or grilled meats. Thanks to the Cajun seasoning, it gets more attention than an ordinary side dish.

—GREG FONTENOT THE WOODLANDS, TX

START TO FINISH: 20 MIN.
MAKES: 10 SERVINGS

- 2 **small eggplants, cut into ½-inch slices**
- ¼ **cup olive oil**
- 2 **tablespoons lime juice**
- 1 **tablespoon Cajun seasoning**

1. Brush eggplant slices with oil on both sides. Drizzle with lime juice; sprinkle with Cajun seasoning. Let stand for 5 minutes.

2. Grill the eggplant slices, covered, over medium heat or broil 4 in. from the heat for 4-5 minutes on each side or until tender.

POTATOES PLUS

On our busy farm, meals need to be ready in a short amount of time. These herb-seasoned potatoes grill up perfectly in only half an hour. They're excellent with steak or chicken.

—JILL JELLETT LEDUC, AB

PREP: 10 MIN. • **GRILL:** 25 MIN.
MAKES: 4 SERVINGS

- 4 **medium red potatoes, cubed**
- 1 **medium onion, cubed**
- 1 **medium sweet red pepper, cubed**
- ½ **teaspoon seasoned salt**
- ¼ **teaspoon garlic powder**
- ¼ **teaspoon each dried basil, dill weed and parsley flakes**
- ¼ **cup butter, cubed**

1. Combine vegetables and seasonings; divide among four pieces of heavy-duty foil (about 12 in. square). Dot with butter. Fold foil around vegetables and seal tightly.

2. Grill, covered, over medium heat for 15 minutes on each side. Open foil carefully to allow steam to escape.

FAST FIX
ZUCCHINI WITH SALSA

I top zucchini slices with homemade chunky salsa to make this scrumptious side dish that cooks on the grill. I fix it often in the summer when I have fresh vegetables on hand from my garden.

—CAROLE HILDEBRAND KELSEYVILLE, CA

START TO FINISH: 30 MIN.
MAKES: 10 SERVINGS

- 4 **medium zucchini, sliced**
- 3 **medium tomatoes, diced**
- 1 **medium onion, diced**
- 3 **green onions, sliced**
- 2 **jalapeno peppers, seeded and minced**
- 2 **garlic cloves, minced**
- 1 **tablespoon minced fresh cilantro**
  Salt and pepper to taste, optional

Divide zucchini between two pieces of heavy-duty foil (about 20x18 in.). In a bowl, combine the remaining ingredients; spoon over zucchini. Fold foil around vegetables and seal tightly. Grill, covered, over indirect heat for 15-20 minutes or until the vegetables are tender.

NOTE *Wear disposable gloves when cutting hot peppers; the oils can burn skin. Avoid touching your face.*

SPICY GRILLED
EGGPLANT

BUTTERY HORSERADISH
CORN ON THE COB

FAST FIX ▶

BUTTERY HORSERADISH CORN ON THE COB

For a July Fourth barbecue a few years ago, I whipped up a butter and horseradish topping for grilled corn. People actually formed a line to get seconds.
—**TRISH LOEWEN** BAKERSFIELD, CA

START TO FINISH: 30 MIN.
MAKES: 12 SERVINGS

- ¾ **cup butter, softened**
- ¼ **cup shredded pepper jack cheese**
- ¼ **cup prepared horseradish**
- 1 **tablespoon dried parsley flakes**
- 3 **teaspoons salt**
- 2 **teaspoons balsamic vinegar**
- ½ **teaspoon pepper**
- ¼ **teaspoon dried thyme**
- 12 **medium ears sweet corn, husks removed**

1. In a small bowl, mix the first eight ingredients until blended; spread over sweet corn. Wrap each with a piece of heavy-duty foil (about 14 in. square), sealing tightly.
2. Grill corn, covered, over medium heat 15-20 minutes or until tender, turning occasionally. Open foil carefully to allow steam to escape.

ONION-BASIL GRILLED VEGETABLES

As the caretaker for a private home, I sometimes cook for the young family who lives there. Although I'm an old-fashioned cook, my job has me trying new flavors. Everyone likes these grilled vegetables.

—JAN OEFFLER DANBURY, WI

PREP: 25 MIN. • **COOK:** 25 MIN.
MAKES: 6 SERVINGS

- 3 **medium ears fresh corn, cut into 3 pieces**
- 1 **pound medium red potatoes, quartered**
- 1 **cup fresh baby carrots**
- 1 **large green pepper, cut into 1-inch pieces**
- 1 **large sweet red pepper, cut into 1-inch pieces**
- 1 **envelope onion soup mix**
- 3 **tablespoons minced fresh basil or 1 tablespoon dried basil**
- 1 **tablespoon olive oil**
- ¼ **teaspoon pepper**
- 1 **tablespoon butter**

1. In a large bowl, combine the first nine ingredients. Toss to coat. Place on a double thickness of heavy-duty foil (about 28x18 in.). Dot with butter. Fold foil around vegetable mixture and seal tightly.
2. Grill, covered, over medium heat for 25-30 minutes or until potatoes are tender, turning once.

ONION-BASIL GRILLED VEGETABLES

FAST FIX
OLIVE QUICK BREAD

It's true! You can make bread on the grill! We cook out all year long, so this round olive-topped loaf is served alongside everything from pork to beef to chicken. It's a nice change of pace from garlic bread and also makes a tempting appetizer.

—PATRICIA GASPER PEORIA, IL

START TO FINISH: 30 MIN.
MAKES: 2 LOAVES (6-8 SERVINGS EACH)

- 1 **can (4¼ ounces) chopped ripe olives**
- ½ **cup chopped pimiento-stuffed olives**
- ¾ **cup shredded Colby-Monterey Jack cheese**
- ¾ **cup grated Parmesan cheese, divided**
- ¼ **cup butter, melted**
- 1 **tablespoon olive oil**
- 2 **garlic cloves, minced**
- 3 **drops hot pepper sauce**
- 2 **cups biscuit/baking mix**
- ⅔ **cup milk**
- 2 **tablespoons minced fresh parsley Paprika**

1. In a bowl, combine the olives, Colby-Monterey Jack cheese, ½ cup Parmesan cheese, butter, oil, garlic and pepper sauce; set aside.
2. In another bowl, combine the biscuit mix, milk, 2 tablespoons Parmesan cheese and parsley just until moistened. Press into two greased 9-in. disposable aluminum pie pans. Top with olive mixture; sprinkle with paprika and remaining Parmesan.
3. Grill bread, covered, over indirect heat for 8-10 minutes or until bottom crust is golden brown when edge of bread is lifted with a spatula.

ROSEMARY GARLIC POTATOES

ROSEMARY GARLIC POTATOES

Red potatoes just need to be scrubbed clean and quartered to start this side dish perfect for two. You can grill or bake the packets with equally tasty results.

—KRISS ERICKSON KALAUEA, HI

PREP: 10 MIN. • **GRILL:** 40 MIN.
MAKES: 2 SERVINGS

- 6 **small red potatoes, quartered**
- 1 **small onion, thinly sliced**
- 6 **whole garlic cloves, peeled**
- 2 **sprigs fresh rosemary or 1 to 2 teaspoons dried rosemary, crushed**
- ½ **teaspoon salt Dash pepper**
- 2 **tablespoons grated Parmesan cheese**
- ¼ **cup olive oil**

1. Place the potatoes, onion and garlic on two pieces of heavy-duty foil (about 12 in. square); top with rosemary, salt, pepper and cheese. Drizzle with oil. Fold in edges of foil and seal tightly.
2. Grill, covered, over medium heat for 40-45 minutes or until potatoes are tender. Carefully open foil to allow steam to escape.
NOTE *To bake the foil packets, place on a baking pan. Bake at 350° for 45 minutes.*

MARINATED ASPARAGUS

BRIQUETTE SCALLOPED POTATOES

Creamy and cheesy with a touch of garlic, these delicious potatoes make a great addition to any meal! Don't worry about leftovers—there won't be any.
—**JUNE DRESS** MERIDIAN, ID

PREP: 20 MIN. • **GRILL:** 70 MIN.
MAKES: 16 SERVINGS (¾ CUP EACH)

- 5 **pounds potatoes (about 6 large), peeled and thinly sliced**
- 3 **cups (12 ounces) shredded cheddar cheese**
- 1 **large onion, chopped**
- ¼ **cup butter, cubed**
- 6 **garlic cloves, minced**
- 2 **teaspoons onion salt**
- ½ **teaspoon salt**
- ½ **teaspoon pepper**
- 1 **cup milk**

1. Prepare grill or campfire for low heat, using 20-24 charcoal briquettes or large wood chips.
2. Line a Dutch oven with heavy-duty aluminum foil; add half of the potatoes. Top with 1½ cups cheese, onion, butter, garlic, onion salt, salt and pepper. Top with remaining potatoes and cheese. Pour milk over the top.
3. Cover Dutch oven. When briquettes or wood chips are covered with white ash, place Dutch oven directly on top of 10 of them. Using long-handled tongs, place the remaining briquettes on the pan's cover.
4. Cook for 70-80 minutes or until bubbly and potatoes are tender. When checking for doneness, use the tongs to carefully lift the cover.

(5) INGREDIENTS

MARINATED ASPARAGUS

Freshly harvested asparagus says spring is in the air...and on your table! If you ask me, eating the tender spears right off the grill is pure pleasure.
—**LESSIE SITES** LIVINGSTON, MT

PREP: 10 MIN. + MARINATING • **GRILL:** 10 MIN.
MAKES: 4 SERVINGS

- 3 **tablespoons balsamic vinegar**
- 2 **tablespoons lemon juice**
- 1 **tablespoon olive oil**
- 1 **tablespoon soy sauce**
- ⅛ **teaspoon pepper**
- 1 **pound fresh asparagus, trimmed**

1. In a large resealable plastic bag, combine the first five ingredients. Add the asparagus; seal bag and turn to coat. Refrigerate for up to 1 hour.
2. Drain asparagus, reserving marinade. Moisten a paper towel with cooking oil; using long-handled tongs, lightly coat the grill rack.
3. Grill asparagus, covered, over medium heat for 6-8 minutes or until crisp-tender, turning and basting occasionally with reserved marinade.

MARVELOUS MEDITERRANEAN VEGETABLES

With so many barbecues in the summer, I created this simple, tasty and colorful dish to complement any entree. I like to prepare it earlier in the day and let it marinate, then I just throw it on the grill.

—CATHY GODBERSON OAKVILLE, ON

PREP: 25 MIN. + MARINATING • **GRILL:** 10 MIN.
MAKES: 9 SERVINGS

- 3 large portobello mushrooms, sliced
- 1 each medium sweet red, orange and yellow peppers, sliced
- 1 medium zucchini, sliced
- 10 fresh asparagus spears, cut into 2-inch lengths
- 1 small onion, sliced and separated into rings
- ¾ cup grape tomatoes
- ½ cup fresh sugar snap peas
- ½ cup fresh broccoli florets
- ½ cup pitted Greek olives
- 1 bottle (14 ounces) Greek vinaigrette
- ½ cup crumbled feta cheese

1. In a large resealable plastic bag, combine the mushrooms, peppers and zucchini. Add the asparagus, onion, tomatoes, peas, broccoli and olives. Pour vinaigrette into bag; seal bag and turn to coat. Refrigerate for at least 30 minutes.

2. Discard marinade. Transfer vegetables to a grill wok or basket. Grill, uncovered, over medium heat for 8-12 minutes or until tender, stirring frequently. Place on a serving plate; sprinkle with cheese.

NOTE *If you do not have a grill wok or basket, use a disposable foil pan. Poke holes in the bottom of the pan with a meat fork to allow liquid to drain.*

MARVELOUS MEDITERRANEAN VEGETABLES

**CILANTRO-LIME CHICKEN
SANDWICHES, PAGE 71**

**SALMON AND SPUD SALAD,
PAGE 95**

**FAJITAS IN PITAS,
PAGE 91**

**SOUTHWESTERN STEAK
SALAD, PAGE 93**

SANDWICHES &
ENTREE SALADS

Take your thrill of the grill
to new heights with hearty
sandwiches and **beefed-up**
salads! Consider the following
meal-in-one favorites when
craving a fiery bite. Whether
served for weekend parties
or **weeknight dinners,** these
savory sensations promise
to satisfy.

CHICKEN & CARAMELIZED ONION GRILLED CHEESE

My grilled cheese sandwich combines chicken with sweet caramelized onions, red peppers, Swiss cheese and sourdough bread. It's "oh my goodness" good!
—KADIJA BRIDGEWATER BOCA RATON, FL

PREP: 40 MIN. • **GRILL:** 15 MIN.
MAKES: 4 SERVINGS

- 2 tablespoons olive oil
- 2 large sweet onions, thinly sliced
- ¾ teaspoon salt, divided
- 1 teaspoon minced fresh rosemary or ¼ teaspoon dried rosemary, crushed
- 2 boneless skinless chicken breast halves (6 ounces each)
- 2 tablespoons lemon juice
- ¼ teaspoon pepper
- ¼ cup mayonnaise
- ⅓ cup finely chopped roasted sweet red peppers
- 8 slices sourdough bread
- 12 slices Swiss cheese
- 2 tablespoons butter, softened

1. In a large skillet, heat the oil over medium heat. Add onions and ¼ teaspoon salt; cook and stir for 6-8 minutes or until softened. Reduce heat to medium-low; cook 30-40 minutes or until deep golden brown, stirring occasionally. Stir in rosemary.

2. Meanwhile, pound chicken with a meat mallet to ½-in. thickness. Drizzle with lemon juice; sprinkle with pepper and remaining salt. Grill, covered, over medium heat or broil 4 in. from heat 5-7 minutes on each side or until no longer pink. Cut into strips.

3. In a small bowl, mix mayonnaise and red peppers. Spread half of the mayonnaise mixture over four slices of bread. Layer with one slice cheese, chicken, onions and two more slices of cheese. Spread remaining mayonnaise mixture over remaining bread; place over top. Spread outsides of sandwiches with butter.

4. Grill sandwiches, covered, over medium heat or broil 4 in. from heat 2-3 minutes on each side or until golden brown and cheese is melted.

CHICKEN & CARAMELIZED ONION GRILLED CHEESE

REUNION STEAK SANDWICHES

Every year, my grandma hosts a family reunion where these flank steak subs always steal the show. They're topped with a "special sauce" that requires only three ingredients. For a quick dinner, serve them with coleslaw and macaroni salad.

—**JAN CLARK** RIDGEWOOD, NJ

PREP: 20 MIN. • **GRILL:** 20 MIN.
MAKES: 6 SERVINGS

- 1 beef flank steak (1½ pounds)
- ¼ teaspoon salt
- ¼ teaspoon pepper
- 2 tablespoons butter, softened
- 6 sesame submarine sandwich buns, split
- 2 medium tomatoes, thinly sliced
- 1 medium onion, thinly sliced
- 6 slices process American cheese

MUSTARD SAUCE
- ½ cup mayonnaise
- 2 tablespoons Dijon mustard
- 4½ teaspoons Worcestershire sauce

1. Sprinkle steak with salt and pepper. Grill, covered, over medium heat for 6-10 minutes on each side or until meat reaches desired doneness (for medium-rare, a thermometer should read 145°; medium, 160°; well-done, 170°). Let the steak stand for 5 minutes before thinly slicing.

2. Spread butter over inside of buns. Place the tomatoes, onion, sliced steak and cheese on bun bottoms. Broil 5-6 in. from the heat for 2-3 minutes or until cheese is melted. In a small bowl, whisk the mayonnaise, mustard and Worcestershire sauce until blended; spoon over cheese. Replace bun tops.

BEEF TENDERLOIN SANDWICHES

Sweet-sour onions and mushrooms are perfect over the tender beef and roasted garlic mayonnaise. It's a combination that's sure to please!

—**RUTH LEE** TROY, ON

PREP: 15 MIN. + MARINATING • **COOK:** 70 MIN.
MAKES: 4 SERVINGS

- 1 tablespoon brown sugar
- 2 garlic cloves, minced
- ½ teaspoon coarsely ground pepper
- ¼ teaspoon salt
- 1 beef tenderloin roast (1 pound)
- 1 whole garlic bulb
- ½ teaspoon canola oil
- ¼ cup fat-free mayonnaise
- ¼ cup plain yogurt

ONION TOPPING
- 1 tablespoon olive oil
- 1 large sweet onion, thinly sliced
- ½ pound sliced fresh mushrooms
- 2 tablespoons balsamic vinegar
- 1½ teaspoons sugar
- ⅛ teaspoon salt
- ⅛ teaspoon pepper
- 4 slices French bread (¾-inch thick)
- 1 cup fresh arugula

1. Combine the first four ingredients; rub over meat. Refrigerate for 2 hours. Remove papery outer skin from garlic (do not peel or separate cloves). Cut top off of whole garlic. Brush with oil.

2. Wrap bulb in heavy-duty foil. Bake at 425° for 30-35 minutes or until softened. Cool bulb for 10-15 minutes. Squeeze garlic into food processor; add mayonnaise and yogurt. Process until smooth; chill.

3. In a large nonstick skillet, heat the olive oil and saute onion for 5 minutes. Reduce heat; cook and stir onion for 10-12 minutes or until golden. Add mushrooms; cook and stir until tender. Add next four ingredients; cook until reduced slightly

4. Moisten a paper towel with cooking oil; using long-handled tongs, rub it on the grill rack to coat lightly. Grill beef, covered, over medium heat or broil 4 in. from the heat for 5-6 minutes on each side or until meat reaches desired doneness (for medium-rare, a thermometer should read 145°; medium, 160°; well-done, 170°). Let stand for 10 minutes before cutting into 4 slices.

5. Serve warm on bread with garlic mayonnaise, arugula and the onion mixture.

FAST FIX

PINEAPPLE CHICKEN SANDWICHES

For a fun handheld summer entree, I grill up these mouthwatering sandwiches. Serve with chips and iced tea for a truly satisfying meal.

—**SANDRA FISHER** MISSOULA, MT

START TO FINISH: 30 MIN.
MAKES: 2 SERVINGS

- 2 bacon strips, halved
- 2 boneless skinless chicken breast halves (5 ounces each)
- 1 tablespoon olive oil
- 2 tablespoons barbecue sauce
- 2 pineapple slices
- 2 kaiser rolls, split
- 2 lettuce leaves, optional
- 2 slices provolone cheese

1. In a small skillet, cook bacon over medium heat until crisp. Remove to paper towels. Flatten chicken to ⅜-in. thickness; brush both sides with oil. Grill, uncovered, over medium heat for 4 minutes. Turn; brush with barbecue sauce. Grill 3-4 minutes longer or until juices run clear.

2. Meanwhile, place the pineapple and rolls cut side down on grill; cook for 3-4 minutes or until browned, turning the pineapple once. Place lettuce, if desired, on roll bottoms; top with chicken, cheese, bacon and pineapple. Replace roll tops.

STEAK SALAD WITH TOMATOES & AVOCADO

FAST FIX ▶
STEAK SALAD WITH TOMATOES & AVOCADO

My family loves a good steak dinner, but having busy schedules, I'm often thinking about ways to put new and simple twists on meals. This salad is flavored with the freshness of lemon and cilantro, and is one of my husband's favorite dishes.

—LYNDSAY WELLS LADYSMITH, BC

START TO FINISH: 30 MIN.
MAKES: 6 SERVINGS

- 1 beef top sirloin steak (1¼-inch thick and 1½ pounds)
- 1 tablespoon olive oil
- 3 teaspoons Creole seasoning
- 2 large tomatoes, chopped
- 1 can (15 ounces) white kidney or cannellini beans, rinsed and drained
- 1 can (15 ounces) black beans, rinsed and drained
- 3 green onions, chopped
- ¼ cup minced fresh cilantro
- 2 teaspoons grated lemon peel
- 2 tablespoons lemon juice
- ¼ teaspoon salt
- 1 medium ripe avocado, peeled and cubed (½ inch)

1. Rub both sides of steak with oil; sprinkle with Creole seasoning. Grill, covered, over medium heat or broil 4 in. from heat 5-8 minutes on each side or until meat reaches desired doneness (for medium-rare, a thermometer should read 145°; medium, 160°; well-done, 170°). Let stand 5 minutes.
2. In a large bowl, combine tomatoes, beans, green onions, cilantro, lemon peel, lemon juice and salt; gently stir in avocado. Cut steak into slices; serve with bean mixture.
NOTE *The following spices may be substituted for 3 teaspoons Creole seasoning: ¾ teaspoon each salt, garlic powder and paprika; and ⅛ teaspoon each dried thyme, ground cumin and cayenne pepper.*

RASPBERRY CHICKEN SANDWICHES

My raspberry barbecue sauce makes these grilled chicken sandwiches special. I also use this sauce on meatballs, chicken wings and pork chops.

—KELLY WILLIAMS FORKED RIVER, NJ

PREP: 25 MIN. • **GRILL:** 15 MIN.
MAKES: 12 SERVINGS

- 1 cup chili sauce
- ¾ cup raspberry preserves
- 2 tablespoons red wine vinegar
- 1 tablespoon Dijon mustard
- 6 boneless skinless chicken breast halves (4 ounces each)
- 2 tablespoons plus ½ cup olive oil, divided
- ½ teaspoon salt
- ¼ teaspoon pepper
- 24 slices French bread (½-inch thick)
- 12 slices Muenster cheese, halved Shredded lettuce

1. In a small saucepan, combine the first four ingredients. Bring to a boil. Reduce heat; simmer, uncovered, for 2 minutes. Set aside 1 cup for serving and remaining sauce for basting.
2. Flatten chicken breasts to ¼-in. thickness. Cut in half widthwise; place in a large resealable plastic bag. Add 2 tablespoons oil, salt and pepper. Seal bag and turn to coat. Brush remaining oil over both sides of bread.
3. Moisten a paper towel with cooking oil; using long-handled tongs, rub it on the grill rack to coat lightly. Grill chicken, uncovered, over medium heat for 5-7 minutes on each side or until no longer pink, basting frequently with sauce. Remove and keep warm.
4. Grill bread, uncovered, 1-2 minutes or until lightly browned on one side. Turn and top each piece of bread with a slice of cheese. Grill 1-2 minutes longer or until bottom of bread is toasted. Place a piece of chicken, lettuce and reserved raspberry sauce on half of bread slices; top with remaining bread.

JAMAICAN JERK TURKEY WRAPS

After tasting these spicy wraps at a neighborhood party, I got the recipe. The grilled turkey tenderloin and light jalapeno dressing made them a hit.

—MARY ANN DELL PHOENIXVILLE, PA

PREP: 20 MIN. • **GRILL:** 20 MIN.
MAKES: 4 SERVINGS

- 2 cups broccoli coleslaw mix
- 1 medium tomato, seeded and chopped
- 3 tablespoons reduced-fat coleslaw dressing
- 1 jalapeno pepper, seeded and chopped
- 1 tablespoon prepared mustard
- 1½ teaspoons Caribbean jerk seasoning
- 2 turkey breast tenderloins (8 ounces each)
- 4 fat-free flour tortillas (8 inches)

1. In a large bowl, toss coleslaw mix, tomato, coleslaw dressing, jalapeno and mustard; set aside.
2. Rub the seasoning over turkey tenderloins. Moisten a paper towel with cooking oil; using long-handled tongs, rub it on grill rack to coat lightly. Grill turkey, covered, over medium heat or broil 4 in. from heat 8-10 minutes on each side or until a thermometer reads 165°. Let stand 5 minutes.
3. Grill tortillas, uncovered, over medium heat 45-55 seconds on each side or until warmed. Thinly slice turkey; place down the center of tortillas. Top with coleslaw mixture and roll up.
NOTE *Wear disposable gloves when cutting hot peppers; the oils can burn skin. Avoid touching your face.*

**OPEN-FACED GRILLED
SANDWICHES**

**OPEN-FACED GRILLED
SALMON SANDWICHES**

(5) INGREDIENTS FAST FIX

OPEN-FACED GRILLED SALMON SANDWICHES

My family loves to fish. What better reward after a day of fishing than eating what you just caught? We make salmon several different ways, and this one is the family favorite.

—**STEPHANIE HANISAK** PORT MURRAY, NJ

START TO FINISH: 30 MIN.
MAKES: 4 SERVINGS

- 4 **salmon fillets (1-inch thick and 5 ounces each), skin removed**
- ¾ **cup mesquite marinade**
- ¼ **teaspoon pepper**
- 4 **slices sourdough bread (½-inch thick)**
- ¼ **cup tartar sauce**
- 4 **iceberg lettuce leaves**
- 4 **lemon wedges, optional**

1. Place fillets in an 8-in. square dish. Pour marinade over fillets; turn fish to coat. Let stand 15 minutes.

2. Drain salmon, discarding marinade. Sprinkle salmon with pepper.

3. Moisten a paper towel with cooking oil; using long-handled tongs, rub it on the grill rack to coat lightly. Grill salmon, covered, over medium heat or broil 4 in. from heat 4-6 minutes on each side or until fish just begins to flake easily with a fork.

4. Grill bread, covered, over medium heat 1-2 minutes on each side or until lightly toasted. Spread with tartar sauce; top with lettuce and salmon. If desired, serve with lemon wedges.

FAST FIX ▶
CHICKEN STRAWBERRY SPINACH SALAD

This pretty spinach salad topped with grilled chicken, strawberries and almonds features a delectably sweet poppy seed dressing. Made in moments, it's a refreshing lunch or light supper for two.
—**GINGER ELLSWORTH** CALDWELL, ID

START TO FINISH: 30 MIN.
MAKES: 2 SERVINGS

- ¾ **pound boneless skinless chicken breasts, cut into strips**
- ¼ **cup reduced-sodium chicken broth**
- ¼ **cup poppy seed salad dressing, divided**
- 2 **cups fresh baby spinach**
- 1 **cup torn romaine**
- 1 **cup sliced fresh strawberries**
- ¼ **cup sliced almonds, toasted**

1. Place chicken on a double thickness of heavy-duty foil (about 18x15 in.). Combine broth and 1 tablespoon poppy seed dressing; spoon over chicken. Fold edges of foil around chicken mixture, leaving center open. Grill, covered, over medium heat for 10-12 minutes or until chicken is no longer pink.
2. In a salad bowl, combine spinach, romaine and strawberries. Add chicken and remaining poppy seed dressing; toss to coat. Sprinkle with almonds.

GRILL SKILL ———

Use a meat thermometer to check the internal temperature of grilled chicken before the recommended cooking time is up. The internal temperature of boneless chicken breasts, for instance, should be 165° before serving.

DEE'S GRILLED TUNA WITH GREENS

FAST FIX ▶
DEE'S GRILLED TUNA WITH GREENS

Slices of moist, tender tuna top this colorful combo of fresh spinach, grape tomatoes, corn and edamame. The tangy vinaigrette takes the salad to an intriguing new level.
—**DE'LAWRENCE REED** DURHAM, NC

START TO FINISH: 30 MIN.
MAKES: 4 SERVINGS

- 1 **pound tuna steaks**
- 2 **teaspoons olive oil**
- ¼ **teaspoon salt**
- ¼ **teaspoon pepper**
- 6 **cups fresh baby spinach**
- 1 **cup grape tomatoes**
- ¾ **cup frozen shelled edamame, thawed**
- ½ **cup frozen corn, thawed**

CITRUS VINAIGRETTE
- 2 **tablespoons olive oil**
- 1 **tablespoon minced fresh basil**
- 1 **tablespoon white wine vinegar**
- 1 **tablespoon honey**
- 1 **tablespoon lime juice**
- 1 **tablespoon lemon juice**
- 1 **tablespoon orange juice**
- ⅛ **teaspoon salt**
- ⅛ **teaspoon pepper**

1. Moisten a paper towel with cooking oil; using long-handled tongs, rub grill rack to coat lightly. Brush tuna with olive oil; sprinkle with salt and pepper. Grill, covered, over high heat or broil 3-4 in. from the heat for 2-3 minutes on each side for rare; cook longer if desired. Let stand for 5 minutes.
2. Meanwhile, in a large bowl, combine spinach, tomatoes, edamame and corn. In a small bowl, whisk the vinaigrette ingredients; drizzle over salad and toss to coat.
3. Divide salad among four plates; slice tuna and arrange over salads. Serve immediately.

THAI PORK SALAD

My husband and I love to try different recipes, like this one. Lime, cilantro and a little bit of heat create a unique Asian salad that's out of this world.

—SHARON DELANEY-CHRONIS
SOUTH MILWAUKEE, WI

PREP: 25 MIN. • **GRILL:** 10 MIN.
MAKES: 2 SERVINGS

- 2½ **cups shredded cabbage**
- ⅓ **cup minced fresh cilantro**
- 2 **tablespoons minced fresh mint**
- 2 **boneless pork loin chops (½-inch thick and 4 ounces each)**
- ¼ **cup thinly sliced onion**
- 1 **tablespoon canola oil**
- ¼ **cup lightly salted cashews**
- ¼ **teaspoon salt**
- ⅛ **to ¼ teaspoon cayenne pepper**
- 2 **tablespoons plus 2 teaspoons lime juice**
- 1½ **teaspoons sugar**

1. In a small bowl, combine the cabbage, cilantro and mint; set aside.
2. Moisten a paper towel with cooking oil; using long-handled tongs, rub the grill rack lightly to coat. Grill pork, covered, over medium heat or broil 4 in. from the heat for 4-5 minutes on each side or until a thermometer reads 160°. Slice pork and keep warm.
3. In a small skillet, saute onion in oil until tender. Add the cashews, salt, cayenne and pork; heat through. Stir in lime juice and sugar until blended. Remove from the heat.
4. Divide cabbage mixture between two serving plates. Top with the pork mixture.

BRUSCHETTA CHICKEN WRAP

FAST FIX
BRUSCHETTA CHICKEN WRAP

As an Italian-American, I love garlic, tomatoes and basil, all of which are musts for good bruschetta. This recipe was created in celebration of the first tomatoes from our home garden.

—GINA RINE CANFIELD, OH

START TO FINISH: 30 MIN.
MAKES: 4 SERVINGS

- 2 **plum tomatoes, finely chopped (about 1 cup)**
- 1 **cup fresh baby spinach, coarsely chopped**
- ¼ **cup finely chopped red onion**
- 1 **tablespoon shredded Parmesan or Romano cheese**
- 1 **tablespoon minced fresh basil**
- 1 **teaspoon olive oil**
- 1 **teaspoon balsamic vinegar**
- ⅛ **teaspoon plus ¼ teaspoon pepper, divided**
  Dash garlic powder
- 4 **boneless skinless chicken breast halves (4 ounces each)**
- ½ **teaspoon salt**
- 2 **ounces fresh mozzarella cheese, cut into 4 slices**
- 4 **whole wheat tortillas (8 inches)**

1. In a small bowl, mix the tomatoes, spinach, onion, Parmesan cheese, basil, oil, vinegar, ⅛ teaspoon pepper and garlic powder.
2. Moisten a paper towel with cooking oil; using long-handled tongs, rub on grill rack to coat lightly. Sprinkle the chicken with salt and the remaining pepper; place on grill rack. Grill, covered, over medium heat 4-6 minutes on each side or until a thermometer reads 165°.
3. Top each chicken breast with one cheese slice; cover and grill 1-2 minutes longer or until cheese is melted. Grill the tortillas over medium heat for 20-30 seconds or until heated through.
4. Place chicken on center of each tortilla; top with about ¼ cup tomato mixture. Fold bottom of tortilla over filling; fold both sides to close.

BUFFALO CHICKEN SANDWICHES

I love grilling chicken because it's often a healthier choice. I put my Joe-style twist on this sandwich with a spicy-sweet marinade and a homemade blue cheese dressing.

—JOE SLATE PORT ST. JOE, FL

PREP: 25 MIN. + MARINATING • **GRILL:** 10 MIN.
MAKES: 4 SERVINGS

- 1 cup Louisiana-style hot sauce
- ½ cup packed brown sugar
- 4 tablespoons butter
- 2 tablespoons cider vinegar
- 1 teaspoon taco seasoning
- 4 boneless skinless chicken breast halves (5 ounces each)
- ¼ cup crumbled blue cheese
- ¼ cup buttermilk
- ¼ cup mayonnaise
- 1 tablespoon shredded Parmesan cheese
- 1 tablespoon minced chives
- 1½ teaspoons lemon juice
- ½ teaspoon balsamic vinegar
- ¼ teaspoon minced garlic
- ¼ teaspoon pepper
- 4 onion rolls, split and toasted
- 4 cooked bacon strips
- 4 slices Colby cheese (¾ ounce each)
- 4 lettuce leaves
- 4 slices tomato
- 4 slices red onion

1. In a small saucepan over medium heat, bring the first five ingredients to a boil; boil, uncovered, for 1 minute. Cool for 10 minutes; set aside ½ cup for basting.

2. Flatten chicken to ½-in. thickness. Pour remaining marinade into a large resealable plastic bag; add chicken. Seal bag and turn to coat; refrigerate for at least 2 hours.

3. Drain and discard marinade from chicken. Grill chicken, covered, over medium heat or broil 4 in. from heat for 5-6 minutes on each side or until a thermometer reads 170°, basting occasionally with reserved marinade.

4. In a small bowl, combine the blue cheese, buttermilk, mayonnaise, Parmesan cheese, chives, lemon juice, vinegar, garlic and pepper. Spread over roll bottoms; top with the chicken, bacon, cheese, lettuce, tomato and onion. Replace roll tops.

BUFFALO CHICKEN SANDWICHES

GRILLED SALMON CAESAR SALAD

Flaky grilled salmon, lettuce, tomatoes and homemade garlic croutons star in this attractive salad. A Caesar-style dressing, seasoned with lemon juice and grated Parmesan cheese, coats this elegant salad.

—CLARA BARRETT MADISON, FL

PREP: 20 MIN. • **GRILL:** 20 MIN. + COOLING
MAKES: 6 SERVINGS

- 2 salmon fillets (1 pound each)
- 3 cups cubed French bread
- 1 tablespoon olive oil
- ¼ teaspoon garlic powder
- 1 bunch romaine, torn
- 2 cups small cherry tomatoes

DRESSING

- 3 tablespoons olive oil
- 2 tablespoons lemon juice
- 4½ teaspoons mayonnaise
- 2¼ teaspoons sugar
- 2 garlic cloves, minced
- ½ teaspoon salt
- ⅛ teaspoon pepper
- 1 tablespoon grated Parmesan cheese

1. Moisten a paper towel with cooking oil; using long-handled tongs, rub on grill rack to coat lightly. Place salmon skin side down on grill. Grill, covered, over medium heat or broil 4 in. from the heat for 15-20 minutes or until the fish flakes easily with a fork. Cool.

2. For croutons, toss the bread cubes, oil and garlic powder in a large bowl. In a nonstick skillet, saute bread cubes for 5-6 minutes or until golden brown, stirring occasionally. Remove from the heat; set aside.

3. Flake salmon into chunks. In a large bowl, combine romaine and tomatoes. In a small bowl, whisk the oil, lemon juice, mayonnaise, sugar, garlic, salt and pepper. Pour over salad and toss to coat. Add the salmon, croutons and cheese; toss gently.

GRILLED CHICKEN ON GREENS WITH CITRUS DRESSING

TURKEY CUTLET SANDWICHES

These sandwiches are a welcome change from the usual hamburger or grilled chicken sandwich. The herbed marinade makes the meat so juicy.

—**MARY DETWEILER** MIDDLEFIELD, OH

PREP: 20 MIN. + MARINATING • **GRILL:** 10 MIN.
MAKES: 6 SERVINGS

- ½ **cup chicken broth**
- ¼ **cup olive oil**
- 4½ **teaspoons finely chopped onion**
- 1 **tablespoon white wine vinegar**
- 2 **teaspoons dried parsley flakes**
- ½ **teaspoon salt**
- ½ **teaspoon rubbed sage**
- ⅛ **teaspoon pepper**
- 6 **turkey breast cutlets (about 1 pound)**
- 6 **whole wheat hamburger buns, split**
- 6 **lettuce leaves**
- 6 **tomato slices**

1. In a large resealable plastic bag, combine the first eight ingredients; add the turkey. Seal bag and turn to coat; refrigerate for 12 hours or overnight, turning occasionally.
2. Drain and discard the marinade. Moisten a paper towel with cooking oil; using long-handled tongs, rub the grill rack to coat lightly.
3. Grill turkey, covered, over indirect medium heat or broil 6 in. from the heat for 3-4 minutes on each side or until the juices run clear. Serve on buns with lettuce and tomato.

FAST FIX

GRILLED CHICKEN ON GREENS WITH CITRUS DRESSING

If you love the flavors of the Southwest, this versatile recipe for grilled chicken with fresh red and green peppers is for you. The spicy dressing also keeps well in the refrigerator, perfect for days when you need a quick salad dressing.

—**THERESE ANDERSON** PINE CITY, MN

START TO FINISH: 30 MIN.
MAKES: 8 SERVINGS

- 1 **pound boneless skinless chicken breasts**

DRESSING
- 1 **cup mayonnaise**
- 1 **cup (8 ounces) sour cream**
- ⅓ **cup orange juice**
- 2 **tablespoons lemon juice**
- 4 **teaspoons grated orange peel**
- 1 **tablespoon ground cumin**
- 1 **tablespoon chili powder**
- 1 **teaspoon pepper**
- 1 **garlic clove, minced**
- ¼ **teaspoon salt**
- ¼ **teaspoon cayenne pepper**

SALAD
- 4 **cups torn leaf lettuce**
- 1 **medium tomato, seeded and chopped**
- 1 **medium red onion, chopped**
- 1 **medium sweet red pepper, chopped**
- 1 **medium green pepper, chopped**
- ½ **cup shredded cheddar cheese**

1. Moisten a paper towel with cooking oil; using long-handled tongs, rub the grill rack lightly to coat. Grill chicken, covered, over medium heat or broil 4 in. from the heat for 5-7 minutes on each side or until a thermometer reads 170°.
2. Meanwhile, in a small bowl, combine the dressing ingredients; set aside. In a large bowl, combine the lettuce, tomato, onion, peppers and cheese; divide among eight plates. Cut chicken into bite-size pieces; place over salad. Serve with dressing.

CILANTRO-LIME CHICKEN SANDWICHES

This is summer's ultimate sandwich! The creamy spread and heart-healthy avocado will wake up your taste buds. Everyone I've shared this sandwich recipe with makes it over and over again.

—DEBBIE SPECKMEYER LAKEWOOD, CA

PREP: 25 MIN. + MARINATING • **GRILL:** 15 MIN.
MAKES: 8 SERVINGS

- ½ cup canola oil
- ¼ cup lime juice
- 4 teaspoons ground cumin
- 8 boneless skinless chicken breast halves (6 ounces each)
- 1 cup fat-free spreadable cream cheese
- ⅓ cup minced fresh cilantro
- ¼ cup chopped red onion
- ⅛ teaspoon salt
- ⅛ teaspoon pepper
- 8 whole wheat hamburger buns, split
- 2 medium tomatoes, sliced
- 1 medium ripe avocado, peeled and thinly sliced

1. In a large resealable plastic bag, combine the oil, lime juice and cumin. Add the chicken; seal bag and turn to coat. Refrigerate for at least 1 hour. In a small bowl, combine the cream cheese, cilantro, onion, salt and pepper; chill until serving.

2. Drain and discard marinade. Grill chicken, covered, over medium heat or broil 4 in. from the heat for 6-8 minutes on each side or until a thermometer reads 170°.

3. Spread cream cheese mixture onto buns. Layer with tomatoes, chicken and avocado; replace bun tops.

CILANTRO-LIME
CHICKEN SANDWICHES

COLESLAW
CHICKEN WRAPS

COLESLAW CHICKEN WRAPS

This portable recipe is perfect for outdoor dining when warm weather arrives. We like the fun, fresh spin on regular coleslaw using pineapple and toasted almonds.
—**BARB AGNEW** MAHNOMEN, MN

PREP: 15 MIN. + MARINATING • **GRILL:** 15 MIN.
MAKES: 8 SERVINGS

- 1 **bottle (16 ounces) reduced-fat poppy seed salad dressing, divided**
- 2 **pounds boneless skinless chicken breasts**
- 1 **can (20 ounces) unsweetened pineapple tidbits, drained**
- 1 **package (14 ounces) coleslaw mix**
- 1 **medium sweet red pepper, finely chopped**
- 8 **whole wheat tortillas (8 inches)**
- ½ **cup sliced almonds, toasted**

1. Place 1 cup dressing in a large resealable plastic bag. Add the chicken; seal bag and turn to coat. Refrigerate for 1 hour.

2. Drain and discard marinade. Moisten a paper towel with cooking oil; using long-handled tongs, rub the grill rack to coat lightly.

3. Grill the chicken, covered, over medium heat or broil 4 in. from the heat for 6-8 minutes on each side or until a thermometer reads 170°. Let stand 5 minutes before slicing.

4. Meanwhile, in a large bowl, combine the pineapple, coleslaw mix, red pepper and remaining dressing; toss to coat. Divide among tortillas; top with the chicken and sprinkle with almonds. Roll up tightly; secure with toothpicks.

EGGPLANT PEPPER SANDWICHES

These filling sandwiches give eggplant new appeal. One bite and you'll be hooked—even my grandchildren like them!
—**PAULA MARCHESI** LENHARTSVILLE, PA

PREP: 50 MIN. • **GRILL:** 15 MIN.
MAKES: 4 SERVINGS

- ½ cup pitted ripe olives
- 2 to 3 tablespoons balsamic vinegar
- 1 garlic clove, minced
- ⅛ teaspoon salt
  Dash pepper
- ¼ cup olive oil

SANDWICHES

- ¼ cup olive oil
- 3 garlic cloves, minced
- 1 teaspoon pepper
- ½ teaspoon salt
- 1 large eggplant, cut lengthwise into ½-inch slices
- 2 large sweet red peppers, quartered
- 8 slices firm white bread (½-inch thick)
- ¼ cup fresh basil leaves, thinly sliced

1. Place the first five ingredients in a food processor; cover and process until pureed. While processing, gradually add oil in a steady stream; process until blended. Set aside.

2. For sandwiches, in a small bowl, combine the oil, garlic, pepper and salt; brush over eggplant and red peppers. Prepare grill for indirect heat, using a drip pan. Arrange vegetables on a grilling grid; place on a grill rack over drip pan.

3. Grill, covered, over indirect medium heat for 10-12 minutes or until tender. Remove and keep warm. Grill bread over medium heat 1-2 minutes on each side or until toasted.

4. Spread olive mixture over toast. Top four slices with vegetables and basil; top with remaining toast.

NOTE *If you do not have a grilling grid, use a disposable foil pan. Poke holes in the bottom of the pan with a meat fork to allow liquid to drain.*

GRILLED TENDERLOIN SALAD

FAST FIX
GRILLED TENDERLOIN SALAD

I rely on crisp, cool salads during the hot summer months. In this recipe, the pork is grilled so I don't have to turn on the oven.
—**ROBERTA WHITESELL** PHOENIX, AZ

START TO FINISH: 30 MIN.
MAKES: 5 SERVINGS

DRESSING

- ½ cup orange juice
- 2 tablespoons olive oil
- 2 tablespoons cider vinegar
- 1 tablespoon grated orange peel
- 2 teaspoons honey
- 2 teaspoons Dijon mustard
- ½ teaspoon coarsely ground pepper

SALAD

- 1 pork tenderloin (1 pound)
- 10 cups torn mixed salad greens
- 2 seedless oranges, sectioned and cut into bite-size pieces
  Chopped pistachios and cashews, optional

1. In a small bowl, combine all dressing ingredients; cover and chill until serving.

2. Moisten a paper towel with cooking oil; using long-handled tongs, rub it on the grill rack to coat lightly. Grill pork, covered, over medium heat or broil 4 in. from the heat for 9-11 minutes on each side or until a thermometer reads 145°. Let stand for 5 minutes before slicing.

3. Thinly slice tenderloin. Just before serving, place greens on a serving plate; top with oranges and pork. Drizzle with dressing. Sprinkle with nuts, if desired.

FAST FIX

DELUXE CHEESEBURGER SALAD

I was planning to grill burgers, and then it dawned on me: How about a Big Mac salad? The original recipe doesn't call for a tomato, but it's awesome here.

—**PAM JEFFERIES** CANTRALL, IL

START TO FINISH: 30 MIN.
MAKES: 4 SERVINGS

- 1 **pound ground beef**
- 2 **teaspoons Montreal steak seasoning**
- 6 **cups torn iceberg lettuce**
- 2 **cups (8 ounces) shredded cheddar cheese**
- 1 **cup salad croutons**
- 1 **medium tomato, chopped**
- 1 **small onion, halved and thinly sliced**
- ½ **cup dill pickle slices**
  Thousand Island salad dressing

1. In a large bowl, combine beef and steak seasoning, mixing lightly but thoroughly. Shape into twenty ½-in.-thick patties. Grill burgers, covered, over medium heat 3-4 minutes on each side or until a thermometer reads 160°.
2. In a large bowl, combine the lettuce, burgers, cheese, croutons, tomato, onion and pickles. Serve with salad dressing.
FREEZE OPTION *Place patties on a plastic wrap-lined baking sheet; wrap and freeze until firm. Remove from sheet and transfer to a resealable plastic freezer bag; return to freezer. To use, cook frozen patties as directed, increasing time as necessary for a thermometer to read 160°.*

FLANK STEAK SALAD

This beautiful salad combines marinated flank steak with a tangy homemade dressing for a satisfying meal. If you have leftovers, keep the meat and greens in separate containers.

—**JENNIFER HUNSAKER** ROY, UT

PREP: 25 MIN. + MARINATING
GRILL: 15 MIN. + STANDING • **MAKES:** 8 SERVINGS

- 2 **tablespoons lime juice**
- 2 **tablespoons reduced-sodium soy sauce**
- 3 **garlic cloves, minced**
- 2 **teaspoons minced fresh gingerroot**
- 1 **beef flank steak (2 pounds)**

VINAIGRETTE

- 2 **tablespoons plus 2 teaspoons white vinegar**
- 1 **tablespoon reduced-sodium soy sauce**
- 1 **teaspoon ketchup**
- 3 **tablespoons chopped onion**
- 1 **tablespoon sugar**
- 1 **small garlic clove, peeled and halved**
- ½ **teaspoon minced fresh gingerroot**
- ¼ **teaspoon salt**
- ¼ **teaspoon pepper**
- 3 **tablespoons canola oil**
- 1 **bunch romaine, torn**
- 1 **cup grape tomatoes**

1. In a large resealable plastic bag, combine the lime juice, soy sauce, garlic and ginger; add the beef. Seal bag and turn to coat; refrigerate for 8 hours or overnight.
2. Drain beef and discard marinade. Moisten a paper towel with cooking oil; using long-handled tongs, rub the grill rack to coat lightly. Grill beef, covered, over medium heat or broil 4 in. from the heat for 6-8 minutes on each side or until meat reaches desired doneness (for medium-rare, a thermometer should read 145°; medium, 160°; well-done, 170°). Let meat stand for 10 minutes. To serve, thinly slice across the grain.
3. Meanwhile, in a blender, combine the vinegar, soy sauce, ketchup, onion, sugar, garlic, ginger, salt and pepper; cover and process until pureed. While processing, gradually add the oil in a steady stream.
4. Place romaine and tomatoes in a large bowl. Drizzle with vinaigrette; toss to coat. Divide among eight plates; top with steak.

MUSTARD TURKEY SANDWICHES

I turn to this recipe when hosting a casual dinner with friends. The turkey cutlets can marinate while you visit with guests, then be popped onto the grill for a mouthwatering meal in no time.

—**MONICA WILCOTT** STURGIS, SK

PREP: 10 MIN. + MARINATING • **GRILL:** 10 MIN.
MAKES: 6 SERVINGS

- ½ **cup olive oil**
- ½ **cup honey**
- ¼ **cup Dijon mustard**
- 1 **tablespoon curry powder**
  Pinch cayenne pepper
- 1 **package (17.6 ounces) turkey breast cutlets**
- 6 **onion or kaiser rolls, split**
  Lettuce leaves

1. In a small saucepan, combine the first five ingredients. Cook and stir over medium heat until the mixture is combined. Cool slightly; set aside ¼ cup. Pour remaining mixture into a large resealable plastic bag; add turkey. Seal bag and refrigerate for at least 2 hours.
2. Drain and discard marinade. Grill turkey for 4 minutes on each side or until no longer pink. Spread cut sides of rolls with reserved honey mixture. Add lettuce and turkey.

**DELUXE
CHEESEBURGER SALAD**

FAST FIX

ORANGE CHICKEN SALAD

This refreshing salad makes a wonderful light supper on a warm evening, or leave out the chicken and serve it as a side dish to perk up a main course.
—STEPHEN MCKENNEY EAGLE, MI

START TO FINISH: 30 MIN.
MAKES: 4 SERVINGS

- 4   boneless skinless chicken breast halves (1 pound)
- ⅓   cup raspberry vinegar
- ¼   cup sugar
- 3   tablespoons orange juice
- 2   tablespoons olive oil
- 2   tablespoons minced fresh parsley
- ½   teaspoon salt
- ¼   teaspoon coarsely ground pepper
- ¼   teaspoon hot pepper sauce
- 6   cups torn mixed salad greens
- 2   celery ribs, thinly sliced
- 1   cup orange sections
- ½   cup thinly sliced red onion
- ¼   cup dried cranberries
- ¼   cup slivered almonds, toasted

1. Grill chicken, uncovered, over medium heat for 6-8 minutes on each side or until the juices run clear. Slice and set aside. In a small bowl, combine the vinegar, sugar, orange juice, oil, parsley, salt, pepper and hot pepper sauce; set aside.

2. In a large bowl, combine the salad greens, celery, orange sections, onion and cranberries. Divide among individual serving plates. Top with the chicken. Drizzle with dressing. Sprinkle with almonds.

HEARTY BREADED FISH SANDWICHES

FAST FIX

HEARTY BREADED FISH SANDWICHES

Fishing for a burger alternative? Consider it caught. A hint of cayenne is cooled by a creamy yogurt and mayo sauce that will put your local drive-thru to shame.
—*TASTE OF HOME* TEST KITCHEN

START TO FINISH: 30 MIN.
MAKES: 4 SERVINGS

- ½   cup dry bread crumbs
- ½   teaspoon garlic powder
- ½   teaspoon cayenne pepper
- ½   teaspoon dried parsley flakes
- 4   cod fillets (6 ounces each)
- 4   whole wheat hamburger buns, split
- ¼   cup plain yogurt
- ¼   cup fat-free mayonnaise
- 2   teaspoons lemon juice
- 2   teaspoons sweet pickle relish
- ¼   teaspoon dried minced onion
- 4   lettuce leaves
- 4   slices tomato
- 4   slices sweet onion

1. In a bowl, combine bread crumbs, garlic powder, cayenne and parsley. Coat fillets with bread crumb mixture.

2. Moisten a paper towel with cooking oil; using long-handled tongs, rub the grill rack to coat lightly. Grill the cod, covered, over medium heat or broil 4 in. from the heat for 4-5 minutes on each side or until fish flakes easily with a fork. Grill buns over medium heat for 30-60 seconds or until toasted.

3. Meanwhile, in a small bowl, combine the yogurt, mayonnaise, lemon juice, relish and minced onion; spread over bun bottoms. Top with cod, lettuce, tomato and onion; replace bun tops.

SALSA FISH SANDWICHES *Omit lemon juice, relish and dried minced onion. Substitute salsa for the plain yogurt. Top the sandwiches with sliced tomato and fresh cilantro.*

SLAW-TOPPED FISH SANDWICHES *Omit relish, lettuce, tomato and onion. Substitute red wine vinegar for lemon juice. Stir 1½ cups coleslaw mix into mayonnaise mixture. Top the cod with slaw mixture.*

FAST FIX ▶
ASPARAGUS SALAD WITH GRILLED SALMON

This salad's a little sweet, a little savory and very refreshing. The grilled asparagus makes it even more fabulous!
—**JENNE DELKUS** DES PERES, MO

START TO FINISH: 30 MIN.
MAKES: 4 SERVINGS

- ⅓ **cup maple syrup**
- 2 **tablespoons Dijon mustard**
- 1 **tablespoon olive oil**
- 1 **teaspoon snipped fresh dill**
- 4 **salmon fillets (4 ounces each)**
- 1 **pound fresh asparagus, trimmed**
- 4 **cups spring mix salad greens**
- 1 **cup shredded carrots**
- 1 **hard-cooked egg, cut into eight wedges**
  Coarsely ground pepper

1. In a small bowl, whisk the syrup, mustard, oil and dill; set aside.

2. Place the salmon skin side down on grill rack. Grill, covered, over medium heat for 5 minutes. Meanwhile, in a shallow bowl, drizzle asparagus with 1 tablespoon dressing; toss to coat. Arrange asparagus on a grilling grid; place on the grill rack with salmon. Spoon 1 tablespoon dressing over the salmon.

3. Grill salmon and asparagus, covered, for 4-6 minutes or until salmon flakes easily with a fork and the asparagus is crisp-tender, turning asparagus once.

4. Divide salad greens among four plates and sprinkle with the carrots. Remove skin from salmon. Arrange the egg wedges, asparagus and salmon over salads. Drizzle with the remaining dressing; sprinkle with pepper.

NOTE *If you do not have a grilling grid, use a disposable foil pan. Poke holes in the bottom of the pan with a meat fork to allow liquid to drain.*

ASPARAGUS SALAD WITH GRILLED SALMON

FAST FIX ▶
CHICKEN CAESAR SALAD

Topping a delicious Caesar salad with a tender grilled chicken breast ensures a healthy lunch that will keep you going throughout the day.
—**KAY ANDERSEN** BEAR, DE

START TO FINISH: 25 MIN.
MAKES: 2 SERVINGS

- 2 **boneless skinless chicken breast halves (4 ounces each)**
- 2 **teaspoons olive oil**
- ¼ **teaspoon garlic salt**
- ¼ **teaspoon paprika**
- ¼ **teaspoon pepper**
- ⅛ **teaspoon dried basil**
- ⅛ **teaspoon dried oregano**
- 4 **cups torn romaine**
- 1 **small tomato, thinly sliced**
- ¼ **cup fat-free creamy Caesar salad dressing**
  Caesar salad croutons, optional

1. Brush chicken with oil. Combine the garlic salt, paprika, pepper, basil and oregano; sprinkle over chicken. Grill, uncovered, over medium heat or broil 4 in. from the heat for 4-7 minutes on each side or until a thermometer reads 170°.

2. Arrange romaine and tomato on plates. Cut chicken into strips; place over the salads. Drizzle with dressing. Sprinkle with croutons if desired.

 **GRILL SKILL**

To test the heat of your charcoal grill, put the cover down and open the vent slightly. Wearing an oven mitt, insert a grill thermometer through the vent.

STRAWBERRY-CHICKEN PASTA SALAD

When I figured out how to recreate this restaurant dish at home, my family celebrated. For a different spin, use fresh peaches or raspberries instead of strawberries.

—JANE OZMENT PURCELL, OK

PREP: 25 MIN. • **GRILL:** 15 MIN.
MAKES: 4 SERVINGS

- ½ **cup sliced fresh strawberries**
- 1 **tablespoon sugar**
- 1 **tablespoon balsamic vinegar**
- ½ **teaspoon salt, divided**
- ¼ **teaspoon pepper, divided**
- 3 **tablespoons olive oil**
- 4 **boneless skinless chicken breast halves (6 ounces each)**

ASSEMBLY

- 1 **package (10 ounces) hearts of romaine salad mix**
- 1 **cup cooked gemelli or spiral pasta**
- 1 **small red onion, halved and thinly sliced**
- 1 **cup sliced fresh strawberries**
- ½ **cup glazed pecans**

1. Place strawberries, sugar, vinegar, ¼ teaspoon salt and ⅛ teaspoon pepper in a blender; cover and process until smooth. While processing, gradually add oil in a steady stream. Refrigerate until serving.

2. Moisten a paper towel with cooking oil; using long-handled tongs, rub it on the grill rack to coat lightly. Sprinkle chicken with the remaining salt and pepper; grill, covered, over medium heat 6-8 minutes on each side or until a thermometer reads 165°.

3. Cut chicken into slices. Divide salad mix among four plates; top with pasta, onion, chicken and strawberries. Drizzle with the vinaigrette; sprinkle with pecans.

STRAWBERRY-CHICKEN PASTA SALAD

FAST FIX
STEAK & NEW POTATO TOSS

I usually use leftover barbecued steak to make this fabulous main dish salad. It's pretty, too, with the red pepper, green broccoli and white potatoes.
—DEYANNE DAVIES ROSSLAND, BC

START TO FINISH: 30 MIN.
MAKES: 4 SERVINGS

- 1 pound small red potatoes, scrubbed and cut into wedges
- 1¼ pounds beef top sirloin steak
- 3 cups fresh broccoli florets
- ¼ cup olive oil
- 2 tablespoons cider vinegar
- 2 green onions, thinly sliced
- 2 garlic cloves, minced
- ½ teaspoon ground mustard
- ½ teaspoon paprika
- ¼ teaspoon pepper
- 1 medium sweet red pepper, chopped

1. Place potatoes in a large saucepan and cover with water. Bring to a boil. Reduce the heat; cover and cook for 10-15 minutes or until tender.
2. Meanwhile, grill steak, covered, over medium heat for 8-11 minutes on each side or until meat reaches the desired doneness (for medium-rare, a thermometer should read 145°; medium, 160°; well-done, 170°). Let stand for 10 minutes before thinly slicing across the grain.
3. Place broccoli florets in a steamer basket. Place in a saucepan over 1 in. of water. Bring to a boil. Cover and steam for 2-3 minutes or until crisp-tender. In a small bowl, combine the oil, vinegar, green onions, garlic, mustard, paprika and pepper.
4. Drain broccoli and potatoes; place in a large bowl. Add beef and red pepper; drizzle with vinaigrette and toss to coat. Serve warm or cold.

PORK FAJITA SALAD

You won't need tortillas to enjoy these fajitas! Your crowd will love the festive layers and creamy guacamole.
—IOLA EGLE BELLA VISTA, AR

PREP: 35 MIN. + MARINATING • **GRILL:** 15 MIN.
MAKES: 6 SERVINGS

- ¼ cup olive oil
- 2 tablespoons lime juice
- 1 teaspoon dried oregano
- 1 teaspoon chili powder
- 4 boneless pork loin chops (1-inch thick, about 1½ pounds)
- 2¼ cups chicken broth
- 1 cup uncooked long grain rice
- 2 ripe avocados, peeled
- 1 tablespoon lemon juice
- 1 medium tomato, seeded and chopped
- 1 jalapeno pepper, seeded and chopped
- 2 tablespoons minced fresh cilantro
- 1 tablespoon finely chopped onion
- 1 head iceberg lettuce, shredded
- 1 can (15 ounces) black beans, rinsed and drained
- 1 cup (4 ounces) shredded sharp cheddar cheese
- 1⅓ cups salsa
- 2 cups (16 ounces) sour cream
  Sliced ripe olives and green onions

1. In a large resealable plastic bag, combine the first four ingredients. Add the pork chops. Seal and turn to coat; refrigerate for 8 hours or overnight, turning occasionally. Drain, discarding marinade. Grill chops, uncovered, over medium heat for 12-14 minutes or until juices run clear, turning once. Thinly slice pork; set aside.
2. In a saucepan, bring broth to a boil; stir in rice. Return to a boil. Reduce heat; cover and simmer for 15 minutes or until rice is tender. Cool.
3. Meanwhile, for guacamole, mash avocados with lemon juice. Stir in the tomato, jalapeno, cilantro and onion. In a 5-qt. glass salad bowl, layer lettuce, beans, cheese, pork and guacamole.

Spread with salsa. Combine rice and sour cream; spread over salsa. Garnish with olives and green onions.
NOTE *Wear disposable gloves when cutting hot peppers; the oils can burn skin. Avoid touching your face.*

VEGGIE TORTILLA WRAPS

These tasty wraps, stuffed with cream cheese and marinated veggies, will have everyone singing their praises.
—MARTA NORTHCUTT LEBANON, TN

PREP: 20 MIN. + MARINATING • **GRILL:** 10 MIN.
MAKES: 4 SERVINGS

- 3 tablespoons red wine vinegar
- 3 tablespoons olive oil
- 1 teaspoon lemon-pepper seasoning
- 1 garlic clove, minced
- ½ teaspoon dried oregano
- ½ teaspoon dried basil
- 2 medium zucchini, cut lengthwise into ¼-inch slices
- 1 medium yellow summer squash, cut lengthwise into ¼-inch slices
- 1 medium sweet red pepper, cut into strips
- 4 ounces cream cheese, softened
- 1 tablespoon prepared pesto
- 4 whole wheat tortillas (8 inches), warmed

1. In a large resealable plastic bag, combine the first six ingredients; add zucchini, yellow squash and red pepper. Seal bag and turn to coat; refrigerate overnight, turning once.
2. In a small bowl, combine the cream cheese and pesto; set aside. Drain and discard marinade. Place vegetables in a grill basket or disposable foil pan with slits cut in the bottom. Grill, covered, over medium heat for 3-4 minutes on each side or until tender.
3. Spread reserved pesto cream cheese over tortillas; top with vegetables. Fold sides over filling. Serve immediately.

HONEY-CITRUS CHICKEN SANDWICHES

PEANUT CHICKEN SALAD

Our former neighbor was originally from Indonesia, and one day shared with us this peanut chicken salad, which she called *sate*. My family liked it so much that after she moved away, I continued to make it.
—**DELLA BYERS** ROSAMOND, CA

PREP: 15 MIN. + MARINATING • **GRILL:** 15 MIN.
MAKES: 6 SERVINGS

- ⅓ cup soy sauce
- 3 tablespoons minced garlic
- 3 tablespoons peanut butter
- ¼ cup minced fresh cilantro
- ½ teaspoon hot pepper sauce
- 4 boneless skinless chicken breast halves (4 ounces each)
- 4 cups torn mixed salad greens
- 4 small tomatoes, seeded and chopped
- 4 green onions, chopped
- 1 cup shredded cabbage
- 1 medium cucumber, sliced
- 1 cup honey-roasted peanuts
- 1 cup ranch salad dressing
- 2 to 4 drops hot pepper sauce

1. In a large saucepan, combine the soy sauce, garlic, peanut butter, cilantro and hot pepper sauce; cook and stir until heated through and blended. Cool to room temperature.

2. Pour the soy sauce mixture into a large resealable plastic bag; add the chicken. Seal bag and turn to coat; refrigerate for 1 hour.

3. Drain and discard marinade. Grill chicken, uncovered, over medium heat for 3 minutes on each side. Grill for 6-8 minutes longer or until a thermometer reads 170°.

4. Place the salad greens, tomatoes, onions, cabbage, cucumber and peanuts on a serving platter. Slice the chicken; arrange over salad.

5. In a small bowl, combine the salad dressing and hot pepper sauce. Serve with salad.

HONEY-CITRUS CHICKEN SANDWICHES

During the summer months, our kids and schedules keep me busy, so I always appreciate when my husband volunteers to cook out. This is his specialty.
—**CLAIRE BATHERSON** WESTCHESTER, IL

PREP: 10 MIN. + MARINATING • **GRILL:** 10 MIN.
MAKES: 6 SERVINGS

- 6 boneless skinless chicken breast halves (4 ounces each)
- ¼ cup orange juice
- ¼ cup lemon juice
- ¼ cup honey
- 2 tablespoons vegetable oil
- 1 tablespoon prepared mustard
- ¼ teaspoon poultry seasoning
- ⅛ to ¼ teaspoon cayenne pepper
- 6 slices Monterey Jack or Muenster cheese, optional
- 6 kaiser rolls, split
- 6 thin tomato slices
- 6 red onion slices
  Shredded lettuce

1. Flatten chicken breasts evenly to ¼-in. thickness; set aside. In a large resealable plastic bag, combine the orange and lemon juices, honey, oil, mustard, poultry seasoning and cayenne pepper. Add chicken breasts; seal bag and turn to coat. Refrigerate for 6-8 hours or overnight.

2. Drain; discard marinade. Grill, uncovered, over medium-low heat, turning occasionally, for 10-12 minutes or until juices run clear. If desired, top each chicken breast with a slice of cheese and grill 1-2 minutes longer or until cheese begins to melt. Serve on rolls with tomato, onion and lettuce.

SALMON SPINACH SALAD

I have always loved the combination of salmon and orange, but feel free to change things up in this salad. If you don't have goat cheese, try feta.

—STEPHANIE MATTHEWS TEMPE, AZ

PREP: 25 MIN. • **GRILL:** 10 MIN.
MAKES: 4 SERVINGS

- 4 **salmon fillets (4 ounces each)**
- 6 **tablespoons thawed orange juice concentrate, divided**
- ½ **teaspoon salt, divided**
- ½ **teaspoon paprika**
- ¼ **teaspoon pepper**
- 5 **cups fresh baby spinach**
- 1 **medium navel orange, peeled and cut into ½-inch pieces**
- 2 **green onions, thinly sliced**
- ¼ **cup chopped walnuts, toasted**
- 4½ **teaspoons balsamic vinegar**
- 1 **tablespoon olive oil**
- 1 **garlic clove, minced**
- ¼ **cup crumbled goat cheese**

1. Brush salmon with 4 tablespoons orange juice concentrate. Sprinkle with ¼ teaspoon salt, paprika and pepper. Moisten a paper towel with cooking oil; using long-handled tongs, rub the grill rack to coat lightly. Grill the salmon, covered, over medium heat or broil 4 in. from the heat for 8-10 minutes or until fish flakes easily with a fork.

2. Meanwhile, in a large bowl, combine the spinach, orange, green onions and walnuts. In a small bowl, whisk the vinegar, oil, garlic, remaining orange juice concentrate and salt. Drizzle over salad; toss to coat.

3. Divide among plates; sprinkle with cheese. Top with salmon.

SPIEDIS

SPIEDIS

This recipe originated in my hometown in the 1930s, and is our favorite cookout dish now. Our meat preference for spiedis is venison, but we use other types of meat when it's not available.

—**GERTRUDE SKINNER** BINGHAMTON, NY

PREP: 10 MIN. + MARINATING • **GRILL:** 10 MIN.
MAKES: 8 SERVINGS

- 1 **cup vegetable oil**
- ⅔ **cup cider vinegar**
- 2 **tablespoons Worcestershire sauce**
- ½ **medium onion, finely chopped**
- ½ **teaspoon salt**
- ½ **teaspoon sugar**
- ½ **teaspoon dried basil**
- ½ **teaspoon dried marjoram**
- ½ **teaspoon dried rosemary, crushed**
- 2½ **pounds boneless lean pork, beef, lamb, venison, chicken or turkey, cut into 1½- to 2-inch cubes**
  Italian rolls or hot dog buns

1. In a glass or plastic bowl, combine first nine ingredients. Add meat and toss to coat. Cover and let marinate for 24 hours, stirring occasionally.

2. When ready to cook, thread meat on metal skewers and grill over hot heat until meat reaches desired doneness, abut 10-15 minutes. Remove meat from skewers and serve on long Italian rolls or hot dog buns.

⑤ INGREDIENTS FAST FIX ▶

CHICKEN PESTO SANDWICHES

I especially favor these sandwiches on game day. They're so easy to prep ahead and assemble later at an event.
—**COLLEEN STURMA** MILWAUKEE, WI

START TO FINISH: 30 MIN.
MAKES: 6 SERVINGS

- 6 boneless skinless chicken breast halves (4 ounces each)
- ¾ cup prepared pesto, divided
- ½ teaspoon salt
- ¼ teaspoon pepper
- 12 slices Italian bread (½-inch thick), toasted
- 1 jar (12 ounces) roasted sweet red peppers, drained
- ¼ pound fresh mozzarella cheese, cut into 6 slices

1. Flatten chicken to ¼-in. thickness. Spread 1 tablespoon pesto over each chicken breast; sprinkle with salt and pepper. Grill chicken, covered, over medium heat for 3-5 minutes on each side or until no longer pink.
2. Spread 3 tablespoons pesto over six slices of toast; layer with red peppers, chicken and cheese. Spread remaining pesto over the remaining toast; place over top.

🍴 GRILL SKILL ─────

Don't waste time scrubbing your grill rack after cooking out. Instead, let the grate cool, and then put it in a clean plastic trash bag. Spray the rack generously with oven cleaner. Close the bag tightly and leave overnight. The next day, washing the grate will be a breeze.
LELAND S. DE QUEEN, AR

PORK TENDERLOIN NECTARINE SALAD

PORK TENDERLOIN NECTARINE SALAD

A bag of fresh nectarines shared by my neighbor inspired this grilled pork recipe. The salad is delicious served with corn bread as a quick lunch or light supper.
—**ROBYN LIMBERG-CHILD** ST. CLAIR, MI

PREP: 25 MIN. + MARINATING • **GRILL:** 5 MIN.
MAKES: 6 SERVINGS

- ¼ cup balsamic vinegar
- ¼ cup maple syrup
- 2 tablespoons olive oil
- 1 pound pork tenderloin, cut into ¼-inch slices

SALAD

- 6 cups spring mix salad greens
- 4 medium nectarines, sliced
- 4 ounces Havarti cheese, cubed
- ½ cup sliced sweet onion
- ¼ cup honey-roasted almonds
- 1 cup honey mustard salad dressing

1. In a large resealable plastic bag, combine the vinegar, syrup and oil. Add the pork; seal bag and turn to coat. Refrigerate for 8 hours or overnight.
2. Drain and discard the marinade. Moisten a paper towel with cooking oil; using long-handled tongs, rub it on the grill rack to coat lightly. Grill the pork, covered, over medium heat or broil 4 in. from the heat for 2-3 minutes on each side or until tender.
3. Divide the salad greens among six plates; top with the pork, nectarines, cheese, onion and almonds. Drizzle with dressing.

STEAK
BRUSCHETTA SALAD

FAST FIX

STEAK BRUSCHETTA SALAD

You'll want to fire up the grill just to make this impressive entree. The steaks cook quickly and the salad prep takes almost no time at all.

—**DEVON DELANEY** WESTPORT, CT

START TO FINISH: 30 MIN.
MAKES: 6 SERVINGS

1½ pounds beef tenderloin steaks
  (1-inch thick)
½ teaspoon salt
¼ teaspoon pepper
6 slices Italian bread (½-inch thick)
3 cups fresh arugula or baby spinach
¾ cup prepared bruschetta topping or
  vegetable salad of your choice
  Crumbled blue cheese, optional
¾ cup blue cheese salad dressing

1. Sprinkle steaks with salt and pepper. Grill, covered, over medium heat for 6-8 minutes on each side or until meat reaches desired doneness (for medium-rare, a thermometer should read 145°; medium, 160°; well-done, 170°). Let stand for 5 minutes.
2. Grill bread, covered, for 1-2 minutes on each side or until toasted; place on salad plates.
3. Thinly slice steak; arrange over the toast. Top with arugula and bruschetta topping; sprinkle with cheese if desired. Drizzle with dressing.
NOTE *Look for bruschetta topping in the pasta aisle or your grocer's deli case.*

THAI SHRIMP SALAD

Here's a deliciously different salad that blends grilled shrimp with the crunch of cucumber and onion. It's tossed and dressed with Thai flavors of sesame, cilantro, lime and refreshing mint.

—**ANNETTE TRAVERSO** SAN RAFAEL, CA

PREP: 25 MIN. • **GRILL:** 10 MIN.
MAKES: 4 SERVINGS

¼ cup lime juice
2 tablespoons sesame oil
2 tablespoons reduced-sodium soy
  sauce
1 tablespoon sesame seeds, toasted
1 tablespoon minced fresh mint
1 tablespoon minced fresh cilantro
⅛ teaspoon crushed red pepper flakes
1 pound uncooked large shrimp,
  peeled and deveined
¼ teaspoon salt
¼ teaspoon pepper
1 sweet onion, sliced
1 medium cucumber, peeled and
  sliced
4 cups torn leaf lettuce

1. In a large bowl, combine the first seven ingredients; set aside. Sprinkle shrimp with salt and pepper; thread onto four metal or soaked wooden skewers.
2. Moisten a paper towel with cooking oil; using long-handled tongs, rub it on the grill rack to coat lightly. Grill the skewers, covered, over medium heat for 2-4 minutes on each side or until shrimp turn pink.
3. Stir the reserved dressing; add the shrimp, onion and cucumber. Toss to coat. Divide lettuce among four salad plates; top with shrimp mixture.

FAST FIX

MEXICAN CHICKEN SANDWICHES

Sure, these grilled bread and melted cheese sandwiches are special, but the best part? They come together in less than 30 minutes!

—**SAMANTHA ANHALT** SPRING LAKE, MI

START TO FINISH: 25 MIN.
MAKES: 4 SERVINGS

3 tablespoons olive oil
4 teaspoons chili powder
½ teaspoon garlic powder
¼ to ½ teaspoon cayenne pepper
4 boneless skinless chicken breast
  halves (4 ounces each)
1½ cups (6 ounces) shredded Mexican
  cheese blend, divided
⅓ cup mayonnaise
8 slices sourdough bread
½ cup salsa

1. In a small bowl, combine the oil and seasonings. Rub over both sides of chicken. Grill, covered, over medium heat for 6-8 minutes on each side or until a thermometer reaches 170°.
2. Meanwhile, combine 1 cup cheese and mayonnaise; set aside. Grill bread on one side until lightly browned. Spread with cheese mixture; grill until cheese is melted.
3. Place chicken on four slices of toast; top with salsa, remaining shredded cheese and remaining toast.

FAST FIX▸

GRILLED FISH SANDWICHES

These fish fillets are seasoned with lime juice and lemon pepper before being charbroiled on the grill. A simple sauce of mayonnaise and honey mustard puts the sandwiches ahead of the rest.
—**VIOLET BEARD** MARSHALL, IL

START TO FINISH: 30 MIN.
MAKES: 4 SERVINGS

- 4 **cod fillets (4 ounces each)**
- 1 **tablespoon lime juice**
- ½ **teaspoon lemon-pepper seasoning**
- ¼ **cup fat-free mayonnaise**
- 2 **teaspoons Dijon mustard**
- 1 **teaspoon honey**
- 4 **hamburger buns, split**
- 4 **lettuce leaves**
- 4 **tomato slices**

1. Brush both sides of fillets with lime juice; sprinkle with lemon-pepper seasoning. Moisten a paper towel with cooking oil; using long-handled tongs, lightly rub on the grill rack. Grill fillets, covered, over medium heat or broil 4 in. from the heat 4-5 minutes on each side or until fish flakes easily with a fork.
2. In a small bowl, combine the mayonnaise, mustard and honey. Spread over the bottom of each bun. Top with a fillet, lettuce and tomato; replace bun tops.

 **GRILL SKILL**

Let fish fillets develop a seared crust before you try to flip them. If you turn them over too soon, you run the risk of the fillets sticking to the grill and ultimately falling apart. Fish is done cooking when it flakes easily with a fork.

SPICY CHICKEN TOMATO PITAS

FAST FIX▸

SPICY CHICKEN TOMATO PITAS

I'm not sure if this is a Mediterranean dish with a Southwestern flair or the other way around. All I know is that it's ideal for a summer dinner. The tomato relish is also yummy as an appetizer with tortilla chips, so you may want to double it.
—**CORI COOPER** BOISE, ID

START TO FINISH: 30 MIN.
MAKES: 4 SERVINGS

TOMATO RELISH
- ¼ **cup lemon juice**
- 1 **tablespoon olive oil**
- 1 **teaspoon ground coriander**
- 1 **teaspoon ground cumin**
- ¼ **teaspoon crushed red pepper flakes**
- 4 **medium tomatoes, seeded and chopped**
- 1 **small onion, chopped**
- ¼ **cup minced fresh parsley**

CHICKEN PITAS
- 1 **tablespoon ground cumin**
- 1 **tablespoon paprika**
- 1½ **teaspoons dried oregano**
- 1½ **teaspoons ground coriander**
- ½ **teaspoon crushed red pepper flakes**
- ¼ **teaspoon salt**
- 4 **boneless skinless chicken breast halves (4 ounces each)**
- 8 **whole wheat pita pocket halves**

1. In a bowl, whisk the first five ingredients. Add the tomatoes, onion and parsley; toss to coat. Refrigerate until serving.
2. Moisten a paper towel with cooking oil; using long-handled tongs, rub on the grill rack to coat lightly. Combine cumin, paprika, oregano, coriander, pepper flakes and salt; rub onto both sides of chicken. Grill chicken, covered, over medium heat or broil 4 in. from heat 4-7 minutes on each side or until a thermometer reads 165°.
3. Cut chicken into slices. Serve in pita halves with relish.

GRILLED VEGETABLE SANDWICHES

Use some of your fresh garden bounty to build these hearty, unique subs. Basil-lemon mayo is so good, you won't even miss the meat in these sandwiches.
—**KATHY HEWITT** CRANSTON, RI

PREP: 30 MIN. • **GRILL:** 20 MIN.
MAKES: 12 SERVINGS

- 3 **large sweet red peppers**
- 3 **medium red onions**
- 3 **large zucchini**
- ¼ **cup olive oil**
- ¾ **teaspoon salt**
- ¾ **teaspoon coarsely ground pepper**
- ¾ **cup reduced-fat mayonnaise**
- ⅓ **cup minced fresh basil**
- 2 **tablespoons lemon juice**
- 6 **garlic cloves, minced**
- 12 **submarine buns, split**
- 24 **slices cheddar cheese**
- 3 **medium tomatoes, sliced**
- ¾ **cup hummus**

1. Cut the red peppers into eighths; cut onions and zucchini into ½-in. slices.

Brush vegetables with oil; sprinkle with salt and pepper. Grill vegetables in batches, covered, over medium heat or broil 4 in. from the heat for 4-5 minutes on each side or until crisp-tender. Cool.
2. Combine the mayonnaise, basil, lemon juice and garlic; spread over bun bottoms. Layer with cheese, grilled vegetables and tomatoes. Spread hummus over bun tops; replace tops.

FAST FIX ▶
GREEK ISLANDS STEAK SALAD

I invented this recipe while watching a movie set on the Greek islands. I like bringing together the grilled steak and sauteed mushrooms with cold salad ingredients.
—**CHRIS WELLS** LAKE VILLA, IL

START TO FINISH: 25 MIN.
MAKES: 2 SERVINGS

- 1 **boneless beef top loin steak (8 ounces)**
- 1 **tablespoon A.1. steak sauce**

MUSHROOMS
- 1½ **cups sliced fresh mushrooms**
- 2 **tablespoons butter**
- 1 **tablespoon sherry or chicken broth**
- ⅛ **teaspoon salt**
- ⅛ **teaspoon pepper**

SALAD
- 4 **cups torn mixed salad greens**
- 10 **cherry tomatoes, halved**
- ⅔ **cup thinly sliced cucumber**
- 10 **pitted Greek olives**
- ¼ **cup finely chopped red onion**
- ½ **cup crumbled feta cheese**
- ¼ **cup prepared balsamic vinaigrette**

1. Rub steak on both sides with steak sauce; let stand for 10 minutes.
2. Meanwhile, in a small skillet, saute the mushrooms in butter until golden brown. Add the sherry, salt and pepper. Cook 1-2 minutes longer or until liquid is evaporated. Set aside and keep warm.
3. Moisten a paper towel with cooking oil; using long-handled tongs, rub on the grill rack to coat lightly. Grill steak, covered, over medium heat or broil 4 in. from the heat for 5-6 minutes on each side or until the meat reaches desired doneness (for medium-rare, a thermometer should read 145°; medium, 160°; well-done, 170°). Let stand for 5 minutes before slicing.
4. Divide salad greens between two plates. Top with tomatoes, cucumber, olives, onion, steak and mushrooms. Sprinkle with cheese. Drizzle with vinaigrette. Serve immediately.
NOTE *Top loin steak may be labeled as strip steak, Kansas City steak, New York strip steak, ambassador steak or boneless club steak in your region.*

GRILLED VEGETABLE SANDWICHES

FAST FIX

BERRY CHICKEN SALAD

You either love the distinct flavor of goat cheese or you don't. If you're a fan, try it with this spinach and berry chicken salad. If not, feta cheese works great, too.
—**WENDY BALL** BATTLE CREEK, MI

START TO FINISH: 20 MIN.
MAKES: 4 SERVINGS

- 4 **boneless skinless chicken breast halves (4 ounces each)**
- ¼ **teaspoon salt**
- ¼ **teaspoon pepper**
- 1 **package (6 ounces) fresh baby spinach**
- 1 **cup fresh raspberries**
- 1 **cup halved fresh strawberries**
- ⅔ **cup crumbled goat cheese**
- 3 **tablespoons chopped pecans, toasted**
- ¼ **cup prepared fat-free raspberry vinaigrette**

1. Sprinkle the chicken with salt and pepper. Moisten a paper towel with cooking oil; using long-handled tongs, rub on grill rack to coat lightly. Grill chicken, covered, over medium heat or broil 4 in. from heat 4-7 minutes on each side or until a thermometer reads 165°.

2. In a large bowl, combine spinach, berries, cheese and pecans. Cut chicken into slices; add to salad. Drizzle with vinaigrette and toss lightly to coat. Serve immediately.

NOTE *To toast nuts, bake in a shallow pan in a 350° oven for 5-10 minutes or cook in a skillet over low heat until lightly browned, stirring occasionally.*

BERRY CHICKEN SALAD

CAJUN CHICKEN SANDWICHES

This is my favorite sandwich! The seasoning mixture is enough to give a mild zip to chicken breasts.

—AMBER PETERSON OAKES, ND

PREP: 10 MIN. + MARINATING • **GRILL:** 10 MIN.
MAKES: 6 SERVINGS

- 6 boneless skinless chicken breast halves (4 ounces each)
- 1 tablespoon olive oil
- ½ teaspoon celery salt
- ½ teaspoon garlic salt
- ½ teaspoon lemon-pepper seasoning
- ¼ teaspoon cayenne pepper
- ¼ teaspoon paprika
- ¼ teaspoon pepper
- 6 kaiser rolls, split and toasted
- 12 slices tomato
- 6 lettuce leaves

1. Flatten chicken to ½-in. thickness. Brush both sides with oil. Combine the seasonings; rub over both sides of chicken. Arrange in a 13x9-in. baking dish. Cover and refrigerate for at least 2 hours or overnight.
2. Moisten a paper towel with cooking oil; using long-handled tongs, rub on the grill rack to coat lightly. Grill the chicken, covered, over medium heat or broil 4 in. from the heat for 3-5 minutes on each side or until no longer pink. Serve on rolls with tomato and lettuce.

GREEK PORK WRAPS

If you like gyros, you'll love these strips of grilled pork wrapped in tortillas. It's a popular dish, especially in the summer, at my home.

—CHRISTINE LONDON KANSAS CITY, MO

PREP: 20 MIN. + MARINATING • **GRILL:** 15 MIN.
MAKES: 4 SERVINGS

- ¼ cup lemon juice
- 2 tablespoons olive oil
- 1 tablespoon prepared mustard
- 1¾ teaspoons minced garlic, divided
- 1 teaspoon dried oregano
- 1 pork tenderloin (1 pound)
- 1 cup chopped peeled cucumber
- 1 cup reduced-fat plain yogurt
- ¼ teaspoon salt
- ¼ teaspoon dill weed
- 8 flour tortillas (6 inches)
- ½ cup chopped green onions

1. In a large resealable plastic bag, combine the lemon juice, oil, mustard, 1¼ teaspoons garlic and oregano; add the pork. Seal bag and turn to coat; refrigerate for 2 hours.
2. In a small bowl, combine the cucumber, yogurt, salt, dill and the remaining garlic; cover and refrigerate until serving.
3. Drain and discard marinade. Moisten a paper towel with cooking oil; using long-handled tongs, rub on the grill rack to coat lightly. Prepare the grill for indirect heat using a drip pan.
4. Grill pork tenderloin, uncovered, over direct medium-high heat for 2-3 minutes on each side. Place meat over drip pan and grill, covered, over indirect medium heat for 10-15 minutes longer or until a thermometer reads 160°. Let stand for 5 minutes.
5. Meanwhile, wrap tortillas in foil; place on grill for 1-2 minutes on each side or until warmed. Slice tenderloin into strips; place on tortillas. Top each with 3 tablespoons yogurt sauce and 1 tablespoon green onions.

BUFFALO STEAK SALAD

We raise buffalo on our ranch, so I cook plenty of buffalo steak as well as other cuts. During the warmer months, this is a change of pace from the heavier meals I feed my crew during other seasons.

—BURT GUENIN CHAPPELL, NE

START TO FINISH: 25 MIN.
MAKES: 4 SERVINGS

- ⅓ cup olive oil
- 2 tablespoons red wine vinegar
- 1 tablespoon lemon juice
- 1 garlic clove, minced
- ½ teaspoon salt
- ⅛ teaspoon pepper
  Dash Worcestershire sauce
- ½ cup crumbled blue cheese
- 2 buffalo sirloin or beef ribeye steaks (about 8 ounces each)
- 6 cups torn salad greens
- 1 medium tomato, thinly sliced
- 1 small carrot, thinly sliced
- ½ cup thinly sliced onion
- ¼ cup sliced pimiento-stuffed olives

1. In a small bowl, combine the first seven ingredients; mix well. Stir in blue cheese. Cover and refrigerate.
2. Grill steaks, uncovered, over medium heat for 6-10 minutes on each side or until the meat reaches desired doneness (for medium-rare, a thermometer should read 145°; medium, 160°; well-done, 170°). Thinly slice meat.
3. On a serving platter or individual salad plates, arrange greens, tomato, carrot, onion and olives. Top with steak and dressing.

**SHRIMP SALAD
WITH PEACHES**

BISTRO TUNA SANDWICHES

Your family and friends will love this fun French twist on a grilled tuna sandwich. Tucked into a crusty baguette, it's fast to prep and packed with veggies.

—**SONYA LABBE** WEST HOLLYWOOD, CA

PREP: 25 MIN. • **GRILL:** 10 MIN.
MAKES: 4 SERVINGS

- 2 tablespoons Greek olives
- 1 tablespoon capers, drained
- 1 tablespoon lemon juice
- 1 teaspoon grated lemon peel
- 1 garlic clove, peeled
- 1 tablespoon plus 2 teaspoons olive oil, divided
- 2 tuna steaks (6 ounces each)
- ¼ teaspoon pepper
- 1 French bread baguette (10½ ounces)
- ⅓ cup reduced-fat mayonnaise
- 2 tablespoons Dijon mustard
- ¼ cup roasted sweet red peppers, drained and cut into strips
- 4 slices red onion
- 4 Boston lettuce leaves

1. Place the olives, capers, lemon juice, peel, garlic and 1 tablespoon oil in a food processor; cover and process until finely chopped. Set aside.
2. Brush tuna with the remaining oil; sprinkle with pepper. Moisten a paper towel with cooking oil; using long-handled tongs, rub on the grill rack to coat lightly. For medium-rare, grill the tuna, covered, over high heat or broil 3-4 inches from the heat 3-4 minutes on each side or until slightly pink in the center.
3. Cut baguette in half horizontally. Grill bread cut side down, uncovered, for 1-2 minutes or until toasted. Slice tuna into ½-in.-thick slices. Combine mayonnaise and mustard until smooth; spread over baguette bottoms. Layer with the peppers, onion, tuna, olive mixture and lettuce; replace tops. Cut into slices.

SHRIMP SALAD WITH PEACHES

My husband doesn't miss his beloved meat and potatoes meals when I cook up this shrimp dish, made light with fresh fruit and greens.

—**GILDA LESTER** MILLSBORO, DE

PREP: 25 MIN. • **GRILL:** 10 MIN.
MAKES: 4 SERVINGS

- ¾ pound uncooked large shrimp
- ½ cup hoisin sauce
- 6 tablespoons olive oil, divided
- ¼ cup lemon juice, divided
- 1 teaspoon hot pepper sauce
- ½ teaspoon ground cumin
- 4 medium peaches, halved
- ¼ teaspoon salt
- 8 cups fresh arugula
- ½ cup fresh cilantro leaves
- ½ cup crumbled goat cheese
- 1 medium lemon, quartered

1. Peel and devein shrimp, leaving tails on. In a large resealable plastic bag, combine the hoisin sauce, 2 tablespoons oil, 2 tablespoons lemon juice, hot sauce and cumin. Add the shrimp; seal bag and turn to coat. Refrigerate for up to 30 minutes. Drain and discard the marinade.
2. Thread shrimp on four metal or soaked wooden skewers. Moisten a paper towel with cooking oil; using long-handled tongs, rub on the grill rack to coat lightly. Brush peach halves with 1 tablespoon oil.
3. Grill shrimp and peaches, covered, over medium heat or broil 4 in. from the heat for 6-8 minutes or until shrimp turn pink, turning once.
4. In a large bowl, combine salt with the remaining oil and lemon juice. Add the arugula and cilantro; toss to coat. Divide among four plates. Top with the peaches, shrimp and goat cheese. Squeeze lemon over salads.

FAST FIX
FAJITAS IN PITAS

For a weekend lunch with company, we grill chicken and peppers to stuff inside pita pockets. The dressing doubles as a grilling sauce and a sandwich spread.

—CLARA COULSON MINNEY
WASHINGTON COURT HOUSE, OH

START TO FINISH: 25 MIN.
MAKES: 4 SERVINGS

- ½ cup mayonnaise
- 1 green onion, chopped
- 4 teaspoons Dijon mustard
- ¼ teaspoon pepper
- 3 boneless skinless chicken breast halves (6 ounces each)
- 2 medium sweet red peppers, halved and seeded
- 2 medium green peppers, halved and seeded
- 8 pita pocket halves, warmed
- 8 lettuce leaves

1. In a small bowl, mix mayonnaise, green onion, mustard and pepper; reserve ⅓ cup for assembling. Spread the remaining mixture over chicken and peppers.
2. Grill chicken and peppers, covered, over medium heat or broil 4 in. from heat for 5-6 minutes on each side or until a thermometer inserted in chicken reads 165° and peppers are tender. Cut chicken into ½-in. slices; cut peppers into 1-in. slices.
3. Spread reserved mayonnaise mixture inside pita halves; fill with lettuce, chicken and peppers.

FAJITAS IN PITAS

**LOADED GRILLED
CHICKEN SANDWICH**

LOADED GRILLED CHICKEN SANDWICH

I threw these ingredients together on a whim and the sandwich turned out so well, I surprised myself! If you're in a rush, microwave the bacon. Be sure to cover it with a paper towel to keep it from splattering too much.

—**DANA YORK** KENNEWICK, WA

START TO FINISH: 30 MIN.
MAKES: 4 SERVINGS

- 4 **boneless skinless chicken breast halves (4 ounces each)**
- 2 **teaspoons Italian salad dressing mix**
- 4 **slices pepper jack cheese**
- 4 **ciabatta or kaiser rolls, split**
- 2 **tablespoons mayonnaise**
- ¾ **teaspoon Dijon mustard**
- 4 **cooked bacon strips, halved**
- 4 **slices tomato**
- ½ **medium ripe avocado, peeled and thinly sliced**
- ½ **pound deli coleslaw (about 1 cup)**

1. Pound chicken with a meat mallet to flatten slightly; sprinkle both sides with dressing mix. Moisten a paper towel with cooking oil; using long-handled tongs, rub on grill rack to coat lightly.
2. Grill chicken, covered, over medium heat or broil 4 in. from heat 4-6 minutes on each side or until a thermometer reads 165°. Place cheese on chicken; grill, covered, 1-2 minutes longer or until cheese is melted. Meanwhile, grill the rolls, cut side down, 1-2 minutes or until toasted.
3. Mix mayonnaise and mustard; spread on roll tops. Layer roll bottoms with chicken, bacon, tomato, avocado and coleslaw. Replace tops.

FAST FIX

TUNA BIBB SALADS

Here, the buttery, sweet taste of Bibb lettuce complements the delicate flavor of tuna steaks. I like to serve the salad with a French baguette on the side.

—**WOLFGANG HANAU** WEST PALM BEACH, FL

START TO FINISH: 30 MIN.
MAKES: 4 SERVINGS

- 1 **pound tuna steaks (¾-inch thick)**
- 2 **teaspoons lime juice**
- ¼ **teaspoon salt**
- ¼ **teaspoon pepper**
- 2 **celery ribs**
- 1 **small sweet red pepper**
- 1 **small sweet yellow pepper**
- 1 **small red onion**
- 4 **cups torn Bibb or Boston lettuce**
- ¼ **cup thinly sliced fresh basil leaves**
- 1 **teaspoon minced fresh rosemary**
    Whole Bibb or Boston lettuce leaves
- ½ **cup reduced-fat ranch salad dressing**

1. Sprinkle tuna with lime juice, salt and pepper. Moisten a paper towel with cooking oil; using long-handled tongs, rub on the grill rack to coat lightly. For medium-rare, grill tuna, covered, over high heat or broil 3-4 in. from the heat for 3-4 minutes on each side or until slightly pink in the center. Cut into 1-in. pieces.

2. Finely chop the celery, peppers and onion; place in a large bowl. Add the torn lettuce, tuna, basil and rosemary; toss to combine.

3. Arrange lettuce leaves on four plates; top each with 2 cups tuna mixture. Drizzle with dressing.

SOUTHWESTERN STEAK SALAD

SOUTHWESTERN STEAK SALAD

I get along just fine with salads, but my boyfriend generally avoids them. This beefed-up pasta salad with steak, peppers and onions makes us both happy.

—**YVONNE STARLIN** HERMITAGE, TN

PREP: 25 MIN. • **GRILL:** 20 MIN.
MAKES: 4 SERVINGS

- 1 **beef top sirloin steak (1-inch thick and ¾ pound)**
- ¼ **teaspoon salt**
- ¼ **teaspoon ground cumin**
- ¼ **teaspoon pepper**
- 3 **poblano peppers, halved and seeded**
- 2 **large ears sweet corn, husks removed**
- 1 **large sweet onion, cut into ½-inch rings**
- 1 **tablespoon olive oil**
- 2 **cups uncooked multigrain bow tie pasta**
- 2 **large tomatoes**

DRESSING
- ¼ **cup lime juice**
- 1 **tablespoon olive oil**
- ¼ **teaspoon salt**
- ¼ **teaspoon ground cumin**
- ¼ **teaspoon pepper**
- ⅓ **cup chopped fresh cilantro**

1. Rub steak with salt, cumin and pepper. Brush poblano peppers, corn and onion with oil. Grill steak, covered, over medium heat or broil 4 in. from heat 6-8 minutes on each side or until meat reaches desired doneness (for medium-rare, a thermometer should read 145°; medium, 160°; well-done, 170°). Grill vegetables, covered, for 8-10 minutes or until crisp-tender, turning occasionally.

2. Cook pasta according to package directions. Meanwhile, cut corn from cob; coarsely chop peppers, onion and tomatoes. Transfer vegetables to a large bowl. In a small bowl, whisk the lime juice, oil, salt, cumin and pepper until blended; stir in cilantro.

3. Drain pasta; add to the vegetable mixture. Drizzle with dressing; toss to coat. Cut the steak into thin slices; add to salad.

**SALMON AND
SPUD SALAD**

FAST FIX

SALMON AND SPUD SALAD

When I decided to live a healthier lifestyle, my first stop was the kitchen. This salmon with veggies salad proves that smart choices can be simple to put together and satisfying to eat.

—MATTHEW TEIXEIRA MILTON, ON

START TO FINISH: 30 MIN.
MAKES: 4 SERVINGS

- 1 **pound fingerling potatoes**
- ½ **pound fresh green beans**
- ½ **pound fresh asparagus**
- 4 **salmon fillets (6 ounces each)**
- 1 **tablespoon plus ⅓ cup red wine vinaigrette, divided**
- ¼ **teaspoon salt**
- ¼ **teaspoon pepper**
- 4 **cups fresh arugula or baby spinach**
- 2 **cups cherry tomatoes, halved**
- 1 **tablespoon minced fresh chives**

1. Cut potatoes lengthwise in half. Trim and cut the green beans and asparagus into 2-in. pieces. Place the potatoes in a 6-qt. stockpot; add water to cover. Bring to a boil. Reduce heat; cook, uncovered, 10-15 minutes or until tender, adding the green beans and asparagus during the last 4 minutes of cooking. Drain.
2. Meanwhile, brush salmon with 1 tablespoon vinaigrette; sprinkle with salt and pepper. Moisten a paper towel with cooking oil; using long-handled tongs, rub on grill rack to coat lightly. Place fish on grill rack, skin side down. Grill, covered, over medium-high heat or broil 4 in. from heat 6-8 minutes or until fish just begins to flake easily with a fork.
3. In a large bowl, combine the potato mixture, arugula, tomatoes and chives. Drizzle with remaining vinaigrette; toss to coat. Serve with salmon.

GROUND BEEF GYROS

FAST FIX

GROUND BEEF GYROS

If your family likes gyros as much as mine, they'll love this quick version that's made with ground beef instead of lamb. A cucumber yogurt sauce adds an authentic finishing touch.

—RUTH STAHL SHEPHERD, MT

START TO FINISH: 30 MIN.
MAKES: 4 SERVINGS

- 1 **cup (8 ounces) plain yogurt**
- ⅓ **cup chopped seeded cucumber**
- 2 **tablespoons finely chopped onion**
- 1 **garlic clove, minced**
- 1 **teaspoon sugar**

FILLING

- 1½ **teaspoons dried oregano**
- 1 **teaspoon garlic powder**
- 1 **teaspoon onion powder**
- 1 **teaspoon salt, optional**
- ¾ **teaspoon pepper**
- 1 **pound ground beef**
- 4 **pita breads (6 inches), halved, warmed**
- 3 **cups shredded lettuce**
- 1 **large tomato, chopped**
- 1 **small onion, sliced**

1. In a small bowl, combine the first five ingredients. Chill. In a large bowl, combine seasonings; crumble beef over the mixture and mix well. Shape into four patties.
2. Grill, covered, over medium heat or broil 4 in. from the heat for 6-7 minutes on each side or until a thermometer reads 160°. Cut patties into thin slices; stuff into pita halves. Add the lettuce, tomato and onion. Serve with the yogurt sauce.

**CHICAGO-STYLE
HOT DOGS, PAGE 101**

SAUSAGE & PEPPER SANDWICHES, PAGE 118

KING BURGERS, PAGE 121

BARBECUED BURGERS, PAGE 124

BURGERS, DOGS & MORE

It's not a barbecue until the **first burger** hits the plate, so you need a go-to recipe to impress. This chapter is filled with flame-broiled favorites, **topped with cheese,** bacon and more. With so many **delicious options,** there won't be a bun left unstacked!

BASIL BURGERS WITH SUN-DRIED TOMATO MAYONNAISE

BASIL BURGERS WITH SUN-DRIED TOMATO MAYONNAISE

Basil thrives in my backyard and I am often blessed with a bumper crop. Here's one of my favorite ways to use some of it. No one can resist the gooey, cheesy centers.

—**VIRGINIA KOCHIS** SPRINGFIELD, VA

PREP: 25 MIN. • **GRILL:** 10 MIN.
MAKES: 6 SERVINGS

- ¼ cup sun-dried tomatoes (not packed in oil)
- 1 cup boiling water
- 1 cup fat-free mayonnaise
- 2 teaspoons Worcestershire sauce
- ¼ cup fresh basil leaves, coarsely chopped
- 2 teaspoons Italian seasoning
- 2 garlic cloves, minced
- ½ teaspoon pepper
- ¼ teaspoon salt
- 1½ pounds lean ground beef (90% lean)
- ¾ cup shredded part-skim mozzarella cheese
- 6 whole wheat hamburger buns, split
   Additional fresh basil leaves, optional

1. In a small bowl, combine tomatoes and water. Let stand for 5 minutes; drain. In a food processor, combine mayonnaise and tomatoes; cover and process until blended. Chill until serving.

2. In a large bowl, combine the Worcestershire sauce, basil, Italian seasoning, garlic, pepper and salt. Crumble beef over mixture and mix well. Shape into 12 thin patties. Place 2 tablespoons cheese on six patties; top with remaining patties and press edges firmly to seal.

3. Moisten a paper towel with cooking oil; using long-handled tongs, lightly rub the grill rack to coat. Grill burgers, covered, over medium heat or broil 4 in. from the heat for 5-7 minutes on each side or until a thermometer reads 160° and juices run clear. Serve on buns with mayonnaise mixture and additional basil, if desired.

FAST FIX ▶

PEPPER JACK VENISON BURGERS

My son, who's an avid hunter, gave me this change-of-pace recipe. Jalapenos and pepper jack cheese give these burgers a kick that is nicely offset by the cool lime-mustard mayonnaise.

—JERRY HONEYAGER NORTH PRAIRIE, WI

START TO FINISH: 30 MIN.
MAKES: 8 SERVINGS

- ⅓ **cup mayonnaise**
- 1 **teaspoon lime juice**
- 1 **teaspoon Dijon mustard**
- ½ **teaspoon grated lime peel**
- ⅓ **cup chopped green onions**
- 3 **tablespoons plain yogurt**
- 2 **tablespoons finely chopped jalapeno pepper**
- ½ **teaspoon salt**
- ½ **teaspoon pepper**
- 2 **pounds ground venison**
- 8 **hamburger buns, split**
- 8 **slices pepper jack cheese**

1. In a small bowl, combine the mayonnaise, lime juice, mustard and lime peel; cover and refrigerate until serving.

2. In a bowl, combine the onions, yogurt, jalapeno, salt and pepper. Crumble meat over mixture and mix well. Shape into eight patties.

3. Pan-fry, grill or broil until meat is no longer pink. Serve on buns; top with cheese and mayonnaise mixture.

NOTE *Wear disposable gloves when cutting hot peppers; the oils can burn skin. Avoid touching your face.*

CHICKEN PARMESAN BURGERS

FAST FIX ▶

CHICKEN PARMESAN BURGERS

We love chicken Parmesan and thought, "Why not make it a grilled burger?" I like to use fresh mozzarella on these. I've also made the burgers with ground turkey.

—CHARLOTTE GEHLE BROWNSTOWN, MI

START TO FINISH: 30 MIN.
MAKES: 4 SERVINGS

- ½ **cup dry bread crumbs**
- ¼ **cup grated Parmesan cheese**
- 3 **garlic cloves, minced**
- 1 **tablespoon minced fresh basil or 1 teaspoon dried basil**
- ½ **teaspoon dried oregano**
- 1 **pound lean ground chicken**
- 1 **cup meatless spaghetti sauce, divided**
- 2 **slices part-skim mozzarella cheese, cut in half**
- 4 **slices Italian bread (¾-inch thick)**

1. In a large bowl, combine the first five ingredients. Add chicken; mix lightly but thoroughly. Shape into four ½-in.-thick oval patties.

2. Grill burgers, covered, over medium heat or broil 4 in. from heat 4-7 minutes on each side or until a thermometer reads 165°. Top burgers with ½ cup of spaghetti sauce and cheese. Cover and grill 30-60 seconds longer or until the cheese is melted.

3. Grill bread, uncovered, over medium heat or broil 4 in. from heat for 30-60 seconds on each side or until toasted. Top with remaining spaghetti sauce. Serve burgers on toasted bread.

FREEZE OPTION *Place patties on a plastic wrap-lined baking sheet; wrap and freeze until firm. Remove from sheet and transfer to a resealable plastic freezer bag; return to freezer. To use, grill frozen patties as directed, increasing time as necessary for a thermometer to read 165°.*

CHICAGO-STYLE
HOT DOGS

FAST FIX ▶
CHICAGO-STYLE HOT DOGS

I decided to give a Chicago-style dog a healthy twist for my family. Our kids love it. You can use other fresh toppings to please just about anyone.

—GREGG MAY COLUMBUS, OH

START TO FINISH: 20 MIN.
MAKES: 4 SERVINGS

- 4 turkey hot dogs
- 4 thin sandwich pickle slices
- ½ medium cucumber, peeled and thinly sliced
- 2 plum tomatoes, cut into thin wedges
- ½ cup chopped sweet onion
- 4 whole wheat tortillas (8 inches), warmed
  Optional toppings: prepared mustard, shredded reduced-fat cheddar cheese and sport peppers or other pickled hot peppers

Grill hot dogs according to package directions. To serve, place pickle, cucumber, tomatoes and onion on center of tortillas. Add hot dogs and toppings as desired. Fold the tortillas over filling.

FAST FIX ▶
BEEF 'N' PORK BURGERS

Ground pork adds an extra dimension to these juicy grilled burgers. I depend on them time and again for summer fun.

—SHARON ADAMCZYK WIND LAKE, WI

START TO FINISH: 25 MIN.
MAKES: 8 SERVINGS

- 4 bacon strips, diced
- 1 large onion, finely chopped
- 1 garlic clove, minced
- 1½ cups soft bread crumbs
- 1 large egg, lightly beaten
- ½ cup water
- 1 tablespoon dried parsley flakes
- 2 to 3 teaspoons salt
- ¼ teaspoon dried marjoram
- ¼ teaspoon paprika
- ¼ teaspoon pepper
- 1 pound ground beef
- 1 pound ground pork
- 8 hamburger buns, split and toasted
  Mayonnaise, lettuce leaves and tomato slices

1. In a small skillet, cook bacon, onion and garlic over medium heat until the bacon is crisp; drain and place in a small bowl. Stir in the bread crumbs, egg, water, parsley, salt, marjoram, paprika and pepper. Crumble beef and pork over the mixture and mix well. Shape into eight ¾-in.-thick patties.
2. Grill burgers, uncovered, over medium heat for 4-5 minutes on each side or until a thermometer reads 160°. Serve on buns with mayonnaise, lettuce and tomato.

PINEAPPLE-STUFFED BURGERS

FAST FIX ▶
PINEAPPLE-STUFFED BURGERS

I enjoy grilling these special burgers with a surprise inside. The homemade sauce, with brown sugar, mustard and ketchup, makes these tropical bites even better.

—ANN COUCH HALIFAX, NC

START TO FINISH: 30 MIN.
MAKES: 2 SERVINGS

- ¼ cup packed brown sugar
- ¼ cup ketchup
- 1 tablespoon prepared mustard
- ½ pound lean ground beef (90% lean)
- 2 slices unsweetened pineapple
- ⅛ teaspoon salt
- ⅛ teaspoon pepper
- 2 hamburger buns, split
- 2 lettuce leaves

1. In a small saucepan, combine the brown sugar, ketchup and mustard. Cook mixture over medium heat for 2-3 minutes, stirring occasionally.
2. Meanwhile, shape beef into four patties. Place pineapple slices on two patties; top with remaining patties. Seal edges; sprinkle with salt and pepper.
3. Moisten a paper towel with cooking oil; using long-handled tongs, rub on grill rack to coat lightly. Grill burgers, covered, over medium heat or broil 4 in. from the heat for 7-9 minutes on each side or until a thermometer reads 160° and juices run clear. Serve on buns with sauce and lettuce.

⚒ HOW-TO TOP IT

There's no need to stick to ketchup and mustard when topping your burger, dog or brat. Sliced avocado, feta cheese, crispy bacon, crushed chips and chopped cucumber all make great toppers. Or get creative with Buffalo wing sauce, a fried egg, mac and cheese, pulled pork or even a salad from the deli department.

FAST FIX ▶

CHICKEN CAESAR BURGERS

I sometimes make these burgers with ground turkey, depending on what's cheaper. Either way, it's a delicious, lean option that will satisfy any burger craving.
—**RACHEL RICCOMINI** SAINT MARYS, KS

START TO FINISH: 30 MIN.
MAKES: 2 SERVINGS

- ¼ cup finely chopped onion
- 2 tablespoons shredded Parmesan cheese, divided
- 1 tablespoon lemon juice
- 1½ teaspoons dried parsley flakes
- 1 garlic clove, minced
- 1 teaspoon Worcestershire sauce
- ¼ teaspoon salt
- ¼ teaspoon pepper
- ½ pound ground chicken
- 2 hamburger buns, split
- ¼ cup torn romaine
- 4 teaspoons fat-free creamy Caesar salad dressing

1. In a small bowl, combine the onion, 1 tablespoon cheese, lemon juice, parsley, garlic, Worcestershire sauce, salt and pepper. Crumble the chicken over mixture and mix well. Shape into two patties.

2. Grill burgers, covered, over medium heat for 5-7 minutes on each side or until a thermometer reads 165° and juices run clear. Sprinkle with the remaining cheese.

3. Serve on buns with romaine and salad dressing.

ALOHA BURGERS

FAST FIX ▶

ALOHA BURGERS

I love hamburgers and pineapple, so it just seemed natural for me to combine them. My family frequently requests these unique sandwiches. It's a nice change of pace from the same old boring burger.
—**JOI MCKIM-JONES** WAIKOLOA, HI

START TO FINISH: 30 MIN.
MAKES: 4 SERVINGS

- 1 can (8 ounces) sliced pineapple
- ¾ cup reduced-sodium teriyaki sauce
- 1 pound ground beef
- 1 large sweet onion, sliced
- 1 tablespoon butter
- 4 lettuce leaves
- 4 sesame seed or onion buns, split and toasted
- 4 slices Swiss cheese
- 4 bacon strips, cooked

1. Drain pineapple juice into a small bowl; add the teriyaki sauce. Place 3 tablespoons in a resealable plastic bag. Add pineapple; toss to coat and set aside.

2. Shape beef into four patties; place in an 8-in. square baking dish. Pour the remaining teriyaki sauce mixture over patties; marinate for 5-10 minutes, turning once.

3. Drain and discard the teriyaki marinade. Grill patties, covered, over medium heat or broil 4 in. from the heat for 6-9 minutes on each side or until a thermometer reads 160° and juices run clear. Meanwhile, in a small skillet, saute onion in butter until tender, about 5 minutes; set aside.

4. Drain and discard the pineapple marinade. Place pineapple on grill or under broiler to heat through. Layer with lettuce and onion on bottom of buns. Top with the burgers, cheese, pineapple and bacon. Replace tops.

SALMON BURGERS WITH TANGY SLAW

I thought I'd made salmon every way possible—until now! Here, honey mustard and a tasty slaw, made with fennel and avocado, add terrific layers of flavor. In addition, the slaw goes well with other grilled seafood dishes.

—AMBER MASSEY ARGYLE, TX

PREP: 25 MIN. + CHILLING • **GRILL:** 10 MIN.
MAKES: 4 SERVINGS

SLAW
- 3 cups thinly sliced cabbage
- 1½ cups thinly sliced fennel bulb
- 1 cup thinly sliced cucumber
- ½ cup thinly sliced red onion
- ¼ cup minced fresh cilantro
- 1 jalapeno pepper, seeded and finely chopped
- ½ teaspoon salt
- ¼ teaspoon pepper
- 2 medium ripe avocados, peeled and cubed
- ¼ cup lime juice

HONEY MUSTARD
- 1 tablespoon Dijon mustard
- 1 tablespoon honey

SALMON BURGERS
- 1 pound skinless salmon fillets, cut into 1-inch pieces, divided
- 2 tablespoons grated lime peel
- 1 tablespoon Dijon mustard
- 3 tablespoons finely chopped shallot
- 2 tablespoons minced fresh cilantro
- 1 tablespoon reduced-sodium soy sauce
- 1 tablespoon honey
- 3 garlic cloves, minced
- ½ teaspoon salt
- ¼ teaspoon pepper
- 4 hamburger buns, split

1. Place the first eight ingredients in a large bowl; toss to combine. In a small bowl, gently toss avocados with lime juice; add to the cabbage mixture. Refrigerate until serving. In a small bowl, mix honey-mustard ingredients.
2. For burgers, place a fourth of the salmon in a food processor. Add lime peel and mustard; process until smooth. Transfer to a large bowl.
3. Place remaining salmon in food processor; pulse until coarsely chopped and add to puree. Fold in the shallot, cilantro, soy sauce, honey, garlic, salt and pepper. Shape into four ½-in.-thick patties.
4. Moisten a paper towel with cooking oil; using long-handled tongs, rub on grill rack to coat lightly. Grill burgers, covered, over medium heat or broil 4 in. from heat 4-5 minutes on each side or until a thermometer reads 145°.
5. Serve on buns with honey mustard; top each with ½ cup slaw. Serve the remaining slaw on the side.
NOTE *Wear disposable gloves when cutting hot peppers; the oils can burn skin. Avoid touching your face.*

FAST FIX
PORK BURGERS

Try something a little different at your next cookout with these patties made of ground pork. They're jazzed up with Parmesan and plenty of seasonings.

—DAWNITA PHILLIPS DREXEL, MO

START TO FINISH: 25 MIN.
MAKES: 6 SERVINGS

- 1 large egg, lightly beaten
- ¾ cup soft bread crumbs
- ¾ cup grated Parmesan cheese
- 1 tablespoon dried parsley flakes
- 2 teaspoons dried basil
- ½ teaspoon salt
- ½ teaspoon garlic powder
- ¼ teaspoon pepper
- 2 pounds ground pork
- 6 hamburger buns, split
  Lettuce leaves, sliced tomato and sweet onion, optional

1. In a large bowl, combine the first eight ingredients. Crumble the pork over mixture and mix well. Shape into six patties.
2. Grill burgers, covered, over medium heat for 4-5 minutes on each side or until a thermometer reads 160°.
3. Serve on buns with lettuce, tomato and onion, if desired.

SALMON BURGERS WITH TANGY SLAW

PORTOBELLO BURGERS

PORTOBELLO BURGERS

Robust portobello mushrooms have such a meaty flavor, so they make the perfect hamburger substitute.
—**THERESA SABBAGH** WINSTON-SALEM, NC

PREP: 10 MIN. + STANDING • **GRILL:** 15 MIN.
MAKES: 2 SERVINGS

- 2 tablespoons balsamic vinegar
- 1 tablespoon olive oil
- 3 garlic cloves, minced
- 1½ teaspoons minced fresh basil or ½ teaspoon dried basil
- 1½ teaspoons minced fresh oregano or ½ teaspoon dried oregano
  Dash salt
  Dash pepper
- 2 large portobello mushrooms, stems removed
- 2 slices reduced-fat provolone cheese
- 2 hamburger buns, split
- 2 lettuce leaves
- 2 slices tomato

1. In a small bowl, whisk the first seven ingredients. Add mushroom caps; let stand for 15 minutes, turning twice. Drain and reserve marinade.
2. Moisten a paper towel with cooking oil; using long-handled tongs, rub on grill rack to coat lightly. Grill mushrooms, covered, over medium heat or broil 4 in. from the heat for 6-8 minutes on each side or until tender, basting with reserved marinade. Top with cheese during the last 2 minutes.
3. Serve on buns with lettuce and tomato.

FAST FIX
GREEK BURGERS

My stepdad's parents were born in Greece, so when I served these to him, he really enjoyed the flavor.
—**MICHELLE CURTIS** BAKER CITY, OR

START TO FINISH: 25 MIN.
MAKES: 4 SERVINGS

- 1 tablespoon Dijon mustard
- 1 tablespoon lemon juice
- 1 tablespoon finely chopped onion
- 1 garlic clove, minced
- ½ teaspoon dried rosemary, crushed
- ½ teaspoon salt
- ¼ teaspoon pepper
- 1 pound ground lamb
- 4 hamburger buns or hard rolls, split
  Sliced cucumbers and tomatoes, optional
  Ranch salad dressing, optional

1. In a large bowl, combine the first seven ingredients. Crumble the lamb over mixture and mix well. Shape into four patties.
2. Pan-fry, grill or broil until no longer pink. Serve on buns with cucumbers, tomatoes and ranch dressing, if desired.

FAST FIX
COLA BURGERS

The unusual combination of cola and French salad dressing gives these hamburgers fabulous flavor. The mixture is also used as a basting sauce on the moist patties, which are a family hit.
—**MELVA BAUMER** MILLMONT, PA

START TO FINISH: 30 MIN.
MAKES: 6 SERVINGS

- 1 large egg
- ½ cup cola, divided
- ½ cup crushed saltines (about 15)
- 6 tablespoons French salad dressing, divided
- 2 tablespoons grated Parmesan cheese
- ¼ teaspoon salt
- 1½ pounds ground beef
- 6 hamburger buns, split

1. In a large bowl, combine egg, ¼ cup cola, cracker crumbs, 2 tablespoons salad dressing, Parmesan cheese and salt. Crumble the beef over mixture and mix well. Shape into six ¾-in.-thick patties (mixture will be moist).
2. In a small bowl, combine the remaining cola and salad dressing; set aside.
3. Grill the patties, uncovered, over medium heat for 3 minutes on each side. Brush with the cola mixture. Grill for 8-10 minutes longer, basting and turning occasionally, or until a thermometer reads 160°. Serve on buns.
NOTE *Diet cola is not recommended for this recipe.*

DAD'S BEST BURGERS

This favorite was created by my father-in-law years ago, then I added a few ingredients of my own. Even my husband, who doesn't care for cream cheese, gobbles up these burgers.
—**MARY ROLANDO** FARMINGTON, IL

PREP: 20 MIN. • **GRILL:** 15 MIN.
MAKES: 8 SERVINGS

- 1 package (3 ounces) cream cheese, softened
- 1 large egg
- 1 medium onion, finely chopped
- ½ cup dry bread crumbs
- 1½ teaspoons dried parsley flakes
- ½ teaspoon seasoned salt
- ¼ teaspoon pepper
- 1 pound ground beef
- 1 pound bulk pork sausage
- 8 hamburger buns, split

1. In a bowl, combine the first seven ingredients. Crumble beef and sausage over mixture; mix well. Shape into eight patties.
2. Grill, uncovered, over medium heat for 4-6 minutes on each side or until no longer pink. Serve on buns.
TO GIVE DAD'S BEST BURGERS AN ITALIAN TWIST, *use seasoned bread crumbs and Italian sausage. Serve with spaghetti or pizza sauce instead of traditional ketchup.*

FAST FIX

TASTY ITALIAN BURGERS

The best flavors of Italy—pesto, basil, tomato and mozzarella—are celebrated in these tempting turkey burgers. Grill some up for an international cookout.

—SHARON NOVIN WEST HILLS, CA

START TO FINISH: 30 MIN.
MAKES: 6 SERVINGS

- 3 tablespoons shredded Parmesan cheese
- 1 garlic clove, minced
- 1 pound lean ground turkey
- ½ pound Italian turkey sausage links, casings removed
- 6 hamburger buns, split
- 3 tablespoons olive oil
- 6 tablespoons prepared pesto
- 6 ounces fresh mozzarella cheese, sliced
- 6 lettuce leaves
- 6 slices tomato
- ¼ cup thinly sliced fresh basil leaves

1. In a large bowl, combine Parmesan cheese and garlic. Crumble turkey and turkey sausage over mixture and mix well. Shape into six patties.

2. Grill the burgers, covered, over medium heat or broil 4 in. from the heat for 5-8 minutes on each side or until a thermometer reads 165° and juices run clear.

3. Brush buns with olive oil; grill, uncovered, for 1-2 minutes or until toasted. Serve burgers on buns with pesto, mozzarella cheese, lettuce, tomato and basil.

TASTY ITALIAN BURGERS

TURKEY BURGERS WITH
AVOCADO SAUCE

2. For sauce, in a small bowl, mash avocado with the sour cream, cilantro, lime juice, garlic and salt. Refrigerate until serving.

3. Moisten a paper towel with cooking oil; using long-handled tongs, rub on grill rack to coat lightly. Grill burgers, covered, over medium heat or broil 4 in. from the heat for 5-7 minutes on each side or until a thermometer reads 165° and juices run clear.

4. Place on buns; top each with about ¼ cup sauce. Serve with the lettuce, cheese, tomato and onion, if desired.

NOTE *Wear disposable gloves when cutting hot peppers; the oils can burn skin. Avoid touching your face.*

FAST FIX

FRENCH ONION BURGERS

I created French Onion Burgers one day when I needed to stretch a pound of hamburger. When we have high school boys help with baling hay, this is one of their favorite foods to enjoy after the hard work is done.

—**BETH JOHNSON** DALTON, OH

START TO FINISH: 20 MIN.
MAKES: 4 SERVINGS

- 1 **can (4 ounces) mushroom stems and pieces, drained and diced**
- 1 **can (2.8 ounces) French-fried onions**
- 1 **tablespoon Worcestershire sauce**
- ½ **teaspoon salt**
- 1 **pound ground beef**
- 4 **hamburger buns, split**
   Lettuce leaves and tomato slices

1. In a large bowl, combine the mushrooms, onions, Worcestershire sauce and salt. Crumble beef over the mixture and mix well. Shape into four patties.

2. Grill, uncovered, over medium heat or broil 4 in. from the heat 6-9 minutes on each side or until a thermometer reads 160° and juices run clear. Serve on buns with lettuce and tomato.

TURKEY BURGERS WITH AVOCADO SAUCE

I love burgers and Southwestern food, so why not combine the two in a light and juicy burger? I like to whip these up, pop them in the fridge and cook them later for a quick weeknight meal!

—**JAN WARREN-RUCKER** CLEMMONS, NC

PREP: 30 MIN. + CHILLING • **GRILL:** 10 MIN.
MAKES: 4 SERVINGS

- 1 **cup fresh or frozen corn, thawed**
- ½ **cup chopped red onion**
- 1 **small sweet red pepper, chopped**
- 2 **jalapeno peppers, seeded and minced**
- 2 **teaspoons olive oil**
- 2 **tablespoons lime juice**
- 2 **garlic cloves, minced**
- ½ **teaspoon salt**
- ½ **teaspoon ground cumin**
- ¼ **teaspoon chili powder**
- ⅛ **teaspoon dried oregano**
- 1 **pound extra-lean ground turkey**

SAUCE
- 1 **medium ripe avocado, peeled**
- ½ **cup fat-free sour cream**
- 2 **tablespoons minced fresh cilantro**
- 2 **teaspoons lime juice**
- 1 **garlic clove, minced**
- ⅛ **teaspoon salt**

SERVING
- 4 **whole wheat hamburger buns, split**
   Shredded lettuce and reduced-fat Mexican cheese blend, optional
   Sliced tomato and red onion, optional

1. In a large skillet, saute the corn, onion and peppers in oil until crisp-tender. Stir in the lime juice, garlic, salt, cumin, chili powder and oregano; cook 1 minute longer. Transfer to a large bowl and cool slightly. Crumble turkey over mixture and mix well. Shape into four burgers. Refrigerate for at least 30 minutes.

TUSCAN BURGERS WITH PESTO MAYO

Everyone needs to bring their appetite when you serve these man-size burgers. They have a bit of Italy in them with the use of pancetta, pesto and mozzarella cheese. Try them and you'll love them!

—RITA COMBS VALDOSTA, GA

PREP: 25 MIN. • **GRILL:** 20 MIN.
MAKES: 4 SERVINGS

- ¼ cup mayonnaise
- ¼ cup prepared pesto, divided
- 3 ounces sliced pancetta, finely chopped
- ¼ teaspoon pepper
- ⅛ teaspoon kosher salt
- 1 pound ground beef
- 1 small red onion, cut into 4 slices
- 1 large tomato, cut into 4 slices
- 1 tablespoon olive oil
- 8 ounces fresh mozzarella cheese, cut into 4 slices
- 4 Italian rolls, split
- 1 cup fresh arugula or fresh baby spinach

1. In a small bowl, combine the mayonnaise and 2 tablespoons pesto; cover and chill until serving. In a large bowl, combine the pancetta, pepper, salt and remaining pesto. Crumble beef over mixture and mix well. Shape into four patties.

2. Brush onion and tomato slices with oil. Grill onion slices over medium heat for 4-6 minutes on each side or until crisp-tender. Grill tomato slices for 1-2 minutes on each side or until lightly browned.

3. Grill burgers, covered, over medium heat for 5-7 minutes on each side or until a thermometer reads 160° and juices run clear. Top the burgers with mozzarella cheese. Grill 1 minute longer or until cheese is melted. Spread cut sides of rolls with pesto mayonnaise; top with the burgers, onion, tomato and arugula.

TUSCAN BURGERS
WITH PESTO MAYO

HONEY-MUSTARD
BRATS

HONEY-MUSTARD BRATS

These dressed-up brats are bursting with honey-mustard flavor. Tailgaters and grill masters alike are sure to love this recipe and ask for more.
—**DENISE HRUZ** GERMANTOWN, WI

PREP: 15 MIN. + MARINATING • **GRILL:** 20 MIN.
MAKES: 8 SERVINGS

- 1 **cup honey mustard**
- ¼ **cup mayonnaise**
- 2 **teaspoons Worcestershire sauce**
- ¼ **teaspoon celery seed**
- 8 **uncooked bratwurst links**
- 8 **brat buns**

1. In a small bowl, combine the honey mustard, mayonnaise, Worcestershire sauce and celery seed. Pour ¾ cup into a large resealable plastic bag; add the bratwurst. Seal bag and turn to coat; refrigerate for 30 minutes.

2. Transfer ¼ cup of the sauce to another bowl; cover and refrigerate until serving. Set aside remaining sauce for basting.

3. Drain and discard brat marinade. Moisten a paper towel with cooking oil; using long-handled tongs, rub on the grill rack to coat lightly. Grill brats, covered, over medium heat or broil 4 in. from the heat for 10 minutes, turning frequently. Baste with 2 tablespoons of reserved sauce; grill 3 minutes longer.

4. Turn and baste with remaining sauce; grill or broil 3-5 minutes longer or until no longer pink. Serve brats on buns; top each with 1½ teaspoons of refrigerated sauce.

BETTY'S BURGERS

I dreamed up these cheese- and vegetable-stuffed burgers for a family barbecue years ago. They're delicious grilled or pan fried. Folks are always thrilled with the tasty surprise inside!

—BETTY CANOLES ATASCADERO, CA

START TO FINISH: 30 MIN.
MAKES: 6 SERVINGS

- 1½ **pounds ground beef**
- 6 **thin slices cheddar cheese**
- 1 **large green pepper, julienned**
- 1 **medium onion, thinly sliced**
- 1 **medium tomato, thinly sliced**
- 6 **thin slices Swiss cheese**
  Salt and pepper to taste
  Lettuce leaves
- 6 **hamburger buns, split**

1. Shape beef into 12 thin patties. Top six patties with a slice of cheddar cheese, green pepper strips and a slice of onion, tomato and Swiss cheese. Top each with another patty and seal edges. Season to taste.

2. Grill beef, covered, over medium heat or broil 4 in. from the heat for 4-5 minutes on each side or until a thermometer reads 160° and juices run clear. Serve on lettuce-lined buns.

BETTY'S BURGERS

 ## HOW TO STUFF BURGERS

Shape 1½ lbs. of ground chuck into eight 3-oz. portions on waxed paper. Press each portion into a 4-in. patty using a fork.

Top four of the patties as directed or use your own toppings. A slice of onion and shredded cheese is a great start. Cover with remaining patties.

Use a fork to tightly seal the edges of the patties. Grill according to the recipe's directions or to your desired doneness.

FAST FIX ▶

BARBECUE ITALIAN SAUSAGES

The tangy barbecue sauce in this recipe is fast, flavorful and extremely versatile. It's fantastic on sausages, but don't stop there; give it a try on ribs, chicken or with pulled pork.

—*TASTE OF HOME* TEST KITCHEN

START TO FINISH: 30 MIN.
MAKES: 4 SERVINGS

- 4 uncooked Italian sausage links
- ½ cup chopped green pepper
- ¼ cup chopped onion
- 1 tablespoon olive oil
- ⅓ cup dry red wine or beef broth
- ½ cup ketchup
- 1 tablespoon cider vinegar
- 1 tablespoon soy sauce
- 1 teaspoon brown sugar
- ¼ teaspoon ground cumin
- ¼ teaspoon chili powder
- ⅛ teaspoon liquid smoke, optional
- 4 hot dog buns, split

1. Grill the sausages, covered, over medium heat for 5-8 minutes on each side or until no longer pink.

2. In a large skillet, saute green pepper and onion in oil for 3-4 minutes or until tender. Stir in the wine. Bring to a boil; cook for 2 minutes or until liquid is evaporated.

3. Stir in the ketchup, vinegar, soy sauce, brown sugar, cumin, chili powder and liquid smoke, if desired. Bring to a boil. Reduce heat; simmer 2-3 minutes or until thickened. Place sausages in buns; serve with sauce.

CHIPOTLE CHEESEBURGERS

FAST FIX ▶

CHIPOTLE CHEESEBURGERS

Heat up a casual meal with these spiced-up burgers. You can substitute ground turkey for the beef and your favorite sliced cheese for the mozzarella.

—**CRYSTAL JO BRUNS** ILIFF, CO

START TO FINISH: 25 MIN.
MAKES: 4 SERVINGS

- 1 small onion, finely chopped
- 2 tablespoons minced fresh cilantro
- 1 chipotle pepper in adobo sauce, finely chopped
- 1 teaspoon onion powder
- 1 teaspoon garlic powder
- 1 teaspoon seasoned salt
- ¼ teaspoon pepper
- 1 pound ground beef
- 4 slices part-skim mozzarella cheese
- 4 hamburger buns, split and toasted
  Lettuce leaves and tomato slices, optional

1. In a small bowl, combine the first seven ingredients. Crumble the beef over mixture and mix well. Shape into four patties.

2. Grill, covered, over medium heat or broil 4 in. from the heat for 5-7 minutes on each side or until a thermometer reads 160° and juices run clear. Top with cheese. Cook 1-2 minutes longer or until cheese is melted. Serve on buns with lettuce and tomato, if desired.

BOURBON BRAT SKEWERS

When we decided to marinate veggies in a tasty bourbon sauce and serve them with grilled bratwurst, this recipe made our VIP tailgate party list!

—MARY LEVERETTE COLUMBIA, SC

PREP: 20 MIN. + MARINATING • **GRILL:** 15 MIN.
MAKES: 6 SKEWERS

- ½ cup reduced-sodium soy sauce
- ½ cup bourbon
- 3 tablespoons brown sugar
- 1 teaspoon seasoned salt
- ¼ teaspoon cayenne pepper
- 2 cups whole mushrooms
- 2 medium sweet red peppers, cut into 1-inch pieces
- 1 medium green pepper, cut into 1-inch pieces
- 1 medium onion, cut into wedges
- 1 package (16 ounces) uncooked bratwurst links, cut into 1-inch slices

1. In a large resealable plastic bag, combine the first five ingredients. Add the vegetables; seal bag and turn to coat. Refrigerate for at least 1 hour.
2. Drain and reserve marinade. On six metal or soaked wooden skewers, alternately thread the vegetables and bratwurst.
3. Spoon some reserved marinade over the vegetables and bratwurst. Grill, covered, over medium heat for 15-20 minutes or until bratwurst is no longer pink and vegetables are tender, turning and basting frequently with reserved marinade during the last 5 minutes.

BOURBON BRAT SKEWERS

FAST FIX
BACON-STUFFED BURGERS

I came across this recipe years ago and added the pork sausage to perk it up. My husband claims these are the best burgers he's ever tasted, and I have to agree. They are great served with crunchy dill pickles.

—SANDY MCKENZIE BRAHAM, MN

START TO FINISH: 30 MIN.
MAKES: 8 SERVINGS

- 4 slices bacon
- ¼ cup chopped onion
- 1 can (4 ounces) mushroom pieces, drained and finely chopped
- 1 pound lean ground beef
- 1 pound bulk pork sausage
- ¼ cup grated Parmesan cheese
- ½ teaspoon pepper
- ¼ teaspoon garlic powder
- 2 tablespoons steak sauce
- 8 hamburger buns, split and toasted
  Leaf lettuce, optional

1. In a large skillet, cook bacon over medium heat until crisp. Remove bacon and discard all but 2 tablespoons drippings. Saute onions in drippings until tender. Crumble bacon; add with mushrooms to skillet and set aside.
2. Meanwhile, combine beef, pork, cheese, pepper, garlic powder and steak sauce in a large bowl. Shape into 16 patties. Divide bacon mixture and place over eight of the patties. Place the remaining patties on top and press edges tightly to seal.
3. Grill over medium heat until well-done (pork sausage in burgers requires thorough cooking). Serve on buns, with lettuce if desired.

SOUTHWEST BURGERS

FAST FIX

SOUTHWEST BURGERS

Whether you're tailgating at the ballpark or hanging out on the patio with friends, these Southwestern-style burgers are great on the grill. Sometimes I make six patties rather than eight out of the ingredients because I like my burgers bigger and better!

—**ROBERT HODGES** SAN DIEGO, CA

START TO FINISH: 30 MIN.
MAKES: 8 SERVINGS

- 1 can (4 ounces) chopped green chilies
- ¼ cup Worcestershire sauce
- ½ teaspoon hickory liquid smoke, optional
- ½ cup crushed butter-flavored crackers (about 12 crackers)
- 4½ teaspoons chili powder
- 3 teaspoons ground cumin
- ½ teaspoon salt
- ½ teaspoon pepper
- 2 pounds lean ground beef (90% lean)
- ½ pound bulk pork sausage
- 8 slices pepper jack cheese
- 8 sesame seed hamburger buns, split
  Lettuce leaves and tomato slices
  Toppings of your choice

1. In a large bowl, combine the first eight ingredients. Crumble beef and sausage over mixture and mix well. Shape into eight patties.

2. Grill, covered, over medium heat for 5-7 minutes on each side or until no longer pink. Top with cheese. Grill for 1 minute longer or until the cheese is melted.

3. Grill the buns, cut side down, for 1-2 minutes or until toasted. Serve burgers on buns with lettuce, tomato and toppings.

5 INGREDIENTS FAST FIX

TERIYAKI BURGERS

I was getting tired of regular hamburgers, so I decided to create something just a little bit different. I love the sweet and salty combination of these patties.

—**TINA BRYAN** ALTOONA, PA

START TO FINISH: 20 MIN.
MAKES: 2 SERVINGS

- ½ pound lean ground beef (90% lean)
- 2 hamburger buns, split
- 4 slices deli ham (¾ ounce each)
- 2 pineapple slices
- 3 tablespoons reduced-sodium teriyaki sauce

Shape beef into two patties. Grill, covered, over medium heat or broil 4 in. from the heat for 4-5 minutes on each side or until a thermometer reads 160° and juices run clear. Serve on buns with ham, pineapple and teriyaki sauce.

BACON-BLUE CHEESE STUFFED BURGERS

These loaded burgers are one hearty meal in a bun. They're sure to satisfy even the biggest of appetites.

—**CHRISTINE KEATING** NORWALK, CA

PREP: 30 MIN. • **GRILL:** 10 MIN.
MAKES: 4 SERVINGS

- 1½ pounds lean ground beef (90% lean)
- 1 package (3 ounces) cream cheese, softened
- ⅓ cup crumbled blue cheese
- ⅓ cup bacon bits
- ½ teaspoon salt
- ½ teaspoon garlic powder
- ¼ teaspoon pepper
- 1 pound sliced fresh mushrooms
- 1 tablespoon olive oil
- 1 tablespoon water
- 1 tablespoon Dijon mustard
- 4 whole wheat hamburger buns, split
- ¼ cup mayonnaise
- 4 romaine leaves
- 1 medium tomato, sliced

1. Shape beef into eight thin patties. Combine the cream cheese, blue cheese and bacon bits; spoon onto the center of four patties. Top with remaining patties and press edges firmly to seal. Combine the salt, garlic powder and pepper; sprinkle over patties.

2. Grill burgers, covered, over medium heat or broil 4 in. from the heat for 5-7 minutes on each side or until a thermometer reads 160° and juices run clear.

3. Meanwhile, in a large skillet, saute mushrooms in oil until tender. Stir in water and mustard.

4. Serve the burgers on buns with mayonnaise, romaine, tomato and mushroom mixture.

GREEK-STUFFED BURGERS *Omit cream cheese, blue cheese and bacon bits. Mix ⅓ cup feta cheese, ⅓ cup chopped tomato, 2 tablespoons chopped red onion, 4 teaspoons chopped ripe olives, 2 teaspoons olive oil and ¼ teaspoon dried oregano. Stuff burgers with feta mixture and proceed as recipe directs.*

 **GRILL SKILL**

To keep grilled burgers from drying out, don't overhandle the meat before cooking. If you add seasonings to the beef, gently mix them in with two forks just until combined. Then shape into 4-in. round patties about ½-in. thick (beef plumps when it cooks). Hamburgers are best cooked over medium heat.

APPLE 'N' PORK BURGERS

BRATS IN BEER

Make these juicy brats at your next barbecue. The flavor of the marinade really comes through in the grilled onions.

—**JILL HAZELTON** HAMLET, IN

PREP: 10 MIN. + MARINATING • **GRILL:** 15 MIN.
MAKES: 8 SERVINGS

- 1 **can (12 ounces) beer or nonalcoholic beer**
- 2 **tablespoons brown sugar**
- 2 **tablespoons soy sauce**
- 1 **tablespoon chili powder**
- 1 **tablespoon prepared mustard**
- ⅛ **teaspoon garlic powder**
- 8 **uncooked bratwurst links**
- 1 **large onion, thinly sliced**
- 8 **brat or hot dog buns, split**

1. In a small bowl, combine the first six ingredients. Pour 1¾ cups into a large resealable plastic bag; add bratwurst. Seal bag and turn to coat; refrigerate for 4 hours or overnight. Cover and refrigerate remaining marinade.

2. Add onion to remaining marinade; toss to coat. Place on a double thickness of heavy-duty foil (about 18 in. square). Fold foil around onion mixture and seal tightly. Drain and discard marinade from bratwurst.

3. Grill bratwurst and onion, covered, over medium heat or broil 4 in. from the heat for 15-20 minutes or until meat is no longer pink and the onion is tender, turning frequently. Open foil carefully to allow steam to escape. Serve brats in buns with onion mixture.

FAST FIX ▶

APPLE 'N' PORK BURGERS

This pork burger recipe is a favorite of ours. We had a similar burger in Hawaii, and once we can home, I created this tasty version that we actually prefer to the original. I like to serve them with a salad or fresh corn on the cob.

—**TRISHA KRUSE** EAGLE, ID

START TO FINISH: 30 MIN.
MAKES: 2 SERVINGS

- ½ **cup shredded peeled apple**
- ¼ **cup finely chopped onion**
- ¼ **cup drained unsweetened crushed pineapple**
- 2 **tablespoons dry bread crumbs**
- 1 **tablespoon reduced-sodium soy sauce**
- 1 **garlic clove, minced**
- ½ **pound ground pork**
- 2 **slices Swiss cheese (¾ ounce each)**
- 2 **hamburger buns, split**
   Lettuce leaves, tomato slices, sliced ripe avocado, mustard and mayonnaise, optional

1. In a small bowl, combine the first six ingredients. Crumble the pork over mixture; mix well. Shape into two patties.

2. Grill, covered, over medium heat for 4-5 minutes on each side or until a thermometer reads 160°. Top with the cheese. Grill 1-2 minutes longer or until cheese is melted.

3. Serve on buns with lettuce, tomato, avocado, mustard and mayonnaise, if desired.

FAST FIX ▶
PHILLY BURGER

The rich cheese topping and crunchy French-fried onions make this recipe a cookout sensation. Simply serve the burgers with potato salad and fresh fruit, and dinner is done!

—MARJORIE CAREY ALAMOSA, CO

START TO FINISH: 30 MIN.
MAKES: 4 BURGERS

- 2 tablespoons Worcestershire sauce, divided
- 4 teaspoons Dijon mustard, divided
- 1 can (2.8 ounces) French-fried onions, divided
- 1 pound ground beef
- 1 package (3 ounces) cream cheese, softened
- 1 jar (2.5 ounces) sliced mushrooms, drained
- 1 teaspoon dried parsley flakes
- 4 kaiser rolls

1. In a bowl, combine 1 tablespoon of Worcestershire sauce, 3 teaspoons of mustard and half of the onions. Crumble beef over mixture; mix well. Form into four patties.

2. Grill, covered, over medium heat or broil 4 in. from the heat 6-9 minutes on each side or until a thermometer reads 160° and juices run clear.

3. Meanwhile, in a small bowl, combine cream cheese, mushrooms, parsley and remaining Worcestershire sauce and mustard. Spread mixture on cooked patties; top with the remaining onions.

4. Grill or broil 30 seconds longer or until onions are crisp-tender. Serve on kaiser rolls.

PHILLY BURGER

WHISKEY CHEDDAR BURGERS

FAST FIX

WHISKEY CHEDDAR BURGERS

This juicy burger has big flavors to satisfy even the heartiest appetites. It always impresses at our cookouts, and no one guesses the secret ingredient: whiskey!
—**AMBER NICHOLSON**
WINOOSKI, VT

START TO FINISH: 30 MIN.
MAKES: 8 SERVINGS

- ¼ cup whiskey
- 1 tablespoon reduced-sodium soy sauce
- 1 tablespoon Worcestershire sauce
- 1 cup (4 ounces) shredded sharp cheddar cheese
- ¼ cup finely chopped onion
- 2 tablespoons seasoned bread crumbs
- 3 garlic cloves, minced
- ½ teaspoon salt
- ½ teaspoon paprika
- ½ teaspoon dried basil
- ½ teaspoon pepper
- 1½ pounds lean ground beef (90% lean)
- 8 onion rolls or hamburger buns, split
  Optional toppings: lettuce leaves, sliced tomato, cheddar cheese slices and barbecue sauce

1. In a large bowl, combine the first 11 ingredients. Add beef; mix lightly but thoroughly. Shape mixture into eight ½-in.-thick patties.

2. Moisten a paper towel with cooking oil; using long-handled tongs, rub on grill rack to coat lightly. Grill burgers, covered, over medium heat or broil 4 in. from heat 4-5 minutes on each side or until a thermometer reads 160°. Serve burgers on rolls with toppings as desired.

FREEZE OPTION *Place patties on a plastic wrap-lined baking sheet; wrap and freeze until firm. Remove from sheet and transfer to a resealable plastic freezer bag; return to freezer. To use, grill frozen patties as directed, increasing time as necessary for a thermometer to read 160°.*

FLORIBBEAN FISH BURGERS
WITH TROPICAL SAUCE

FAST FIX ▶
HERB & CHEESE-STUFFED BURGERS

Tired of the same old ground-beef burgers? This quick-fix alternative, with its creamy cheese filling, will wake up your taste buds.

—SHERRI COX LUCASVILLE, OH

START TO FINISH: 30 MIN.
MAKES: 4 SERVINGS

- ¼ cup shredded cheddar cheese
- 2 tablespoons cream cheese, softened
- 2 tablespoons minced fresh parsley
- 3 teaspoons Dijon mustard, divided
- 2 green onions, thinly sliced
- 3 tablespoons dry bread crumbs
- 2 tablespoons ketchup
- ½ teaspoon salt
- ½ teaspoon dried rosemary, crushed
- ¼ teaspoon dried sage leaves
- 1 pound lean ground beef (90% lean)
- 4 hard rolls, split
  Lettuce leaves and tomato slices, optional

1. In a small bowl, combine the cheddar cheese, cream cheese, parsley and 1 teaspoon mustard; set aside.
2. In another bowl, combine the onions, bread crumbs, ketchup, salt, rosemary, sage and remaining mustard. Crumble the beef over mixture and mix well.
3. Shape into eight thin patties. Spoon cheese mixture onto center of four patties; top with remaining patties and press edges firmly to seal.
4. Grill burgers, covered, over medium heat or broil 4 in. from the heat for 5-7 minutes on each side or until a thermometer reads 160° and juices run clear. Serve on rolls with lettuce and tomato, if desired.

FLORIBBEAN FISH BURGERS WITH TROPICAL SAUCE

I like to make fish burgers because they are usually lower in saturated fat and cholesterol than beef patties. I add some avocado because there's not much fat in the burgers.

—VIRGINIA ANTHONY JACKSONVILLE, FL

PREP: 35 MIN. • **GRILL:** 10 MIN.
MAKES: 6 SERVINGS

- ½ cup fat-free mayonnaise
- 1 tablespoon minced fresh cilantro
- 1 tablespoon minced chives
- 1 tablespoon sweet pickle relish
- 1 tablespoon lime juice
- 1 teaspoon grated lime peel
- 1½ teaspoons Caribbean jerk seasoning
- ⅛ teaspoon hot pepper sauce

BURGERS
- 1 large egg white, lightly beaten
- 4 green onions, chopped
- ⅓ cup soft bread crumbs
- 2 tablespoons minced fresh cilantro
- 2 teaspoons Caribbean jerk seasoning
- 1 garlic clove, minced
- ⅛ teaspoon salt
- 1½ pounds grouper or red snapper fillets
- 6 kaiser rolls, split
- 6 lettuce leaves
- 1 medium ripe avocado, peeled and cut into 12 slices

1. In a small bowl, combine the first eight ingredients; cover and refrigerate until serving.
2. In a large bowl, combine the egg white, onions, bread crumbs, cilantro, jerk seasoning, garlic and salt. Place fish in a food processor; cover and process until finely chopped. Add to egg white mixture and mix well. Shape into six burgers.
3. Spray both sides of burgers with cooking spray. Moisten a paper towel with cooking oil; using long-handled tongs, lightly rub on the grill rack to coat. Grill the burgers, covered, over medium heat or broil 4 in. from the heat for 4-5 minutes on each side or until a thermometer reads 160°.
4. Serve each on a roll with lettuce, avocado and 5 teaspoons tropical sauce.

SAUSAGE & PEPPER SANDWICHES

Pick a dark, malty lager for simmering these sausages. Next, grill 'em, split 'em and load 'em on toasted buns with garlicky peppers and onions. Yum!

—JEANNE HORN DULUTH, MN

PREP: 30 MIN. • **GRILL:** 5 MIN.
MAKES: 8 SERVINGS

- 2 **bottles (12 ounces each) beer or nonalcoholic beer**
- 2 **tablespoons prepared mustard**
- 1 **tablespoon ketchup**
- 8 **fresh Italian sausage, bratwurst or Polish sausage links**
- 1 **large onion, thinly sliced**
- 1 **tablespoon olive oil**
- 1 **medium sweet red pepper, coarsely chopped**
- 1 **medium green pepper, coarsely chopped**
- 1 **medium onion, chopped**
- 1 **garlic clove, minced**
- 1 **teaspoon Italian seasoning**
- ½ **teaspoon salt**
- ¼ **teaspoon pepper**
- 8 **hot dog buns, split**
  Spicy brown mustard

1. In a 6-qt. stockpot, combine beer, prepared mustard and ketchup. Add sausages, sliced onion and, if necessary, water to cover. Bring to a simmer and cook, uncovered, for 10-12 minutes or until a thermometer inserted in sausage reads 160°.

2. Meanwhile, in a large skillet, heat oil over medium heat. Add the peppers and chopped onion; cook and stir 6-8 minutes or until tender. Stir in the garlic and seasonings; cook for 30 seconds longer. Remove from heat.

3. Remove sausages from beer mixture. Grill sausages, covered, over medium heat or broil 4 in. from heat 1-2 minutes on each side or until lightly browned. Cut each sausage lengthwise in half. Serve in buns with pepper mixture and brown mustard.

SAUSAGE & PEPPER SANDWICHES

GYRO BURGERS

A blend of mild seasonings gives these burgers mass appeal. I find that pita bread is a creative change of pace from the usual hamburger buns.

—KATIE KOZIOLEK HARTLAND, MN

PREP: 35 MIN. + CHILLING • **GRILL:** 15 MIN.
MAKES: 4 SERVINGS

CUCUMBER SAUCE
- 2 cups (16 ounces) plain yogurt
- 1¼ cups chopped seeded peeled cucumber
- ¼ teaspoon salt
- 2 tablespoons olive oil
- 2 tablespoons white vinegar
- 1 garlic clove, minced

GYRO BURGERS
- 2 tablespoons plain yogurt
- 2 garlic cloves, minced
- 1 teaspoon dried rosemary, crushed
- ½ teaspoon lemon-pepper seasoning
- ¼ teaspoon salt
- 1 pound ground lamb or pork
- 4 pita breads, halved
  Sliced cucumber

1. For the cucumber sauce, line a fine mesh strainer with two layers of cheesecloth. Place yogurt in strainer over a large bowl. Cover and refrigerate for at least 4 hours or overnight.

2. Drain and discard liquid; set yogurt aside. Place cucumber in a colander over another bowl; sprinkle with salt. Let stand for 15 minutes; discard liquid.

3. In a large bowl, whisk the oil and vinegar until blended. Stir in the garlic, reserved yogurt and cucumber; cover and refrigerate until serving.

4. For gyro burgers, in a large bowl, combine the yogurt, garlic, rosemary, lemon pepper and salt. Crumble meat over mixture and mix well. Shape into four oval patties.

5. Grill, covered, over medium heat for 6-7 minutes on each side or until a thermometer reads 160°. Serve in pita bread with sliced cucumber and cucumber sauce.

THE PERFECT HAMBURGER

FAST FIX

THE PERFECT HAMBURGER

We think these burgers are perfect and make them often for friends and extended family. Check out the three variations, too!

—SHIRLEY KIDD NEW LONDON, MN

START TO FINISH: 20 MIN.
MAKES: 4 SERVINGS

- 1 large egg, lightly beaten

SEASONINGS
- 2 tablespoons chili sauce
- 1 teaspoon dried minced onion
- 1 teaspoon prepared horseradish
- 1 teaspoon Worcestershire sauce
- ½ teaspoon salt
  Dash pepper

BURGER
- 1 pound lean ground beef (90% lean)
- 4 hamburger buns, split

TOPPINGS
  Sliced tomato, onion, pickles and condiments, optional

1. In a large bowl, combine egg and seasonings. Crumble beef over mixture and mix well. Shape into four ¾-in.-thick patties.

2. Moisten a paper towel with cooking oil; using long-handled tongs, rub lightly on the grill rack to coat. Grill, covered, over medium heat or broil 4 in. from the heat for 5-7 minutes on each side or until a thermometer reads 160° and juices run clear. Serve on buns with toppings, if desired.

BACON BURGER *Replace the seasonings with ½ cup shredded cheddar cheese, 1 small chopped onion, 2 tablespoons ketchup, 1 tablespoon each Parmesan cheese and Worcestershire sauce, ½ teaspoon salt and pepper. Shape into six patties. Wrap 1 bacon strip around each patty and secure with a toothpick. Grill as directed.*

HERBED BURGERS *Omit egg. Replace seasoning mix with 5 teaspoons sour cream, ¾ teaspoon dried parsley flakes, ½ teaspoon salt and ⅛ teaspoon pepper. Shape into four patties. Grill as directed.*

TACO BURGERS *Replace seasoning mix with 3 tablespoons taco seasoning mix, 2 teaspoons instant minced onion and ¾ cup finely crushed corn chips. Shape into six patties. Grill as directed.*

KING BURGERS

My husband is a grill master, and we make up recipes together. The sauce for this juicy burger tastes even better when it's been refrigerated overnight.

—**MARY POTTER** STERLING HEIGHTS, MI

START TO FINISH: 30 MIN.
MAKES: 6 SERVINGS

- 2 tablespoons butter
- ¼ cup mayonnaise
- 2 tablespoons prepared horseradish
- 2 tablespoons Dijon mustard
- ⅛ teaspoon salt
- ⅛ teaspoon pepper
- BURGERS
- 1½ pounds ground beef
- ⅓ cup beef broth
- 2½ teaspoons hamburger seasoning, divided
- 6 hamburger buns, split
- 3 tablespoons butter, softened
  Toppings: shredded lettuce, sliced tomato and red onion

1. Cut butter into six slices. Place on a small plate; freeze until firm. For sauce, in a small bowl, mix the mayonnaise, horseradish, mustard, salt and pepper until blended.
2. In a large bowl, combine the beef, broth and 1½ teaspoons hamburger seasoning, mixing together lightly but thoroughly. Shape into six patties. Place a frozen butter slice in the center of each; shape beef around butter, forming ¾-in.-thick patties. Sprinkle patties with remaining hamburger seasoning.
3. Grill burgers, covered, over medium heat 5-7 minutes on each side or until a thermometer reads 160°.
4. Spread buns with softened butter. Grill buns over medium heat, cut side down, for 30-60 seconds or until toasted. Serve burgers on buns with sauce and toppings.

FREEZE OPTION *Place patties on a plastic wrap-lined baking sheet; wrap and freeze until firm. Remove from sheet and transfer to a resealable plastic freezer bag; return to freezer. To use, cook frozen patties as directed, increasing time as necessary for a thermometer to read 160°.*

PROVOLONE BURGERS

Grilled hamburgers that are seasoned with garlic, onion and herbs and topped with melted cheese are a summertime staple for us. A delicious alternative to American or cheddar, mild provolone cheese is great on these beef patties.

—**CHERYL WILT** EGLON, WV

START TO FINISH: 25 MIN.
MAKES: 8 SERVINGS

- 1 medium onion, finely chopped
- 2 large eggs, lightly beaten
- 3 teaspoons dried basil
- 2 garlic cloves, minced
- 1 teaspoon dried oregano
- ½ teaspoon salt
- ¼ teaspoon pepper
- 3 pounds ground beef
- 8 slices provolone cheese
- 8 sandwich rolls, split
  Lettuce leaves

1. In a large bowl, combine the first seven ingredients. Crumble the beef over mixture and mix well. Shape into eight patties.
2. Grill, covered, over medium heat for 5-7 minutes on each side or until a thermometer reaches 160°.
3. Top each patty with a cheese slice; grill 1 minute longer or until cheese is melted. Grill rolls cut-side down for 1-2 minutes or until toasted. Top each with a burger and lettuce.

HAWAIIAN HONEY BURGERS

These nicely spiced burgers were a favorite of mine when I was growing up. Fresh fruit and buttery corn on the cob are ideal accompaniments.

—**SHERYL CREECH** LANCASTER, CA

START TO FINISH: 25 MIN.
MAKES: 8 SERVINGS

- ½ cup honey
- ¼ teaspoon ground cinnamon
- ¼ teaspoon paprika
- ¼ teaspoon curry powder
- ⅛ teaspoon ground ginger
- ⅛ teaspoon ground nutmeg
- 2 pounds ground beef
- ¼ cup reduced-sodium soy sauce
- 1 can (20 ounces) sliced pineapple, drained
- 8 hamburger buns, split and toasted
  Lettuce leaves, optional

1. In a large bowl, combine the first six ingredients. Crumble beef over mixture and mix well. Shape into eight ¾-in.-thick patties.
2. Grill, uncovered, over medium heat for 3 minutes on each side. Brush with the soy sauce. Continue grilling for 4-6 minutes or until juices run clear, basting and turning several times.
3. During the last 4 minutes, grill the pineapple slices until browned, turning once. Serve burgers and pineapple on buns with lettuce, if desired.

ZESTY SOUTHWESTERN BURGERS

We love burgers and have them every Saturday in summer. We also have a favorite burrito recipe. One day, we got the bright idea to combine the two favorites. Voila! Our Southwestern burgers were born.

—**TAMMY FORTNEY** DEER PARK, WA

START TO FINISH: 30 MIN.
MAKES: 8 SERVINGS

- 1 can (4 ounces) chopped green chilies
- 4 teaspoons ground cumin
- 1 teaspoon chili powder
- ¾ teaspoon garlic powder
- ¾ teaspoon salt
- ½ teaspoon pepper
- 2 pounds lean ground beef
- ¾ pound bulk pork sausage
- 8 slices Monterey Jack cheese
- 8 hamburger buns, split, toasted
- 8 lettuce leaves
- 1 large tomato, sliced
- 1 to 2 ripe avocados, peeled and sliced
  Mayonnaise or mustard, optional

1. In a large bowl, combine the first six ingredients. Crumble beef and sausage over mixture; mix well. Shape into eight patties.

2. Grill, covered, over medium heat for 5 minutes on each side or until a thermometer reads 160° and juices run clear. Top each burger with a slice of cheese.

3. Grill 1-2 minutes longer or until cheese begins to melt. Serve on buns with the lettuce, tomato, avocado and mayonnaise or mustard, if desired.

DILLY TURKEY BURGERS

DILLY TURKEY BURGERS

Dill is a great herb to enhance the flavor of turkey, and it certainly adds a lot to these burgers! You can also try this recipe with ground lamb.

—**ANDREA ROS** MOON TOWNSHIP, PA

START TO FINISH: 20 MIN.
MAKES: 4 SERVINGS

- 1 large egg, lightly beaten
- 2 tablespoons lemon juice
- 1 to 2 tablespoons snipped fresh dill or 1 to 2 teaspoons dill weed
- 1 garlic clove, minced
- ½ teaspoon salt
- ½ teaspoon dried oregano
- ¼ teaspoon pepper
- ½ cup soft bread crumbs
- 1 pound ground turkey
- 4 hamburger buns, split
  Lettuce leaves
- 8 slices tomato, optional
- 2 tablespoons mayonnaise, optional

1. In a large bowl, combine the first eight ingredients. Crumble turkey over mixture and mix well. Shape into four patties.

2. Grill, covered, over medium heat or broil 4 in. from heat for 8-10 minutes or until a thermometer reads 165°, turning once. Serve on buns with lettuce, tomato and mayonnaise, if desired.

 **GRILL SKILL**

Avoid the temptation to press on burgers with a spatula while grilling. Doing so squeezes out the juices, decreasing flavor and increasing the chances of drying out the patties.

JALAPENO POPPER BURGERS

What do you get when you combine a jalapeno popper and a juicy burger? This fantastic recipe! It takes the classic components of a popper and encases them in a beef patty for a burst of flavor in every bite.

—**JO DAVISON** NAPLES, FL

PREP: 30 MIN. • **GRILL:** 15 MIN.
MAKES: 4 SERVINGS

- 3 **jalapeno peppers, halved lengthwise and seeded**
- 1 **teaspoon olive oil**
- 6 **bacon strips, cooked and crumbled**
- 1 **package (3 ounces) cream cheese, softened**
- 2 **garlic cloves, minced**
- 1 **teaspoon salt**
- 1 **teaspoon lemon-pepper seasoning**
- ½ **teaspoon pepper**
- ¼ **teaspoon paprika**
- 2 **pounds ground beef**
- 4 **slices pepper jack cheese**
- 4 **hamburger buns, split**
- 4 **lettuce leaves**
- 1 **large tomato, sliced**
- ¾ **cup guacamole**

1. Brush the jalapenos with oil. Grill, covered, over medium heat for 3-5 minutes or until tender, turning occasionally. When cool enough to handle, finely chop. In a small bowl, combine the bacon, cream cheese and jalapeno until blended.

2. In a large bowl, combine the garlic, salt, lemon pepper, pepper and paprika. Crumble beef over mixture and mix well. Shape into eight thin patties. Spoon bacon mixture onto center of four patties; top with remaining patties and press edges firmly to seal.

3. Grill burgers, covered, over medium heat or broil 4 in. from the heat for 6-7 minutes on each side or until a thermometer reads 160° and juices run clear. Top with pepper jack cheese. Cover and cook 1-2 minutes longer or until cheese is melted.

4. Grill buns, cut side down, over medium heat for 30-60 seconds or until toasted. Serve burgers on buns with lettuce, tomato and guacamole.

NOTE *Wear disposable gloves when cutting hot peppers; the oils can burn skin. Avoid touching your face.*

JALAPENO POPPER BURGERS

BARBECUED BURGERS

I can't take all the credit for these winning burgers. My husband's uncle passed down the special barbecue sauce recipe. We love it on everything—it seemed only natural to try it on, and in, burgers!

—RHODA TROYER GLENFORD, OH

PREP: 25 MIN. • **GRILL:** 15 MIN.
MAKES: 6 SERVINGS

SAUCE
- 1 cup ketchup
- ½ cup packed brown sugar
- ⅓ cup sugar
- ¼ cup honey
- ¼ cup molasses
- 2 teaspoons prepared mustard
- 1½ teaspoons Worcestershire sauce
- ¼ teaspoon salt
- ¼ teaspoon liquid smoke
- ⅛ teaspoon pepper

BURGERS
- 1 large egg, lightly beaten
- ⅓ cup quick-cooking oats
- ¼ teaspoon onion salt
- ¼ teaspoon garlic salt
- ¼ teaspoon pepper
- ⅛ teaspoon salt
- 1½ pounds ground beef
- 6 hamburger buns, split
  Toppings of your choice

1. In a small saucepan, combine the first 10 ingredients. Bring to a boil. Remove from the heat. Set aside 1 cup barbecue sauce to serve with burgers.

2. In a large bowl, combine the egg, oats, ¼ cup of the remaining barbecue sauce, onion salt, garlic salt, pepper and salt. Crumble beef over mixture and mix well. Shape into six patties.

3. Grill, covered, over medium heat for 6-8 minutes on each side or until a thermometer reads 160°, basting with ½ cup barbecue sauce during the last 5 minutes. Serve on buns with toppings of your choice and the reserved barbecue sauce.

FAST FIX ▶
CANTONESE CHICKEN BURGERS

Ground chicken is perked up with onion, chopped peanuts and carrots for these delectable chicken burgers that can be served year-round. These sandwiches may take a little more work than the regular burgers, but the taste is worth it.

—BETTY CARR HUNTSVILLE, OH

START TO FINISH: 30 MIN.
MAKES: 4 SERVINGS

- 1 **large egg**
- 1 **teaspoon sesame oil**
- 1 **teaspoon soy sauce**
- ⅓ **cup dry bread crumbs**
- ¼ **cup chopped salted peanuts**
- 2 **tablespoons sliced green onion**
- 2 **tablespoons shredded carrot**
- ⅛ **teaspoon garlic powder**
- 1 **pound ground chicken**
- 4 **hamburger buns, split and toasted**
- ½ **cup plum sauce**
- 8 **spinach leaves, chopped**

1. In a large bowl, whisk the egg, oil and soy sauce. Stir in the bread crumbs, peanuts, onion, carrot and garlic powder. Crumble chicken over mixture and mix well. Shape into four patties.
2. Grill, uncovered, over medium heat or broil 3-4 in. from the heat for 8-10 minutes on each side or until juices run clear. Serve on buns, topped with plum sauce and spinach.

BACON-WRAPPED HOT DOGS

BACON-WRAPPED HOT DOGS

Here's a juicy, delicious and savory meal in a bun! I make it for tailgate parties, picnics and barbecues, and it always gets compliments. To transport, wrap the hot dogs in foil and then in paper.

—PETER HALFERTY CORPUS CHRISTI, TX

PREP: 25 MIN. • **GRILL:** 10 MIN.
MAKES: 8 SERVINGS

- 12 **bacon strips**
- 8 **cheese beef hot dogs**
- 8 **bakery hot dog buns, split and toasted**
- ¼ **cup chopped red onion**
- 2 **cups sauerkraut, rinsed and well drained**
  Optional condiments: mayonnaise, ketchup or Dijon mustard

1. In a large skillet, cook bacon over medium heat until partially cooked but not crisp. Remove to paper towels to drain; cool slightly. Wrap 1½ strips of bacon around each hot dog, securing with toothpicks as needed. (Do not wrap tightly or the bacon may tear during grilling.)
2. Grill, covered, over medium heat or broil 4 in. from heat for 6-8 minutes or until bacon is crisp and hot dogs are heated through, turning frequently. Discard toothpicks. Serve hot dogs in buns with onion and sauerkraut; top with condiments of your choice.

FAST FIX ▶
HORSERADISH BURGERS

My husband and I love to grill burgers year-round. This variation with a creamy horseradish filling is a hit with our family and friends.

—CHRIS ANDERSON MORTON, IL

START TO FINISH: 30 MIN.
MAKES: 8 SERVINGS

- 2 **pounds ground beef**
- 2 **tablespoons steak sauce**
- ¾ **teaspoon seasoned salt**
- 1 **package (3 ounces) cream cheese, softened**
- 1 **to 2 tablespoons prepared horseradish**
- 1 **teaspoon prepared mustard**
- 8 **hamburger buns, split**

1. In a large bowl, combine beef, steak sauce and seasoned salt; mix well. Shape into 16 thin patties. In a small bowl, combine the cream cheese, horseradish and mustard. Spoon about 1 tablespoonful onto center of eight patties; top with remaining patties. Press edges to seal.
2. Grill, covered, over medium heat for 6-7 minutes on each side or until a thermometer reads 160° and juices run clear. Serve on buns.

GRILLED HONEY BRATS

SOFT TACO BURGERS

I love to grill these sandwiches for quick summer meals or impromptu get-togethers around the pool. They're a snap to prepare, and no one ever guesses that they're low in fat.

—JOAN HALLFORD
NORTH RICHLAND HILLS, TX

START TO FINISH: 25 MIN.
MAKES: 8 SERVINGS

- 1 cup fat-free refried beans
- 1 can (4 ounces) chopped green chilies, drained, divided
- ¼ cup chopped onion
- ¼ teaspoon salt
- 1½ pounds lean ground beef (90% lean)
- 1 cup (4 ounces) shredded reduced-fat cheddar cheese
- 8 flour tortillas (6 inches), warmed
- 1 cup chopped lettuce
- 1 medium tomato, chopped
- ½ cup salsa

1. In a large bowl, combine the beans, 2 tablespoons green chilies, onion and salt. Crumble the beef over mixture and mix well. Shape into eight 5-in. patties. Top each patty with 2 tablespoons cheddar cheese; fold in half and press edges to seal, forming a half moon.
2. Moisten a paper towel with cooking oil; using long-handled tongs, rub lightly on the grill rack to coat. Grill burgers, uncovered, over medium heat or broil 4 in. from heat for 7-9 minutes on each side or until a thermometer reads 160° and juices run clear. Serve on tortillas with lettuce, tomato, salsa and remaining chilies.

GRILLED HONEY BRATS

Our honey-mustard glaze gives every bite of these brats a sweet and punchy flavor. Everyone who tries them agrees they're delicious.

—LILY JULOW LAWRENCEVILLE, GA

START TO FINISH: 25 MIN.
MAKES: 4 SERVINGS

- ¼ cup Dijon mustard
- ¼ cup honey
- 2 tablespoons mayonnaise
- 1 teaspoon steak sauce
- 4 uncooked bratwurst links
- 4 brat buns, split

1. In a small bowl, mix mustard, honey, mayonnaise and steak sauce.
2. Grill bratwurst, covered, over medium heat 15-20 minutes or until a thermometer reads 160°, turning occasionally; brush frequently with mustard mixture during the last 5 minutes. Serve on buns.

SWEET AND SASSY TURKEY BURGERS

These are scrumptious! I served them at our last family reunion and they were a huge hit. Cranberry sauce with turkey is a match made in heaven.

—MARLA CLARK MORIARTY, NM

PREP: 25 MIN. • **GRILL:** 15 MIN.
MAKES: 6 SERVINGS

- 6 **turkey bacon strips, diced and cooked**
- ¼ **cup dried cranberries**
- 1 **tablespoon maple syrup**
- 1 **teaspoon rubbed sage**
- ⅛ **teaspoon pepper**
- 1¼ **pounds extra-lean ground turkey**
- 1 **Italian turkey sausage link (4 ounces), casing removed**
- 3 **slices part-skim mozzarella cheese, cut in half**
- 6 **onion rolls, split**
- 6 **tablespoons jellied cranberry sauce**
- 6 **tablespoons fat-free mayonnaise**
- 6 **lettuce leaves**

1. In a large bowl, combine the first five ingredients. Crumble the turkey and sausage over mixture and mix well. Shape into six burgers.

2. Moisten a paper towel with cooking oil; using long-handled tongs, lightly rub on the grill rack to coat. Grill the burgers, covered, over medium heat or broil 4 in. from the heat for 5-7 minutes on each side or until a thermometer reads 165° and juices run clear. Top with cheese; cook 1-2 minutes longer or until cheese is melted.

3. Toast the rolls; spread warm rolls with cranberry sauce and mayonnaise. Serve burgers on rolls with lettuce.

FAST FIX
BBQ BACON BURGERS

With a slice of bacon inside and a tasty barbecue-mayo sauce on top, these are definitely not ordinary burgers. I think you'll agree.

—JOAN SCHOENHERR EASTPOINTE, MI

START TO FINISH: 30 MIN.
MAKES: 4 SERVINGS

- ¼ **cup mayonnaise**
- ¼ **cup barbecue sauce**
- 4 **bacon strips, cooked and crumbled**
- 1½ **teaspoons dried minced onion**
- 1½ **teaspoons steak seasoning**
- 1 **pound ground beef**
- 4 **slices Swiss cheese**
- 4 **hamburger buns, split**
  Lettuce leaves and tomato slices

1. In a small bowl, combine the mayonnaise and barbecue sauce. In another bowl, combine the bacon, 2 tablespoons mayonnaise mixture, onion and steak seasoning; crumble beef over mixture and mix well. Shape into four patties.

2. Grill burgers, covered, over medium heat for 5-7 minutes on each side or until a thermometer reads 160° and juices run clear. Top with cheese. Cover and cook 1-2 minutes longer or until cheese is melted. Spread remaining mayonnaise mixture over cut sides of bun bottoms. Layer with a lettuce, burger and tomato. Replace tops.

BBQ BACON BURGERS

ALL-AMERICAN BACON CHEESEBURGERS

FAST FIX

ALL-AMERICAN BACON CHEESEBURGERS

Where can you get a juicy bacon cheeseburger that is so superior to drive-thru fare? Right in your backyard with this delicious recipe.

—**JACKIE BURNS** KETTLE FALLS, WA

START TO FINISH: 30 MIN.
MAKES: 4 SERVINGS

- 2 **tablespoons finely chopped onion**
- 2 **tablespoons ketchup**
- 1 **garlic clove, minced**
- 1 **teaspoon sugar**
- 1 **teaspoon Worcestershire sauce**
- 1 **teaspoon steak sauce**
- ¼ **teaspoon cider vinegar**
- 1 **pound ground beef**
- 4 **slices sharp cheddar cheese**
- 4 **hamburger buns, split and toasted**
- 8 **cooked bacon strips**
  Optional toppings: lettuce leaves and tomato, onion and pickle slices

1. In a large bowl, combine the first seven ingredients. Crumble beef over the mixture and mix well. Shape into four patties.

2. Grill burgers, covered, over medium heat or broil 3 in. from the heat for 4-7 minutes on each side or until a thermometer reads 160° and juices run clear. Top with cheese. Grill 1 minute longer or until cheese is melted. Serve on buns with bacon and toppings of your choice.

TUNA LOUIE BURGERS

My father and brother are avid fishermen who keep me supplied with fresh fish from the Pacific. I came up with this recipe that blends Louie sauce with grilled tuna to make a very yummy sandwich.

—CLEO GONSKE REDDING, CA

PREP: 30 MIN. • **GRILL:** 10 MIN.
MAKES: 4 SERVINGS

- 4 tuna steaks (6 ounces each)
- ¼ cup Italian salad dressing
- 1 teaspoon lemon-pepper seasoning

LOUIE SAUCE

- ¼ cup mayonnaise
- 1 tablespoon sweet pickle relish
- 1 tablespoon ketchup
- 1 tablespoon chili sauce
- 1½ teaspoons finely chopped onion
- 1 teaspoon capers, drained
- ½ teaspoon grated horseradish
- ¼ teaspoon Worcestershire sauce

BURGERS

- 4 lemon wedges
- 4 hard rolls, split
- 2 tablespoons butter, softened
- 1 large tomato, sliced
- 4 lettuce leaves

1. Brush tuna steaks with salad dressing; sprinkle with lemon-pepper seasoning. Let the steaks stand at room temperature for 15 minutes. Meanwhile, in a small bowl, combine the sauce ingredients; set aside.

2. Moisten a paper towel with cooking oil; using long-handled tongs, lightly rub on the grill rack to coat. Grill tuna, covered, over high heat or broil 3-4 in. from the heat for 3-4 minutes on each side for medium-rare or until slightly pink in the center. Squeeze lemon over tuna.

3. Spread rolls with butter. Grill, covered, over high heat for 2-3 minutes or until toasted. Serve tuna on rolls with Louie sauce, tomato and lettuce.

STUFFED PIZZA BURGERS

STUFFED PIZZA BURGERS

For years, I used this recipe to make pizza meat loaf, which was absolutely killer. I decided to try it as burgers for a party, and they were a smashing success. Everyone left with the recipe.

—DENNIS BARTER REEDSBURG, WI

PREP: 30 MIN. • **GRILL:** 10 MIN.
MAKES: 8 SERVINGS

- 2 large eggs, lightly beaten
- 1 medium onion, finely chopped
- 1 medium green pepper, finely chopped
- ½ cup crushed cornflakes
- ½ cup chopped fresh mushrooms
- 1 tablespoon minced fresh basil or 1 teaspoon dried basil
- 1 tablespoon minced fresh oregano or 1 teaspoon dried oregano
- 2 garlic cloves, minced
- 2 pounds lean ground turkey
- 1 cup pizza sauce, divided
- ½ cup finely chopped turkey pepperoni
- ½ cup shredded part-skim mozzarella cheese
- 8 hamburger buns, split

1. In a large bowl, combine the first eight ingredients. Crumble the turkey over mixture and mix well. Shape into 16 patties. Layer 1 tablespoon pizza sauce, the pepperoni and cheese onto the center of each of eight patties. Top with remaining patties and press edges firmly to seal.

2. Moisten a paper towel with cooking oil; using long-handled tongs, lightly rub the grill rack to coat. Grill burgers, covered, over medium heat or broil 4 in. from the heat for 4-6 minutes on each side or until a thermometer reads 165° and juices run clear. Serve on buns with remaining pizza sauce.

RIBEYES WITH BROWNED
GARLIC BUTTER, PAGE 141

MEAT 'N' POTATO KABOBS, PAGE 145

GRILLED FAJITAS, PAGE 139

PINWHEEL FLANK STEAKS, PAGE 147

FLAME-BROILED BEEF

Looking to sink your teeth into a juicy spice-rubbed steak? How about a **thick filet** seared to perfection? From **colorful kabobs** to perfectly tender ribeyes, your beefy entrees will be the best that summer has to offer with the **succulent steaks** and roasts found here.

BEEF GRILLING CHART

When cooking beef, check for doneness with a food thermometer. A food thermometer should read 145° for medium-rare, 160° for medium and 170° for well-done. Ground beef patties are done at 160°. For direct grilling, turn meat halfway through the grilling time. The cooking times below are given as general guidelines and are for medium-rare to medium doneness.

CUT	WEIGHT OR THICKNESS	HEAT	APPROXIMATE COOKING TIME (IN MINUTES)
RIBEYE STEAK	1 in. thick 1½ in. thick	medium/direct medium/direct	11 to 14 17 to 22
T-BONE, PORTERHOUSE OR TOP LOIN STEAK (BONELESS STRIP)	¾ in. thick 1 in. thick 1½ in. thick	medium/direct medium/direct medium/direct	10 to 12 15 to 18 19 to 23
TENDERLOIN STEAK	1 in. thick 1½ in. thick	medium/direct medium/direct	13 to 15 14 to 16
TOP SIRLOIN STEAK (BONELESS)	1 in. thick 1½ in. thick	medium/direct medium/direct	17 to 21 22 to 26
FLANK STEAK	1½ to 2 lbs.	medium/direct	12 to 15
SHOULDER TOP BLADE STEAK (FLAT IRON)	8 oz. and ¾ to 1¼ in.	medium/direct	10 to 16
SKIRT STEAK	¼ to ½ in.	high/direct	6 to 8
TOP ROUND STEAK	1in.	medium/direct	16 to 18
CHUCK SHOULDER STEAK	1in.	medium/direct	16 to 20
TENDERLOIN ROAST	2 to 3 lbs. 4 to 5 lbs.	medium/indirect medium/indirect	45 to 60 60 to 75
TRI-TIP ROAST	2 to 3 lbs.	medium-low/indirect	60 to 90
GROUND BEEF OR VEAL PATTY	4 oz. and ½ in.	medium/direct	11 to 14

GRILL SKILL

Grilling over indirect heat is used for foods that need to be cooked for a long time over medium or medium-low heat. For a gas grill, remove the cooking grates and set a foil drip pan over the center of the burners. After preheating, turn off the center burner if possible. For charcoal grills, place a drip pan in the center of the bottom charcoal grate, adding a little water to the pan. Arrange hot coals in a circle around the drip pan. Place food in the center of the cooking grate over the drip pan.

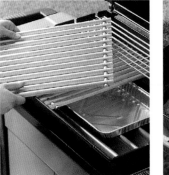

SIZZLING TEX-MEX FAJITAS

My family likes garlic, so I dreamed up this delicious marinade for our fajita dinners. The marinade only needs 8 hours to work its magic, but it's even better when left overnight. Try it on chicken breasts, too.
—**KARYN "KIKI" POWER** ARLINGTON, TX

PREP: 30 MIN. + MARINATING • **GRILL:** 10 MIN.
MAKES: 6 SERVINGS

- ⅓ cup beef broth
- ¼ cup lime juice
- 3 tablespoons olive oil, divided
- 4 garlic cloves, minced
- 2 teaspoons Worcestershire sauce
- 1 teaspoon salt
- 1 envelope savory herb with garlic soup mix, divided
- 1 teaspoon Dijon mustard
- ½ teaspoon pepper
- ½ teaspoon cayenne pepper
- ½ teaspoon liquid smoke, optional
- 2 pounds beef skirt steak, cut into 4- to 6-inch portions
- 2 large onions, sliced
- 1 medium green pepper, sliced
- 1 medium sweet yellow pepper, sliced
- 12 flour tortillas (8 inches)
  Salsa, shredded cheese, guacamole and sour cream, optional

1. In a large resealable plastic bag, combine the beef broth, lime juice, 1 tablespoon oil, garlic, Worcestershire sauce, salt, 1 teaspoon soup mix, mustard, pepper, cayenne and liquid smoke if desired. Add the steaks; seal bag and turn to coat. Refrigerate for 8 hours or overnight.

2. In a large bowl, combine onions, green pepper, yellow pepper and remaining oil and soup mix. Place half of mixture on each of two double thicknesses of heavy-duty foil (about 12 in. square). Fold foil around vegetables and seal tightly.

3. Drain beef and discard marinade. Grill steaks and vegetable packets, covered, over medium heat for 10-13 minutes or until meat reaches desired

SIZZLING TEX-MEX FAJITAS

doneness (for medium-rare, a thermometer should read 145°; medium, 160°; well-done, 170°) and vegetables are tender, turning the steaks once.

4. Open foil packets carefully to allow steam to escape. Thinly slice steaks; place beef and vegetables on tortillas. Serve with salsa, cheese, guacamole and sour cream if desired.

BARBECUED
BEEF BRISKET

BARBECUED BEEF BRISKET

My husband and I used to run an RV park and marina. A guest at the park gave me this flavorful brisket recipe. It's become the star of countless gatherings, from potlucks to holiday dinners. My family looks forward to it as much as to our Christmas turkey.

—**BETTYE MILLER** OKLAHOMA CITY, OK

PREP: 20 MIN. • **GRILL:** 2¼ HOURS
MAKES: 6 SERVINGS

- ½ cup packed brown sugar
- ½ cup ketchup
- ¼ cup water
- ¼ cup cider vinegar
- ¼ cup canola oil
- 3 tablespoons dark corn syrup
- 2 tablespoons prepared mustard
- 1 tablespoon prepared horseradish
- 1 garlic clove, minced

BRISKET

- 2 tablespoons canola oil
- 1 fresh beef brisket (2 to 2½ pounds), trimmed

1. In a small saucepan, combine the first nine ingredients; cook and stir over medium heat 3-4 minutes or until brown sugar is dissolved. Transfer to a disposable foil pan.

2. In a large skillet, heat oil over medium heat. Brown brisket on both sides. Place in foil pan, turning to coat with sauce. Cover pan tightly with foil.

3. Place pan on grill rack over indirect medium heat. Grill, covered, 2 to 2¼ hours or until meat is tender.

4. Remove from heat. Remove brisket from pan; tent with foil and let stand 10 minutes. Meanwhile, skim fat from sauce in pan. Cut brisket diagonally across the grain into thin slices; serve with sauce.

NOTE *This is a fresh beef brisket, not corned beef.*

PEANUTTY BEEF SKEWERS

For my husband and me, this recipe is a summer staple. The aroma of the skewers cooking on the grill is simply heavenly!

—**VICTORIA CADDY** WINTERVILLE, NC

PREP: 10 MIN. + MARINATING • **GRILL:** 10 MIN.
MAKES: 2 SERVINGS

- ¼ cup chopped green onions
- ¼ cup peanut butter
- 2 tablespoons lemon juice
- 2 tablespoons reduced-sodium soy sauce
- 4½ teaspoons brown sugar
- 1 tablespoon water
- 4 garlic cloves, minced
- 1 teaspoon ground coriander
- ⅛ to ¼ teaspoon cayenne pepper
- ¾ pound beef top sirloin steak, cut into ½-inch cubes

1. In a bowl, combine the first nine ingredients; mix ingredients well. Pour 6 tablespoons marinade into a large resealable plastic bag; add the beef. Seal bag and turn to coat; refrigerate for at least 2 hours or overnight, turning occasionally. Cover and refrigerate remaining marinade for basting.

2. Drain and discard marinade from beef. Thread beef onto four metal or soaked wooden skewers. Grill, uncovered, over medium heat or broil 4 in. from the heat for 8-10 minutes or until meat reaches desired doneness, turning and basting frequently with reserved marinade.

CHEESEBURGER PIZZA

I combined our daughter's two favorite foods, pizza and grilled cheeseburgers, to create this main dish. It's a fun change of pace for a backyard cookout.

—**TANYA GUTIERRO** BEACON FALLS, CT

PREP: 25 MIN. • **GRILL:** 15 MIN.
MAKES: 4-6 SERVINGS

- ¾ pound ground beef
- 1 cup ketchup
- 2 tablespoons prepared mustard
- 1 prebaked 12-inch pizza crust
- 1 medium tomato, thinly sliced
- ⅛ teaspoon salt
- ⅛ teaspoon pepper
- 1 small sweet onion, thinly sliced
- ½ cup dill pickle slices
- 1 cup (4 ounces) shredded cheddar cheese
- 1 cup (4 ounces) shredded part-skim mozzarella cheese
- 1 cup shredded lettuce

1. Shape beef into three ½-in.-thick patties. Grill, covered, over medium-hot heat for 5 minutes on each side or until a meat thermometer reads 160° and meat is no longer pink. Cut burgers into ½-in. pieces; set aside.

2. Combine ketchup and mustard; spread over pizza crust to within 1 in. of edges. Top with tomato, burger pieces, onion, pickles and cheeses; sprinkle with salt and pepper.

3. Place pizza on a 16-in. square piece of heavy-duty foil. Prepare grill for indirect heat. Grill pizza, covered, over medium indirect heat for 12-15 minutes or until cheese is melted and crust is lightly browned. Let stand for 5 minutes before slicing. Sprinkle with lettuce.

GRILLED MEAT LOAVES

I created this yummy recipe one day when I wanted meatloaf but didn't want to turn on the oven. It's a huge time saver, and the scrumptious sauce drizzled over the top keeps the patties wonderfully moist.
—**JENNIFER SHELLER** LEBANON, PA

PREP: 15 MIN. • **GRILL:** 20 MIN.
MAKES: 4 SERVINGS

- 1   **egg white**
- ⅓   **cup fat-free milk**
- 1   **tablespoon prepared horseradish**
- 1   **slice rye bread, crumbled**
- ¼   **cup grated carrot**
- 1½   **teaspoons dried minced onion**
- 1   **teaspoon minced fresh parsley**
- ½   **teaspoon salt**
- ⅛   **teaspoon pepper**
- 1   **pound lean ground beef**

SAUCE

- 2   **tablespoons ketchup**
- 4½   **teaspoons brown sugar**
- 1   **tablespoon prepared mustard**

1. In a large bowl, combine the egg white, milk and horseradish. Stir in the bread, carrot, onion, parsley, salt and pepper. Crumble beef over mixture and mix well. Shape into four small loaves.
2. Grill loaves, covered, over medium-hot heat or broil 4-6 in. from the heat for 8 minutes on each side.
3. In a small bowl, combine the sauce ingredients; spoon over loaves. Cook for 2-3 minutes longer or until a meat thermometer reads 160°.

PINEAPPLE BEEF KABOBS

PINEAPPLE BEEF KABOBS

These skewers are easy and colorful, and basting helps keep the sirloin steak oh-so juicy and tender. I came up with this recipe after reading a similar one in a health magazine. It's a keeper.
—**MARGUERITE SHAEFFER** SEWELL, NJ

PREP: 20 MIN. + MARINATING • **GRILL:** 10 MIN.
MAKES: 6 SERVINGS

- 1   **can (6 ounces) unsweetened pineapple juice**
- ⅓   **cup honey**
- ⅓   **cup soy sauce**
- 3   **tablespoons cider vinegar**
- 1½   **teaspoons minced garlic**
- 1½   **teaspoons ground ginger**
- 1½   **pounds beef top sirloin steak, cut into 1-inch pieces**
- 1   **fresh pineapple, peeled and cut into 1-inch chunks**
- 12   **large fresh mushrooms**
- 1   **medium sweet red pepper, cut into 1-inch pieces**
- 1   **medium sweet yellow pepper, cut into 1-inch pieces**
- 1   **medium red onion, cut into 1-inch pieces**
- 2½   **cups uncooked instant rice**

1. In a small bowl, combine first six ingredients. Pour ¾ cup into a large resealable plastic bag; add beef. Seal bag and turn to coat; refrigerate 1-4 hours. Cover and refrigerate remaining marinade for basting.
2. Drain and discard marinade. On 12 metal or soaked wooden skewers, alternately thread the beef, pineapple, mushrooms, peppers and onion. Moisten a paper towel with cooking oil; using long-handled tongs rub on grill rack to coat lightly.
3. Grill, covered, over medium-hot heat 8-10 minutes or until meat reaches desired doneness, turning occasionally and basting skewers frequently with reserved marinade.
4. Cook rice according to package directions; serve with kabobs.

RIBEYES WITH HERB BUTTER

I grill these ribeyes for special occasions. The tantalizing fragrance of the herbes de Provence is unforgettable. The seasoning and herb butter go well with filet mignon, T-bone and steak strips, too.

—JOHN BARANSKI BALDWIN CITY, KS

PREP: 25 MIN. + MARINATING • **GRILL:** 10 MIN.
MAKES: 4 SERVINGS

- ¼ cup olive oil
- ¼ cup dry red wine
- 1 tablespoon minced fresh rosemary or 1 teaspoon dried rosemary, crushed
- 1 tablespoon red wine vinegar
- 1 tablespoon Dijon mustard
- 1 teaspoon coarsely ground pepper
- 1 teaspoon Worcestershire sauce
- 2 garlic cloves, minced
- 4 beef ribeye steaks (¾ pound each)

STEAK SEASONINGS
- 2 teaspoons kosher salt
- 1 teaspoon sugar
- 1 teaspoon herbes de Provence
- 1 teaspoon coarsely ground pepper

HERB BUTTER
- ¼ cup butter, softened
- 1 tablespoon minced fresh parsley
- 1 teaspoon prepared horseradish

1. In a large resealable plastic bag, combine the first eight ingredients. Add the steaks; seal bag and turn to coat. Refrigerate overnight.

2. Drain and discard marinade. Combine the steak seasonings; sprinkle over steaks.

3. Grill steaks, covered, over medium heat or broil 3-4 in. from the heat for 5-7 minutes on each side or until meat reaches desired doneness (for medium-rare, a thermometer should read 145°; medium, 160°; well-done, 170°).

4. For herb butter, in a small bowl, beat the butter, parsley and horseradish until blended. Spoon 1 tablespoon herb butter over each steak.

NOTE *Look for herbes de Provence in the spice aisle.*

FAST FIX

SPICY GRILLED STEAKS

Rubs are a wonderful way to add flavor to meat when you don't have time to marinate. Meat lovers will be in their glory when they see, smell and hear these steaks sizzling on the grill.

—TASTE OF HOME TEST KITCHEN

START TO FINISH: 20 MIN.
MAKES: 4 SERVINGS

- 1 tablespoon paprika
- 2 teaspoons dried thyme
- 1 teaspoon onion powder
- 1 teaspoon garlic powder
- ½ teaspoon rubbed sage
- ½ teaspoon salt
- ½ teaspoon pepper
- ½ teaspoon cayenne pepper
- 4 boneless beef top loin steaks (12 ounces each)

1. In a small bowl, combine the first eight ingredients. Rub about 1 teaspoon of spice mixture over each side of the steaks.

2. Grill, covered, over medium heat for 6-8 minutes on each side or until meat reaches desired doneness (for medium-rare, a thermometer should read 145°; medium, 160°; well-done, 170°).

NOTE *Top loin steak may be labeled as strip steak, KS City steak, NY strip steak, ambassador steak or boneless club steak in your region.*

RIBEYES WITH HERB BUTTER

GRILLED FAJITAS

GRILLED FAJITAS

A special marinade gives the meat in these fajitas an outstanding flavor that always pleases my family. It's a fun and satisfying summer main dish using garden-fresh peppers and onions.

—CHERYL SMITH THE DALLES, OR

PREP: 20 MIN. + MARINATING • **GRILL:** 10 MIN.
MAKES: 4 SERVINGS

- 1 envelope onion soup mix
- ¼ cup canola oil
- ¼ cup lime juice
- ¼ cup water
- 2 garlic cloves, minced
- 1 teaspoon grated lime peel
- 1 teaspoon ground cumin
- ½ teaspoon dried oregano
- ¼ teaspoon pepper
- 1 beef flank steak (about 1 pound)
- 1 medium onion, thinly sliced
   Green, sweet red and/or yellow peppers, julienned
- 1 tablespoon canola oil
- 8 flour tortillas (8 inches), warmed
   Sour cream and lime wedges, optional

1. In a large resealable plastic bag, combine the first nine ingredients; add steak. Seal bag; turn to coat. Cover and refrigerate 4 hours or overnight.

2. Drain and discard marinade. Grill over high heat until meat reaches desired doneness (for medium-rare, a thermometer should read 145°; medium, 160°; well-done, 170°).

3. Meanwhile, in a small skillet, saute onion and peppers if desired in oil for 3-4 minutes or until crisp-tender.

4. Slice meat into thin strips across the grain; place on tortillas. Top with vegetables. Serve with sour cream and lime wedges if desired.

MARINATED RIBEYES

MARINATED RIBEYES

When we go camping, we put frozen steaks with this marinade into a sealed plastic container at the bottom of our cooler. By the second night, they're thawed, tender and ready to cook.

—LOUISE GRAYBIEL TORONTO, ON

PREP: 10 MIN. + MARINATING • **GRILL:** 10 MIN.
MAKES: 4 SERVINGS

- ½ cup barbecue sauce
- 3 tablespoons olive oil
- 3 tablespoons Worcestershire sauce
- 2 tablespoons steak sauce
- 1 tablespoon red wine vinegar
- 1 tablespoon reduced-sodium soy sauce
- 2 teaspoons steak seasoning
- 1 teaspoon hot pepper sauce
- 1 garlic clove, minced
- 4 beef ribeye steaks (8 ounces each)

1. In a large resealable plastic bag, combine the first nine ingredients. Add the steaks; seal bag and turn to coat. Refrigerate for 4 hours or overnight.

2. Drain and discard marinade. Grill steaks, covered, over medium-hot heat for 5-7 minutes on each side or until meat reaches desired doneness (for medium-rare, a thermometer should read 145°; medium, 160°; well-done, 170°).

NOTE *This recipe was tested with McCormick's Montreal Steak Seasoning. Look for it in the spice aisle.*

MOROCCAN BEEF KABOBS

FAST FIX ▶

STEAKS WITH MANGO SALSA

Carrots add beautiful color and texture to this very flavorful mango salsa, which is served over well-seasoned New York strips. Here's a tasty dish to make you the star of the cookout!

—**TASTE OF HOME** TEST KITCHEN

START TO FINISH: 25 MIN.
MAKES: 4 SERVINGS

- 1 **cup chopped carrots**
- 1 **cup chopped peeled mango**
- 1 **medium ripe avocado, peeled and diced**
- ¼ **cup chopped sweet red pepper**
- 5 **teaspoons lime juice**
- 2 **tablespoons minced fresh cilantro**
- ⅛ **teaspoon salt**
- ⅛ **teaspoon ground cumin**
- 1 **tablespoon taco seasoning**
- 4 **boneless beef top loin steaks (8 ounces each)**

1. Place ½ in. of water in a small saucepan; add carrots. Bring to a boil. Reduce heat; cover and simmer for 7-9 minutes or until crisp-tender. Drain and cool.

2. In a small bowl, combine the mango, avocado, red pepper, lime juice, cilantro, salt, cumin and carrots. Refrigerate until serving.

3. Sprinkle taco seasoning over both sides of steaks. Grill, covered, over medium-hot heat for 5-7 minutes on each side or until meat reaches desired doneness (for medium-rare, a thermometer should read 145°; medium, 160°; well-done, 170°). Serve with mango salsa.

NOTE *Top loin steak may be labeled as strip steak, KS City steak, NY strip steak, ambassador steak or boneless club steak in your region.*

MOROCCAN BEEF KABOBS

Here, my grandmother's homemade marinade adds tang to beef kabobs. Best of all, her blend of herbs and spices punches up the flavor without adding lots of calories.

—**JENNIFER SHAW** DORCHESTER, MA

PREP: 25 MIN. + MARINATING • **GRILL:** 10 MIN.
MAKES: 8 SERVINGS

- 1 **cup chopped fresh parsley**
- 1 **cup chopped fresh cilantro**
- ¼ **cup grated onion**
- 3 **tablespoons lemon juice**
- 2 **tablespoons olive oil**
- 1 **tablespoon ground cumin**
- 1 **tablespoon ground coriander**
- 1 **tablespoon paprika**
- 1 **tablespoon cider vinegar**
- 1 **tablespoon ketchup**
- 2 **garlic cloves, minced**
- 1 **teaspoon minced fresh gingerroot**
- 1 **teaspoon Thai red chili paste**
  Dash salt and pepper
- 2 **pounds beef top sirloin steak, cut into 1-inch pieces**

1. In a large resealable plastic bag, combine the parsley, cilantro, onion, lemon juice, oil, cumin, coriander, paprika, vinegar, ketchup, garlic, ginger, chili paste, salt and pepper; add beef. Seal bag and turn to coat; refrigerate for 8 hours or overnight.

2. Drain and discard marinade. On eight metal or soaked wooden skewers, thread beef cubes. Moisten a paper towel with cooking oil; using long-handled tongs, lightly coat the grill rack with oil.

3. Grill beef, covered, over medium-high heat or broil 4 in. from the heat for 8-12 minutes or until meat reaches desired doneness, turning occasionally.

⑤INGREDIENTS **FAST FIX**

RIBEYES WITH BROWNED GARLIC BUTTER

All it takes is the smoke of the grill to flavor these ribeyes. Served alongside a garlicky butter, they make a standout entree.
—**ARGE SALVATORI** WALDWICK, NJ

START TO FINISH: 25 MIN.
MAKES: 8 SERVINGS

- 6 tablespoons unsalted butter, cubed
- 2 garlic cloves, minced
- 4 beef ribeye steaks (about 1 inch thick and 12 ounces each)
- 1½ teaspoons salt
- 1½ teaspoons pepper

1. In a small heavy saucepan, melt butter with garlic over medium heat. Heat 4-6 minutes or until butter is golden brown, stirring constantly. Remove from heat.
2. Season steaks with salt and pepper. Grill, covered, over medium heat or broil 4 in. from heat 5-7 minutes on each side or until meat reaches desired doneness (for medium-rare, a thermometer should read 145°; medium, 160°; well-done, 170°).
3. Gently warm garlic butter over low heat. Cut steaks into thick slices; serve with garlic butter.

 **GRILL SKILL**

To test a steak for doneness, insert an instant-read thermometer horizontally from the side, making sure the reading is from the center of the meat.

RIBEYES WITH BROWNED GARLIC BUTTER

**GRILLED STEAKS WITH
MARINATED TOMATOES**

GRILLED STEAKS WITH MARINATED TOMATOES

The tomatoes in this dish get even more flavorful after marinating overnight. I could eat them all by themselves! Our family likes these steaks served with cheesy potatoes or glazed green beans.
—**ANNA DAVIS** SPRINGFIELD, MO

PREP: 25 MIN. + MARINATING • **GRILL:** 20 MIN.
MAKES: 6 SERVINGS

¼ cup light beer
3 tablespoons raspberry vinaigrette
3 tablespoons olive oil
1 tablespoon torn fresh basil
1 tablespoon cider vinegar
2 teaspoons garlic powder
2 teaspoons coriander seeds, crushed
1½ teaspoons minced fresh oregano
1 teaspoon sugar
½ teaspoon salt
½ teaspoon pepper
3 large tomatoes, sliced

RUB
2 teaspoons Montreal steak seasoning
2 teaspoons chili powder
1 teaspoon salt
1 teaspoon celery seed
1 teaspoon smoked paprika
½ teaspoon pepper
2 beef top sirloin steaks (1 inch thick and 1 pound each)

1. In a small bowl, whisk the first 11 ingredients until blended. Place tomatoes in a 13x9-in. dish; pour beer mixture over top. Cover and refrigerate at least 1 hour.

2. Meanwhile, mix rub seasonings; rub over steaks. Grill steaks, covered, over medium heat or broil 4 in. from heat 8-10 minutes on each side or until meat reaches desired doneness (for medium-rare, a thermometer should read 145°; medium, 160°; well-done, 170°). Let stand 5 minutes before cutting each steak into thirds.

3. Place steaks on a platter. Top with tomatoes; drizzle with any remaining beer mixture.

STEAK PINWHEELS

This elegant-looking entree is easy to make, but looks like you fussed. You can prepare it in advance, too.

—TASTE OF HOME COOKING SCHOOL

PREP: 20 MIN. + MARINATING • **GRILL:** 20 MIN.
MAKES: 6 SERVINGS

- 1½ **pounds beef flank steak**
- ¼ **cup olive oil**
- 2 **tablespoons red wine vinegar**
- 2 **teaspoons Worcestershire sauce**
- 2 **teaspoons Italian seasoning**
- 1½ **teaspoons garlic powder**
- 1½ **teaspoons salt, divided**
- 1½ **teaspoons pepper, divided**
- ½ **cup shredded cheddar cheese**
- 2 **garlic cloves, minced**
- ¼ **cup finely chopped onion**
- ¼ **cup minced fresh parsley**

1. Flatten beef to ¼-in. thickness. In a large resealable plastic bag, combine the oil, vinegar, Worcestershire sauce, Italian seasoning, garlic powder and 1 teaspoon each salt and pepper; add steak. Seal bag and turn to coat; refrigerate for 8 hours or overnight.

2. Drain and discard marinade. Combine the cheese, garlic, onion, parsley and remaining salt and pepper; sprinkle over steak to within 1 in. of edges. Roll up jelly-roll style, starting with a long side; tie with kitchen string at 1-in. intervals. Insert a skewer into each piece where it is tied. Cut into 1¼-in. rolls.

3. Using long-handled tongs, moisten a paper towel with cooking oil and lightly coat the grill rack. Grill over medium heat for 6-8 minutes on each side until meat reaches desired doneness (for medium-rare, a thermometer should read 145°; medium, 160°; well-done, 170°).

PEPPERED FILETS WITH CHERRY PORT SAUCE FOR 2

FAST FIX

PEPPERED FILETS WITH CHERRY PORT SAUCE FOR 2

I like to serve my peppery beef steaks with a light vegetable side dish. You can substitute dried cranberries for the cherries and feta for the blue cheese.

—BARBARA LENTO HOUSTON, PA

START TO FINISH: 30 MIN.
MAKES: 2 SERVINGS

- 2 **beef tenderloin steaks (8 ounces each)**
- 2 **teaspoons coarsely ground pepper**
- 1 **cup dry red wine**
- ½ **cup chopped red onion**
- ⅓ **cup golden raisins**
- ⅓ **cup dried cherries**
- 2 **tablespoons sugar**
- 1½ **teaspoons cornstarch**
- ¼ **teaspoon ground mustard**
- **Dash salt**
- 2 **teaspoons cold water**
- ¼ **cup crumbled blue cheese**

1. Sprinkle steaks with pepper. Grill, covered, over medium heat or broil 4 in. from the heat for 6-8 minutes on each side or until meat reaches desired doneness (for medium-rare, a thermometer should read 145°; medium, 160°; well-done, 170°).

2. Meanwhile, in a small saucepan, combine the wine, onion, raisins, cherries and sugar. Bring to a boil; cook until liquid is reduced by half.

3. Combine the cornstarch, mustard, salt and water until smooth. Gradually stir into the pan. Bring to a boil; cook and stir for 2 minutes or until thickened. Serve sauce with steaks; sprinkle with cheese.

MEAT 'N' POTATO
KABOBS

FAST FIX
MEAT 'N' POTATO KABOBS

These meal-in-one kabobs really stick to your ribs! A microwave makes quick work of cooking the potatoes, so the grilling is done in a flash.

—TASTE OF HOME TEST KITCHEN

START TO FINISH: 30 MIN.
MAKES: 4 SERVINGS

- 1 **pound beef top sirloin steak, cut into 1-inch cubes**
- 1½ **teaspoons steak seasoning, divided**
- 1 **garlic clove, minced**
- 1 **cup cola**
- 3 **small red potatoes (about 8 ounces), cubed**
- 1 **tablespoon water**
- 1 **cup cherry tomatoes**
- 1 **medium sweet orange pepper, cut into 1-inch pieces**
- 1 **teaspoon canola oil**
- 1 **cup pineapple chunks**

1. Sprinkle beef with 1 teaspoon steak seasoning and garlic. Place cola in a large bowl. Add beef; toss to coat. Set mixture aside.
2. Place the potatoes and water in a microwave-safe bowl. Microwave, covered, on high for 4-5 minutes or just until tender; drain. Return to bowl. Add tomatoes, pepper, oil and remaining steak seasoning; gently toss to coat.
3. Drain beef, discarding marinade. On eight metal or soaked wooden skewers, alternately thread beef, vegetables and pineapple.
4. Grill, covered, over medium heat or broil 4 in. from heat 6-8 minutes or until beef reaches desired doneness and pepper is crisp-tender, turning skewers occasionally.
NOTE *This recipe was tested in a 1,100-watt microwave with McCormick's Montreal Steak Seasoning. Look for it in the spice aisle.*

STEAK TERIYAKI QUESADILLAS

The slight smoky flavor of savory steak in these quesadillas pairs perfectly with the sweet pineapple. They embody the definition of cheesy deliciousness.

—LISA HUFF WILTON, CT

PREP: 20 MIN. + MARINATING • **GRILL:** 15 MIN.
MAKES: 18 WEDGES

- ⅓ **cup reduced-sodium soy sauce**
- ⅓ **cup reduced-sodium chicken broth**
- 1 **tablespoon brown sugar**
- 1 **teaspoon minced fresh gingerroot**
- ½ **teaspoon onion powder**
- 1 **garlic clove, minced**
- 1 **beef top sirloin steak (1 inch thick and ¾ pound)**
- ½ **cup finely chopped fresh pineapple**
- ½ **cup finely chopped red onion**
- ½ **cup finely chopped green pepper**
- 2 **cups (8 ounces) shredded part-skim mozzarella cheese**
- 6 **flour tortillas (8 inches)**

1. In a small bowl, combine the first six ingredients; set aside 3 tablespoons for filling. Pour remaining mixture into a large resealable plastic bag. Add the steak; seal bag and turn to coat. Refrigerate for 2 hours.
2. Drain steak and discard marinade. Grill steak, covered, over medium heat or broil 4 in. from the heat for 8-11 minutes on each side or until meat reaches desired doneness (for medium-rare, a thermometer should read 145°; medium, 160°; well-done, 170°).
3. Remove steak from the grill and cool slightly; cut into bite-size pieces. In a large bowl, combine the pineapple, red onion, green pepper and beef.
4. Sprinkle half the cheese over three tortillas. Using a slotted spoon, top with beef mixture. Drizzle with reserved soy mixture. Sprinkle with remaining cheese; top with remaining tortillas.
5. Grill quesadillas over medium heat for 1-2 minutes on each side or until cheese is melted. Cut each into six wedges; serve immediately.

FAST FIX
THYME LEMON SIRLOINS

We love to grill steaks when friends drop by. The tangy lemon herb rub in this recipe really makes everyone's taste buds come to attention.

—SUZANNE WHITAKER KNOXVILLE, TN

START TO FINISH: 25 MIN.
MAKES: 4 SERVINGS

- 2 **teaspoons grated lemon peel**
- 2 **garlic cloves, minced**
- 1 **teaspoon dried thyme**
- ¼ **teaspoon salt**
- ¼ **teaspoon pepper**
- 2 **tablespoons butter**
- 1 **tablespoon lemon juice**
- 4 **boneless beef top sirloin steaks (1 inch thick and about 2 pounds)**

1. In a small bowl, combine the lemon peel, garlic, thyme, salt and pepper. Set aside 1 tablespoon seasoning mixture for steaks. In a small saucepan, melt butter; stir in lemon juice and the rest of the seasoning mixture. Set aside and keep warm.
2. Rub steaks with reserved seasoning mixture. Grill steaks, uncovered, over medium heat for 8-12 minutes on each side or until meat reaches desired doneness (for medium-rare, a thermometer should read 145°; medium, 160°; well-done, 170°). Serve with reserved butter sauce.

 **GRILL SKILL**

When heating up a charcoal grill, leave the vents open; this actually creates higher temperatures because fire needs oxygen to burn. The air escapes through the top vent, which draws air in through the bottom vent and heats up the coals. Then close up the vents for actual grilling.

MIXED GRILL KABOBS

These hearty skewers combine beef and sausage, two of my favorite foods. Both the meat and vegetables are marinated before they're grilled, which makes this meal extra flavorful. Be sure to fire up your grill and try these soon!

—GLENDA ADAMS VANNDALE, AR

PREP: 20 MIN. + MARINATING • **GRILL:** 15 MIN.
MAKES: 10-12 SERVINGS

- 3 **cups pineapple juice**
- 1 **cup cider vinegar**
- 1 **cup canola oil**
- ¼ **cup sugar**
- ¼ **cup reduced-sodium soy sauce**
- 1 **tablespoon browning sauce, optional**
- ½ **teaspoon garlic powder**
- ¼ **teaspoon lemon-pepper seasoning**
- 2 **pounds beef tenderloin, cut into 1-inch cubes**
- 1 **pound smoked kielbasa or Polish sausage, cut into 1-inch chunks**
- 3 **to 4 medium tomatoes, quartered**
- 3 **to 4 medium green peppers, quartered**
- 1 **jar (4½ ounces) whole mushrooms, drained**
- 5 **medium onions, quartered**

1. In a small bowl, combine the first eight ingredients. Pour half into a large resealable plastic bag; add meat. Seal the bag and turn to coat. Pour the rest of the marinade into another large resealable plastic bag; add tomatoes, peppers, mushrooms, and onions. Seal bag and turn to coat. Refrigerate meat and vegetables overnight.

2. Drain and discard marinade. Alternately thread the beef, sausage and vegetables onto metal or soaked wooden skewers.

3. Grill, covered, over medium-hot heat for 6-8 minutes. Turn kabobs; cook 6-8 minutes longer or until beef reaches desired doneness.

SEASONED STEAKS WITH
HORSERADISH CREAM

FAST FIX

SEASONED STEAKS WITH HORSERADISH CREAM

My buttery tenderloin dish is summer comfort at its best. The recipe is simple, but it's a big treat anytime. Add a few fresh sides to pull dinner together fast.

—JENNA EWALD OCONOMOWOC, WI

START TO FINISH: 30 MIN.
MAKES: 4 SERVINGS

- ½ **teaspoon salt**
- ½ **teaspoon garlic powder**
- ¼ **teaspoon dried parsley flakes**
- ¼ **teaspoon chili powder**
- ¼ **teaspoon pepper**
- 4 **beef tenderloin steaks (6 ounces each)**

HORSERADISH CREAM

- 2 **tablespoons butter, softened**
- 1 **tablespoon prepared horseradish**
- 1 **garlic clove, minced**
- 2 **tablespoons heavy whipping cream**

1. Moisten a paper towel with cooking oil; using long-handled tongs, rub on grill rack to coat lightly. Mix salt, garlic powder, parsley flakes, chili powder and pepper. Rub over both sides of steaks.

2. Grill steaks, covered, over medium heat or broil 4 in. from heat 6-8 minutes on each side or until meat reaches desired doneness (for medium-rare, a thermometer should read 145°; medium, 160°; well-done, 170°).

3. Meanwhile, in a small bowl, mix butter, horseradish and garlic until blended; gradually whisk in cream. Serve with steaks.

PINWHEEL FLANK STEAKS

Here's a way to prepare steak that's fancy enough for company but a breeze to grill up. Most of the preparation can be done the day before—a plus for a busy mom like me with two active little girls and a husband who enjoys eating.

—NANCY TAFOYA FORT COLLINS, CO

PREP: 20 MIN. + MARINATING • **GRILL:** 20 MIN.
MAKES: 6 SERVINGS

- 1½ pounds beef flank steak
- ¼ cup olive oil
- 2 tablespoons red wine vinegar
- 2 teaspoons Italian seasoning
- 2 teaspoons Worcestershire sauce
- 1½ teaspoons garlic powder
- 1½ teaspoons pepper, divided
- 1 teaspoon seasoned salt
- 8 bacon strips, cooked and crumbled
- 2 garlic cloves, minced
- ¼ cup minced fresh parsley
- ¼ cup finely chopped onion
- ½ teaspoon salt

1. Cut steak horizontally from a long side to within ½ in. of opposite side. Open meat so it lies flat; cover with plastic wrap. Flatten to ¼-in. thickness. Remove plastic and set aside.

2. In a large resealable plastic bag, combine the oil, vinegar, Italian seasoning, Worcestershire sauce, garlic powder, 1 teaspoon pepper and seasoned salt; add steak. Seal bag and turn to coat; refrigerate overnight.

3. Drain and discard marinade. Combine the bacon, garlic, parsley, onion, salt and remaining pepper; sprinkle over steak to within 1 in. of edges. With the grain of the meat going from left to right, roll up jelly-roll style; tie with kitchen string at 1-in. intervals. Cut into six 1¼-in. rolls.

4. Moisten a paper towel with cooking oil; using long-handled tongs, lightly coat the grill rack. Grill steak rolls, covered, over medium heat or broil 4-6 in. from the heat for 5-7 minutes on each side or until meat reaches desired doneness (for medium-rare, a thermometer should read 145°; medium, 160°; well-done, 170°). Cut string and remove before serving.

HERBED LONDON BROIL

My stepfather passed this recipe along to me. It's good whether you grill or broil the meat, and I've never met anyone who didn't enjoy it as much as we do. Try it alongside grilled asparagus.

—SHARON PATNOE ELKINS, AR

PREP: 10 MIN. + MARINATING • **GRILL:** 15 MIN.
MAKES: 2 SERVINGS

- ¼ cup chopped onion
- ¼ cup lemon juice
- 2 tablespoons canola oil
- 1 garlic clove, minced
- ¼ teaspoon each celery seed, salt, dried thyme and oregano
- ¼ teaspoon dried rosemary, crushed
  Dash pepper
- ½ pound beef flank steak

1. In a large resealable bag, combine onion, lemon juice, oil, garlic and seasonings; add steak. Seal bag and turn to coat; refrigerate several hours or overnight, turning once.

2. Drain and discard marinade. Grill the steak, covered, over medium heat 6-7 minutes on each side or until meat reaches desired doneness (for medium-rare, a thermometer should read 145°; medium, 160°; well-done, 170°). Slice thinly across the grain.

PINWHEEL FLANK STEAKS

FAST FIX

BEEF TENDERLOIN WITH MUSHROOM SAUCE

We treat our guests to a spectacular entree when we grill steaks sprinkled with pepper, then pass a sauce that's rich with wine and mushrooms.

—**TERESA SEAMAN** PICKERINGTON, OH

START TO FINISH: 20 MIN.
MAKES: 4 SERVINGS

- 4 **beef tenderloin steaks (1½ inches thick and 6 ounces each)**
- 1 **tablespoon coarsely ground pepper**
- ½ **pound sliced fresh mushrooms**
- ⅓ **cup butter, cubed**
- ½ **teaspoon minced garlic**
- 2 **tablespoons all-purpose flour**
- 1 **cup beef broth**
- ¾ **cup dry red wine or additional beef broth**
- ⅛ **teaspoon salt**

1. Rub pepper on both sides of steaks. Grill, covered, over medium heat or broil 4 in. from the heat for 6-8 minutes on each side or until meat reaches desired doneness (for medium-rare, a thermometer should read 145°; medium, 160°; well-done, 170°).

2. Meanwhile, in a large skillet, saute mushrooms in butter for 3-4 minutes or until tender. Add garlic; cook mushrooms 1 minute longer. Stir in flour until blended. Gradually stir in the broth, wine and salt. Bring to a boil; cook and stir for 2-3 minutes or until thickened. Serve with steaks.

BEEF TENDERLOIN WITH MUSHROOM SAUCE

TACOS ON A STICK

Kids like assembling these creative kabobs almost as much as they like devouring them. The whole family is sure to enjoy this dinner with a twist on the taco theme.

—DIXIE TERRY GOREVILLE, IL

PREP: 15 MIN. + MARINATING • **GRILL:** 15 MIN.
MAKES: 6 SERVINGS

- 1 **envelope taco seasoning**
- 1 **cup tomato juice**
- 2 **to 4 tablespoons canola oil**
- 2 **pounds beef top sirloin, cut into 1-inch cubes**
- 1 **medium green pepper, cut into chunks**
- 1 **medium sweet red pepper, cut into chunks**
- 1 **large onion, cut into wedges**
- 16 **cherry tomatoes**

1. In a large resealable plastic bag, combine the taco seasoning, tomato juice and oil; mix well. Remove ½ cup for basting; refrigerate. Add beef to the bag; seal and turn to coat. Refrigerate for at least 5 hours.
2. Drain and discard marinade from beef. On metal or soaked wooden skewers, alternately thread beef, peppers, onion and tomatoes.
3. Grill, uncovered, over medium heat for 3 minutes on each side. Baste with reserved marinade. Continue turning and basting for 8-10 minutes or until meat reaches desired doneness.

**FLANK STEAK
WITH CILANTRO &
BLUE CHEESE BUTTER**

FLANK STEAK WITH CILANTRO & BLUE CHEESE BUTTER

I love the wonderful contrast between the citrus marinade sweetness and the strong blue cheese butter tang. And my kids just love the flank steak!

—GWEN WEDEL AUGUSTA, MI

PREP: 15 MIN. + MARINATING • **GRILL:** 15 MIN.
MAKES: 8 SERVINGS

- ½ **cup canola oil**
- ¼ **cup cider vinegar**
- ¼ **cup honey**
- 1 **tablespoon reduced-sodium soy sauce**
- ½ **teaspoon paprika**
- 1 **beef flank steak (2 pounds)**
- **BLUE CHEESE BUTTER**
- ¾ **cup crumbled blue cheese**
- 3 **tablespoons butter, softened**
- 1 **green onion, finely chopped**
- 1 **tablespoon minced fresh cilantro**
- ⅛ **teaspoon salt**
- ⅛ **teaspoon pepper**

1. In a large resealable plastic bag, combine the first five ingredients. Add steak; seal bag and turn to coat. Refrigerate 2-4 hours.
2. Drain beef, discarding marinade. Grill steak, covered, over medium heat or broil 4 in. from heat 6-8 minutes on each side or until meat reaches desired doneness (for medium-rare, a thermometer should read 145°; medium, 160°; well-done, 170°). Let steak stand 5 minutes before thinly slicing across the grain.
3. In a small bowl, beat blue cheese butter ingredients until blended. Serve steak with butter.

LEMON BEEF KABOBS

FOUR-PEPPER RIBEYE ROAST

Serve up a tender prime rib for your next special meal. For more robust flavor, let the seasoned roast set overnight.
—*TASTE OF HOME* TEST KITCHEN

PREP: 15 MIN. + CHILLING
GRILL: 2 HOURS + STANDING
MAKES: 12 SERVINGS

- 1 tablespoon paprika
- 1 tablespoon coarsely ground pepper
- 1 teaspoon kosher salt
- 1 teaspoon fennel seed, crushed
- ½ teaspoon white pepper
- ¼ teaspoon cayenne pepper
- 1 beef ribeye roast (4 to 5 pounds)
- 2 tablespoons olive oil
- 2 cups soaked wood chips, optional

1. In a small bowl, combine the first six ingredients. Tie the roast at 1½-in. to 2-in. intervals with kitchen string. Rub with seasonings; cover and refrigerate 8 hours or overnight.
2. Remove roast from refrigerator 30 minutes before grilling; brush with oil. Prepare grill for indirect heat, using a drip pan. Add wood chips to grill according to manufacturer's directions if desired.
3. Place roast over drip pan and grill, covered, over indirect medium-low heat for 2 to 2½ hours or until meat reaches desired doneness (for medium-rare, a thermometer should read 145°; medium, 160°; well-done, 170°). Let stand for 15 minutes before slicing.

LEMON BEEF KABOBS

These kabobs bring the bright flavor of lemon to the table, and you don't even have to heat up the kitchen. My family loves the mix of tender meat and mushrooms with tasty green pepper.
—**JANE TURNER** CANTON, OH

PREP: 25 MIN. + MARINATING • **GRILL:** 10 MIN.
MAKES: 4 KABOBS

- ⅓ cup lemon juice
- ⅓ cup canola oil
- 1 small onion, finely chopped
- 1 teaspoon Worcestershire sauce
- 1 garlic clove, minced
- ½ teaspoon salt
- ¼ teaspoon curry powder
- ¼ teaspoon ground ginger
- ⅛ teaspoon pepper
- 1 bay leaf
- ¾ pound boneless beef sirloin steak, cut into 1-inch cubes
- 1 cup medium fresh mushrooms
- 1 small green pepper, cut into 1-inch pieces
- ½ cup pearl onions

1. In a large resealable plastic bag, combine the first 10 ingredients; add beef and mushrooms. Seal bag and turn to coat; refrigerate for up to 2 hours. Drain and discard the marinade and the bay leaf.
2. On four metal or soaked wooden skewers, alternately thread beef and vegetables.
3. Grill, covered, over medium heat for 8-10 minutes or until beef reaches desired doneness, turning occasionally.

GARLIC-RUBBED T-BONES WITH BURGUNDY MUSHROOMS

T-bone steak is a fairly tender cut, so there's no need to marinate. Punch up the flavor using loads of garlic.

—**KEVIN BLACK** CEDAR RAPIDS, IA

START TO FINISH: 25 MIN
MAKES: 4 SERVINGS

- 12 garlic cloves, minced or sliced
- 1 tablespoon olive oil
- 1 teaspoon salt
- 4 beef T-bone or porterhouse steaks (¾ inch thick and 12 ounces each)
- ½ cup butter, cubed
- 1 pound baby portobello mushrooms, thickly sliced
- ½ cup Burgundy wine or reduced-sodium beef broth

1. In a small bowl, combine the garlic, oil and salt; rub over both sides of steaks. Grill steaks, covered, over medium heat or broil 4 in. from the heat for 4-7 minutes on each side or until meat reaches desired doneness (for medium-rare, a thermometer should read 145°; medium, 160°; well-done, 170°).

2. Meanwhile, in a large skillet, melt butter over medium-high heat. Add mushrooms; cook and stir mixture for 3-5 minutes or until almost tender. Stir in wine; bring to a boil. Cook until liquid is reduced by half, stirring occasionally. Serve over steaks.

GARLIC-RUBBED T-BONES WITH BURGUNDY MUSHROOMS

**TANGY
SIRLOIN STRIPS**

TANGY SIRLOIN STRIPS

My love of cooking started when I was trying to earn my Girl Scout cooking badge. Today my family savors the sweet sauce on these bacon-wrapped strips.
—JOANNE HALDENMAN BAINBRIDGE, PA

PREP: 5 MIN. + MARINATING • **GRILL:** 10 MIN.
MAKES: 4 SERVINGS

- ¼ cup canola oil
- 2 tablespoons Worcestershire sauce
- 1 garlic clove, minced
- ½ teaspoon onion powder
- ½ teaspoon salt
- ¼ teaspoon pepper
- 1 pound beef top sirloin steak (1 inch thick)
- 4 bacon strips
  Lemon-pepper seasoning

GLAZE
- ½ cup barbecue sauce
- ½ cup steak sauce
- ½ cup honey
- 1 tablespoon molasses

1. In a large resealable plastic bag, combine the first six ingredients. Cut steak into four wide strips; add to the marinade. Seal bag and turn to coat; refrigerate for 2-3 hours or overnight, turning once.

2. Drain and discard marinade. Wrap a bacon strip around each steak piece; secure with a toothpick. Sprinkle pieces with lemon-pepper. Using a long-handled tongs, moisten a paper towel with cooking oil and lightly coat the grill rack.

3. Grill steak, covered, over medium-low heat or broil 4 in. from the heat for 10-15 minutes, turning occasionally, until meat reaches desired doneness (for medium-rare, a thermometer should read 145°; medium, 160°; well-done, 170°).

4. Combine the glaze ingredients; brush over steaks. Grill until glaze is heated. Discard toothpicks.

BARBECUED BEEF SHORT RIBS

These sweet-spicy ribs are always a hit. The barbecue sauce is also excellent on other meat like pork ribs.

—PAULA ZSIRAY LOGAN, UT

PREP: 5 MIN. + MARINATING
BAKE: 2 HOURS 10 MIN.
MAKES: 10 SERVINGS

- 1 **cup sugar**
- ½ **cup packed brown sugar**
- 2 **tablespoons salt**
- 2 **tablespoons garlic powder**
- 2 **tablespoons paprika**
- 2 **teaspoons pepper**
- ¼ **teaspoon cayenne pepper**
- 7 **pounds bone-in beef short ribs**

SAUCE

- 1 **small onion, finely chopped**
- 2 **teaspoons canola oil**
- 1½ **cups water**
- 1 **cup ketchup**
- 1 **can (6 ounces) tomato paste**
- 2 **tablespoons brown sugar**
  Pepper to taste

1. In a large bowl, combine the first seven ingredients; rub over ribs. Place in two large resealable plastic bags; seal and refrigerate overnight.
2. Line two 15x10x 1-in. baking pans with foil; grease the foil. Place ribs in prepared pans. Bake, uncovered, at 325° for 2 hours or until meat is tender.
3. Meanwhile, in a large saucepan, saute onion in oil until tender. Stir in the water, ketchup, tomato paste, brown sugar and pepper. Bring the sauce to a boil. Reduce heat; cover and simmer for 1 hour.
4. Remove ribs from the oven. Grill ribs, covered, over indirect medium heat for 20 minutes, turning and basting frequently with sauce.

ANCHO GARLIC STEAKS WITH SUMMER SALSA

FAST FIX ▶
ANCHO GARLIC STEAKS WITH SUMMER SALSA

The first time I tasted this, I was amazed how well the blueberries and watermelon go with the peppery steak. Use whatever fruits are in season so you can serve the grilled entree anytime.

—VERONICA CALLAGHAN GLASTONBURY, CT

START TO FINISH: 30 MIN.
MAKES: 4 SERVINGS

- 2 **boneless beef top loin steaks (1¼ inches thick and 8 ounces each)**
- 2 **teaspoons ground ancho chili pepper**
- 1 **teaspoon garlic salt**

SALSA

- 1 **cup seeded chopped watermelon**
- 1 **cup fresh blueberries**
- 1 **medium tomato, chopped**
- ¼ **cup finely chopped red onion**
- 1 **tablespoon minced fresh mint**
- 1½ **teaspoons grated fresh gingerroot**
- ¼ **teaspoon salt**

1. Rub steaks with chili pepper and garlic salt. Grill, covered, over medium heat or broil 4 in. from heat 7-9 minutes on each side or until meat reaches desired doneness (for medium-rare, a thermometer should read 145°; medium, 160°; well-done, 170°).
2. In a bowl, combine salsa ingredients. Cut steak into thin slices; serve with the salsa.
NOTE *Top loin steak may be labeled as strip steak, KS City steak, NY strip steak, ambassador steak or boneless club steak in your region.*

SOUTHWEST
STEAK & POTATOES

SOUTHWEST STEAK & POTATOES

Here, bold seasonings give meat and potatoes a simple Southwest twist. Feel free to adjust the heat factor by using more or less chili powder.

—KENNY FISHER CIRCLEVILLE, OH

START TO FINISH: 30 MIN.
MAKES: 4 SERVINGS

- 4 **medium Yukon Gold potatoes**
- 2 **teaspoons cider vinegar**
- 1 **teaspoon Worcestershire sauce**
- 1 **beef top round steak (1 inch thick and about 1½ pounds)**
- 1 **tablespoon brown sugar**
- 1 **tablespoon chili powder**
- 1½ **teaspoons ground cumin**
- 1 **teaspoon garlic powder**
- 1 **teaspoon salt, divided**
- ⅛ **teaspoon cayenne pepper**
- ⅛ **teaspoon pepper**

1. Pierce potatoes; place on a microwave-safe plate. Microwave, uncovered, on high 4-5 minutes or until almost tender, turning once. Cool slightly.

2. Meanwhile, mix vinegar and Worcestershire sauce; brush over steak. Mix brown sugar, chili powder, cumin, garlic powder, ½ teaspoon salt and cayenne until blended; sprinkle over both sides of steak.

3. Cut potatoes into ½-in. slices. Sprinkle with pepper and remaining salt. Grill potatoes and steak, covered, turning occasionally, over medium heat 12-17 minutes or until potatoes are tender and a thermometer inserted in beef reads 145° for medium-rare.

4. Cut steak into thin slices. Serve with the potatoes.

SIMPLE MARINATED RIBEYES

When spring arrives, the grill comes out at our house! My husband does a great job cooking these steaks to perfection. They taste so terrific, we have them as often as once a week.

—SONJA KANE WENDELL, NC

PREP: 10 MIN. + MARINATING • **GRILL:** 10 MIN.
MAKES: 6 SERVINGS

- ½ **cup butter, melted**
- ¼ **cup lemon juice**
- ¼ **cup ketchup**
- 2 **tablespoons Worcestershire sauce**
- 2 **tablespoons cider vinegar**
- 2 **tablespoons olive oil**
- 4 **garlic cloves, minced**
- 1 **teaspoon salt**
- 1 **teaspoon sugar**
- ½ **teaspoon hot pepper sauce**
  Dash cayenne pepper
- 6 **beef ribeye steaks (about 1 inch thick and 12 ounces each)**

1. In a large resealable bag, combine the first 11 ingredients. Add the steaks. Seal bag and turn to coat; refrigerate for 6 hours or overnight.

2. Drain and discard marinade. Grill steaks, uncovered, over medium-hot heat for 5-7 minutes on each side or until the meat reaches desired doneness (for medium-rare, a thermometer should read 145°; medium, 160°; well-done, 170°).

SESAME BEEF 'N' VEGGIE KABOBS

This is a favorite with my family. Chalk it up to the fact that the kabobs deliver great flavor and tender chunks of meat with a picture-pretty presentation!

—FRANCES KLINGEMANN OMAHA, NE

PREP: 25 MIN. + MARINATING • **GRILL:** 10 MIN.
MAKES: 8 SERVINGS

- ½ **cup reduced-sodium soy sauce**
- ¼ **cup white wine or unsweetened apple juice**
- 3 **medium green peppers, cut into 1-inch pieces, divided**
- 1 **medium onion, cut into wedges**
- 1 **garlic clove, peeled**
- ½ **teaspoon ground ginger**
- 1 **tablespoon sesame seeds**
- 2 **pounds beef top sirloin steak, cut into 1-inch pieces**
- 32 **medium fresh mushrooms**
- 32 **cherry tomatoes**
- 1 **tablespoon canola oil**

1. In a blender, combine the soy sauce, wine, ½ cup green pepper, onion, garlic and ginger; cover and process until smooth. Stir in sesame seeds.

2. Cover and refrigerate ⅓ cup mixture for basting. Pour remaining mixture into a large resealable plastic bag; add the beef. Seal bag and turn to coat; refrigerate overnight. Refrigerate remaining peppers.

3. Drain and discard marinade. On 16 metal or soaked wooden skewers, thread the beef, mushrooms, tomatoes and remaining peppers alternately. Brush lightly with oil.

4. Moisten a paper towel with cooking oil; using long-handled tongs, lightly coat the grill rack. Grill kabobs, covered, over medium heat or broil 4 in. from the heat for 10-15 minutes or until beef reaches desired doneness, turning occasionally and basting with reserved marinade.

BARBECUED CHUCK ROAST

Whether I serve this roast for church dinners, company or family, it's always a hit. My family likes scalloped potatoes, tossed salad and pie to round out the menu. Use up the leftovers for tasty sandwiches the next day!

—ARDIS GAUTIER LAMONT, OK

PREP: 25 MIN. + MARINATING
GRILL: 1 HOUR 20 MIN.
MAKES: 6-8 SERVINGS

- ⅔ cup cider vinegar
- ½ cup ketchup
- ¼ cup canola oil
- ¼ cup soy sauce
- 2 tablespoons Worcestershire sauce
- 2 teaspoons garlic powder
- 2 teaspoons salt
- 2 teaspoons prepared mustard
- ½ teaspoon pepper
- 1 boneless beef chuck roast (2½-3 pounds)
- ½ cup unsweetened applesauce

1. In a large bowl, combine the first nine ingredients. Pour half of the marinade into a large resealable plastic bag; add roast. Seal bag and turn to coat; refrigerate for at least 3 hours. Cover and refrigerate remaining marinade.
2. Drain and discard marinade. Grill roast, covered, over indirect heat for 20 minutes, turning occasionally.
3. Add applesauce to reserved marinade; brush over roast. Continue basting and turning the roast several times for 1 to 1½ hours or until meat reaches desired doneness (for medium-rare, a thermometer should read 145°; medium, 160°; well-done, 170°).

CHIPOTLE BEEF TENDERLOIN

CHIPOTLE BEEF TENDERLOIN

Head outside for your Sunday dinner and grill this tender steak that's kicked up with a smoky homemade picante sauce. Try the sauce as a chip dip, too.

—GENE PETERS EDWARDSVILLE, IL

PREP: 40 MIN. • **GRILL:** 10 MIN.
MAKES: 6 SERVINGS

- ¾ cup chopped sweet onion
- ¾ cup chopped green pepper
- 1 jalapeno pepper, seeded and minced
- 1 chipotle pepper in adobo sauce, minced
- 2 tablespoons olive oil
- 3 cups seeded chopped tomatoes
- 1 tablespoon chipotle hot pepper sauce
- 2 teaspoons sugar
- 1 teaspoon salt
- 1 teaspoon chili powder
- ½ teaspoon ground cumin
- 2 tablespoons minced fresh cilantro
- 1 teaspoon liquid smoke, optional
- 6 beef tenderloin steaks (1½ inches thick and 6 ounces each)
- 2 teaspoons steak seasoning

1. In a Dutch oven, saute the onion, green pepper, jalapeno and chipotle pepper in oil until tender. Add the tomatoes, pepper sauce, sugar, salt, chili powder and cumin. Bring to a boil. Reduce heat; simmer, uncovered, for 30 minutes or until thickened, stirring mixture frequently.
2. Remove from the heat; stir in cilantro and liquid smoke if desired.
3. Meanwhile, sprinkle steaks with steak seasoning. Grill over medium heat for 7-8 minutes on each side or until meat reaches desired doneness (for medium-rare, a thermometer should read 145°; medium, 160°; well-done, 170°). Serve with sauce.

STEAKHOUSE STRIP STEAKS WITH CHIMICHURRI

Chilies and lime juice give this version of chimichurri sauce a zesty Southwest flair that's dynamite with cumin-rubbed steaks. You've got to try the thick herb sauce with salmon, too!

—GILDA LESTER MILLSBORO, DE

PREP: 30 MIN. • **GRILL:** 10 MIN.
MAKES: 4 SERVINGS

- 4 **boneless beef top loin steaks (8 ounces each)**
- 1 **tablespoon olive oil**
- 2 **teaspoons ground cumin**
- 1 **teaspoon salt**
- 1 **teaspoon coarsely ground pepper**

CHIMICHURRI

- 2½ **cups chopped green onions**
- 3 **garlic cloves, minced**
- 5 **tablespoons olive oil, divided**
- 1 **cup packed fresh parsley sprigs**
- ½ **cup fresh cilantro leaves**
- ½ **cup loosely packed basil leaves**
- 2 **tablespoons canned chopped green chilies**
- ¼ **teaspoon salt**
- ¼ **teaspoon coarsely ground pepper**
- ¼ **cup reduced-sodium chicken broth**
- 3 **tablespoons lime juice**
  Lime wedges

1. Brush steaks with oil. Combine the cumin, salt and pepper. Rub over steaks; set aside.

2. In a large skillet, saute onions and garlic in 2 tablespoons oil until tender. Cool slightly.

3. In a food processor, combine the onion mixture, herbs, chilies, salt and pepper; cover and process until finely chopped. Add broth and lime juice. While processing, gradually add remaining oil in a steady stream.

4. Grill steaks, covered, over medium heat or broil 4 in. from the heat for 5-7 minutes on each side or until meat reaches desired doneness (for medium-rare, a thermometer should read 145°; medium 160°; well-done 170°). Serve with chimichurri and lime wedges.

NOTE *Top loin steak may be labeled as strip steak, KS City steak, NY strip steak, ambassador steak or boneless club steak in your region.*

STEAKHOUSE STRIP STEAKS WITH CHIMICHURRI

---

⑤INGREDIENTS

HOBO DINNER

The meat and vegetables in this effortless supper are wrapped in a piece of foil and cooked together. The recipe yields a single serving, but you could make as many of the meal-in-one packets as you need.

—PAT WALTER PINE ISLAND, MN

PREP: 5 MIN. • **BAKE:** 45 MIN.
MAKES: 1 SERVING.

- ¼ **pound ground beef**
- 1 **potato, sliced**
- 1 **carrot, sliced**
- 2 **tablespoons chopped onion**
- 1 **sheet heavy-duty aluminum foil (18 x 13 inches)**
  Salt and pepper to taste, optional

Shape beef into a patty; place in the center of foil with potato, carrot and onion. Sprinkle with salt and pepper if desired. Fold foil over and seal well. Grill, covered, over medium heat for 45-60 minutes or until potato is tender. Open the foil packet carefully.

JUICY & DELICIOUS
MIXED SPICE BURGERS

FAST FIX ▸
JUICY & DELICIOUS MIXED SPICE BURGERS

Not your average burgers, these Middle Eastern patties are seasoned with fresh herbs and warm spices such as cinnamon, pepper and nutmeg. Serving them with tzatziki sauce is optional, but you won't regret it if you do.

—**ANNE HENRY** TORONTO, ON

START TO FINISH: 30 MIN.
MAKES: 6 SERVINGS

- 1 medium onion, finely chopped
- 3 tablespoons minced fresh parsley
- 2 tablespoons minced fresh mint
- 1 garlic clove, minced
- ¾ teaspoon ground allspice
- ¾ teaspoon pepper
- ½ teaspoon ground cinnamon
- ½ teaspoon salt
- ¼ teaspoon ground nutmeg
- 1½ pounds lean ground beef (90% lean)
  Refrigerated tzatziki sauce, optional

1. In a large bowl, combine the first nine ingredients. Add beef; mix lightly but thoroughly. Shape into six 4x2-in. oblong patties.
2. Grill patties, covered, over medium heat or broil 4 in. from heat 4-6 minutes on each side or until a thermometer reads 160°. If desired, serve with sauce.

EASY GRILLED FLANK STEAK

We've made this flank steak over an open fire pit, which is really fabulous, and also on a gas grill. Try serving it with onions, peppers and potatoes grilled in a foil pack.

—**VALERIE CHIPMAN** LISBON, ME

PREP: 20 MIN. + MARINATING • **GRILL:** 15 MIN.
MAKES: 4 SERVINGS

- 1 small onion, chopped
- ½ cup dry red wine or reduced-sodium beef broth
- 2 tablespoons olive oil
- 2 garlic cloves, minced
- 1 teaspoon brown sugar
- ¼ teaspoon pepper
- 2 fresh sage leaves, thinly sliced or ¾ teaspoon dried sage leaves
- ½ teaspoon salt
- ½ teaspoon minced fresh gingerroot
- 1 beef flank steak (1 pound)

1. In a large resealable plastic bag, combine the first nine ingredients. Score the surface of the beef, making diamond shapes ¼ in. deep; place in bag. Seal bag and turn to coat; refrigerate for 8 hours or overnight.
2. Drain and discard marinade. Using long-handled tongs, moisten a paper towel with cooking oil and lightly coat the grill rack. Grill steak, covered, over medium heat or broil 4 in. from the heat for 6-8 minutes on each side or until meat reaches desired doneness (for medium-rare, a thermometer should read 145°; medium, 160°; well-done, 170°).
3. Let stand for 5 minutes; thinly slice across the grain.

BEEF AND PEPPER KABOBS

I've traveled to many different countries and am always on the lookout for new cookbooks. This recipe was adapted from a Turkish book. It brings rave reviews whenever I serve it. Try offering the kabobs alongside rice pilaf and a freshly tossed salad.

—**JANET WOOD** WINDHAM, NH

PREP: 15 MIN. + MARINATING • **GRILL:** 15 MIN.
MAKES: 6-8 SERVINGS

- 3 tablespoons lemon juice
- 2 tablespoons canola oil
- 1 large onion, finely chopped
- 1½ teaspoons dried thyme
- ½ teaspoon salt
- ¼ teaspoon pepper
- 2 pounds beef top sirloin steak, cut into 1-inch cubes
- 1 each medium sweet green, yellow, orange and red peppers

1. In a large heavy-duty resealable plastic bag, combine the lemon juice, oil, onion, thyme, salt and pepper. Add meat; seal bag and turn to coat. Refrigerate for 6 hours or overnight.
2. Cut peppers into 1-in. squares and thread onto metal or soaked wooden skewers alternately with meat.
3. Grill kabobs over medium heat for 12-15 minutes or until the meat reaches desired doneness, turning often.
NOTE *Boneless lamb can be substituted for the beef.*

✹ HOW TO CREATE PERFECT GRILL MARKS

The trick to creating diamond-shaped grill marks is to sear the meat just long enough to create solid grill lines, then rotate the food 90 degrees (as seen at left). Continue searing until you have a second set of grill lines. Generally, only one side of a steak has such marks. Searing both sides in such a manner could dry out the beef. Once the steak is nicely marked, move it to a cooler area of the grill to finish cooking.

FIRE BEEF

FIRE BEEF

I first made this peppery beef using a recipe from my boss, who lived in Korea during the 1950s. Freeze the ribeyes first to make slicing them a cinch.

—**LINDA McCANE** CHESAPEAKE, VA

PREP: 20 MIN. + MARINATING • **GRILL:** 10 MIN.
MAKES: 10 SERVINGS

- 3 **pounds beef ribeye steaks**
- 3 **tablespoons sugar**
- ⅓ **cup reduced-sodium soy sauce**
- ¼ **cup canola oil**
- 3 **tablespoons toasted sesame seeds, crushed**
- 2 **garlic cloves, minced**
- 1½ **teaspoons hot pepper sauce**
- ¼ **teaspoon crushed red pepper flakes**
  Thinly sliced green onions, optional

1. Freeze steaks until firm, about 30 minutes. Cut steaks crosswise into ¼-inch slices. Sprinkle with sugar; place in a large resealable plastic bag. Add soy sauce, oil. sesame seeds, garlic, pepper sauce and pepper flakes; seal bag and turn to coat. Refrigerate for 4 hours or overnight.
2. Thread beef onto 10 metal or soaked wooden skewers; discard any remaining marinade. Grill meat, covered, over medium heat 4-5 minutes on each side or until beef reaches desired doneness. If desired, sprinkle with green onions.

BBQ BRISKET FLATBREAD PIZZAS

Preparing beef brisket pizza takes time, but when you take that first smoky, rich and juicy bite, you'll know it's worth it.

—AARON REYNOLDS FOX RIVER GROVE, IL

PREP: 3 HOURS + MARINATING • **GRILL:** 20 MIN.
MAKES: 2 FLATBREAD PIZZAS (6 SLICES EACH)

- 2 **cups barbecue sauce, divided**
- ½ **cup cider vinegar**
- ½ **cup chopped green onions, divided**
- ½ **cup minced fresh cilantro, divided**
- 2 **pounds fresh beef brisket**
- 1 **teaspoon salt**
- 1 **teaspoon pepper**
- 1 **large red onion, cut into thick slices**
- 1 **teaspoon olive oil**
- 2 **cups (8 ounces) shredded smoked Gouda cheese**

DOUGH
- 2¾ to 3¼ **cups all-purpose flour**
- 1 **tablespoon sugar**
- 3 **teaspoons salt**
- 1 **package (¼ ounce) quick-rise yeast**
- 1¼ **cups warm water (120° to 130°)**
- 2 **tablespoons olive oil**

1. In a large resealable plastic bag, combine 1 cup barbecue sauce, vinegar, ¼ cup green onions and ¼ cup of cilantro. Sprinkle brisket with salt and pepper; add to bag. Seal bag and turn to coat. Refrigerate meat for 8 hours or overnight.

2. Drain and discard marinade. Prepare grill for indirect heat, using a drip pan. Place brisket over pan; grill, covered, over indirect low heat for 1 hour. Add 10 briquettes to coals. Cover and grill about 1¼ hours longer or until meat is fork-tender, adding more briquettes if needed. When cool enough to handle, shred meat with two forks; set aside.

3. Meanwhile, in a large bowl, combine 2¾ cups flour, sugar, salt and yeast. Add water and oil; beat just until smooth. Stir in enough remaining flour to form a soft dough (dough will be sticky).

4. Turn onto a floured surface; knead until smooth and elastic, about 6-8 minutes. Place in a greased bowl, turning once to grease the top. Cover and let rise in a warm place until doubled, about 1 hour. Punch dough down; divide into two portions. Roll each into a 15-in. circle.

5. Grill each circle, covered, over medium heat for 1-2 minutes on one side or until lightly browned. Set crusts aside. Brush onion with oil; grill for 4-5 minutes or until tender, turning once. Remove from the heat; chop and set aside.

6. Spread the grilled side of each crust with remaining barbecue sauce. Top with shredded brisket, onion, cheese and remaining green onions and cilantro.

7. Place one pizza on grill; cover and cook over indirect medium heat for 8-10 minutes or until crust is lightly browned and cheese is melted. Rotate pizza halfway through cooking to ensure an evenly browned crust. Repeat with remaining pizza.

BBQ BRISKET FLATBREAD PIZZAS

STEAK WITH CITRUS SALSA

3. Combine salsa ingredients in a bowl. Cut steak across the grain into thin slices. Serve with salsa.

NOTE *Wear disposable gloves when cutting hot peppers; the oils can burn skin. Avoid touching your face.*

ASIAN FLANK STEAK

Friends and family keep asking me to make this great recipe that combines ginger and steak to make an Asian-flavored favorite. You'll enjoy it too!!
—**WARREN PAULSON** MESA, AZ

PREP: 10 MIN. + MARINATING • **GRILL:** 15 MIN.
MAKES: 4 SERVINGS

- ¼ **cup thinly sliced green onions**
- ¼ **cup unsweetened pineapple juice**
- ¼ **cup soy sauce**
- ¼ **cup ketchup**
- ¼ **cup plum sauce**
- 2 **tablespoons minced fresh cilantro**
- 3 **garlic cloves, minced**
- 1 **tablespoon minced fresh gingerroot**
- 1 **beef flank steak (1¼ pounds)**

1. In a small bowl, combine the first eight ingredients. Pour ¾ cup marinade into a large resealable plastic bag; add the steak. Seal bag and turn to coat; refrigerate for 4 hours or overnight. Cover and refrigerate remaining marinade.
2. Drain and discard marinade. Grill steak, covered, over medium heat for 6-8 minutes on each side or until meat reaches desired doneness (for medium-rare, a thermometer should read 145°; medium, 160°; well-done, 170°), basting occasionally with reserved marinade. To serve, thinly slice across the grain.

STEAK WITH CITRUS SALSA

A lime juice marinade really perks up these grilled steaks. And the snappy, light citrus salsa is a delightful change from the usual heavy steak sauce.
—**KATHLEEN SMITH** PITTSBURGH, PA

PREP: 15 MIN. + MARINATING • **GRILL:** 15 MIN.
MAKES: 4-6 SERVINGS

- ½ **cup soy sauce**
- ¼ **cup chopped green onions**
- 3 **tablespoons lime juice**
- 2 **tablespoons brown sugar**
- ⅛ **teaspoon hot pepper sauce**
- 1 **garlic clove, minced**
- 1½ **pounds beef top sirloin steak (about 1 inch thick)**

SALSA
- 2 **navel oranges, peeled, sectioned and chopped**
- ¼ **cup chopped green onions**
- 2 **tablespoons orange juice**
- 2 **tablespoons red wine vinegar**
- 2 **tablespoon chopped lemon**
- 1 **tablespoon chopped lime**
- 1 **tablespoon sugar**
- 1 **tablespoon minced fresh cilantro**
- 1 **teaspoon minced jalapeno pepper**
- ½ **teaspoon grated lemon peel**
- ½ **teaspoon grated lime peel**
- ⅛ **teaspoon salt**

1. In a large resealable plastic bag, combine the first six ingredients; add beef. Seal and refrigerate for 2 hours or overnight, turning occasionally.
2. Drain and discard marinade. Broil or grill steak, uncovered, over medium heat for 4-6 minutes on each side or until meat reaches desired doneness (for medium-rare, a thermometer should read 145°; medium, 160°; well-done, 170°).

FAST FIX ▶

SUBLIME LIME BEEF

It's fun to watch the happy reactions of others when they try my lime beef kabobs. The meat on the skewers is so good, it's hard not to smile after the first bite!

—DIEP NGUYEN HANFORD, CA

START TO FINISH: 25 MIN.
MAKES: 4 SERVINGS

- ⅓ cup lime juice
- 2 teaspoons sugar
- 2 garlic cloves, minced
- 1 beef top sirloin steak (1 inch thick and 1 pound)
- 1½ teaspoons pepper
- ¾ teaspoon salt
- 2 tablespoons unsalted dry roasted peanuts, chopped
- 3 cups hot cooked brown rice

1. In a small bowl, mix lime juice, sugar and garlic until blended; set aside. Cut steak into 2x1x¾-in. pieces; toss with pepper and salt. Thread beef onto four metal or soaked wooden skewers.
2. Grill kabobs, covered, over medium heat or broil 4 in. from heat 2-4 minutes on each side or until beef reaches desired doneness. Add peanuts to sauce; serve with kabobs and rice.

GRILL SKILL

When working with uncooked beef, always have a clean serving platter at the ready for the cooked food. Don't reuse the dish you carried the food out to the grill. It's also safest to baste food with a sauce after it's been flipped once on the grill. This way, the basting brush isn't touching the uncooked beef and then contaminating the sauce when you set the brush back into the container.

SUBLIME LIME BEEF

BEEF & BACON KABOBS

Many times, I come up with recipes based simply on whatever I have on hand. This improvization is one of those dishes. It's become my husband's favorite entree.
—**DOLORES LUEKEN** FERDINAND, IN

PREP: 15 MIN. + MARINATING • **GRILL:** 10 MIN.
MAKES: 4 SERVINGS

- 1 bottle (8 ounces) French or Russian salad dressing
- 2 tablespoons lemon juice
- 2 tablespoons Worcestershire sauce
- ⅛ teaspoon garlic powder
- ⅛ teaspoon pepper
- 1 pound beef top sirloin steak, cut into 1½-inch cubes
- 8 to 10 bacon strips, cut in half
- 1 sweet red pepper, cut into chunks
- 1 green pepper, cut into chunks
- 2 small zucchini squash, cut into chunks
- 8 medium fresh mushrooms
- 1 large onion, quartered, optional

1. In a small bowl, whisk the first five ingredients. Place half of marinade in a large resealable plastic bag. Add beef; seal bag and turn to coat. Refrigerate 8 hours or overnight. Cover and refrigerate remaining marinade.
2. Drain beef, discarding marinade in bag. Wrap bacon around beef cubes. On four metal or soaked wooden skewers, alternately thread beef and vegetables.
3. Grill, covered, over medium heat 10-15 minutes or until beef reaches desired doneness and vegetables are tender, turning occasionally and basting kabobs frequently with the reserved marinade.

CUMIN-CHILI SPICED FLANK STEAK

CUMIN-CHILI SPICED FLANK STEAK

Share this wonderful dish with friends and family. They'll rave about the sizzling grilled steak with flavorful jalapeno and tomato salsa. Couscous makes it a meal.
—**YVONNE STARLIN** WESTMORELAND, TN

PREP: 40 MIN. • **COOK:** 15 MIN.
MAKES: 4 SERVINGS

- 2 small sweet red peppers, cut into 2-inch strips
- 1 small sweet yellow pepper, cut into 2-inch strips
- 2 cups grape tomatoes
- 1 small onion, cut into ½-inch wedges
- 2 jalapeno peppers, halved and seeded
- 2 tablespoons olive oil, divided
- ¾ teaspoon salt, divided
- ¾ teaspoon pepper, divided
- 2 teaspoons ground cumin
- 1 teaspoon chili powder
- 1 beef flank steak (1½ pounds)
- 2 to 3 teaspoons lime juice
   Hot cooked couscous
   Lime wedges

1. Preheat broiler. Place the first five ingredients in a greased 15x10x1-in. baking pan. Toss with 1 tablespoon oil, ¼ teaspoon salt and ¼ teaspoon pepper. Broil vegetables 4 in. from heat 10-12 minutes or until they are tender and begin to char, turning once.
2. Meanwhile, mix salt, pepper, cumin, chili powder and the remaining oil; rub over both sides of steak. Grill, covered, over medium heat or broil 4 in. from heat 6-9 minutes on each side or until meat reaches desired doneness (for medium-rare, a thermometer should read 145°; medium, 160°; well-done, 170°). Let stand 5 minutes.
3. For salsa, chop broiled onion and jalapenos; place in a small bowl. Stir in tomatoes and lime juice. Thinly slice steak across the grain; serve with salsa, broiled peppers, couscous and lime wedges.
NOTE *Wear disposable gloves when cutting hot peppers; the oils can burn skin. Avoid touching your face.*

LIP-SMACKIN'
BBQ CHICKEN, PAGE 181

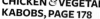
CHICKEN & VEGETABLE KABOBS, PAGE 178

CAN-CAN CHICKEN,
PAGE 171

TAPENADE-STUFFED
CHICKEN BREASTS,
PAGE 177

CHARBROILED CHICKEN & TURKEY

There's sure to be a lot of **Southern "flare"** in the air when BBQ chicken breasts, smoky turkey legs and other **juicy poultry staples** hit the grill. Put down that fork and knife, because these saucy **finger-licking** entrees are calling for you to get your hands dirty!

POULTRY GRILLING CHART

When cooking poultry, check for doneness with a food thermometer. Bone-in chicken breasts are done at 170°; whole chickens at 170° to 175° as measured in the thigh. Boneless chicken breasts, chicken sausages and chicken patties are done at 165° For direct grilling, turn meat halfway through grilling time. The cooking times below are general guidelines.

CUT	WEIGHT OR THICKNESS	HEAT	APPROXIMATE COOKING TIME (IN MINUTES)
CHICKEN			
BROILER/FRYER, WHOLE	3 to 4 lbs.	medium/indirect	1 to 1¼ hours
ROASTER, WHOLE	5 to 6 lbs.	medium/indirect	1¾ to 2¼ hours
MEATY BONE-IN PIECES, BREAST HALVES, LEGS, QUARTERS	1¼ to 1½ lbs.	medium/indirect medium/direct	35 to 45 minutes 40 to 50 minutes
BONE-IN THIGHS, DRUMSTICKS, WINGS	3 to 7 oz. each	medium-low/direct medium/indirect	15 to 30 minutes 20 to 30 minutes
BREAST HALVES, BONELESS	6 oz. each	medium/direct	10 to 15 minutes
KABOBS	1-in. cubes	medium/direct	10 to 15 minutes
CORNISH GAME HENS	1½ to 2 lbs.	medium/indirect	45 to 55 minutes
TURKEY			
WHOLE, UNSTUFFED	8 to 11 lbs. 12 to 16 lbs.	medium/indirect medium/indirect	2 to 2½ hours 2½ to 3 hours
BREAST (BONE-IN)	4 to 5 lbs.	medium/indirect	1½ to 2 hours
BREAST (BONELESS)	1¼ to 1¾ lbs.	medium/indirect	1 to 1¼ hours
TENDERLOINS	8 oz. each	medium/direct	15 to 20 minutes
DRUMS OR THIGHS	½ to 1½ lbs.	medium/indirect	45 to 75 minutes
PATTY	4 oz. and ½ in.	medium/direct	8 to 10 minutes

 **GRILL SKILL**

Grilling chicken kabobs? Due to variations in size, the chicken on a kabob is done when its juices run clear. For best results, consider grilling chicken and veggies on separate skewers.

CHICKEN-CHILE RELLENO TACOS

A local restaurant makes awesome charred tacos that are a lot like these. Their marinade recipe's a secret, so I invented my own. Light the coals and have them anytime of day.

—DENISE KLIBERT SHREVEPORT, LA

PREP: 30 MIN. + MARINATING
GRILL: 30 MIN. + STANDING • **MAKES:** 8 SERVINGS

- ⅓ **cup olive oil**
- ⅓ **cup lime juice**
- ⅓ **cup red wine vinegar**
- 2 **teaspoons sugar**
- 2 **teaspoons salt**
- 2 **teaspoons pepper**
- 1 **cup coarsely chopped fresh cilantro**
- 2 **tablespoons finely chopped chipotle peppers in adobo sauce**
- 2 **pounds boneless skinless chicken thighs**

TACOS
- 4 **poblano peppers**
- 1 **tablespoon olive oil**
- 8 **flour tortillas (8 inches)**
- 2 **cups (8 ounces) shredded Monterey Jack cheese**

1. In a small bowl, whisk the first six ingredients until blended; stir in cilantro and chipotles. Transfer ⅔ cup marinade to a large resealable plastic bag. Add the chicken; seal bag and turn to coat. Refrigerate 8 hours or overnight. Cover and refrigerate the remaining marinade.

2. Brush poblanos with 1 tablespoon oil. Grill peppers, covered, over high heat 8-10 minutes or until blistered and blackened, turning as needed. Immediately place peppers in a small bowl; let stand, covered, 20 minutes. Reduce temperature to medium heat.

3. Drain chicken, discarding marinade in bag. Grill chicken, covered, over medium heat 6-8 minutes on each side or until a thermometer reads 170°.

4. Peel off and discard charred skin from peppers. Cut peppers lengthwise in half; carefully remove stems and seeds. Cut chicken into slices. Warm reserved marinade; add chicken and toss to coat.

5. To assemble, place one pepper half in center of each tortilla; top with ½ cup chicken and ¼ cup cheese. Fold tortillas in half over filling. Grill, covered, on medium heat 2-3 minutes on each side or until heated through.

CHICKEN-CHILE RELLENO TACOS

CAN-CAN
CHICKEN

CAN-CAN CHICKEN

Here's a fun take on the popular beer-can chicken. To add color and flavor, try spraying the chicken with a mixture of 2 cups apple cider and 1 tablespoon balsamic vinegar as it grills. If you're frequently opening up the grill, you may need to increase the cooking time a bit.
—**STEVE BATH** LINCOLN, NE

PREP: 30 MIN. + CHILLING
GRILL: 1¼ HOURS + STANDING
MAKES: 6 SERVINGS

- 1 **tablespoon kosher salt**
- 1 **teaspoon sugar**
- 1 **teaspoon onion powder**
- 1 **teaspoon garlic powder**
- 1 **teaspoon cayenne pepper**
- 1 **teaspoon paprika**
- 1 **teaspoon ground mustard**
- 1 **broiler/fryer chicken (3½-4 pounds)**
- 1 **can (12 ounces) beer**

1. In a small bowl, combine the first seven ingredients. With fingers, carefully loosen skin from chicken; rub spice mixture under and over skin. Tuck wings under chicken. Refrigerate for 1 hour.

2. Prepare grill for indirect grilling. Completely cover all sides of an 8- or 9-in. baking pan with foil. Place a beer-can chicken rack in pan. Remove half of the beer from can; save for another use. Using a can opener, make additional large holes in top of can. Add beer can to rack.

3. Place the chicken vertically onto rack. Place pan on grill rack. Grill, covered, over indirect medium heat for 1¼-1½ hours or until a thermometer inserted in thigh reads 180°.

4. Remove pan from grill; tent chicken with foil. Let stand 10 minutes. Carefully remove chicken from rack.

MAPLE CRANBERRY CHICKEN

(5) INGREDIENTS FAST FIX
MAPLE CRANBERRY CHICKEN

Canned cranberry sauce gets a makeover to become a wonderfully sweet-tart glaze that really jazzes up chicken or even pork.
—**MARGARET WILSON** SUN CITY, CA

START TO FINISH: 25 MIN.
MAKES: 6 SERVINGS

- ½ **cup maple syrup**
- 1 **can (14 ounces) whole-berry cranberry sauce, divided**
- 6 **boneless skinless chicken breast halves (4 ounces each)**
- ½ **teaspoon salt**

1. In a small bowl, combine syrup and ¾ cup cranberry sauce; set aside. Sprinkle chicken with salt.

2. Moisten a paper towel with cooking oil; using long-handled tongs, lightly coat the grill rack. Grill chicken, covered, over medium heat or broil 4 in. from the heat for 6-8 minutes on each side or until a thermometer reads 165°, basting frequently with syrup mixture.

3. Warm the remaining cranberry sauce; serve with chicken.

GRILL SKILL

If you like to have professional-looking grill marks on your chicken, add a little honey to your marinade or sauce. The sugar in the honey caramelizes when heated on the grill, creating sear marks. You will need about 1 teaspoon to 1 tablespoon, depending on the amount of marinade or sauce. It even works on the stovetop. Simply brush the chicken with honey and saute in a nonstick pan coated with cooking spray to give it a golden-brown color.
LISA M. SPRING VALLEY, NY

COLA BARBECUED CHICKEN

I'm always looking for fun, great-tasting foods that will feed a crowd. To reduce the sugar content of this recipe, I sometimes use diet cola.

—MILDRED DIEFFENBACH
WOMELSDORF, PA

PREP: 25 MIN. + MARINATING • **GRILL:** 40 MIN.
MAKES: 8 SERVINGS

- 1   can (12 ounces) cola
- 1   can (6 ounces) tomato paste
- 2   tablespoons finely chopped onion
- 1   tablespoon red wine vinegar
- 1   tablespoon Worcestershire sauce
- ¼   teaspoon salt
- 2   broiler/fryer chickens (3 pounds each), cut in half

1. In a small saucepan, combine the cola, tomato paste, onion, vinegar, Worcestershire sauce and salt. Bring to a boil. Reduce heat; simmer, uncovered, for 15 minutes. Set aside ½ cup for basting; cover and refrigerate.

2. Carefully loosen the skin of the chicken; brush the remaining sauce under skin. Cover and refrigerate for 30 minutes.

3. Prepare grill for indirect heat, using a drip pan. Using long-handled tongs, moisten a paper towel with cooking oil and lightly coat the grill rack. Place chicken over drip pan and grill, uncovered, over indirect medium heat for 25 minutes on each side or until chicken juices run clear, basting occasionally with reserved sauce.

SPANISH TURKEY TENDERLOINS

SPANISH TURKEY TENDERLOINS

If you're hungry for warm-weather fare, give this a try! The grilled turkey and the bright, sunny colors of the relish look and taste like summer.

—ROXANNE CHAN ALBANY, CA

PREP: 20 MIN. • **GRILL:** 15 MIN.
MAKES: 6 SERVINGS

- 1   package (20 ounces) turkey breast tenderloins
- 1   tablespoon olive oil
- ½   teaspoon salt
- ½   teaspoon pepper
- ¼   teaspoon paprika

RELISH

- 1   plum tomato, chopped
- 1   large navel orange, peeled, sectioned and chopped
- ¼   cup sliced pimiento-stuffed olives
- 1   green onion, finely chopped
- 2   tablespoons minced fresh oregano or 2 teaspoons dried oregano
- 2   tablespoons sliced almonds
- 2   tablespoons minced fresh parsley
- 1   large garlic clove, minced
- 1   tablespoon capers, drained
- 1   teaspoon lemon juice
- ½   teaspoon grated lemon peel
- ¼   teaspoon salt

1. Rub turkey with oil; sprinkle with salt, pepper and paprika.

2. Grill, covered, over medium heat or broil 4 in. from the heat 15-20 minutes or until a thermometer reads 170°, turning occasionally. Let stand for 5 minutes before slicing.

3. Meanwhile, in a small bowl, combine the relish ingredients. Serve with turkey.

POTATO-SAUSAGE FOIL PACKS

We had these satisfying campfire bundles at a friend's house for dinner and loved the simplicity of this great summer meal. Now we commonly make it for weeknight dinners in the summer.

—ALISSA KEITH LYNCHBURG, VA

PREP: 20 MIN. • **GRILL:** 30 MIN.
MAKES: 4 SERVINGS

- 1 package (14 ounces) smoked turkey kielbasa, sliced
- 2 large potatoes, cut into wedges
- 1 each medium green, sweet red and yellow peppers, cut into 1-inch pieces
- 1 medium onion, chopped
- 4 teaspoons lemon juice
- 4 teaspoons olive oil
- ½ teaspoon garlic powder
- ½ teaspoon pepper
- ¼ teaspoon salt

1. Divide the kielbasa, potatoes, peppers and onion among four double thicknesses of heavy-duty foil (about 18x12 in.). Drizzle with lemon juice and oil; sprinkle with garlic powder, pepper and salt.

2. Fold foil around kielbasa mixture and seal tightly. Grill, covered, over medium heat for 30-35 minutes or until potatoes are tender. Open foil carefully to allow steam to escape.

POTATO-SAUSAGE FOIL PACKS

CHICKEN PIZZA PACKETS

Basil, garlic, pepperoni and mozzarella give plenty of pizza flavor to these individual chicken dinners. This speedy supper is a tasty way to get little ones to eat their veggies.

—AMBER ZURBRUGG ALLIANCE, OH

PREP: 15 MIN. • **GRILL:** 20 MIN.
MAKES: 4 SERVINGS

- 1 pound boneless skinless chicken breasts, cut into 1-inch pieces
- 2 tablespoons olive oil
- 1 small zucchini, thinly sliced
- 16 pepperoni slices
- 1 small green pepper, julienned
- 1 small onion, sliced
- ½ teaspoon dried oregano
- ½ teaspoon dried basil
- ¼ teaspoon salt
- ¼ teaspoon garlic powder
- ¼ teaspoon pepper
- 1 cup halved cherry tomatoes
- ½ cup shredded part-skim mozzarella cheese
- ½ cup shredded Parmesan cheese

1. In a large bowl, combine the first 11 ingredients. Coat four pieces of heavy-duty foil (about 12 in. square) with cooking spray. Place a quarter of the chicken mixture in the center of each piece. Fold foil around mixture and seal tightly.

2. Grill, covered, over medium-hot heat for 15-18 minutes or until chicken is no longer pink.

3. Carefully open each packet. Sprinkle with tomatoes and cheeses. Seal loosely; grill 2 minutes longer or until cheese is melted.

BARBECUED
CHICKEN BREASTS

BARBECUED CHICKEN BREASTS

It's fun to have my family over so I can prepare their favorite foods, such as this saucy barbecued chicken. The moist and plump pieces always bring enthusiastic compliments from our four grown children and three grandkids.

—BARBARA BLICKENS DERFER
EDGEWATER, FL

PREP: 15 MIN. + MARINATING
COOK: 35 MIN. • **MAKES:** 6 SERVINGS

- 1 large onion, chopped
- ⅔ cup butter, melted
- 6 tablespoons cider vinegar
- 4 teaspoons sugar
- 1 tablespoon chili powder
- 2 teaspoons salt
- 2 teaspoons Worcestershire sauce
- 1½ teaspoons pepper
- 1½ teaspoons ground mustard
- ½ teaspoon hot pepper sauce
- 2 garlic cloves, minced
- 6 bone-in chicken breast halves (4 to 5 pounds), skin removed

1. In a bowl, combine the first 11 ingredients. Cover and refrigerate ⅓ cup for basting. Place the chicken in a large resealable plastic bag; add remaining marinade. Refrigerate for at least 1 hour, turning occasionally.
2. Drain and discard marinade from chicken. Grill chicken, covered, over indirect medium heat for 20 minutes. Turn; grill 15-25 minutes longer or until juices run clear, basting occasionally with reserved marinade.

GRILLED APPLE-BRINED TURKEY

Producing a juicy amber-colored turkey infused with flavor is possible with this brine. You won't regret planning for the long marinating time. This uncommonly tasty turkey is worth every minute.

—TRUDY WILLIAMS SHANNONVILLE, ON

PREP: 30 MIN. + MARINATING
GRILL: 3 HOURS + STANDING
MAKES: 12-14 SERVINGS

- 2 quarts unsweetened apple juice
- 2½ cups packed brown sugar
- 1 cup kosher salt
- 4 ounces fresh gingerroot, peeled and thinly sliced
- 15 whole cloves
- 6 garlic cloves, crushed
- 3 bay leaves
- 3 medium oranges, quartered
- 3 quarts cold water
- 1 turkey (12 to 14 pounds)
- 2 tablespoons canola oil

1. In a large kettle, combine the first seven ingredients. Bring to a boil; cook and stir until salt and sugar are dissolved. Stir in oranges. Remove from the heat. Add cold water to cool the marinade to room temperature.
2. Remove giblets from turkey (discard or save for another use). Place a turkey-size oven roasting bag inside a second roasting bag; add turkey. Pour cooled marinade into bag. Squeeze out as much air as possible; seal bags and turn to coat. Place in a roasting pan or other large container. Refrigerate for 18-24 hours, turning occasionally.
3. Prepare grill for indirect heat. Drain and discard marinade. Rinse turkey under cold water; pat dry. Rub oil over skin. Skewer turkey openings; tie the drumsticks together.
4. Place breast side up on a rack in a disposable foil roasting pan. Grill, covered, over indirect medium heat for 1½ hours. Tent turkey with foil; grill 1½-2 hours longer or until a thermometer reads 180°. Cover and let stand for 15 minutes before carving.
NOTE *This recipe was tested with Morton brand kosher salt. It is best not to use a prebasted turkey for this recipe. However, if you do, omit the salt in the recipe.*

JIM'S MAPLE BARBECUE

I created a pleasantly sweet marinade out of my fondness for maple syrup. It's perfect with chicken, and the flavors offer a great change from traditional poultry marinades and basting sauces.

—JIM BODLE CANASTOTA, NY

PREP: 5 MIN. + MARINATING • **GRILL:** 50 MIN.
MAKES: 4 SERVINGS

- ¾ cup maple syrup
- ½ cup white vinegar
- 3 tablespoons Worcestershire sauce
- 1 garlic clove
- 4 bone-in chicken breast halves (8 ounces each)

1. In a blender, combine syrup, vinegar, Worcestershire sauce and garlic; process for 30 seconds. Reserve ⅓ cup for basting; cover and refrigerate. Place chicken in a large resealable plastic bag; pour remaining sauce over chicken. Seal bag and turn to coat; cover and refrigerate overnight.
2. Drain and discard marinade. Grill, covered, over medium-low heat for 40 minutes or until juices run clear, turning and basting with reserved marinade during the last 10 minutes.

CHICKEN SATAY

2. In a small bowl, whisk the sauce ingredients until blended. Cover and refrigerate until serving. Drain and discard marinade. Thread two chicken strips onto each metal or soaked wooden skewer.

3. Grill, uncovered, over medium-hot heat for 2-3 minutes on each side or until chicken juices run clear. Serve with peanut butter sauce.

NOTE *Wear disposable gloves when cutting hot peppers; the oils can burn skin. Avoid touching your face.*

LIME HERB CHICKEN

This tangy chicken recipe uses pantry staples, which is convenient for a weeknight meal. Lime juice is key to its bright, refreshing flavor.

—**JENNIFER PARTIN** REPTON, AL

PREP: 15 MIN. + MARINATING
GRILL: 40 MIN. • **MAKES:** 6 SERVINGS

- 1 cup lime juice
- ⅔ cup Italian salad dressing
- 2 teaspoons minced garlic
- 2 teaspoons dried basil
- 1 teaspoon dried thyme
- ½ teaspoon salt
- ½ teaspoon pepper
- 1 broiler/fryer chicken (3 to 4 pounds), cut up

1. In a large bowl, combine the first seven ingredients. Pour 1 cup marinade into a large resealable plastic bag; add the chicken. Seal bag and turn to coat; marinate for 15 minutes. Set aside remaining marinade for basting.

2. Drain and discard marinade. Grill chicken, covered, over medium heat for 40-45 minutes or until juices run clear, basting occasionally with ½ cup reserved marinade. Brush the remaining marinade over chicken just before serving.

CHICKEN SATAY

These golden skewered chicken snacks are marinated and grilled, then served with a zesty Thai-style peanut butter sauce.

—**SUE GRONHOLZ** BEAVER DAM, WI

PREP: 15 MIN. + MARINATING • **GRILL:** 5 MIN.
MAKES: 8 SERVINGS (1 CUP SAUCE)

- 2 pounds boneless skinless chicken breasts
- ½ cup 2% milk
- 6 garlic cloves, minced
- 1 tablespoon brown sugar
- 1 tablespoon each ground coriander, ground turmeric and ground cumin
- 1 teaspoon salt
- 1 teaspoon white pepper
- ⅛ teaspoon coconut extract

PEANUT BUTTER SAUCE
- ⅓ cup peanut butter
- ⅓ cup 2% milk
- 2 green onions, chopped
- 1 small jalapeno pepper, seeded and finely chopped
- 2 to 3 tablespoons lime juice
- 2 tablespoons reduced-sodium soy sauce
- 1 garlic clove, minced
- 1 teaspoon sugar
- 1 teaspoon minced fresh cilantro
- 1 teaspoon minced fresh gingerroot
- ⅛ teaspoon coconut extract

1. Flatten chicken to ¼-in. thickness; cut lengthwise into 1-in.-wide strips. In a large resealable plastic bag, combine milk, garlic, brown sugar, seasonings and extract. Add the chicken; seal bag and turn to coat. Refrigerate for 8 hours or overnight.

FAST FIX

TAPENADE-STUFFED CHICKEN BREASTS

I created this recipe for my husband, who absolutely loves olives. I usually make a larger batch of the olive tapenade and serve it with bread or crackers as a snack or appetizer.

—JESSICA LEVINSON NYACK, NY

START TO FINISH: 30 MIN. • **MAKES:** 4 SERVINGS

- 4 **oil-packed sun-dried tomatoes**
- 4 **pitted Greek olives**
- 4 **pitted Spanish olives**
- 4 **pitted ripe olives**
- ¼ **cup roasted sweet red peppers, drained**
- 4 **garlic cloves, minced**
- 1 **tablespoon olive oil**
- 2 **teaspoons balsamic vinegar**
- 4 **boneless skinless chicken breast halves (6 ounces each)**
  Grated Parmesan cheese

1. Place the first eight ingredients in a food processor; pulse until tomatoes and olives are coarsely chopped. Cut a pocket horizontally in the thickest part of each chicken breast. Fill with olive mixture; secure with toothpicks.

2. Moisten a paper towel with cooking oil; using long-handled tongs, rub on grill rack to coat lightly. Grill chicken, covered, over medium heat or broil 4 in. from heat 8-10 minutes on each side or until a thermometer inserted in stuffing reads 165°. Sprinkle with cheese. Discard toothpicks before serving.

TAPENADE-STUFFED CHICKEN BREASTS

GRILL SKILL

Before broiling up dinner the first time of the season, make sure to clean the entire grill as well as possible. Check the manufacturer's directions for the best way to do this, because if the grill is not cleaned properly, it could start a fire from built-up grease on the bottom and/or sides of the grill. Take out and clean the grill grate, the burners and grease trap. Replace any aluminum foil drip pans or grease traps as well.

CHICKEN & VEGETABLE KABOBS

In the summer, my husband and I love to cook out, and we especially enjoy grilling vegetables. These kabobs not only taste delicious but they look great, too!

—**TINA OLES** NASHWAUK, MN

START TO FINISH: 30 MIN.
MAKES: 4 SERVINGS

- 1 **pound boneless skinless chicken breasts, cut into 1½-inch cubes**
- 1 **medium sweet red pepper, cut into 1½-inch pieces**
- 1 **medium zucchini, cut into 1½-inch pieces**
- 1 **medium red onion, cut into thick wedges**
- ⅔ **cup sun-dried tomato salad dressing, divided**

1. In a large bowl, combine chicken and vegetables. Drizzle with ⅓ cup dressing and toss to coat. Alternately thread chicken and vegetables onto four metal or soaked wooden skewers.

2. Grill the kabobs, covered, over medium heat or broil 4 in. from heat 8-10 minutes or until chicken is no longer pink, turning occasionally and basting with remaining dressing during the last 3 minutes.

CHICKEN & VEGETABLE KABOBS

**APPLE-MARINATED
CHICKEN & VEGETABLES**

BOMBAY CHICKEN

This barbecue dinner always turns out moist and tender. The marinade has a slightly exotic flair, giving the chicken a robust flavor.
—**JUNE THOMAS** CHESTERTON, IN

PREP: 10 MIN. + MARINATING • **GRILL:** 25 MIN.
MAKES: 8 SERVINGS

- 1½ **cups (12 ounces) plain yogurt**
- ¼ **cup lemon juice**
- 2 **tablespoons chili powder**
- 2 **tablespoons paprika**
- 2 **tablespoons olive oil**
- 1½ **teaspoons salt**
- ½ **to 1 teaspoon cayenne pepper**
- ½ **teaspoon garlic powder**
- ¼ **teaspoon ground ginger**
- ¼ **teaspoon ground cardamom**
- ⅛ **teaspoon ground cinnamon**
- 4 **to 5 pounds bone-in chicken thighs and legs, skin removed**

1. In a large resealable plastic bag, combine the first 11 ingredients. Add the chicken; seal bag and turn to coat. Refrigerate overnight.

2. Moisten a paper towel with cooking oil; using long-handled tongs, lightly coat the grill rack or coat with cooking spray before starting the grill. Drain and discard marinade.

3. Grill chicken, covered, over medium-hot heat for 10-15 minutes on each side or until a thermometer reads 180°.

BOMBAY CHICKEN

APPLE-MARINATED CHICKEN & VEGETABLES

I actually created this at a campground, so you know it's easy. Using the same marinade for the chicken and veggies keeps it simple so we can spend more time outside and less time making dinner.
—**JAYME SCHERTZ** CLINTONVILLE, WI

PREP: 20 MIN. + MARINATING • **GRILL:** 25 MIN.
MAKES: 6 SERVINGS

- 1 **cup apple juice**
- ½ **cup canola oil**
- ¼ **cup packed brown sugar**
- ¼ **cup reduced-sodium soy sauce**
- 3 **tablespoons lemon juice**
- 2 **tablespoons minced fresh parsley**
- 3 **garlic cloves, minced**
- 6 **boneless skinless chicken breast halves (6 ounces each)**
- 4 **large carrots**
- 2 **medium zucchini**
- 2 **medium yellow summer squash**

1. In a small bowl, whisk the first seven ingredients until blended. Place 1 cup marinade and chicken in a large resealable plastic bag; seal bag and turn to coat. Refrigerate 6 hours or overnight. Cover and refrigerate remaining marinade.

2. Cut carrots, zucchini and squash lengthwise into quarters; cut crosswise into 2-in. pieces. Toss with ½ cup reserved marinade.

3. Drain chicken, discarding marinade in bag. Grill chicken, covered, over medium heat or broil 4 in. from heat 6-8 minutes on each side or until a thermometer reads 165°, basting frequently with remaining marinade during the last 5 minutes. Keep warm.

4. Transfer vegetables to a grill wok or basket; place on grill rack. Grill, covered, over medium heat for 10-12 minutes or until crisp-tender, stirring frequently. Serve with chicken.

LIP-SMACKIN'
BBQ CHICKEN

LIP-SMACKIN' BBQ CHICKEN

When we have friends over for barbecued chicken, the kids always say, "Prepare to lick your lips!" This is the first recipe I ever created, and I'm proud to say that it's also one of my best.
—**SUE THOMAS** MOORE, SC

PREP: 1¼ HOURS • **GRILL:** 25 MIN.
MAKES: 12 SERVINGS

- 2 **cups ketchup**
- 1 **cup cider vinegar**
- 1 **cup water**
- ¼ **cup packed brown sugar**
- ¼ **cup reduced-sodium soy sauce**
- ¼ **cup molasses**
- ¼ **cup honey**
- 2 **tablespoons prepared mustard**
- 3 **teaspoons ground cumin**
- ¼ **teaspoon salt**
- ¼ **teaspoon pepper**
- 6 **pounds assorted bone-in chicken pieces**

1. In a large saucepan, combine the first 11 ingredients; bring to a boil. Reduce heat; simmer, uncovered, 1-1½ hours or until thickened, stirring occasionally. Remove half of the sauce; reserve for brushing chicken. Keep remaining sauce warm for serving.

2. Grill chicken, covered, over medium heat 25-35 minutes or until juices run clear, turning occasionally and brushing with reserved sauce during the last 10 minutes. Serve with remaining sauce.

GRILLED BROWN SUGAR-MUSTARD CHICKEN

⑤INGREDIENTS FAST FIX

GRILLED BROWN SUGAR-MUSTARD CHICKEN

I came up with this recipe in college, and it's been a household staple ever since. I throw it together in a snap with items I usually have on hand.
—**KENDRA DOSS** COLORADO SPRINGS, CO

START TO FINISH: 20 MIN.
MAKES: 8 SERVINGS

- ½ **cup yellow or Dijon mustard**
- ⅓ **cup packed brown sugar**
- ½ **teaspoon ground allspice**
- ¼ **teaspoon crushed red pepper flakes**
- 8 **boneless skinless chicken thighs (about 2 pounds)**

1. In a large bowl, mix mustard, brown sugar, allspice and pepper flakes. Remove ¼ cup mixture for serving. Add chicken to remaining mixture; toss to coat.

2. Grill chicken, covered, over medium heat or broil 4 in. from heat 6-8 minutes on each side or until a thermometer reads 170°. Serve with reserved mustard mixture.

HONEY ORANGE CHICKEN

I couldn't get enough of the sweet-and-citrusy marinade that flavors this grilled chicken, so I saved some to drizzle on top.
—**MARY HART EASTERLING**
SANTA CLARITA, CA

PREP: 15 MIN. + MARINATING
GRILL: 15 MIN. • **MAKES:** 4 SERVINGS

- 1 cup chicken broth
- 1 cup orange juice
- ½ cup honey
- 1 tablespoon lemon juice
- 1 tablespoon cider vinegar
- 1 tablespoon reduced-sodium soy sauce
- 1 teaspoon grated orange peel
- 1 teaspoon ground ginger
- ½ teaspoon salt
- 4 bone-in chicken breast halves (10 ounces each)
- 1 tablespoon cornstarch
- 2 tablespoons water
- 4 cups hot cooked rice
  Chopped green onions, orange slices and parsley sprigs, optional

1. In a saucepan, combine the first nine ingredients. Bring to a boil. Remove from heat; cool. Pour 1⅓ cups marinade into a large resealable plastic bag; add chicken. Seal bag and turn to coat; refrigerate for 4-8 hours or overnight, turning occasionally. Cover and refrigerate remaining marinade.
2. Drain chicken, discarding marinade. Grill, covered, over medium heat for 12-15 minutes on each side or until juices run clear. Meanwhile, combine cornstarch and water in a small saucepan until smooth; stir in reserved marinade. Bring to a boil; cook and stir for 2 minutes or until thickened.
3. Remove and discard skin from chicken. Serve chicken over rice; drizzle with sauce. Garnish with green onions, orange slices and parsley if desired.

GRILLED CORNISH HENS

GRILLED CORNISH HENS

I like experimenting with different foods and adapting them to my own tastes. These hens are one of my specialties, an entree I concocted by combining a few different recipes. The moist meat has a pleasant grilled flavor that's accented with cloves and ginger.
—**DAVID BARUCH** WESTON, FL

PREP: 15 MIN. • **GRILL:** 50 MIN.
MAKES: 4 SERVINGS

- ¼ cup butter, softened
- 2 green onions, finely chopped
- 2 tablespoons minced fresh parsley
- 2 tablespoons grated fresh gingerroot
- 3 garlic cloves, minced
- 1 teaspoon salt, divided
- ½ teaspoon pepper, divided
- 4 Cornish game hens (20 to 24 ounces each)

1. In a small bowl, combine the butter, green onions, minced parsley, grated ginger, garlic, ½ teaspoon salt and ¼ teaspoon pepper.
2. Rub mixture under the skin and over the top of each game hen. Sprinkle remaining salt and pepper inside the hen cavities.
3. Using long-handled tongs, moisten a paper towel with cooking oil and lightly coat the grill rack. Prepare grill for indirect heat, using a drip pan.
4. Place hens breast side up over drip pan; grill, covered, over indirect medium heat for 45-60 minutes or until a thermometer reads 180° and the meat juices run clear.

GRILLED TURKEY TENDERLOIN

"This turkey melts in your mouth," is what my guests say whenever they bite into my grilled specialty.

—DENISE NEBEL WAYLAND, IA

PREP: 5 MIN. + MARINATING • **GRILL:** 20 MIN.
MAKES: 4 SERVINGS

- ¼ **cup apple juice**
- ¼ **cup reduced-sodium soy sauce**
- ¼ **cup canola oil**
- 2 **tablespoons lemon juice**
- 2 **tablespoons dried minced onion**
- 1 **teaspoon vanilla extract**
- ¼ **teaspoon ground ginger**
  Dash each garlic powder and pepper
- 2 **turkey breast tenderloins (½ pound each)**

1. In a large resealable plastic bag, combine the apple juice, soy sauce, oil, lemon juice, onion, vanilla, ginger, garlic powder and pepper; add the turkey. Seal bag and turn to coat. Refrigerate for at least 2 hours.

2. Drain and discard marinade. Grill turkey, covered, over medium heat for 8-10 minutes on each side or until a thermometer reads 170°.

GRILLED TURKEY TENDERLOIN

SOUTHERN BARBECUED CHICKEN

Nothing says Texas like outdoor grilling. And summer is a prime time for patio picnics featuring my barbecued chicken. Friends are surprised to find the basis for my "mystery marinade" is simply a little vinegar and oil.

—REVONDA STROUD FORT WORTH, TX

PREP: 25 MIN. + MARINATING • **GRILL:** 40 MIN.
MAKES: 4 SERVINGS

- 2 **cups cider vinegar**
- 1 **cup canola oil**
- 1 **large egg, lightly beaten**
- 2 **tablespoons hot pepper sauce**
- 1 **tablespoon garlic powder**
- 1 **tablespoon poultry seasoning**
- 2 **teaspoons salt**
- 1 **teaspoon pepper**
- 1 **broiler/fryer chicken (3 to 4 pounds), cut up**

1. In a large saucepan, combine the first eight ingredients. Bring to a boil, stirring constantly. Reduce heat; simmer, uncovered, for 10 minutes, stirring often. Cool.

2. Pour 1⅔ cups marinade into a large resealable plastic bag; add the chicken. Seal bag and turn to coat; refrigerate overnight, turning occasionally. Cover and refrigerate the remaining marinade for basting.

3. Prepare grill for indirect heat, using a drip pan. Drain and discard marinade from chicken. Place skin side down over pan. Grill, covered, over indirect medium heat for 20-25 minutes on each side or until juices run clear, basting occasionally with reserved marinade.

**SMOKY
GRILLED CHICKEN**

SMOKY GRILLED CHICKEN

Instant coffee is the secret to my sweet and spicy barbecue sauce. Don't be surprised when folks tell you this is the best chicken they've ever had!

—**KATHY WHIPPLE** TWIN FALLS, ID

PREP: 5 MIN. • **GRILL:** 45 MIN.
MAKES: 4 SERVINGS

- ¼ **cup packed brown sugar**
- 1 **tablespoon ground mustard**
- 1 **tablespoon instant coffee granules**
- ½ **cup hot water**
- 1 **bottle (14 ounces) ketchup**
- 1 **tablespoon Worcestershire sauce**
- 1 **tablespoon liquid smoke, optional**
- 1 **broiler/fryer chicken (3½-4 pounds), quartered**

1. In a large bowl, dissolve sugar, mustard and coffee in hot water. Stir in ketchup, Worcestershire sauce, and liquid smoke if desired. Reserve 1 cup for basting; refrigerate the remaining sauce.

2. Moisten a paper towel with cooking oil; using long-handled tongs, lightly coat the grill rack with oil. Grill the chicken, covered, over medium heat, for 30 minutes, turning and basting with sauce frequently. Grill, covered, 15 minutes longer, turning and basting occasionally or until juices run clear. Serve with reserved sauce.

 **GRILL SKILL**

Lots of barbecue recipes call for mustard. Ground mustard (referred to as "dry mustard" in some recipes) is made from mustard seeds that have been finely ground. When a recipe calls for prepared mustard, use yellow or brown mustard commonly served as a condiment.

SESAME CHICKEN BREASTS

The aroma and flavor of grilled food really says "summer" to me. I even take leftovers from this dish and turn them into crisp entree salads or toss them into pasta.

—**CATHERINE ALLAN** TWIN FALLS, ID

PREP: 10 MIN. + MARINATING • **GRILL:** 15 MIN.
MAKES: 12 SERVINGS

- 1 **cup olive oil**
- 1 **cup white grape juice**
- 1 **cup soy sauce**
- 1 **cup chopped green onions**
- ⅓ **cup sesame seeds, toasted**
- 2 **tablespoons ground mustard**
- 2 **tablespoons grated fresh gingerroot**
- 2 **teaspoons pepper**
- 8 **garlic cloves, minced**
- 12 **boneless skinless chicken breast halves (4 ounces each)**

1. In a large resealable plastic bag, combine the first nine ingredients. Remove ½ cup for basting; cover and refrigerate. Add chicken to the bags; seal and turn to coat. Refrigerate for 6-8 hours.

2. Drain and discard marinade from chicken. Grill, covered, over medium heat for 6-8 minutes on each side or until a thermometer reads 170°, basting occasionally with reserved marinade.

CITRUS GRILLED TURKEY BREAST

Instead of the usual outdoor fare, treat your guests to a sit-down dinner featuring this delicious grilled entree with a luscious herb-and-citrus gravy.

—**TASTE OF HOME** TEST KITCHEN

PREP: 10 MIN. • **GRILL:** 1½ HOURS + STANDING
MAKES: 10-12 SERVINGS

- 1 **bone-in turkey breast (5 to 6 pounds)**
- ¼ **cup fresh parsley sprigs**
- ¼ **cup fresh basil leaves**
- 3 **tablespoons butter**
- 4 **garlic cloves, halved**
- ½ **teaspoon salt**

- 1 **medium lemon, thinly sliced**
- 1 **medium orange, thinly sliced**
- 1 **tablespoon cornstarch**
- 2 **tablespoons water**
- 1 **cup orange juice**
- 1 **teaspoon grated orange peel**
- 1 **teaspoon grated lemon peel**
- ¼ **teaspoon pepper**

1. Using fingers, carefully loosen the skin from both sides of turkey breast. In a food processor or blender, combine the parsley, basil, butter, garlic and salt; cover and process until smooth. Spread under turkey skin; arrange lemon and orange slices over herb mixture. Secure the skin to the underside of the breast with toothpicks.

2. Using long-handled tongs, moisten a paper towel with cooking oil and lightly coat the grill rack. Prepare grill for indirect heat, using a drip pan.

3. Place turkey over drip pan. Grill, covered, over indirect medium heat for 1½-2 hours or until a thermometer reads 170°. Cover and let stand for 10 minutes.

4. Meanwhile, pour pan drippings into a measuring cup; skim fat. In a small saucepan, combine cornstarch and water until smooth. Add the orange juice, orange peel, lemon peel, pepper and pan drippings. Bring to a boil; cook and stir for 2 minutes or until thickened.

5. Discard the skin, lemon and orange slices from turkey breast. Remove herb mixture from turkey; stir into gravy. Slice turkey and serve with gravy.

**MAPLE-THYME
CHICKEN THIGHS**

GRILLED THIGHS AND DRUMSTICKS

This chicken is juicy, has great barbecue flavor and makes a big batch, so it's just perfect for all of our summer picnics and family reunions.

—**BRENDA BEACHY** BELVIDERE, TN

PREP: 10 MIN. + MARINATING • **GRILL:** 30 MIN.
MAKES: 12-14 SERVINGS

- 2½ **cups packed brown sugar**
- 2 **cups water**
- 2 **cups cider vinegar**
- 2 **cups ketchup**
- 1 **cup canola oil**
- 4 **tablespoons salt**
- 3 **tablespoons prepared mustard**
- 4½ **teaspoons Worcestershire sauce**
- 1 **tablespoon reduced-sodium soy sauce**
- 1 **teaspoon pepper**
- 1 **teaspoon Liquid Smoke, optional**
- 10 **pounds bone-in chicken thighs and chicken drumsticks**
- ½ **teaspoon seasoned salt**

1. In a large bowl, combine the first 11 ingredients. Pour into two large resealable plastic bags; add equal amounts of chicken to each bag. Seal the bags and turn to coat; refrigerate overnight.
2. Drain and discard marinade. Prepare grill for indirect heat. Using long-handled tongs, moisten a paper towel with cooking oil and lightly coat the grill rack. Sprinkle chicken with seasoned salt. Grill chicken skin side down, covered, over indirect medium heat for 15-20 minutes on each side or until a thermometer reads 170°-175°.

(5) INGREDIENTS **FAST FIX**

MAPLE-THYME CHICKEN THIGHS

We eat a lot of chicken at our house, and figuring out different ways to serve it gets challenging. My family went nuts for the cozy maple flavor in this recipe, so now I share it at potlucks, too.

—**LORRAINE CALAND** SHUNIAH, ON

START TO FINISH: 15 MIN.
MAKES: 6 SERVINGS

- 2 **tablespoons stone-ground mustard**
- 2 **tablespoons maple syrup**
- 1 **teaspoon minced fresh thyme or ½ teaspoon dried thyme**
- ½ **teaspoon salt**
- ½ **teaspoon pepper**
- 6 **boneless skinless chicken thighs (about 1½ pounds)**

1. In a small bowl, mix the first five ingredients. Moisten a paper towel with cooking oil; using long-handled tongs, rub on grill rack to coat lightly.
2. Grill chicken, covered, over medium heat 4-5 minutes on each side or until a thermometer reads 170°. Brush frequently with mustard mixture during the last 4 minutes of cooking.

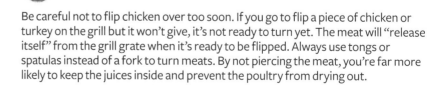 **GRILL SKILL**

Be careful not to flip chicken over too soon. If you go to flip a piece of chicken or turkey on the grill but it won't give, it's not ready to turn yet. The meat will "release itself" from the grill grate when it's ready to be flipped. Always use tongs or spatulas instead of a fork to turn meats. By not piercing the meat, you're far more likely to keep the juices inside and prevent the poultry from drying out.

KIELBASA CHICKEN KABOBS

You can substitute orange juice for the pineapple juice or beef for the chicken. Just about any veggie, especially mushrooms, works well.

—CRISTI SMAY CLEARFIELD, PA

PREP: 20 MIN. + MARINATING • **GRILL:** 20 MIN.
MAKES: 16 KABOBS

- ¾ **cup unsweetened pineapple juice**
- ¼ **cup cider vinegar**
- ¼ **cup canola oil**
- 2 **tablespoons sugar**
- 2 **tablespoons soy sauce**
- ½ **teaspoon garlic powder**
- ¼ **teaspoon lemon-pepper seasoning**
- 2 **pounds boneless skinless chicken breasts, cut into 1-inch cubes**
- 1 **pound smoked kielbasa or Polish sausage, thickly sliced**
- 1 **can (20 ounces) unsweetened pineapple chunks, drained**
- 2 **medium green peppers, quartered**
- 2 **cups grape tomatoes**
- 2 **medium red onions, quartered**

1. In a small bowl, combine the first seven ingredients. Remove ½ cup for basting; cover and refrigerate. Divide remaining marinade between two large resealable plastic bags. Add chicken to one bag; add the kielbasa, pineapple and vegetables to the other bag. Seal bags and turn to coat; refrigerate for at least 2 hours.

2. On 16 metal or soaked wooden skewers, alternately thread the chicken, kielbasa, pineapple and vegetables.

3. Using long-handled tongs, moisten a paper towel with cooking oil and lightly coat the grill rack. Grill kabobs, covered, over medium heat or broil 4 in. from the heat for 10-15 minutes or until chicken is no longer pink, turning frequently and basting with reserved marinade.

KIELBASA CHICKEN KABOBS

CHINESE TAKEOUT-ON-A-STICK

FAST FIX

CHINESE TAKEOUT-ON-A-STICK

I like to serve chicken and broccoli with rice, along with a side of pineapple or other fresh fruit. Leftovers, if there are any, are great the next day when used in a salad or wrapped in a flour tortilla with a little mayonnaise.

—BETHANY SEELEY WARWICK, RI

START TO FINISH: 30 MIN.
MAKES: 4 SERVINGS

- 3 tablespoons reduced-sodium soy sauce
- 3 tablespoons sesame oil
- 4 teaspoons brown sugar
- 4 teaspoons minced fresh gingerroot
- 2 garlic cloves, minced
- ½ teaspoon crushed red pepper flakes
- 1 pound boneless skinless chicken breasts, cut into 1-inch cubes
- 3 cups fresh broccoli florets

1. In a large bowl, combine the first six ingredients; remove 3 tablespoons for basting. Add chicken to remaining soy sauce mixture; toss to coat. On four metal or soaked wooden skewers, alternately thread chicken and broccoli.
2. Moisten a paper towel with cooking oil; using long-handled tongs, lightly coat the grill rack. Grill skewers, covered, over medium heat or broil 4 in. from the heat for 10-15 minutes or until chicken is no longer pink, turning occasionally; baste with reserved soy mixture during the last 4 minutes of cooking.

BRAZILIAN-STYLE TURKEY WITH HAM

Grilling is a different and fun way to prepare whole turkey. My mom has served this main dish for special occasions, Christmas in July and weddings at her home.

—CAROL MARRIOTT CENTREVILLE, VA

PREP: 30 MIN. + MARINATING
BAKE: 2 HOURS AND 30 MIN. + STANDING
MAKES: 16 SERVINGS

- 1 **whole turkey (12 pounds)**
- 4½ **teaspoons salt**
- 2 **teaspoons pepper**
- 3 **garlic cloves, minced**
- 1½ **cups white vinegar**
- 1 **cup olive oil**
- 4 **medium tomatoes, seeded and chopped**
- 4 **medium green peppers, seeded and chopped**
- ½ **cup minced fresh parsley**
- 2 **pounds smoked ham, thinly sliced**

1. Remove giblets from turkey and discard. Place a turkey-size oven roasting bag inside a second roasting bag; add turkey. Place in a roasting pan. Combine the salt, pepper and garlic; rub over turkey.

2. In a large bowl, combine the vinegar, oil, tomatoes, peppers and parsley. Pour over turkey and into cavity. Squeeze out as much air as possible from the bag; seal and turn to coat. Refrigerate for 12-24 hours, turning several times.

3. Drain and discard marinade. Skewer turkey openings; tie drumsticks together. Prepare grill for indirect heat, using a drip pan. Using long-handled tongs, moisten a paper towel with cooking oil and lightly coat the grill rack.

4. Place turkey over drip pan and grill, covered, over indirect medium heat for 2-2½ hours or until a thermometer reads 180°, tenting turkey with foil after about 1 hour.

5. Let stand for 20 minutes before slicing. Meanwhile, warm the ham. Layer turkey and ham slices on a serving platter.

MARGARITA CHICKEN

⑤ INGREDIENTS

MARGARITA CHICKEN

Marinated in the flavors of garlic and lime, this tangy chicken is ready to go whenever the coals are hot! Serve with roasted corn on the cob and lemonade for summer dining at its most relaxed.

—KELLY BRUNEMAN CEDAR PARK, TX

PREP: 10 MIN. + MARINATING • **GRILL:** 10 MIN.
MAKES: 4 SERVINGS

- 1 **can (10 ounces) frozen non-alcoholic margarita mix, thawed**
- 3 **tablespoons lime juice**
- 3 **garlic cloves, minced**
- 4 **boneless skinless chicken breast halves (6 ounces each)**
- ¼ **teaspoon salt**
- ¼ **teaspoon pepper**

1. In a small bowl, combine the margarita mix, lime juice and garlic. Pour 1 cup marinade into a large resealable plastic bag. Add the chicken; seal bag and turn to coat. Refrigerate for 2-4 hours. Cover and refrigerate remaining marinade.

2. Drain and discard marinade. Sprinkle chicken with salt and pepper. Using long-handled tongs, moisten a paper towel with cooking oil and lightly coat the grill rack.

3. Grill the chicken, covered, over medium heat or broil 4 in. from the heat for 5-7 minutes on each side or until a thermometer reads 160°, basting frequently with reserved marinade.

PINEAPPLE TERIYAKI CHICKEN

(5) INGREDIENTS

PINEAPPLE TERIYAKI CHICKEN

I like to marinate this delicious chicken entree overnight, then pop it on the grill for a breezy taste of the islands that my family and friends really love.
—**VICKI ROBERTS** JACKSONVILLE, FL

PREP: 10 MIN. + MARINATING • **GRILL:** 15 MIN.
MAKES: 4 SERVINGS

- 1 can (20 ounces) sliced pineapple
- ½ cup teriyaki sauce
- 4 boneless skinless chicken breast halves (4 ounces each)
- 4 slices provolone cheese (1 ounce each)

1. Drain pineapple, reserving juice; refrigerate pineapple. In a small bowl, combine teriyaki sauce and reserved juice. Pour ¾ cup marinade into a large resealable plastic bag; add chicken. Seal bag and turn to coat. Refrigerate for 8 hours or overnight. Cover and refrigerate the remaining marinade for basting.
2. Drain and discard marinade. Grill the chicken, covered, over medium heat or broil 4 in. from the heat for 4-6 minutes on each side or until a thermometer reads 170°, basting frequently with some of the remaining marinade.

3. Grill eight pineapple slices for 2 minutes on each side or until lightly browned, basting with remaining marinade (save remaining pineapple for another use).
4. Top each piece of chicken with cheese and two pineapple slices. Grill, covered, for 1-2 minutes or until cheese is melted.

CURRIED PEANUT CHICKEN

This is a nice change from traditional grilled items. I sprinkle coconut and currants over a tasty combination of chicken and peppers.
—**JENNIFER MYERS** HAVERTOWN, PA

PREP: 15 MIN. + MARINATING • **GRILL:** 10 MIN.
MAKES: 4 SERVINGS

- 1½ cups orange juice
- ¾ cup peanut butter
- 2 tablespoons curry powder
- 4 boneless skinless chicken breast halves (6 ounces each)
- 2 medium sweet red peppers, cut in half
- ¼ cup flaked coconut, toasted
- ¼ cup dried currants
  Hot cooked rice

1. In a small bowl, combine the orange juice, peanut butter and curry powder. Pour ⅔ cup marinade into a large resealable plastic bag; add chicken. Seal bag and turn to coat; refrigerate for 8 hours or overnight. Cover and refrigerate remaining marinade.
2. Drain chicken and discard marinade. Grill chicken and peppers, covered, over medium heat for 5-8 minutes on each side or until a thermometer reads 165° and peppers are tender.
3. Warm the reserved marinade. Cut chicken and peppers into ½-in. strips; sprinkle with coconut and currants. Serve with rice and reserved marinade.

CILANTRO & LEMON MARINATED CHICKEN SKEWERS

I like to grill the onions in this recipe first so there's plenty of room for the chicken skewers. Give the whole platter a spritz of lemon for a sunshiny delight.
—**MOUMITA GHOSH** KOLKATA, WEST BENGAL

PREP: 40 MIN. + MARINATING • **GRILL:** 20 MIN.
MAKES: 6 SERVINGS

- 1½ pounds boneless skinless chicken breasts, cut into 1-inch pieces
- 3 tablespoons lemon juice
- 1½ teaspoons salt
- ½ cup water
- ¼ cup plain yogurt
- 1 cup fresh cilantro leaves
- ⅓ cup fresh mint leaves
- 2 serrano peppers, sliced
- 1 piece fresh gingerroot (1 inch), coarsely chopped
- 4 garlic cloves, sliced
- 3 medium sweet onions, cut crosswise into ½-inch slices
- 4 tablespoons canola oil, divided
  Lemon wedges

1. In a large bowl, toss chicken with lemon juice and salt; let stand 15 minutes. Meanwhile, place water, yogurt, herbs, peppers, ginger and garlic in a blender; cover and process until smooth. Stir into chicken mixture; refrigerate, covered, 2 hours.
2. Moisten a paper towel with cooking oil; using long-handled tongs, rub on grill rack to coat lightly. Brush onions with 2 tablespoons oil. Grill, covered, over medium heat or broil 4 in. from heat 10-12 minutes or until tender, turning occasionally.
3. Remove chicken from marinade; discard marinade. Thread chicken onto six metal or soaked wooden skewers. Grill, covered, over medium heat or broil 4 in. from heat 10-12 minutes or until chicken is no longer pink, turning occasionally and brushing with remaining oil during the last 4 minutes. Serve with onions and lemon wedges.

CILANTRO & LEMON
MARINATED CHICKEN
SKEWERS

SOUTHWESTERN SKEWERS

Garlic and spices dress up a store-bought vinaigrette for this recipe's spicy, quick-to-make marinade. These kabobs have a nice kick.

—**LARRY SMITH** YOUNGSTOWN, OH

PREP: 20 MIN. + MARINATING • **GRILL:** 10 MIN.
MAKES: 4 SERVINGS

- 1 **bottle (8 ounces) reduced-fat Italian salad dressing**
- 10 **garlic cloves, minced**
- 1 **teaspoon white pepper**
- 1 **teaspoon chili powder**
- 1 **teaspoon ground cumin**
- 1 **teaspoon paprika**
- ½ **teaspoon cayenne pepper**
- 1 **medium green pepper, cut into 1-inch pieces**
- 1 **medium sweet red pepper, cut into 1-inch pieces**
- 1 **medium onion, cut into 1-inch pieces**
- 8 **large fresh mushrooms**
- 8 **cherry tomatoes**
- 1 **pound boneless skinless chicken breasts, cut into 1-inch cubes**

1. In a large bowl, combine the first seven ingredients. Pour half into a large resealable plastic bag; add vegetables. Seal bag and turn to coat. Pour the remaining marinade into another large resealable plastic bag; add chicken. Seal bag and turn to coat. Refrigerate vegetables and chicken for at least 2-3 hours.

2. Drain chicken, discarding marinade. Drain vegetables, reserving marinade for basting. On eight metal or soaked wooden skewers, alternately thread chicken and vegetables.

3. Using long-handled tongs, moisten a paper towel with cooking oil and lightly coat the grill rack. Grill, covered, over medium heat or broil 4 in. from the heat for 6-8 minutes on each side or until chicken is no longer pink and vegetables are tender, basting frequently with reserved marinade.

CITRUS CHICKEN WITH SALSA

CITRUS CHICKEN WITH SALSA

I know summer has arrived when I make this grilled chicken dish with all its fresh ingredients. The salsa is bursting with zesty flavor!

—**JULIE SIMPSON** NORTH AURORA, IL

PREP: 25 MIN. + MARINATING • **GRILL:** 10 MIN.
MAKES: 4 SERVINGS (3 CUPS SALSA)

- ¼ **cup lemon juice**
- 2 **tablespoons lime juice**
- 2 **tablespoons orange juice**
- 1 **tablespoon canola oil**
- 1 **teaspoon sugar**
- ½ **teaspoon dried oregano**
- ½ **teaspoon salt**
- ¼ **teaspoon pepper**
- 4 **boneless skinless chicken breast halves (4 ounces each)**

TOMATO-PINEAPPLE SALSA

- 4 **plum tomatoes, chopped**
- 1 **cup cubed fresh pineapple**
- ½ **cup chopped sweet red pepper**
- ⅓ **cup chopped red onion**
- ¼ **cup lime juice**
- 3 **tablespoons minced fresh cilantro**
- 1 **jalapeno pepper, seeded and finely chopped**

1. In a large resealable plastic bag, combine the first eight ingredients; add chicken. Seal bag and turn to coat; refrigerate for 4 hours. Meanwhile, in a small bowl, combine salsa ingredients. Cover and refrigerate until serving.

2. Drain and discard marinade. Grill chicken, covered, over medium heat for 5-6 minutes on each side or until a thermometer reads 170°. Serve with salsa.

NOTE *Wear disposable gloves when cutting hot peppers; the oils can burn skin. Avoid touching your face.*

HONEY-CILANTRO GAME HENS

I love to cook and bake just about everything, but grilling is my specialty. These game hens pick up wonderful flavor from a sweet and refreshing marinade.

—KRISS ERICKSON KALAUEA, HI

PREP: 5 MIN. + MARINATING • **GRILL:** 35 MIN.
MAKES: 4 SERVINGS

- 2 **Cornish game hens (20 to 24 ounces each), split lengthwise**
- ½ **cup olive oil**
- ⅔ **cup white wine vinegar**
- 8 **garlic cloves, minced**
- ⅓ **cup minced fresh cilantro**
- ⅓ **cup honey**
- ⅓ **cup reduced-sodium soy sauce**
- 2 **to 3 tablespoons ground ginger**
- ½ **teaspoon crushed red pepper flakes**
  Dash pepper

1. Place hens in a large resealable plastic bag. In a small bowl, combine the remaining ingredients. Pour half into bag; add the hens. Seal bag and turn to coat. Refrigerate for at least 1 hour. Cover and refrigerate the remaining marinade.

2. Drain and discard marinade from hens. Place hens in a 13x9-in. aluminum pan. Pour reserved marinade over hens; cover pan.

3. Grill, covered, over medium-hot heat for 35-40 minutes or until a thermometer reads 180° and meat juices run clear, basting frequently.

4. Place hens directly over heat for the last 3-4 minutes of cooking time, turning once.

HONEY-CILANTRO GAME HENS

ORANGE CHICKEN AND VEGGIES

Here's a summer dish with a tasty twist! A mild maple marinade seasons the chicken, vegetables and fruit in this delightfully seasonal supper.

—VIOLET KLAUSE ONOWAY, AB

PREP: 15 MIN. + MARINATING • **GRILL:** 15 MIN.
MAKES: 6 SERVINGS

- 1 **can (6 ounces) frozen orange juice concentrate, thawed**
- ¾ **cup maple syrup**
- 4 **teaspoons canola oil**
- ¾ **teaspoon curry powder**
- ¼ **teaspoon cayenne pepper**
- 6 **boneless skinless chicken breast halves (1½ pounds)**
- 2 **medium sweet red peppers, halved and seeded**
- 1 **medium green pepper, halved and seeded**
- 3 **medium zucchini, halved lengthwise**
- 1 **fresh pineapple, peeled and cut into ½-inch slices**
- 2 **unpeeled medium oranges, cut into ½-inch slices**

1. In a small bowl, combine the orange juice concentrate, syrup, oil, curry and cayenne. Place chicken in a large resealable plastic bag; add half of the marinade. Seal bag and turn to coat. Place the peppers, zucchini, pineapple and oranges in another resealable bag; add remaining marinade. Seal bag and turn to coat. Refrigerate chicken and vegetables for 8 hours or overnight, turning occasionally.

2. Drain chicken and discard marinade. Drain vegetables and fruits, reserving marinade for basting. Grill the chicken, vegetables and fruits, uncovered, over medium heat for 3 minutes on each side. Baste with reserved marinade. Continue turning and basting 6-8 minutes longer or until chicken juices run clear, vegetables are tender and fruits are golden brown.

FAMOUS
BBQ CHICKEN

FAMOUS BBQ CHICKEN

This chicken is topped with a sticky, finger-lickin' sauce that everyone, including my kids, loves. I make it in big batches now and give jars of it to family and friends.

—STACEY NERNESS SPENCER, IA

PREP: 45 MIN. • **GRILL:** 40 MIN.
MAKES: 4 SERVINGS PLUS 3 CUPS LEFTOVER SAUCE

- 2½ cups ketchup
- ½ cup packed brown sugar
- ½ cup honey
- ¼ cup liquid smoke
- ¼ cup molasses
- 1 serrano pepper, finely chopped
- 2 tablespoons prepared mustard
- 1 tablespoon white wine vinegar
- 1 tablespoon Worcestershire sauce
- 2 teaspoons onion powder
- 2 teaspoons garlic powder
- ¼ teaspoon cayenne pepper
- 4 chicken leg quarters
- ½ teaspoon salt
- ½ teaspoon pepper

1. In a large saucepan, combine the first 12 ingredients. Bring to a boil. Reduce heat; simmer, uncovered, for 30 minutes to allow flavors to blend. Set aside ½ cup sauce for basting; cover and refrigerate the remaining sauce for later use.
2. Sprinkle chicken with salt and pepper. Moisten a paper towel with cooking oil; using long-handled tongs, rub on grill rack to coat lightly.
3. Prepare the grill for indirect heat, using a drip pan. Place chicken skin side down over drip pan; grill, covered, over indirect medium heat for 20 minutes. Turn; grill 20-30 minutes longer or until a thermometer reads 170°-175°, basting occasionally with reserved sauce.
NOTE *Wear disposable gloves when cutting hot peppers; the oils can burn skin. Avoid touching your face.*

MUSTARD-HERB CHICKEN BREASTS

The Dijon mayonnaise makes this grilled entree tender and flavorful. Even though I learned to cook when I was young and helped make supper for our family, I didn't really enjoy it until now. My husband appreciates my new interest in finding and trying new recipes.

—TERRI WEME SMITHERS, BC

PREP: 10 MIN. + MARINATING • **GRILL:** 15 MIN.
MAKES: 4 SERVINGS

- ¼ cup chopped green onions
- ¼ cup Dijon-mayonnaise blend
- 2 tablespoons lemon juice
- 1 garlic clove, minced
- ½ teaspoon salt
- ½ teaspoon dried thyme
- ¼ teaspoon pepper
- 4 boneless skinless chicken breast halves (4 ounces each)

1. In a large resealable plastic bag, combine the first seven ingredients; add chicken. Seal bag and turn to coat. Refrigerate for 2 hours, turning once.
2. Grill chicken, covered, over medium heat for 6-8 minutes on each side or until a thermometer reads 170°.

TURKEY LIME KABOBS

My husband loves to grill these deliciously different turkey kabobs, and everyone gets a kick out of the zing from the limes and jalapenos. The tongue-tingling combination of flavors makes this one company dish that always draws compliments.

—SHELLY JOHNSTON ROCHESTER, MN

PREP: 20 MIN. + MARINATING • **GRILL:** 20 MIN.
MAKES: 8 SERVINGS

- 3 cans (6 ounces each) orange juice concentrate, thawed
- 1¼ cups lime juice
- 1 cup honey
- 4 to 5 jalapeno peppers, seeded and chopped
- 10 garlic cloves, minced
- 3 tablespoons ground cumin
- 2 tablespoons grated lime peel
- 1 teaspoon salt
- 2 pounds boneless turkey, chicken or pork, cut into 1¼-inch cubes
- 4 medium sweet red or green peppers, cut into 1-inch pieces
- 1 large red onion, cut into 1-inch pieces
- 3 small zucchini, cut into ¾-inch slices
- 8 ounces fresh mushrooms
- 3 medium limes, cut into wedges

1. In a bowl, combine the first eight ingredients. Pour half of marinade into a large resealable plastic bag; add meat and turn to coat. Pour remaining marinade into another large resealable plastic bag. Add vegetables and turn to coat. Seal and refrigerate for 8 hours or overnight, turning occasionally.
2. Drain meat, discarding marinade. Drain vegetables, reserving marinade for basting. On metal or soaked wooden skewers, alternate meat, vegetables and lime wedges.
3. Grill, uncovered, over medium heat for 4-5 minutes on each side. Baste with reserved marinade. Continue turning and basting for 10-12 minutes or until the meat juices run clear and vegetables are tender.
NOTE *Wear disposable gloves when cutting hot peppers; the oils can burn skin. Avoid touching your face.*

 **GRILL SKILL**

Always discard marinade after uncooked meat has sat in it. Never use such marinade for basting. Instead, reserve a small amount of the marinade before adding the meat. Refrigerate this reserved marinade in a separate container for basting.

**PORK MEDALLIONS
WITH PEAR SALSA, PAGE 220**

COUNTRY-STYLE
GRILLED RIBS, PAGE 218

ULTIMATE GRILLED
PORK CHOP,
PAGE 215

BARBECUED PORK, LAMB & MORE

There's nothing like digging in to a stack of barbecued ribs to signal the start of summer. Here you'll find plenty of grilled **pork favorites** as well as tasty takes on **lamb, sausages** and other mouthwatering staples. So what are you waiting for? **Sizzle up a feast** tonight!

SWISS HAM
KABOBS, PAGE 200

PORK & LAMB GRILLING CHART

The cooking times given are guidelines. Check for doneness with a food thermometer. Pork chops and roasts are done at 145°, including stand time. Ribs and shoulder (butt) roast are done when tender. Ground pork (patties, sausages) are done at 160°. Cooked sausages are done when heated through.

Always grill ground lamb to 160°. For direct grilling, turn meat halfway through the grilling time. Grill lamb roasts and chops with the grill's lid covered. For large cuts of lamb, if desired, sear over medium direct heat before cooking over indirect heat.

CUT	WEIGHT OR THICKNESS	HEAT	APPROXIMATE COOKING TIME
PORK			
LOIN OR RIB CHOP (BONE-IN OR BONELESS)	³/₄ to 1 in. thick 1¹/₄ to 1¹/₂ in. thick	medium/direct medium/direct	8 to 10 minutes 12 to 18 minutes
BACK RIBS OR SPARERIBS	3 to 4 lbs.	medium/indirect	1¹/₂ to 2 hours
TENDERLOIN	³/₄ to 1 lb.	medium-high/indirect medium/direct	25 to 40 minutes 18 to 22 minutes
LOIN ROAST (BONE-IN OR BONELESS)	3 to 5 lbs.	medium/indirect	1¹/₂ hours
KABOBS	1 in. cubes	medium/direct	10 to 15 minutes
SAUSAGE, COOKED	—	medium/direct	3 to 7 minutes or until heated through
SAUSAGE, FRESH	4 oz.	medium/indirect	20 to 30 minutes
PORK PATTIES	4 oz. and ¹/₂ in.	medium/direct	8 to 10 minutes
LAMB			
RIB OR LOIN CHOPS	1 in.	medium/direct	10 to 18 minutes
LEG OF LAMB (BONE-IN)	5 to 7 lbs.	medium-low/indirect	1³/₄ to 2³/₄ hours
LEG OF LAMB (BONELESS)	3 to 4 lbs.	medium-low/indirect	1¹/₂ to 2¹/₂ hours
RACK OF LAMB	1 to 1¹/₂ lbs.	medium/direct	25 to 35 minutes
KABOBS	1 in. cubes	medium/direct	8 to 12 minutes
LAMB PATTIES	4 oz. and ¹/₂ in.	medium/direct	8 to 10 minutes

GRILLED SAUSAGES WITH SUMMER VEGETABLES

Our grilled sausage and veggies dish is a superstar at any summer potluck, barbecue or get-together.

—**NANCY DAUGHERTY** CORTLAND, OH

PREP: 35 MIN. • **GRILL:** 25 MIN.
MAKES: 12 SERVINGS

- ¾ **cup peach preserves**
- ½ **cup reduced-sodium soy sauce**
- 3 **tablespoons minced fresh gingerroot**
- 3 **tablespoons water**
- 3 **garlic cloves, minced**
 Dash hot pepper sauce, optional
- 4 **medium sweet red peppers**
- 1 **medium eggplant**
- 3 **small zucchini**
- 2 **small yellow summer squash**
- 12 **hot Italian pork or turkey sausage links (4 ounces each)**

1. Place the first five ingredients in a blender; if desired, add pepper sauce. Cover and process until blended.

2. Cut peppers lengthwise in half; remove seeds. Cut the eggplant lengthwise into ½-in.-thick slices. Cut zucchini and yellow squash lengthwise into quarters. Place all vegetables in a large bowl; drizzle with ½ cup of the sauce and toss to coat.

3. Moisten a paper towel with cooking oil; using long-handled tongs, rub on the grill rack to coat lightly. Grill vegetables, covered, over medium heat for 8-10 minutes or until tender and lightly charred, turning once. Cool slightly. Reduce grill temperature to medium-low heat.

4. Cut vegetables into bite-size pieces. Toss with additional ¼ cup sauce; keep warm.

5. Grill the sausages, covered, over medium-low heat for 15-20 minutes or until a thermometer reads 160° for pork sausages (165° for turkey ausages), turning occasionally. Remove sausages from grill; toss with remaining sauce. Serve with vegetables.

GRILLED SAUSAGES WITH SUMMER VEGETABLES

FAST FIX

SWISS HAM KABOBS

With juicy pineapple and tender ham, these kabobs are my daughter's birthday dinner request every year. They're a fantastic way to start grilling season.
—**HELEN PHILLIPS** HORSEHEADS, NY

START TO FINISH: 20 MIN.
MAKES: 4 SERVINGS

- 1 **can (20 ounces) pineapple chunks**
- ½ **cup orange marmalade**
- 1 **tablespoon prepared mustard**
- ¼ **teaspoon ground cloves**
- 1 **pound fully cooked ham, cut into 1-inch cubes**
- ½ **pound Swiss cheese, cut into 1-inch cubes**
- 1 **medium green pepper, cut into 1-inch pieces, optional**

1. Drain the pineapple, reserving 2 tablespoons juice; set pineapple aside. In a small bowl, mix the marmalade, mustard, cloves and reserved pineapple juice. On eight metal or soaked wooden skewers, alternately thread ham, cheese, pineapple and, if desired, green pepper.
2. Moisten a paper towel with cooking oil; using long-handled tongs, rub on grill rack to coat lightly. Grill kabobs, uncovered, over medium heat or broil 4 in. from heat for 5-7 minutes or until heated through, turning and basting frequently with marmalade sauce. Serve with remaining sauce.

LEMONADE PORK CHOPS

These melt-in-your-mouth pork chops are always a hit with my family and with our guests, too. Lemonade concentrate gives them such a wonderfully tangy flavor.
—**ANGELA OELSCHLAEGER** TONGANOXIE, KS

PREP: 15 MIN. + MARINATING • **GRILL:** 10 MIN.
MAKES: 6 SERVINGS

- 1 **can (12 ounces) frozen lemonade concentrate, thawed**
- ⅔ **cup soy sauce**
- 2 **teaspoons seasoned salt**
- 1 **teaspoon celery salt**
- ¼ **teaspoon garlic powder**
- 6 **boneless butterflied pork chops (½-inch thick and 6 ounces each)**

1. In a small bowl, combine lemonade concentrate, soy sauce, seasoned salt, celery salt and garlic powder. Pour 1½ cups mixture into a large resealable plastic bag; add pork chops. Seal bag and turn to coat; refrigerate for at least 4 hours. Cover and refrigerate remaining marinade for basting.
2. Drain and discard marinade from pork. Moisten a paper towel with cooking oil; using long-handled tongs, rub on grill rack to coat lightly. Grill the pork chops, covered, over medium heat or broil 4-5 in. from the heat for 3-4 minutes on each side or until a thermometer reads 145°, basting occasionally with reserved marinade. Let meat stand for 5 minutes before serving.

HONEY-AND-HERB GRILLED PORK ROAST

This pork roast is so hearty and satisfying, thanks to its great grilled flavor and easy marinade. Serve with a salad or garlic bread and dinner is ready! It's also great to slice up for big parties.
—**CATHY IRWIN** ONTARIO, NY

PREP: 5 MIN. + MARINATING
GRILL: 1½ HOURS + STANDING
MAKES: 8-10 SERVINGS

- ¾ **cup ginger ale**
- ⅓ **cup Dijon mustard**
- ⅓ **cup honey**
- 2 **tablespoons canola oil**
- 2 **tablespoons chopped onion**
- ¾ **teaspoon dried rosemary, crushed**
- ½ **teaspoon salt**
- ¼ **teaspoon garlic powder**
- ⅛ **teaspoon pepper**
- 1 **boneless pork loin roast (2½-3 pounds)**

1. In a large resealable plastic bag, combine the first nine ingredients; add pork roast. Seal bag and turn to coat. Refrigerate overnight, turning bag occasionally.
2. Drain and discard marinade. Place roast in a disposable foil pan. Prepare grill for indirect heat.
3. Grill pork, covered, over indirect medium-low heat for 1½ hours or until a thermometer reads 160°. Let stand for 10 minutes before slicing.

🍴 EASY IGNITION

Always use the pyramid method when lighting charcoal briquettes. Start by arranging the briquettes in a pyramid in the grill. Pour lighter fluid over the coals. Recap the fluid and place away from grill. Light briquettes.

If you have an electric starter, arrange briquettes in a pyramid in the grill. Insert the starter into the middle of coals. Plug in the starter. Ash will form on coals in 8-10 minutes. At that point, unplug the starter and remove from briquettes. The starter will be hot, so place it out of the way on a heatproof surface.

SWISS HAM KABOBS

MARINATED OSTRICH STEAK

We raise ostriches on our farm on the Eastern Shore of Maryland, so we have an abundance of meat on hand to use for a variety of dishes. It's a lean meat that tastes similar to beef. My mother-in-law gave me this marinade recipe, and I use it with our ostrich meat.

—**JENNIE SCHMIDT** SUDLERSVILLE, MD

PREP: 30 MIN. + MARINATING
MAKES: 4 SERVINGS

- ¾ **cup vegetable oil**
- ⅓ **cup soy sauce**
- ¼ **cup cider or white wine vinegar**
- 3 **tablespoons lemon juice**
- 2 **tablespoons Worcestershire sauce**
- 1 **tablespoon ground mustard**
- 1 **teaspoon salt**
- 1 **teaspoon pepper**
- 1 **teaspoon dried parsley flakes**
- ½ **teaspoon garlic powder**
- 4 **ostrich or beef tenderloin steaks (4 ounces each)**

1. In a resealable plastic bag or shallow glass container, combine the first 10 ingredients; mix well. Add meat to marinade and turn to coat. Seal bag or cover container; refrigerate meat overnight, turning it occasionally. Drain and discard marinade.

2. Grill, covered, over medium heat for 5 minutes. Turn and cook 6-8 minutes longer or until the meat reaches desired doneness (for medium-rare, a thermometer should read 145°; medium, 160°; and well done, 170°).

CHINESE COUNTRY-STYLE PORK RIBS

These pork ribs are so tangy and tender. The Chinese-style glaze gives them a unique taste.

—**JAMIE WETTER** BOSCOBEL, WI

PREP: 25 MIN. • **GRILL:** 10 MIN.
MAKES: 8 SERVINGS

- 4 **pounds bone-in country-style pork ribs**
- ½ **cup water**
- 1 **tablespoon liquid smoke, optional**
- ½ **teaspoon onion powder**
- ½ **cup chili sauce**
- ¼ **cup hoisin sauce**
- 2 **tablespoons honey**
- ⅛ **teaspoon cayenne pepper**

1. Cut ribs into serving-size pieces; place in a 3-qt. microwave-safe dish with water, liquid smoke if desired and onion powder. Cover and microwave on high for 15-20 minutes or until meat is tender.

2. Meanwhile, in a small saucepan, combine the remaining ingredients. Bring to a boil. Reduce heat; simmer, uncovered, for 5-8 minutes or until the sauce is slightly thickened, stirring occasionally.

3. Drain ribs. Moisten a paper towel with cooking oil; using long-handled tongs, rub on grill rack to coat lightly. Grill ribs, covered, over medium heat for 8-10 minutes or until browned, turning occasionally and basting with the sauce.

FREEZE OPTION *Place cooled ribs in a resealable freezer bag and freeze up to 3 months. To use, thaw in refrigerator overnight. Place in a baking pan; cover and bake at 325° for 35-40 minutes or until heated through.*

NOTE *This recipe was tested in a 1,100-watt microwave.*

CHINESE COUNTRY-STYLE PORK RIBS

JAMAICAN PORK TENDERLOIN

This recipe is perfect for both weeknight dinner and backyard barbecues! A spicy citrus marinade adds plenty of flavor to the tenderloin overnight. Then you can grill the meat in just minutes the next day.
—**ROSE HOCKETT** COLORADO SPRINGS, CO

PREP: 10 MIN. + MARINATING • **GRILL:** 20 MIN.
MAKES: 6 SERVINGS

- ⅓ **cup orange juice**
- ⅓ **cup reduced-sodium soy sauce**
- 3 **tablespoons lemon juice**
- 2 **tablespoons olive oil**
- 1 **large onion, chopped**
- 1 **cup chopped green onions**
- 1 **jalapeno pepper**
- 3 **tablespoons minced fresh thyme or**
  2 teaspoons dried thyme
- ¾ **teaspoon salt**
- ¾ **teaspoon each ground allspice,**
  cinnamon and nutmeg
- ¼ **teaspoon ground ginger**
- ¼ **teaspoon pepper**
- 2 **pork tenderloins (1 pound each)**

1. In a food processor, combine the orange juice, soy sauce, lemon juice, oil, onion, green onions, jalapeno, thyme, salt, allspice, cinnamon, nutmeg, ginger and pepper. Cover and process until smooth. Pour into a large resealable plastic bag; add the pork. Seal bag and turn to coat; refrigerate overnight.

2. Drain and discard the marinade. Moisten a paper towel with cooking oil; using long-handled tongs, rub it on the grill rack to coat lightly. Prepare the grill for indirect heat using a drip pan.

3. Place pork over drip pan and grill, covered, over indirect medium heat for 20-25 minutes or until a thermometer reads 160°. Let stand for 5 minutes before slicing.

NOTE *Wear disposable gloves when cutting hot peppers; the oils can burn skin. Avoid touching your face.*

HERB MARINATED LAMB CHOPS

HERB MARINATED LAMB CHOPS

The fresh herb marinade lends wonderful flavor to these grilled lamb chops. I also use it on pork chops with equally delicious results. Give them a try!
—**JAN BRIGGS** GREENFIELD, WI

PREP: 10 MIN. + MARINATING • **COOK:** 15 MIN.
MAKES: 4 SERVINGS

- ¼ **cup dry red wine or beef broth**
- 2 **tablespoons reduced-sodium soy**
  sauce
- 1½ **teaspoons minced fresh mint or**
  ½ teaspoon dried mint
- 1 **teaspoon minced fresh basil or**
  ¼ teaspoon dried basil
- ½ **teaspoon pepper**
- 1 **garlic clove, minced**
- 4 **bone-in lamb loin chops (1-inch**
  thick and 6 ounces each)

1. In a large resealable plastic bag, combine the wine or broth, soy sauce, mint, basil, pepper and garlic; add the lamb chops. Seal bag and turn to coat; refrigerate for 8 hours or overnight.

2. Drain and discard marinade. Grill lamb chops, uncovered, over medium heat or broil 4-6 in. from the heat for 5-7 minutes on each side or until meat reaches desired doneness (for medium, a thermometer should read 160°; well-done, 170°).

SPICE-RUBBED RIBS

Here's the rub I always recommend for grilling ribs. If you have some left after making the ribs, put it in a shaker and use it another day on pork or beef roasts. It's great alone or under sauce.

—**CHERYL EWING** ELLWOOD CITY, PA

PREP: 10 MIN. • **GRILL:** 1 HOUR
MAKES: 10 SERVINGS

- 3 **tablespoons paprika**
- 2 **tablespoons plus 1 teaspoon salt**
- 2 **tablespoons plus 1 teaspoon garlic powder**
- 2 **tablespoons cayenne pepper**
- 4 **teaspoons onion powder**
- 4 **teaspoons dried oregano**
- 4 **teaspoons dried thyme**
- 4 **teaspoons pepper**
- 10 **pounds pork baby back ribs**

1. In a small bowl, combine the seasonings; rub over ribs.
2. Prepare grill for indirect heat, using a drip pan. Grill ribs, covered, over indirect medium heat for 1 hour or until meat is tender, turning occasionally.

SPICE-RUBBED RIBS

COLA PORK CHOPS

I created this dish after my husband brought home something similar for me to try. I'm happy to say that not only did my version win raves at home, but it received a blue ribbon at the local fair!

—**RUTH REAZIN** LYONS, KS

PREP: 10 MIN. + MARINATING • **GRILL:** 10 MIN.
MAKES: 6 SERVINGS

- 1 **can (12 ounces) cola**
- ¼ **cup soy sauce**
- ¾ **teaspoon garlic powder**
- ¾ **teaspoon ground ginger**
- ¾ **teaspoon ground mustard**
- ½ **teaspoon salt**
- ½ **teaspoon pepper**
- 6 **bone-in pork loin chops (¾-inch thick and 8 ounces each)**

1. In a 2-cup measuring cup, combine the first seven ingredients. Pour 1½ cups into a large resealable plastic bag; add pork chops. Seal bag and turn to coat; refrigerate for 8 hours or overnight. Cover and refrigerate the remaining marinade for basting.
2. Drain marinade from chops and discard. Grill, covered, over medium heat 4-5 minutes on each side or until a thermometer reads 145°, basting occasionally with reserved marinade. Let stand 5 minutes before serving.

LAMB WITH SPINACH AND ONIONS

Grilling is a wonderful way to prepare lamb. This marinade and the onion sauce enhance the meat's naturally terrific taste.

—**SARAH VASQUES** MILFORD, NH

PREP: 25 MIN. + MARINATING • **GRILL:** 10 MIN.
MAKES: 6 SERVINGS

- ½ **cup lime juice**
- ¼ **cup dry red wine or 1 tablespoon red wine vinegar**
- 1 **small onion, chopped**
- 2 **tablespoons minced fresh rosemary or 2 teaspoons dried rosemary, crushed**
- 2 **tablespoons olive oil**
- 2 **tablespoons Worcestershire sauce**
- 3 **garlic cloves, minced**
- 1 **tablespoon minced fresh thyme or 1 teaspoon dried thyme**
- ¼ **teaspoon pepper**
  Dash liquid smoke, optional
- 12 **rib lamb chops (1-inch thick)**

ONION SAUCE
- 2 **tablespoons finely chopped green onions**
- 1 **teaspoon butter**
- 1 **cup balsamic vinegar**
- 1 **cup dry red wine or ½ cup beef broth and grape juice**
- ½ **cup loosely packed fresh mint leaves, chopped**
- 1 **tablespoon sugar**
- 1 **large sweet onion, cut into quarters**
  Olive oil
  Salt and pepper to taste

SPINACH
- ¼ **cup finely chopped green onions**
- 3 **garlic cloves, minced**
- 3 **tablespoons olive oil**
- 3 **tablespoons butter**
- 12 **cups fresh baby spinach**
  Salt and pepper to taste

1. In a large resealable plastic bag, combine the first 10 ingredients; add lamb chops. Seal bag and turn to coat; refrigerate for 8 hours or overnight.
2. In a saucepan, saute green onions in butter until tender. Add vinegar and wine or broth and grape juice; bring to a boil. Add mint and sugar. Reduce heat; simmer, uncovered, for 30 minutes or until sauce is reduced to ¾ cup. Strain; discard mint. Set sauce aside.
3. Thread onion wedges onto metal or soaked wooden skewers. Brush with the oil, salt and pepper. Discard the marinade. Grill chops, covered, over medium heat for 5-6 minutes on each side or until meat reaches desired doneness (for medium, a thermometer should read 160°; well done, 170°). Grill onion skewers for 2-3 minutes or until tender.

4. In a large skillet, saute green onions and garlic in oil and butter until tender. Add the spinach, salt and pepper; saute for 2-3 minutes or until spinach just begins to wilt and is heated through. Place on a serving platter. Remove onion from skewers; place onion and lamb chops over spinach.

LOW COUNTRY KABOBS

We took the ingredients from a traditional Carolina low country grill and threaded them onto skewers for a fun and festive presentation.

—**TASTE OF HOME** TEST KITCHEN

PREP: 30 MIN. • **GRILL:** 10 MIN.
MAKES: 12 KABOBS

- 12 **small red potatoes, quartered**
- 3 **medium ears sweet corn, cut into 1-inch slices**
- ⅓ **cup butter, melted**
- 2 **tablespoons olive oil**
- 1 **teaspoon salt**
- 1 **teaspoon garlic powder**
- 1 **teaspoon seafood seasoning**
- 1 **pound smoked kielbasa or Polish sausage, cut into 1-inch slices**
- 1½ **pounds uncooked medium shrimp, peeled and deveined**

1. Place potatoes in a Dutch oven and cover with water. Bring to a boil. Reduce heat; cover and cook for 5 minutes. Add the corn; cook for 3-5 minutes longer or until potatoes are tender. Drain.
2. In a small bowl, combine the butter, oil, salt, garlic powder and seafood seasoning.
3. On 12 metal or soaked wooden skewers, alternately thread kielbasa, shrimp, potatoes and corn. Grill, covered, over medium heat or broil 4 in. from the heat for 3-4 minutes on each side or until shrimp turn pink, basting with butter mixture.

CHIPOTLE-ORANGE PORK CHOPS

BARBECUED LAMB KABOBS

This is a recipe I brought with me from western Pennsylvania. To fully enjoy this dish, serve it with some hot bread and a cold beverage. It can be made the day before, and it also freezes well.

—GLORIA JARRETT LOVELAND, OH

PREP: 20 MIN. + MARINATING • **GRILL:** 15 MIN.
MAKES: 8-10 SERVINGS

MARINADE
- ½ tablespoon dried parsley flakes
- ½ tablespoon dried minced onion
- 1 teaspoon salt
- ½ teaspoon black pepper
- ½ cup lemon juice
- ½ cup white wine or broth of choice
- 2 tablespoons soy sauce
- 2½ pounds boneless leg of lamb, cut into 1-inch cubes

DIPPING SAUCE
- ½ cup canola oil
- ½ cup lemon juice
- 1 large onion, chopped
- 2 garlic cloves, minced
  Salt to taste
  Pepper to taste
  Hot peppers to taste, chopped

1. Combine marinade ingredients in heavy plastic bag; add the lamb and marinate overnight or at least 5 hours, turning bag occasionally.
2. Drain and discard marinade. Thread lamb cubes on skewers; broil or grill on medium for 7-8 minutes on each side or until meat reaches desired doneness (for medium-rare, a thermometer should read 145°; medium, 160°; well-done, 170°).
3. For the dipping sauce, in a blender, add all the sauce ingredients. Cover and process on high until smooth. Serve with lamb.

(5)INGREDIENTS FAST FIX

CHIPOTLE-ORANGE PORK CHOPS

Orange juice concentrate and maple syrup add a one-two punch of sweetness to grilled flavors. With a method that's as easy as "whisk and grill," you'd be crazy not to fix extras.

—BILLY HENSLEY MOUNT CARMEL, TN

START TO FINISH: 30 MIN.
MAKES: 8 SERVINGS

- ½ cup maple syrup
- ½ cup thawed orange juice concentrate
- 3 tablespoons chopped chipotle peppers in adobo sauce
- 1 teaspoon salt
- 1 teaspoon pepper
- 8 bone-in pork loin chops (8 ounces each and ¾-inch thick)

1. In a small bowl, combine the first five ingredients. Set aside ⅓ cup sauce for serving.
2. Moisten a paper towel with cooking oil; using long-handled tongs, rub on grill rack to coat lightly. Grill chops, covered, over medium heat or broil 4-5 in. from the heat for 4-5 minutes on each side or until a thermometer reads 145°, basting frequently with orange mixture. Let chops stand for 5 minutes before serving with reserved sauce.

FAST FIX

MIXED GRILL FAJITAS

Everyone will love these fajitas with their assortment of tasty fillings. The recipe is my original creation, and I found that through trial, you cannot make an error!
—**KAREN HAEN** STURGEON BAY, WI

START TO FINISH: 30 MIN.
MAKES: 12 SERVINGS

- 1 each medium green, sweet red and yellow peppers, julienned
- 2 medium red onions, sliced
- 3 tablespoons olive oil
- 1 cup (8 ounces) sour cream
- 2 teaspoons ground cumin
- 2 garlic cloves, minced
- ½ teaspoon salt
- ½ teaspoon pepper
- ½ teaspoon chili powder
- 3 Italian sausage links
- 6 boneless skinless chicken breast halves (4 ounces each)
- 2 beef cube steaks (4 ounces each)
- 24 flour tortillas (8 inches), warmed
- 6 cups (24 ounces) shredded cheddar cheese

1. In a large skillet, saute peppers and onions in oil until tender; keep warm. In a small bowl, combine the sour cream, cumin and garlic; chill until serving.

2. Combine the salt, pepper and chili powder; sprinkle over sausages, chicken and steaks. Grill the sausages and chicken, covered, over medium heat for 5-8 minutes on each side or until a thermometer inserted into chicken reads 170° and the sausage is no longer pink. Slice and keep warm.

3. Grill steaks, covered, over medium heat for 2-3 minutes on each side or until meat reaches desired doneness (for medium-rare, a thermometer should read 145°; medium, 160°; well-done, 170°). Slice and keep warm.

4. Divide meats and vegetables among tortillas; sprinkle with cheese. Roll up; serve with sour cream mixture.

MIXED GRILL
FAJITAS

DIRECT HEAT HOW-TO

When a recipe calls for foods to be grilled over direct heat, simply spread out the preheated coals in an even layer. For a gas grill, preheat the grill with all the burners on high. Place food on cooking grate directly over the heat source. Adjust burners to desired temperature.

**GRILLED MAPLE
PORK CHOPS**

(5) INGREDIENTS

GRILLED MAPLE
PORK CHOPS

Pork chops on the grill are hard to beat.
The marinade is simple, and so good.
—**NICHOLAS KING** DULUTH, MN

PREP: 5 MIN. + MARINATING • **GRILL:** 15 MIN.
MAKES: 4 SERVINGS

- 6 **tablespoons maple syrup**
- 6 **tablespoons balsamic vinegar**
- ¾ **teaspoon salt**
- ¾ **teaspoon coarsely ground pepper**
- 4 **boneless pork loin chops (1½-inch
  thick and 12 ounces each)**

1. In a small bowl, whisk maple syrup,
vinegar, salt and pepper until blended.
Pour ½ cup marinade into a large
resealable plastic bag. Add pork chops;
seal bag and turn to coat. Refrigerate
1 hour. Reserve remaining marinade
for basting.
2. Drain pork chops, discarding the
marinade in bag. Moisten a paper towel
with cooking oil; using long-handled
tongs, rub it on grill rack to coat lightly.
3. Grill pork chops, covered, over
medium heat or broil 4 in. from heat
13-17 minutes or until a thermometer
reads 145°, turning occasionally and
basting with reserved marinade during
the last 5 minutes. Let stand 5 minutes
before serving.

COUNTRY PORK RIBS

These hearty ribs feature a lip-smacking sauce that's deliciously tangy with just the right hint of sweetness. The marinade is absolutely terrific for country-style ribs, but I've found it's great with other meats, too.

—**BRIAN JOHNSON** LAGRANGE, GA

PREP: 10 MIN. + MARINATING • **GRILL:** 35 MIN.
MAKES: 8 SERVINGS

- 1 cup grapefruit or orange juice
- 1 cup ketchup
- ½ cup cider vinegar
- ¼ cup soy sauce
- ¼ cup Worcestershire sauce
- 2 tablespoons prepared horseradish
- 2 tablespoons prepared mustard
- 2 teaspoons ground ginger
- 1 to 2 teaspoons hot pepper sauce
- ½ teaspoon garlic powder
- 4 to 5 pounds country-style pork ribs
- ¼ cup honey
- 2 tablespoons brown sugar

1. In a bowl, combine the first 10 ingredients; mix well. Pour 1½ cups marinade into a large resealable plastic bag; add the ribs. Seal and turn to coat; refrigerate for at least 4 hours. Cover and refrigerate remaining marinade.
2. Drain and discard marinade from the ribs. Grill, covered, over indirect medium heat for 20 minutes on each side. Meanwhile, in a saucepan, combine the honey, brown sugar and reserved marinade. Bring to a boil; cook and stir for 2 minutes or until slightly thickened.
3. Baste ribs with some of the sauce. Grill 15-20 minutes longer or until a thermometer reads 160°, turning and basting occasionally. Serve with the remaining sauce.

GRILLED BOURBON CHOPS

FAST FIX ▶
GRILLED BOURBON CHOPS

My husband is a grill master and loves a good bourbon, making this recipe the perfect combination of both! Sometimes we use thicker chops. If you do, too, remember to cook them long enough to reach 145°.

—**DONNA BRYAN** COLUMBIA FALLS, MT

START TO FINISH: 25 MIN.
MAKES: 4 SERVINGS

- ¼ cup bourbon or unsweetened apple juice
- 2 tablespoons brown sugar
- 2 tablespoons Dijon mustard
- 3 garlic cloves, minced
- 1 teaspoon onion powder
- ½ teaspoon salt
- ¼ teaspoon pepper
- 4 bone-in pork loin chops (½-inch thick and 8 ounces each)

1. In a small saucepan, mix bourbon, brown sugar, mustard and garlic; bring to a boil. Reduce heat; simmer, uncovered, for 2-3 minutes or until slightly thickened.
2. Mix onion powder, salt and pepper; sprinkle over pork chops. Grill, covered, over medium heat or broil 4 in. from heat 3-5 minutes on each side or until a thermometer reads 145°. Let stand 5 minutes before serving. Serve with the sauce.

LAMB CHOPS WITH WINE SAUCE

You don't need fancy ingredients to create an elegant entree. Here, roasted tomatoes complement grilled chops beautifully.

—**KAREN GORMAN** GUNNISON, CO

PREP: 25 MIN. • **GRILL:** 30 MIN.
MAKES: 4 SERVINGS

- 2 tablespoons finely chopped sweet onion
- 3 teaspoons olive oil, divided
- 1 cup dry red wine
- 1 teaspoon butter
- 1 teaspoon minced fresh thyme or ¼ teaspoon dried thyme
- 1 cup cherry tomatoes
- 6 whole unpeeled garlic cloves
- 2 garlic cloves, minced
- ¼ teaspoon salt
- ¼ teaspoon pepper
- 4 lamb rib or loin chops (6 ounces each)

1. In a small saucepan, saute onion in 1 teaspoon oil until tender; add the wine. Bring to a boil; cook until liquid is reduced to 2 tablespoons. Stir in butter and thyme. Remove from the heat; keep warm.

2. Place cherry tomatoes on a double thickness of heavy-duty foil. Drizzle with 1 teaspoon oil. Fold foil around the tomatoes and seal tightly; set aside. Repeat with whole garlic cloves and the remaining oil. Grill garlic, covered, over medium heat for 30 minutes.

3. Meanwhile, combine the minced garlic, salt and pepper; rub over chops. Grill lamb and tomato packet, covered, over medium heat for 6-8 minutes on each side or until the lamb reaches desired doneness (for medium-rare, a thermometer should read 145°; medium, 160°; well-done, 170°).

4. Open tomato packet carefully to allow steam to escape; place tomatoes in a small bowl. When garlic is cool enough to handle, squeeze softened garlic over tomatoes; toss to coat. Serve lamb with tomatoes and wine sauce.

GRILLED HAM STEAKS

These savory ham steaks are marinated and basted in a molasses-clove sauce and grilled to perfection.

—**SANDY MORRIS** LITITZ, PA

PREP: 10 MIN. + MARINATING • **GRILL:** 10 MIN.
MAKES: 12 SERVINGS

- 1½ cups orange juice
- ½ cup cider vinegar
- ¼ cup packed brown sugar
- 1 tablespoon ground cloves
- 1 tablespoon molasses
- 2 to 3 teaspoons ground mustard
- 2 to 3 teaspoons ground ginger
- 3 bone-in fully cooked ham steaks (1 pound each and ⅜-inch thick)

1. In a small bowl, combine the first seven ingredients. Pour 1½ cups into a large resealable plastic bag; add the ham steaks. Seal bag and turn to coat; refrigerate for 1-2 hours. Cover and refrigerate the remaining marinade for basting.

2. Drain and discard ham marinade. Moisten a paper towel with cooking oil; using long-handled tongs, rub it on grill rack to coat lightly. Grill ham steaks, covered, over medium heat or broil 4 in. from the heat for 10-15 minutes or until heated through, turning and basting frequently with reserved marinade.

PEACH-CHIPOTLE BABY BACK RIBS

My son and I created this recipe years ago. Cooking these sweet and spicy ribs with him has been a wonderful bonding experience.

—**REBECCA SUASO** WEAVERVILLE, NC

PREP: 15 MIN. • **COOK:** 2¾ HOURS
MAKES: 8 SERVINGS (2 CUPS SAUCE)

- 3 tablespoons brown sugar
- 2 tablespoons kosher salt
- 1 teaspoon pepper
- ½ teaspoon cayenne pepper
- 8 pounds pork baby back ribs (about 3 racks)
- 6 medium peaches, peeled and sliced
- 2 tablespoons olive oil
- 2 large sweet onions, finely chopped
- ⅔ cup packed brown sugar
- 4 finely chopped chipotle peppers in adobo sauce plus 2 tablespoons sauce
- 3 tablespoons white vinegar
- 4 teaspoons ground mustard

1. Preheat oven to 325°. In a small bowl, combine brown sugar, salt, pepper and cayenne. If necessary, remove the thin membrane from back ribs; discard membrane. Rub brown sugar mixture over ribs. Transfer to large roasting pans. Add 1 in. hot water. Bake, covered, 2½-3 hours or until ribs are tender.

2. Meanwhile, place peaches in a blender; cover and process until smooth.

3. In a large saucepan, heat oil over medium heat. Add onions; cook and stir 12-15 minutes or until tender. Add brown sugar, chipotle peppers, adobo sauce, vinegar, mustard and peach puree; bring to a boil. Reduce heat; simmer, uncovered, 25-30 minutes or until slightly thickened.

4. Drain ribs. Moisten a paper towel with cooking oil; using long-handled tongs, rub it on grill rack to coat lightly. Grill ribs, pork side down, covered, over medium heat for 5-7 minutes or until browned. Turn ribs; brush with 2 cups sauce. Cook 5-7 minutes longer or until sauce is thickened. Serve with the remaining sauce.

PEACH-CHIPOTLE
BABY BACK RIBS

DIJON LEG OF LAMB

This grilled entree is always on our Easter table, and I serve it for other events throughout the year. I first tasted this delicious lamb at a dinner party given by a friend who happily shared the recipe.

—CHRISTY PORTER ENGLEWOOD, CO

PREP: 10 MIN. + MARINATING
GRILL: 1½ HOURS + STANDING
MAKES: 9 SERVINGS

- 1 **boneless leg of lamb (4-5 pounds)**
- 1 **cup Dijon mustard**
- ½ **cup soy sauce**
- 2 **tablespoons olive oil**
- 1 **tablespoon chopped fresh rosemary or 1 teaspoon dried rosemary, crushed**
- 1 **teaspoon ground ginger**
- 1 **garlic clove, minced**

1. Cut leg of lamb horizontally from one long side to within 1 in. of opposite side. Open meat so it lies flat; trim and discard fat. Place the lamb in a large resealable plastic bag. In a small bowl, whisk the mustard, soy sauce, oil and seasonings. Pour 1 cup of marinade over lamb. Seal the bag and turn to coat; refrigerate overnight. Cover and refrigerate remaining marinade.
2. Drain and discard marinade from the lamb. Moisten a paper towel with cooking oil; using long-handled tongs, rub it on the grill rack to coat lightly. Prepare grill for indirect heat using a drip pan.
3. Place lamb over drip pan and grill, covered, over medium-low heat for 1½-2½ hours or until meat reaches desired doneness (for medium-rare, a thermometer should read 145°; medium, 160°; well-done, 170°). Let stand for 10 minutes before slicing. Warm reserved mustard sauce; serve with lamb.

EASY GRILLED PORK TENDERLOIN

(5) **INGREDIENTS** FAST FIX

EASY GRILLED PORK TENDERLOIN

We've been making this dish for years and everyone who tastes it requests the recipe. We often double it and serve the leftovers on a mixed green salad.

—DEBBIE WIGLE WILLIAMSON, NY

PREP: 10 MIN. + MARINATING • **GRILL:** 25 MIN.
MAKES: 4 SERVINGS

- ½ **cup Italian salad dressing**
- ¼ **cup reduced-sodium soy sauce**
- 1 **pork tenderloin (1 pound)**
- ½ **teaspoon steak seasoning**

1. In a large resealable plastic bag, combine salad dressing and soy sauce; add pork. Seal bag and turn to coat; refrigerate for up to 4 hours.
2. Drain and discard marinade. Rub pork with steak seasoning. Moisten a paper towel with cooking oil; using long-handled tongs, rub it on the grill rack to coat lightly.
3. Prepare grill for indirect heat. Grill pork, covered, over indirect medium heat for 25-40 minutes or until a thermometer reads 160°. Let stand for 5 minutes before slicing.
NOTE *This recipe was tested with McCormick's Montreal Steak Seasoning. Look for it in the spice aisle.*

 **GRILL SKILL**

Marinades have an acidic ingredient, seasonings, oil and salt. Acidic ingredients such as salad dressing, wine or vinegar tenderize meats, retain juices and add flavors. Seasonings such as herbs, soy sauce and sugar provide primary flavors. Oil carries seasoning flavors and keeps meat moist. Salt carries moisture and seasoning in meats. If a salty seasoning such as soy sauce is included, hold back on additional salt.

PORK CHOPS WITH MAPLE BUTTER

This recipe takes some time to prepare, but after one taste you'll agree it's worth the extra effort. The maple butter and the nutty apple-and-onion topping always get rave reviews at my house.

—ANITA ALFORD MADISONVILLE, KY

PREP: 30 MIN. • **GRILL:** 10 MIN.
MAKES: 4 SERVINGS

MAPLE BUTTER
- 1 teaspoon minced green onion
- 8 tablespoons butter, divided
- ¼ cup apple juice
- ½ cup heavy whipping cream
- ½ cup maple syrup
- ½ teaspoon salt
- ½ teaspoon pepper

- 2 large tart apples, peeled and sliced
- ½ cup sliced onion
- 2 tablespoons butter
- 2 tablespoons brown sugar

CHOPS
- 8 bone-in pork loin chops (½-inch thick and 4 ounces each)
- ½ teaspoon pepper
- 2 teaspoons canola oil
- ¼ cup coarsely chopped pecans, toasted

1. In a saucepan, saute green onion in 1 tablespoon butter. Add apple juice; cook until reduced by half. Add cream, syrup, salt and pepper; cook until reduced by half and mixture is caramel-like. Add the remaining butter, 1 tablespoon at a time, stirring mixture until melted.

2. In a large skillet, cook the apples, onion, butter and brown sugar over medium heat for 3 minutes or until onion is crisp-tender and apples are softened; set aside.

3. Sprinkle chops with pepper. Brush each side with oil. Grill, uncovered, over medium heat for 4-5 minutes on each side or until a thermometer reads 145°. Let meat stand for 5 minutes before serving.

4. Rewarm maple butter and glazed apples. Divide apples among four plates; top each with two chops and a fourth of the maple butter. Sprinkle with pecans.

FAST FIX
KIELBASA APPLE KABOBS

I use sausage to make these colorful kabobs different from the rest. The meaty chunks are skewered with tart apples and colorful peppers, then basted with a mild, sweet glaze.

—EDNA HOFFMAN HEBRON, IN

START TO FINISH: 25 MIN.
MAKES: 8 SERVINGS

- ¼ cup sugar
- 1 tablespoon cornstarch
- ¾ cup cranberry juice
- 2 tablespoons cider vinegar
- 2 teaspoons soy sauce
- 1 pound smoked kielbasa or Polish sausage, cut into 1½-inch pieces
- 2 medium tart apples, cut into wedges
- 1 medium sweet red pepper, cut into 1-inch pieces
- 1 medium green pepper, cut into 1-inch pieces

1. In a large saucepan, combine sugar and cornstarch. Stir in cranberry juice, vinegar and soy sauce. Bring to a boil; cook and stir for 1-2 minutes or until thickened.

2. On metal or soaked wooden skewers, alternately thread sausage, apples and peppers. Grill, uncovered, over indirect heat for 8 minutes or until heated through, turning and brushing with glaze occasionally.

PORK CHOPS WITH MAPLE BUTTER

FAST FIX

GRILLED SAUSAGE-BASIL PIZZAS

These easy little pizzas are a wonderful change of pace from the classic cookout menu. Let each person top his or her own and watch for all the smiles of satisfaction.

—**MARY LISA SPEER** PALM BEACH, FL

START TO FINISH: 30 MIN.
MAKES: 4 SERVINGS

- 4 Italian sausage links (4 ounces each)
- 4 naan flatbreads or whole pita breads
- ¼ cup olive oil
- 1 cup tomato basil pasta sauce
- 2 cups (8 ounces) shredded part-skim mozzarella cheese
- ½ cup grated Parmesan cheese
- ½ cup thinly sliced fresh basil

1. Grill sausages, covered, over medium heat 10-12 minutes or until a thermometer reads 160°, turning occasionally. Cut into ¼-in. slices.
2. Brush both sides of flatbreads with oil. Grill flatbreads, covered, over medium heat 2-3 minutes or until bottoms are lightly browned.
3. Remove from grill. Layer grilled sides with sauce, sausage, cheeses and basil. Return to grill; cook, covered, 2-3 minutes longer or until cheese is melted.

GRILLED SAUSAGE-BASIL PIZZAS

ULTIMATE GRILLED PORK CHOP

turn to coat chops. Place in a 13x9-in. baking dish. Refrigerate 8-12 hours.
3. Remove chops from brine; rinse and pat dry. Discard brine. Brush both sides of chops with oil. In a small bowl, mix rub ingredients; rub over pork chops. Let stand at room temperature for 30 minutes.
4. Moisten a paper towel with cooking oil; using long-handled tongs, rub it on grill rack to coat lightly. Grill the chops, covered, over medium heat 4-6 minutes on each side or until a thermometer reads 145°. Let chops stand 5 minutes before serving.

GREEK PORK CHOPS

My in-laws taught me a lot about cooking, so any time I come across a great new recipe, I enjoy making it for them. These tasty grilled chops always get rave reviews from everyone!
—GERI LIPCZYNSKI OAK LAWN, IL

PREP: 15 MIN. + MARINATING • **GRILL:** 10 MIN.
MAKES: 4 SERVINGS

- 2 **tablespoons olive oil**
- 4 **teaspoons lemon juice**
- 1 **tablespoon Worcestershire sauce**
- 2 **teaspoons dried oregano**
- 1 **teaspoon salt**
- 1 **teaspoon onion powder**
- 1 **teaspoon garlic powder**
- 1 **teaspoon pepper**
- ½ **teaspoon ground mustard**
- 4 **boneless pork loin chops (¾-inch thick and 4 ounces each)**

1. In a large resealable plastic bag, combine the first nine ingredients; add the pork. Seal bag and turn to coat; refrigerate for 8 hours or overnight.
2. Drain and discard the marinade. Moisten a paper towel with cooking oil; using long-handled tongs, rub on grill rack to coat lightly. Grill pork, covered, over medium heat or broil 4-5 in. from the heat for 4-5 minutes on each side or until a thermometer reads 145°. Let stand for 5 minutes before serving.

ULTIMATE GRILLED PORK CHOP

A little brining and a special dry rub go a long way to making the perfect pork chop. Once you've mastered the techniques, you'll be enjoying them all summer long.
—MATTHEW HASS FRANKLIN, WI

PREP: 20 MIN. + BRINING • **GRILL:** 10 MIN.
MAKES: 4 SERVINGS

- ¼ **cup kosher salt**
- ¼ **cup sugar**
- 2 **cups water**
- 2 **cups ice water**
- 4 **bone-in pork center-cut rib chops (1-inch thick and 8 ounces each)**
- 2 **tablespoons canola oil**

BASIC RUB
- 3 **tablespoons paprika**
- 1 **teaspoon each garlic powder, onion powder, ground cumin and ground mustard**
- 1 **teaspoon coarsely ground pepper**
- ½ **teaspoon ground chipotle pepper**

1. In a large saucepan, combine salt, sugar and 2 cups water; cook and stir over medium heat until salt and sugar are dissolved. Remove from heat. Add 2 cups ice water to cool brine to room temperature.
2. Place pork chops in a large resealable plastic bag; add cooled brine. Seal bag, pressing out as much air as possible;

**GRILLED CURRY PORK CHOPS
WITH APRICOT SAUCE**

MINTED LAMB 'N' VEGGIE KABOBS

Mint leaves give these lamb kabobs an enticing flavor and aroma. Served with brown rice, the eye-catching meat and vegetable skewers look and taste special enough to dish out to guests.

—**MICHAEL ROSE** GRAND PRAIRIE, TX

PREP: 30 MIN. + MARINATING • **GRILL:** 10 MIN.
MAKES: 4 SERVINGS

- 3 **tablespoons olive oil**
- 2 **tablespoons lemon juice**
- 4 **garlic cloves, minced**
- 2 **teaspoons dried basil**
- 1 **teaspoon dried oregano**
- 1 **teaspoon pepper**
- ½ **teaspoon salt**
- ½ **teaspoon dried thyme**
- 1 **pound boneless leg of lamb, cut into 1-inch cubes**
- 1 **medium sweet red pepper, cut into 1-inch pieces**
- 1 **medium sweet yellow pepper, cut into 1-inch pieces**
- 1 **medium zucchini, cut into ¼-inch slices**
- 1 **small red onion, cut into chunks**
- 16 **medium fresh mushrooms**
- 1 **cup fresh mint leaves**
  Hot cooked brown rice

1. In a large resealable plastic bag, combine the oil, lemon juice, garlic, basil, oregano, pepper, salt and thyme; add lamb. Seal bag and turn to coat; refrigerate for 30 minutes.
2. On eight metal or soaked wooden skewers, alternately thread the lamb and vegetables with mint leaves.
3. Grill, covered, over medium heat or broil 4 in. from the heat for 4-5 minutes on each side or until meat reaches desired doneness and vegetables are tender. Serve with rice.

FAST FIX

GRILLED CURRY PORK CHOPS WITH APRICOT SAUCE

A little curry powder and some fresh cilantro take this best-loved flavor combo—pork chops with apricots—in a whole new direction. The recipe's so easy and so fantastic, frequent requests are a sure bet.

—**JULIE HANSON** CHARLESTON, ME

START TO FINISH: 25 MIN.
MAKES: 4 SERVINGS

- ¼ **cup apricot preserves**
- 2 **teaspoons curry powder**
- 4 **bone-in pork loin chops (¾-inch thick and 7 ounces each)**

SAUCE

- 1 **cup canned apricot halves, chopped**
- 2 **tablespoons apricot preserves**
- 2 **teaspoons minced fresh cilantro**

1. In a small bowl, mix preserves and curry powder; brush over pork chops. Moisten a paper towel with cooking oil; using long-handled tongs, rub on grill rack to coat lightly.
2. Grill pork chops, covered, over medium heat or broil 4 in. from heat 8-10 minutes or until a thermometer reads 145°, turning occasionally. Let rest 5 minutes before serving.
3. Meanwhile, in a small bowl, mix sauce ingredients. Serve pork chops with sauce.

BRATWURST SUPPER

This meal-in-one grills to perfection in heavy-duty foil packets and is ideal for camping. Loaded with chunks of bratwurst, red potatoes, mushrooms and carrots, it's easy to season with onion soup mix and a little soy sauce.
—JANICE MEYER MEDFORD, WI

PREP: 10 MIN. • **GRILL:** 45 MIN.
MAKES: 12 SERVINGS

- 3 **pounds uncooked bratwurst links**
- 3 **pounds small red potatoes, cut into wedges**
- 1 **pound baby carrots**
- 1 **large red onion, sliced and separated into rings**
- 2 **jars (4½ ounces each) whole mushrooms, drained**
- ¼ **cup butter, cubed**
- 1 **envelope onion soup mix**
- 2 **tablespoons soy sauce**
- ½ **teaspoon pepper**

1. For each of two foil packets, arrange a double thickness of heavy-duty foil (about 17x15 in.) on a flat surface.
2. Cut brats into thirds. Divide the brats, potatoes, carrots, onion and mushrooms evenly between the two double-layer foil pieces. Dot with butter. Sprinkle with soup mix, soy sauce and pepper. Bring edges of foil together; crimp to seal tightly, forming two large packets. Turn to coat.
3. Grill, covered, over medium heat for 23-28 minutes on each side or until vegetables are tender and sausage is no longer pink.

BRATWURST SUPPER

COUNTRY-STYLE
GRILLED RIBS

COUNTRY-STYLE GRILLED RIBS

A sweet and tangy barbecue sauce, sprinkled with celery seed, coats these tender ribs. Chili powder and hot pepper sauce contribute to the mouthwatering appeal of these tender ribs.

—**MARILYN BEERMAN** WORTHINGTON, OH

PREP: 1½ HOURS + STANDING • **GRILL:** 10 MIN.
MAKES: 6 SERVINGS

- 4 **pounds bone-in country-style pork ribs**
- 1 **cup water**
- 1 **cup ketchup**
- ¼ **cup packed brown sugar**
- ¼ **cup cider vinegar**
- ¼ **cup Worcestershire sauce**
- 1 **tablespoon celery seed**
- 1 **teaspoon chili powder**
- ⅛ **teaspoon hot pepper sauce**
  Dash pepper

1. Preheat oven to 325°. Place ribs in a shallow roasting pan. Bake, covered, 1½-2 hours or until meat is tender.

2. In a small saucepan, combine the remaining ingredients. Bring to a boil. Reduce heat; simmer, uncovered, for 5 minutes, stirring occasionally. Pour 1 cup sauce over ribs; turn to coat. Let stand 15 minutes.

3. Drain and discard sauce from ribs. Grill ribs, uncovered, over medium heat 10-12 minutes or until browned, basting with 1 cup sauce and turning occasionally. Serve with remaining sauce.

LAMB AND BEEF KABOBS

A lemon-olive oil marinade gives these tasty kabobs a nice tang. This is a great recipe for a summer meal made on the grill.

—WEDA MOSELLIE PHILLIPSBURG, NJ

PREP: 25 MIN. + MARINATING • **GRILL:** 10 MIN.
MAKES: 8 SERVINGS

- ¼ cup minced fresh parsley
- 2 tablespoons olive oil
- 4 teaspoons salt
- 2 teaspoons pepper
- 2 teaspoons lemon juice
- 2 pounds boneless lamb, cut into 1½-inch cubes
- 1 pound beef top sirloin steak, cut into 1½-inch cubes
- 6 small onions, cut into wedges
- 2 medium sweet red peppers, cut into 1-inch pieces
- 16 large fresh mushrooms
- 6 pita breads (6 inches), cut into wedges

1. In a small bowl, combine first five ingredients. Place the lamb and beef in a large resealable plastic bag; add half of the marinade. Place vegetables in another large resealable plastic bag; add the remaining marinade. Seal bags and turn to coat; refrigerate 1 hour.

2. On eight metal or soaked wooden skewers, alternately thread lamb, beef, onions, red peppers and mushrooms. Grill, covered, over medium heat for 5-6 minutes on each side or until meat reaches desired doneness and the vegetables are tender. Serve with pita bread wedges.

PORK CHOPS WITH APRICOT GLAZE

FAST FIX ▶
PORK CHOPS WITH APRICOT GLAZE

This quick recipe is fantastic! The seasonings add just the right amount of flavor, and the apricot preserves offer a touch of sweetness. The glaze is also tasty on grilled chicken.

—KATHY HARDING RICHMOND, MO

START TO FINISH: 30 MIN.
MAKES: 6 SERVINGS

- 1½ teaspoons ground ginger
- 1 teaspoon salt
- ½ teaspoon garlic powder
- ½ teaspoon pepper
- 6 boneless pork loin chops (6 ounces each)
- 1 cup apricot preserves
- 2 tablespoons hoisin sauce
- ½ teaspoon crushed red pepper flakes
- 2 green onions, chopped
- 3 tablespoons chopped unsalted peanuts

1. Mix ginger, salt, garlic powder and pepper; rub onto both sides of chops. In a small saucepan, combine preserves, hoisin sauce and pepper flakes; cook and stir over medium heat until blended. Reserve ½ cup for brushing chops after grilling.

2. Moisten a paper towel with cooking oil; using long-handled tongs, rub on grill rack to coat lightly. Grill the pork, covered, over medium heat or broil 4 in. from heat 4-5 minutes on each side or until a thermometer reads 145°, basting frequently with reserved sauce during the last 4 minutes of cooking. Let stand 5 minutes before serving. Brush chops with remaining sauce; sprinkle with green onions and peanuts.

PORK MEDALLIONS WITH PEAR SALSA

My husband and I have been in a dinner group with three other couples for a few years. One of the couples served this pork, and I decided to "pear" it with this fabulous salsa.

—**SUZAN WARD** COEUR D'ALENE, ID

PREP: 15 MIN. + MARINATING • **GRILL:** 15 MIN.
MAKES: 8 SERVINGS

- ¼ cup lime juice
- 2 tablespoons olive oil
- 2 garlic cloves, minced
- 1½ teaspoons ground cumin
- 1½ teaspoons dried oregano
- ½ teaspoon pepper
- 2 pounds pork tenderloin, cut into ¾-inch slices

PEAR SALSA

- 4 cups chopped peeled pears (about 4 medium)
- ⅓ cup chopped red onion
- 2 tablespoons chopped fresh mint or 2 teaspoons dried mint
- 2 tablespoons lime juice
- 1 tablespoon grated lime peel
- 1 jalapeno pepper, seeded and chopped
- 1 teaspoon sugar
- ½ teaspoon pepper

1. In a large resealable plastic bag, combine the lime juice, oil, garlic, cumin, oregano and pepper; add pork. Seal bag and turn to coat; refrigerate overnight. Drain and discard marinade.
2. Grill pork, uncovered, over medium heat for 4-6 minutes on each side or until juices run clear.
3. In a bowl, combine the salsa ingredients. Serve with the pork.
NOTE *Wear disposable gloves when cutting hot peppers; the oils can burn skin. Avoid touching your face.*

FAST FIX
SOUTHWESTERN GRILLED LAMB

Jalapeno peppers are quite abundant in this area of the country, and there are numerous ranches here that raise lambs. People seem to be eating food that's a little hotter nowadays, so I think this recipe will appeal to them.

—**MARGARET PACHE** MESA, AZ

START TO FINISH: 30 MIN.
MAKES: 2 SERVINGS

- 1 cup salsa
- ½ cup chopped onion
- ¼ cup molasses
- ¼ cup fresh lime juice (about 2 limes)
- ¼ cup chicken broth
- 2 garlic cloves, minced
- 1 to 3 tablespoons chopped seeded jalapeno peppers
- 2 teaspoons sugar
- 4 lamb chops (1-inch thick)
  Sour cream

1. In a saucepan, combine the first eight ingredients. Simmer, uncovered, for 15-20 minutes.
2. Meanwhile, grill the lamb chops, turning once, over medium heat for 10-14 minutes for medium-rare, 14-16 minutes for medium or 16-20 minutes for well-done. Brush with sauce during the last few minutes of grilling.
3. Serve with sour cream.
NOTE *Wear disposable gloves when cutting hot peppers; the oils can burn skin. Avoid touching your face.*

GREEK LAMB KABOBS

We have a gas grill and use it year-round, especially to make these tender, juicy kabobs. The lamb marinates overnight, and the attractive skewers are quickly assembled the following day.

—**KATHY HERROLA** MARTINEZ, CA

PREP: 10 MIN. + MARINATING • **GRILL:** 10 MIN.
MAKES: 4 SERVINGS

- ½ cup lemon juice
- 2 tablespoons dried oregano
- 4 teaspoons olive oil
- 6 garlic cloves, minced
- 1 pound boneless lamb, cut into 1-inch cubes
- 16 cherry tomatoes
- 1 large green pepper, cut into 1-inch pieces
- 1 large onion, cut into 1-inch wedges

1. In a small bowl, combine the lemon juice, oregano, oil and garlic. Set aside ¼ cup marinade for basting; cover and refrigerate. Pour remaining marinade into a large resealable plastic bag. Add the cubed lamb; seal bag and turn to coat. Refrigerate 8 hours or overnight, turning occasionally.
2. Drain lamb, discarding marinade in bag. On eight metal or soaked wooden skewers, alternately thread the lamb, tomatoes, green pepper and onion. Moisten a paper towel with cooking oil; using long-handled tongs, rub on grill rack to coat lightly.
3. Grill kabobs, covered, over medium heat or broil 4 in. from heat 5-6 minutes on each side or until lamb reaches desired doneness and vegetables are crisp-tender, turning occasionally and basting with reserved marinade.

PORK MEDALLIONS
WITH PEAR SALSA

GRILLED VENISON AND VEGETABLES

My husband enjoys hunting, and it's my challenge to find new ways to serve venison. This recipe makes hearty kabobs perfect for grilling. The marinade reduces the "wild" taste, so guests often don't realize they're eating venison.

—EVA MILLER-VIDETICH
CEDAR SPRINGS, MI

PREP: 10 MIN. + MARINATING • **GRILL:** 15 MIN.
MAKES: 4-6 SERVINGS

- 1 cup red wine vinegar
- ½ cup honey
- ½ cup soy sauce
- ¼ cup ketchup
  Dash pepper
  Dash garlic powder
- 1½ pounds boneless venison steak, cut into 1¼-inch cubes
- 8 to 12 cherry tomatoes
- 8 to 12 fresh mushrooms, optional
- ½ medium green or sweet red pepper, cut into 1½ inch pieces
- 1 to 2 small zucchini, cut into 1-inch chunks
- 1 large onion, cut into wedges
- 8 to 12 small new potatoes, parboiled

1. In a glass bowl or plastic bag, combine vinegar, honey, soy sauce, ketchup, pepper and garlic powder; set aside ¼ cup for vegetables. Set aside ¾ cup for basting. Add meat to bowl or bag; stir or shake to coat. Cover (or close bag) and refrigerate for 4 hours. One hour before grilling, toss vegetables with ¼ cup reserved marinade. Drain and discard marinade from meat.

2. Thread meat and vegetables alternately on skewers. Grill over medium-hot heat for 15-20 minutes or until a meat thermometer inserted in the venison reads 160°, turning and basting frequently with reserved ¾ cup marinade.

MARINATED PORK MIXED GRILL

FAST FIX

MARINATED PORK MIXED GRILL

My whole family gets so happy when they see me prepping this simple meal. When we have leftovers, it's sandwich heaven.

—MARIA BARAL BOZRAH, CT

START TO FINISH: 30 MIN.
MAKES: 4 SERVINGS

- 2 medium onions, cut into ½-inch-thick slices
- 2 medium sweet red peppers, cut into 1½-inch strips
- 2 medium green peppers, cut into 1½-inch strips
- 2 medium zucchini, cut lengthwise into ½-inch-thick slices
- ½ cup balsamic vinaigrette
- 1 peppercorn pork tenderloin (1 pound), halved lengthwise
- 1 loaf (10 ounces) frozen garlic bread
  Additional balsamic vinaigrette, optional

1. In a large bowl, combine vegetables and vinaigrette. Grill pork, covered, over medium heat 4 minutes. Turn; add vegetables. Grill 4-5 minutes longer or until a thermometer inserted into pork reads 145°. Remove pork from grill; tent with foil.

2. Place garlic bread on grill rack, cut side up. Turn vegetables; grill, covered, over medium heat 4-6 minutes longer or until vegetables are tender, the garlic bread is heated through and the bottom is toasted.

3. Cut tenderloin and garlic bread into serving-size pieces. Serve with the vegetables and, if desired, additional vinaigrette.

TENDER PORK CHOPS WITH MANGO SALSA

To save time, I make the salsa and season the pork in the morning so it's ready to throw on the grill later. For a spicier topping, I add jalapenos to the salsa.
—**ANDREA RIVERA** WESTBURY, NY

PREP: 15 MIN. + MARINATING • **GRILL:** 10 MIN.
MAKES: 4 SERVINGS

- 3 **tablespoons cider vinegar**
- 1 **tablespoon salt-free steak grilling blend**
- 1 **tablespoon olive oil**
- 4 **bone-in pork loin chops (7 ounces each)**

SALSA

- 2 **medium mangoes, peeled and chopped**
- 1 **cup chopped sweet onion**
- 1 **jalapeno pepper, seeded and finely chopped**
- 1 **tablespoon lemon juice**
- 2 **teaspoons honey**

1. In a large resealable plastic bag, combine the vinegar, grilling blend and oil. Add the pork; seal bag and turn to coat. Refrigerate for at least 2 hours.

2. Drain and discard marinade. Grill pork chops, covered, over medium heat or broil 4-5 in. from the heat for 4-5 minutes on each side or until a thermometer reads 145°. Let stand for 5 minutes before serving.

3. Meanwhile, in a small bowl, combine the salsa ingredients. Serve with chops.

NOTE *Wear disposable gloves when cutting hot peppers; the oils can burn skin. Avoid touching your face.*

TENDER PORK CHOPS WITH MANGO SALSA

GRILLED RACK OF LAMB

Whenever my husband and I really want to impress guests, we make this rack of lamb. It never fails to please!
—**GAIL CAWSEY** GENESEO, IL

PREP: 20 MIN. + MARINATING • **GRILL:** 20 MIN.
MAKES: 8 SERVINGS

- 2 **cups apple cider or juice**
- ⅔ **cup cider vinegar**
- ⅔ **cup thinly sliced green onions**
- ½ **cup canola oil**
- ⅓ **cup honey**
- ¼ **cup steak sauce**
- 2 **teaspoons dried tarragon**
- 2 **teaspoons salt**
- ½ **teaspoon pepper**
- 4 **racks of lamb (1½-2 pounds each)**

1. In a large saucepan, combine the first nine ingredients. Bring to a boil. Reduce heat; simmer, uncovered, for 20 minutes. Cool to room temperature. Remove 1 cup for basting; cover and refrigerate. Pour the remaining marinade into a large resealable plastic bag; add lamb. Seal bag and turn to coat; refrigerate for 2-3 hours or overnight, turning once or twice.

2. Drain and discard the marinade. Cover the rib ends of lamb with foil. Moisten a paper towel with cooking oil; using long-handled tongs, rub the grill rack to coat lightly. Grill lamb, covered, over medium heat or broil 4 in. from the heat for 15 minutes.

3. Baste with reserved marinade. Grill or broil 5-10 minutes longer or until meat reaches desired doneness (for medium-rare, a thermometer should read 145°; medium, 160°; well-done, 170°), basting occasionally.

GRILLED WHISKEY CHOPS

This is a family favorite for summertime. The molasses butter nicely contrasts with the whiskey and peppercorn taste of the chops.

—KELLY HODSON ANDERSON, IN

START TO FINISH: 25 MIN.
MAKES: 4 SERVINGS

- ¼ **cup butter, softened**
- 1 **tablespoon molasses**
- ½ **teaspoon ground cinnamon**
- ½ **teaspoon lemon juice**
- 3 **tablespoons coarsely ground pepper**
- ⅓ **cup whiskey**
- ½ **teaspoon salt**
- 4 **bone-in pork loin chops (¾-inch thick)**

1. In a small bowl, mix the butter, molasses, cinnamon and lemon juice; refrigerate until serving.

2. Place pepper in a shallow bowl. In a separate shallow bowl, mix whiskey and salt. Dip chops in whiskey mixture, then in pepper.

3. Moisten a paper towel with cooking oil; using long-handled tongs, rub on grill rack to coat lightly. Grill chops, covered, over medium heat or broil 4 in. from heat 4-5 minutes on each side or until a thermometer reads 145°. Let stand for 5 minutes. Serve with the molasses butter.

**GRILLED
WHISKEY CHOPS**

PORK MEDALLIONS WITH HOT MUSTARD

This soy-marinated tenderloin tastes like Chinese food, especially when the slices are dipped in the zippy mustard sauce. It's terrific served warm or cold.
—**KYLE SPENCER** HAVRE, MT

PREP: 5 MIN. + MARINATING • **GRILL:** 25 MIN.
MAKES: 6 SERVINGS

- ¼ **cup reduced-sodium soy sauce**
- 2 **tablespoons dry red wine or chicken broth**
- 1 **tablespoon brown sugar**
- 1 **tablespoon honey**
- ½ **teaspoon ground cinnamon**
- 2 **pork tenderloins (¾ pound each)**

HOT MUSTARD
- ¼ **cup Dijon mustard**
- 1 **tablespoon honey**
- 1 **teaspoon prepared horseradish**
- 2 **teaspoons sesame seeds, toasted**

In a large resealable plastic bag, combine the soy sauce, wine, brown sugar, honey and cinnamon; add pork. Seal bag and turn to coat; refrigerate for 8 hours or overnight. Drain and discard the marinade. Grill the pork, covered, over indirect medium heat for 25-40 minutes or until a thermometer reads 160°. Let stand for 5 minutes before slicing. In a small bowl, combine the mustard, honey and horseradish. Slice pork; sprinkle with sesame seeds. Serve with hot mustard.

BABY BACK RIBS

A grilling goal of mine has been to cook barbecued ribs to tender perfection. These are the most tender and best tasting ribs I have ever made. Everyone who tries them agrees!
—**JOANNE PARKS** STEGER, IL

PREP: 15 MIN. • **GRILL:** 1 HOUR 20 MIN.
MAKES: 4 SERVINGS

- 2 **racks pork baby back ribs (about 4½ pounds)**
- 2 **tablespoons olive oil**
- ¼ **cup packed brown sugar**
- ¼ **cup paprika**
- 1 **tablespoon pepper**
- 1 **teaspoon onion powder**
- 1 **teaspoon garlic powder**
- ½ **teaspoon cayenne pepper**

SAUCE
- ½ **cup barbecue sauce**
- ¼ **cup beer or beef broth**

1. Rub ribs with oil. In a small bowl, combine the brown sugar, paprika, pepper, onion powder, garlic powder and cayenne; rub over ribs. Wrap in a large piece of heavy-duty foil (about 28x18-in.). Seal the edges of foil. In a small bowl, combine barbecue sauce and beer; set aside.
2. Prepare grill for indirect heat. Grill ribs, covered, over indirect medium heat for 1 hour. Carefully remove ribs from foil. Place over direct heat; baste with sauce mixture. Grill 20 minutes or until the meat is tender, turning and basting occasionally with sauce.

GRILLED PINEAPPLE PORK & VEGETABLES

Celebrate the weekend with a tasty grilled dinner. The pork takes just an hour to marinate, so you'll enjoy a little hands-free time with this carefree meal.
—*TASTE OF HOME* TEST KITCHEN

PREP: 25 MIN. + MARINATING • **GRILL:** 15 MIN.
MAKES: 5 SERVINGS

- 1 **can (8 ounces) unsweetened pineapple chunks, undrained**
- ¼ **cup olive oil, divided**
- 2 **garlic cloves, peeled and halved**
- 2 **teaspoons ground cumin**
- 2 **teaspoons dried oregano**
- ¾ **teaspoon pepper, divided**
- ¾ **teaspoon salt, divided**
- 2 **pounds pork tenderloin, cut into ¾-inch slices**
- 1 **pound fresh asparagus, trimmed**
- 4 **medium carrots, halved lengthwise**
- 1 **large sweet red pepper, halved**
- 1 **bunch green onions, trimmed**

GRILLED PINEAPPLE PORK & VEGETABLES

1. Place the pineapple, 2 tablespoons oil, garlic, cumin, oregano, ½ teaspoon pepper and ¼ teaspoon salt in a blender; cover and process until blended. Place in a large resealable plastic bag; add pork. Seal bag and turn to coat; refrigerate 1 hour.
2. Drain and discard the marinade. Moisten a paper towel with cooking oil; using long-handled tongs, rub on the grill rack to coat lightly. Grill the pork, uncovered, over medium heat for 3-4 minutes on each side or until a thermometer reads 145°. Let stand for 5 minutes before serving.
3. Place vegetables in a grill wok or basket. Brush with the remaining oil; sprinkle with the remaining salt and pepper.
4. Grill, uncovered, over medium heat for 6-8 minutes or until tender, stirring frequently. Cut vegetables into 2-in. pieces. Serve with pork.

ORANGE BBQ BABY BACK RIBS

⑤ INGREDIENTS FAST FIX ▶

MARMALADE HAM STEAKS

Orange marmalade and maple syrup combine to give these ham steaks a terrific taste. I even like to serve leftovers at brunch the next day. My children love it with fruit and scrambled eggs.

—**BONNIE HAWKINS** ELKHORN, WI

START TO FINISH: 20 MIN.
MAKES: 4 SERVINGS

- ½ cup orange marmalade
- 2 tablespoons maple syrup
- 4½ teaspoons orange juice
- 1½ teaspoons chili powder
- 4 boneless fully cooked ham steaks (5 ounces each)

1. In a small bowl, combine the marmalade, syrup, orange juice and chili powder.
2. Grill the ham steaks, covered, over medium heat or broil 4 in. from the heat for 3-4 minutes on each side or until heated through, brushing occasionally with marmalade mixture.

 **EASY IDEA** ⎯⎯⎯⎯⎯

When adding marinade to meat, put the meat in a resealable plastic bag, then set the bag in a baking dish. Doing so makes pouring the marinade into the bag a bit easier, and cleanup is a snap should you spill any. In addition, the dish will catch any marinade if the bag leaks while in the refrigerator.

ORANGE BBQ BABY BACK RIBS

I avoid long and complicated recipes during the summer months (I'd rather be out by the pool with my family!), so I came up with this simple citrus twist on barbecue. I also use the sauce when I make chicken fondue.

—**KELLIE SEAMANS** CHANDLER, AZ

PREP: 2¼ HOURS • **GRILL:** 15 MIN.
MAKES: 4 SERVINGS

- 4 pounds pork baby back ribs
- 1 bottle (18 ounces) honey barbecue sauce
- 1 cup orange juice
- 2 tablespoons grated orange peel

1. Place ribs bone side down on a rack in a shallow roasting pan. Cover and bake at 325° for 2-2½ hours or until tender; drain.
2. In a small bowl, combine the barbecue sauce, orange juice and peel; set aside 1 cup for serving. Moisten a paper towel with cooking oil; using long-handled tongs, rub on the grill rack to coat lightly.
3. Place ribs over direct heat; baste with some of the sauce. Grill, covered, over medium heat for 15-20 minutes or until browned, turning and basting occasionally. Serve with reserved sauce.

INDONESIAN PORK TENDERLOIN

Marinated in soy sauce, lime juice, red pepper and ginger, the meat takes on plenty of flavor, which makes it special enough for company.

—MARGARET HAUGH HEILMAN
HOUSTON, TX

PREP: 5 MIN. + MARINATING • **GRILL:** 15 MIN.
MAKES: 4 SERVINGS

- 3 **tablespoons lime juice**
- 3 **tablespoons reduced-sodium soy sauce**
- 3 **tablespoon stir-fry sauce**
- 4½ **teaspoons grated fresh gingerroot**
- 1 **teaspoon crushed red pepper flakes**
- 3 **garlic cloves, minced**
- 1 **pork tenderloin (1 pound)**

In a bowl, combine the first six ingredients. Place the pork in a large resealable plastic bag; add half of the marinade. Seal bag and turn to coat; refrigerate for 2 hours, turning bag occasionally. Cover and refrigerate remaining marinade for basting. Drain and discard marinade from bag. Grill pork, covered, over hot heat for 15-20 minutes or until a thermometer reads 160° and juices run clear, basting occasionally with reserved marinade.

INDONESIAN PORK TENDERLOIN

CAJUN BOIL ON
THE GRILL, PAGE 239

SMOKED HONEY-PEPPERCORN
SALMON, PAGE 245

SOUTHWESTERN
CATFISH, PAGE 243

BARBECUED SHRIMP &
PEACH KABOBS, PAGE 237

FIERY FISH & SEAFOOD

Turn your dinner into the **bayou's best** with these full-flavored entrees. The fiery favorites found here offer the **tangy, zesty** and mouthwatering appeal you'd expect from fresh fish and seafood **grilled to perfection** in your very own backyard.

FISH & SEAFOOD GRILLING CHART

When cooking fish, check for doneness with a food thermometer or other appropriate doneness test. Fish is done when it begins to flake easily with a fork. Scallops are done when they turn firm and opaque, and shrimp are done when they turn pink. Watch closely to avoid overcooking. For direct grilling, turn steaks, whole fish, shrimp and scallops halfway through grilling time. Fillets generally do not need to be turned. To ease turning, use a grill basket. The cooking times below are given as general guidelines.

CUT	WEIGHT OR THICKNESS	HEAT	APPROXIMATE COOKING TIME (IN MINUTES)
FISH			
FILLETS OR STEAKS	¼ to ½ in. thick ½ to 1 in. thick	high/direct high/direct	3 to 5 minutes 5 to 10 minutes
DRESSED FISH	1 lb. ¾ to 1 lb.	medium/direct medium/indirect	10 to 15 minutes 20 to 30 minutes
FISH KABOBS	1-in. cubes	medium/direct	8 to 12 minutes
SEAFOOD			
SEA SCALLOPS	1 lb.	medium/direct	5 to 8 minutes
SHRIMP, MEDIUM	1 lb.	medium/direct	5 to 8 minutes

⑤ INGREDIENTS FAST FIX

GRILLED LEMON-DILL SHRIMP

This grilled shrimp is one of my go-to recipes when I stare at the freezer and draw a blank. Add veggies if desired, but grill them separately.

—JANE WHITTAKER PENSACOLA, FL

START TO FINISH: 30 MIN.
MAKES: 4 SERVINGS

- ¼ cup olive oil
- 1 tablespoon lemon juice
- 2 teaspoons dill weed
- 2 garlic cloves, minced
- ¾ teaspoon salt
- ½ teaspoon pepper
- 1 pound uncooked shrimp (31-40 per pound), peeled and deveined

1. In a large bowl, whisk the first six ingredients until blended. Reserve 3 tablespoons marinade for basting. Add shrimp to remaining marinade; toss to coat. Refrigerate, covered, 15 minutes.

2. Drain shrimp, discarding any remaining marinade. Thread shrimp onto four or eight metal or soaked wooden skewers. Grill, covered, over medium heat or broil 4 in. from heat 2-4 minutes on each side, basting with reserved marinade during the last minute of cooking.

GRILLED LEMON-DILL SHRIMP

GINGER SALMON WITH CUCUMBER LIME SAUCE

Lime and ginger are one of my favorite flavor combos, especially with grilled salmon. Even with the addition of the cucumber sauce, this recipe is always a cinch to put together.

—NOELLE MYERS GRAND FORKS, ND

PREP: 30 MIN. • **GRILL:** 10 MIN.
MAKES: 10 SERVINGS

- 1 tablespoon grated lime peel
- ¼ cup lime juice
- 2 tablespoons olive oil
- 2 tablespoons rice vinegar or white wine vinegar
- 4 teaspoons sugar
- ½ teaspoon salt
- ½ teaspoon ground coriander
- ½ teaspoon freshly ground pepper
- ⅓ cup chopped fresh cilantro
- 1 tablespoon finely chopped onion
- 2 teaspoons minced fresh gingerroot
- 2 garlic cloves, minced
- 2 large cucumbers, peeled, seeded and chopped

SALMON
- ⅓ cup minced fresh gingerroot
- 1 tablespoon lime juice
- 1 tablespoon olive oil
- ½ teaspoon salt
- ½ teaspoon freshly ground pepper
- 10 salmon fillets (6 ounces each)

1. Place the first 13 ingredients in a blender. Cover and process until pureed.

2. In a small bowl, mix ginger, lime juice, oil, salt and pepper. Rub over flesh side of salmon fillets.

3. Moisten a paper towel with cooking oil; using long-handled tongs, rub on grill rack to coat lightly. Place salmon on grill rack, skin side down. Grill, covered, over medium-high heat 10-12 minutes or until fish just begins to flake easily with a fork. Serve with sauce.

GINGER SALMON WITH
CUCUMBER LIME SAUCE

LEMON-BASIL GRILLED
SHRIMP & COUSCOUS

LEMON-BASIL GRILLED SHRIMP & COUSCOUS

Lemon and basil make delicious partners, particularly when used to season these delightful shrimp kabobs. I take the shrimp off the skewers and serve them with quick and easy couscous. Yum!

—**TRISHA KRUSE** EAGLE, ID

START TO FINISH: 30 MIN.
MAKES: 6 SERVINGS

- 1½ cups uncooked pearl (Israeli) couscous
- ⅓ cup lemon juice
- ¼ cup olive oil
- 2 tablespoons Dijon mustard
- 3 garlic cloves, minced
- ½ teaspoon salt
- ¼ teaspoon pepper
- ½ cup minced fresh basil, divided
- 2 pounds uncooked large shrimp, peeled and deveined
- 2 teaspoons grated lemon peel

1. Cook couscous according to package directions; remove from heat. Meanwhile, in a large bowl, whisk lemon juice, oil, mustard, garlic, salt and pepper until blended; stir in ¼ cup basil. Stir ¼ cup dressing into cooked couscous; reserve remaining dressing.
2. Thread shrimp onto metal or soaked wooden skewers. Moisten a paper towel with cooking oil; using long-handled tongs, rub on grill rack to coat lightly. Grill shrimp, covered, over medium-high heat 2-3 minutes on each side or until shrimp turn pink.
3. Remove shrimp from skewers; toss with reserved dressing. Serve with couscous. Sprinkle with lemon peel and remaining basil.

GRILLED SALMON WITH BLACK BEAN SALSA

This fantastic fish dish features tender salmon, colorful salsa and juicy grapes. It's sure to be a winner with family and friends.

—**DIANE HALFERTY** CORPUS CHRISTI, TX

PREP: 20 MIN. + MARINATING • **GRILL:** 10 MIN.
MAKES: 6 SERVINGS

- ¼ cup white wine or reduced-sodium chicken broth
- ¼ cup reduced-sodium soy sauce
- 1½ teaspoons brown sugar
- 1 garlic clove, minced
- 6 salmon fillets (4 ounces each)

SALSA

- 1 can (15 ounces) black beans, rinsed and drained
- 1 cup frozen corn, thawed
- 1 medium sweet red pepper, diced
- ½ cup seedless red grapes, chopped
- ¼ cup fat-free Italian salad dressing
- 1 tablespoon canned chopped green chilies
- 1 teaspoon brown sugar

1. In a small bowl, combine the wine, soy sauce and brown sugar. Set aside 2 tablespoons mixture for basting. Stir garlic into remaining mixture. Place in a large resealable plastic bag; add the salmon. Seal bag and turn to coat; refrigerate for 30 minutes, turning occasionally.
2. Meanwhile, in a small bowl, combine the salsa ingredients. Cover and chill until serving.
3. Drain and discard marinade. Using long-handled tongs, moisten a paper towel with cooking oil and lightly coat the grill rack. Place salmon skin side down on grill rack.
4. Grill, covered, over medium heat for 10-12 minutes or until fish flakes with a fork, basting occasionally with reserved wine mixture. Serve with the salsa.

HONEY-DIJON SALMON AND ASPARAGUS

This is my family's favorite salmon recipe. It's easy, nutritious and delicious. Plus, cleanup is a snap!

—**BETTY STEWART** LEOLA, PA

START TO FINISH: 25 MIN.
MAKES: 2 SERVINGS

- 1½ teaspoons cornstarch
- 2¼ teaspoons butter, melted
- 1 teaspoon Worcestershire sauce
- 2 tablespoons honey
- 1 tablespoon Dijon mustard
  Dash white pepper
- 2 salmon fillets (4 ounces each)
- ¼ cup chopped walnuts
- ½ pound fresh asparagus, trimmed

1. In a small bowl, combine cornstarch, butter and Worcestershire sauce until smooth. Stir in honey, Dijon mustard and pepper.
2. Place each of the salmon fillets on a double thickness of heavy-duty foil (about 18 x12 in.). Drizzle with honey mixture and sprinkle with walnuts. Place asparagus around salmon. Fold foil around salmon and seal tightly. Grill, covered, over medium heat for 15-20 minutes or until fish flakes easily with a fork.

HONEY-DIJON SALMON AND ASPARAGUS

SMOKED SHRIMP & WILD MUSHROOM FETTUCCINE

We smoke these prawns in-house, but a grill works just as well. The broccoli and tomatoes add color to the flavorful prawns and mushrooms.
—**BARBARA SIDWAY** BAKER CITY, OR

PREP: 20 MIN. • **COOK:** 25 MIN.
MAKES: 5 SERVINGS

  2 **cups soaked mesquite wood chips**
 10 **uncooked jumbo shrimp, peeled and deveined**
  1 **package (12 ounces) fettuccine**
 1½ **cups fresh broccoli florets**
  2 **large portobello mushrooms, sliced**
  2 **tablespoons olive oil**
  3 **garlic cloves, minced**
  ¼ **teaspoon salt**
  ½ **cup white wine or chicken broth**
  2 **cups heavy whipping cream**
  1 **medium tomato, chopped**

1. Add wood chips to grill according to manufacturer's directions.
2. Using long-handled tongs, moisten a paper towel with cooking oil and lightly coat the grill rack. Thread shrimp onto two metal or soaked wooden skewers. Grill, covered, over medium heat for 5-8 minutes or until shrimp turn pink, turning once.
3. Meanwhile, cook fettuccine according to package directions. In a large skillet, saute broccoli and mushrooms in oil until tender. Add garlic and salt; cook 1 minute longer. Add wine, stirring to loosen browned bits from pan. Gradually stir in cream. Bring to a boil. Reduce heat; simmer, uncovered, for 10-12 minutes or until thickened.
4. Drain fettuccine. Add to sauce mixture with shrimp. Cook and stir until heated through; gently stir in the chopped tomato.

TILAPIA WITH LEMON-BASIL VINAIGRETTE

FAST FIX
TILAPIA WITH LEMON-BASIL VINAIGRETTE

We aren't big fish eaters, but a friend made this tasty dish for us, and we couldn't believe how wonderful it was! Now we eat it regularly. I love making it for guests because it's simple, looks lovely and tastes restaurant-worthy.
—**BETH COOPER** COLUMBUS, OH

START TO FINISH: 25 MIN.
MAKES: 4 SERVINGS

  3 **tablespoons lemon juice**
  3 **tablespoons minced fresh basil, divided**
  2 **tablespoons olive oil**
  2 **garlic cloves, minced**
  2 **teaspoons capers, drained**
  ½ **teaspoon grated lemon peel**
  4 **tilapia fillets (6 ounces each)**
  ½ **teaspoon salt**
  ¼ **teaspoon pepper**

1. For vinaigrette, in a small bowl, whisk the lemon juice, 2 tablespoons basil, olive oil, garlic, capers and lemon peel; set aside 2 tablespoons for sauce. Sprinkle fillets with salt and pepper. Brush both sides of fillets with remaining vinaigrette.
2. Moisten a paper towel with cooking oil; using long-handled tongs, rub on grill rack to coat lightly. Grill, covered, over medium heat or broil 4 in. from the heat for 3-4 minutes on each side or until fish flakes easily with a fork. Brush with reserved vinaigrette and sprinkle with remaining basil.

GLAZED ASIAN-STYLE SALMON FILLET

I love to cook and usually try a new recipe at least once a week. This salmon has wonderful flavor. I've served it many times over the years, and people always love it.
—**SHERRY WEST** NEW RIVER, AZ

START TO FINISH: 20 MIN.
MAKES: 6 SERVINGS

- ¼ cup reduced-sodium soy sauce
- 2 tablespoons brown sugar
- ¼ teaspoon crushed red pepper flakes
- ¼ teaspoon ground ginger
- ⅛ teaspoon sesame oil
- 1 salmon fillet (1½ pounds)

1. In a large bowl, combine the first five ingredients. Using long-handled tongs, moisten a paper towel with cooking oil and lightly coat the grill rack.

2. Grill salmon, covered, over medium heat or broil 4 in. from the heat for 5-6 minutes on each side or until salmon flakes easily with a fork, basting frequently with glaze.

TUNA VEGGIE KABOBS

This is a quick and easy summer meal. My children love to help cut up the veggies and assemble the skewers. I serve the kabobs over brown rice cooked in chicken broth. I like to garnish the platter with parsley and lemon wedges.
—**LYNN CARUSO** SAN JOSE, CA

PREP: 30 MIN. + MARINATING • **GRILL:** 10 MIN.
MAKES: 8 KABOBS

- 2 pounds tuna steaks, cut into 1½-inch cubes
- 16 large fresh mushrooms
- 3 medium green peppers, seeded and cut into 2-inch pieces
- 3 medium ears sweet corn, cut into 2-inch pieces
- 3 medium zucchini, cut into 1-inch slices
- ¼ cup olive oil
- 2 tablespoons lemon juice
- 2 tablespoons finely chopped shallot
- 1 tablespoon rice vinegar
- 1 tablespoon minced garlic
- 1 teaspoon salt
- 1 teaspoon dried rosemary, crushed
- 1 teaspoon dried thyme
- ½ teaspoon pepper

1. Place tuna in a large resealable plastic bag; place the vegetables in another large resealable plastic bag. In a small bowl, combine the remaining ingredients. Place half of the marinade in each bag. Seal bags and turn to coat; refrigerate for 1 hour.

2. Drain and discard marinade. On eight metal or soaked wooden skewers, alternately thread tuna and vegetables. Using long-handled tongs, moisten a paper towel with cooking oil and lightly coat the grill rack.

3. Grill tuna, covered, over medium heat or broil 4 in. from the heat for 5-6 minutes on each side for medium-rare or until fish is slightly pink in the center and vegetables are crisp-tender.

GRILL SKILL

Mushrooms are perfect additions to grilled kabobs. Remove dirt from mushrooms by brushing or wiping them with a damp paper towel. Or rinse them under cold water, and quickly drain and pat dry with paper towels. Do not peel mushrooms. Trim stems. For shiitake mushrooms, remove and discard stems. For enoki, trim base and separate stems.

GLAZED ASIAN-STYLE SALMON FILLET

GRILLED SPICED FISH

These moist flaky fillets provide a welcome change of pace at summer cookouts. I pepper a savory herb rub with cayenne, then work it into the fish. Even steak lovers will be smacking their lips after one bite!

—CHRIS MCBEE XENIA, OH

PREP: 5 MIN. + MARINATING • **GRILL:** 10 MIN.
MAKES: 4 SERVINGS

- 4 red snapper fillets (6 ounces each)
- 1 tablespoon olive oil
- 2 teaspoons paprika
- 1 teaspoon salt
- 1 teaspoon onion powder
- 1 teaspoon garlic powder
- ½ teaspoon cayenne pepper
- ¼ teaspoon white pepper
- ¼ teaspoon each dried oregano, basil and thyme

1. Spoon oil over fish. In a small bowl, combine the seasonings; sprinkle over fish and press into both sides. Cover and refrigerate for 30 minutes.
2. Using long-handled tongs, moisten a paper towel with cooking oil and lightly coat the grill rack. Grill fillets, covered, over medium heat or broil 4 in. from the heat for 3-5 minutes on each side or until fish flakes with a fork.

ORANGE-GLAZED SALMON

Give guests a special treat with tender grilled salmon fillets served in a delectable glaze. The marinade takes moments to mix together but has a big impact.

—MILDRED SHERRER FORT WORTH, TX

PREP: 10 MIN. + MARINATING • **GRILL:** 20 MIN.
MAKES: 6 SERVINGS

- ½ cup barbecue sauce
- ⅓ cup thawed orange juice concentrate
- 7 teaspoons soy sauce
- 4½ teaspoons sherry or apple juice
- 4½ teaspoons Dijon mustard
- 1 tablespoon minced fresh gingerroot
- 2 teaspoons brown sugar
- 2 teaspoons red wine vinegar
- 1½ teaspoons canola oil
- ½ teaspoon minced garlic
- 1 salmon fillet (2 pounds and ¾ inch thick)

1. In a small bowl, combine the first 10 ingredients. Set aside ½ cup marinade for basting; cover and refrigerate. Pour remaining marinade into a large resealable plastic bag; add salmon. Seal bag and turn to coat; refrigerate for 1 hour, turning occasionally.
2. Drain and discard marinade. Using long-handled tongs, moisten a paper towel with cooking oil and lightly coat the grill rack. Place salmon skin side down on grill rack. Grill, covered, over medium heat for 5 minutes. Spoon reserved marinade over fish. Grill 15-20 minutes longer or until fish flakes easily with a fork, basting frequently.

BASIL TUNA STEAKS

⑤INGREDIENTS FAST FIX

BASIL TUNA STEAKS

One of my favorite creations is this simple five-ingredient recipe. Tuna is delicious and can be grilled in minutes.

—LINDA MCLYMAN SYRACUSE, NY

START TO FINISH: 20 MIN.
MAKES: 6 SERVINGS

- 6 tuna steaks (6 ounces each)
- 4½ teaspoons olive oil
- 3 tablespoons minced fresh basil
- ¾ teaspoon salt
- ¼ teaspoon pepper

1. Drizzle both sides of tuna steaks with oil. Sprinkle with the basil, salt and pepper.
2. Using long-handled tongs, moisten a paper towel with cooking oil and lightly coat the grill rack. Grill tuna, covered, over medium heat or broil 4 in. from the heat for 4-5 minutes on each side for medium-rare or until slightly pink in the center.

🔧 GRILL SKILL

Prepare salmon according to the recipe, leaving the skin on (this makes it easier to remove the fish from the grill). Lightly oil the hot grill to prevent sticking, then place the whole fillet, skin side down, onto the grill. Cover and cook until done. There is no need to turn the fillet during cooking. Gently remove the salmon with a spatula. The cooked fish easily separates from the skin.

BARBECUED SHRIMP & PEACH KABOBS

Shrimp grilled with peaches and green onions really sets off fireworks! This spicy dish won a ribbon at the county fair.

—JEN SMALLWOOD PORTSMOUTH, VA

PREP: 25 MIN. • **GRILL:** 10 MIN.
MAKES: 4 SERVINGS

- 1 tablespoon packed brown sugar
- 1 teaspoon paprika
- ½ to 1 teaspoon ground ancho chili pepper
- ½ teaspoon ground cumin
- ¼ teaspoon salt
- ¼ teaspoon freshly ground pepper
- ⅛ to ¼ teaspoon cayenne pepper
- 1 pound uncooked shrimp (16-20 per pound), peeled and deveined
- 3 medium peaches, each cut into 8 wedges
- 8 green onions (light green and white portion only), cut into 2-inch pieces
  Olive oil-flavored cooking spray
  Lime wedges

1. Mix brown sugar and seasonings. Place shrimp, peaches and green onions in a large bowl; sprinkle with brown sugar mixture and toss to coat. On four or eight metal or soaked wooden skewers, alternately thread shrimp, peaches and green onions.

2. Lightly spritz both sides of kabobs with cooking spray. Grill, covered, over medium heat or broil 4 in. from heat 3-4 minutes on each side or until shrimp turn pink. Squeeze lime wedges over kabobs.

BARBECUED SHRIMP & PEACH KABOBS

**SEAFOOD
BROCHETTES**

FAST FIX ▶

HICKORY BARBECUED SALMON WITH TARTAR SAUCE

Guests of all ages love this succulent seafood dish. The idea to use hickory chips came from my dad. He always prepared his salmon this way.

—LINDA CHEVALIER BATTLE GROUND, WA

START TO FINISH: 30 MIN.
MAKES: 8 SERVINGS (1 CUP SAUCE)

- ½ **cup butter, cubed**
- 2 **garlic cloves, minced**
- 1 **salmon fillet (3 pounds)**
- 2 **medium lemons, thinly sliced**
- 2 **cups soaked hickory chips**

TARTAR SAUCE
- 1 **cup mayonnaise**
- ¼ **cup chopped sweet pickles**
- 1 **teaspoon finely chopped onion**
- ¾ **teaspoon ground mustard**
- ¼ **teaspoon Worcestershire sauce**

1. In a small saucepan, combine butter and garlic; cook and stir over medium heat until butter is melted. Drizzle 2 tablespoons butter mixture over salmon; top with lemon slices. Set aside remaining butter mixture for basting.
2. Coat grill rack with cooking spray before starting the grill. Add wood chips to grill according to the manufacturer's directions. Place the salmon skin side down on grill rack. Grill, covered, over medium heat for 5 minutes.
3. Carefully spoon some of the reserved butter mixture over salmon. Cover and grill 15-20 minutes longer or until fish flakes easily with a fork, basting occasionally with remaining butter mixture.
4. Meanwhile, in a small bowl, combine the tartar sauce ingredients. Serve with the salmon.

SEAFOOD BROCHETTES

Shrimp, halibut and sea scallops are matched up with bacon and an herb butter in this easy-to-grill entree. The tomatoes offer a fun burst of color, and the mild chive butter is delicious on the side.

—NELLA PARKER HERSEY, MI

PREP: 30 MIN. • **GRILL:** 5 MIN.
MAKES: 1 DOZEN

- 24 **medium fresh mushrooms**
- 24 **cherry tomatoes**
- 8 **bacon strips, cut into thirds**
- 1 **pound halibut, cut into 1-inch pieces**
- 1 **pound uncooked large shrimp, peeled and deveined**
- 1 **pound sea scallops**
- ½ **cup butter, melted**

CHIVE BUTTER
- 1 **cup butter, melted**
- 2 **to 3 tablespoons minced chives**

1. On 12 metal or soaked wooden skewers, alternately thread two mushrooms, two tomatoes and two pieces of bacon with four pieces of fish or seafood. Brush with melted butter.
2. Grill, covered, over medium-hot heat for 5-7 minutes or until shrimp turn pink and scallops are opaque, turning once. Combine butter and chives; serve with brochettes.

FAST FIX

CAJUN BOIL ON THE GRILL

I came up with these everything-in-one seafood packets for a family reunion, since the recipe can be increased to feed a large crowd. The foil steams up inside, so be sure to open the packs carefully.

—ALLISON BROOKS FORT COLLINS, CO

START TO FINISH: 30 MIN.
MAKES: 4 SERVINGS

- 1 package (20 ounces) refrigerated red potato wedges
- 2 salmon fillets (6 ounces each), halved
- ¾ pound uncooked shrimp (31-40 per pound), peeled and deveined
- ½ pound summer sausage, cubed
- 2 medium ears sweet corn, halved
- 2 tablespoons olive oil
- 1 teaspoon seafood seasoning
- ½ teaspoon salt
- ¼ teaspoon pepper
- 1 medium lemon, cut into 4 wedges

1. Divide potatoes, salmon, shrimp, sausage and corn among four pieces of heavy-duty foil (about 18x12-in. rectangle). Drizzle with oil; sprinkle with seasonings. Squeeze lemon juice over top; place squeezed wedges in packets. Fold foil around mixture, sealing tightly.

2. Grill, covered, over medium heat 12-15 minutes or until fish just begins to flake easily with a fork, shrimp turn pink and potatoes are tender. Open foil carefully to allow steam to escape.

**CAJUN BOIL
ON THE GRILL**

FIRECRACKER GRILLED SALMON

FIRECRACKER GRILLED SALMON

Let this sensational salmon perk up dinner tonight. With a glaze that kicks you right in the taste buds, this weeknight dish is anything but boring.

—MELISSA ROGERS TUSCALOOSA, AL

PREP: 20 MIN. + MARINATING
GRILL: 5 MIN. • **MAKES:** 4 SERVINGS

- 2 **tablespoons balsamic vinegar**
- 2 **tablespoons reduced-sodium soy sauce**
- 1 **green onion, thinly sliced**
- 1 **tablespoon olive oil**
- 1 **tablespoon maple syrup**
- 2 **garlic cloves, minced**
- 1 **teaspoon ground ginger**
- 1 **teaspoon crushed red pepper flakes**
- ½ **teaspoon sesame oil**
- ¼ **teaspoon salt**
- 4 **salmon fillets (6 ounces each)**

1. In a small bowl, combine the first ten ingredients. Pour ¼ cup marinade into a large resealable plastic bag. Add the salmon; seal bag and turn to coat. Refrigerate for up to 30 minutes. Cover and refrigerate remaining marinade.
2. Drain salmon, discarding marinade. Using long-handled tongs, moisten a paper towel with cooking oil and lightly coat the grill rack. Place salmon skin side down on grill rack. Grill, covered, over high heat or broil 3-4 in. from the heat for 5-10 minutes or until fish flakes easily with a fork, basting occasionally with remaining marinade.

FAST FIX

SALMON WITH HERB BUTTER

Fishing for salmon is our livelihood, so we eat it four or more times a week. This recipe is quick, has tasty seasonings and really lets the goodness of grilled salmon come through.

—JENNY ROTH HOMER, AK

START TO FINISH: 25 MIN.
MAKES: 6-8 SERVINGS

- ½ cup butter, cubed
- ⅓ cup lemon juice
- 2 tablespoons minced parsley
- 1½ teaspoons soy sauce
- 1½ teaspoons Worcestershire sauce
- 1 teaspoon dried oregano
- ½ teaspoon garlic powder
- ¼ teaspoon salt
- ⅛ teaspoon pepper
- 1 salmon fillet (2½-3 pounds and ¾ inch thick)

1. In a small saucepan, combine the first nine ingredients. Cook and stir over low heat until butter is melted; set aside.

2. Using long-handled tongs, moisten a paper towel with cooking oil and lightly coat the grill rack. Place salmon skin side down on grill. Grill, covered, over medium-hot heat or broil 4 in. from the heat for 5 minutes. Baste with butter sauce. Grill or broil 10-15 minutes longer or until fish flakes easily with a fork, basting frequently.

HEAVENLY GREEK TACOS

The first time I made these, my fiance and I were in heaven! I don't think I've ever said "Mmm" so many times. They're sure to satisfy at your home, too.

—MEAGAN JENSEN RENO, NV

PREP: 30 MIN. + MARINATING • **GRILL:** 10 MIN.
MAKES: 6 SERVINGS

- ⅓ cup lemon juice
- 2 tablespoons olive oil
- 4 teaspoons grated lemon peel
- 3 garlic cloves, minced, divided

HEAVENLY GREEK TACOS

- 1 teaspoon dried oregano
- ¼ teaspoon salt
- ¼ teaspoon pepper
- 2 pounds mahi mahi
- 1½ cups shredded red cabbage
- ½ medium red onion, thinly sliced
- ½ medium sweet red pepper, julienned
- ½ cup crumbled feta cheese
- 6 tablespoons chopped pitted Greek olives, divided
- ¼ cup minced fresh parsley
- 1½ cups plain Greek yogurt
- ½ medium English cucumber, cut into 1-inch pieces
- 1 teaspoon dill weed
- ½ teaspoon ground coriander
- 12 whole wheat tortillas (8 inches), warmed

1. In a large resealable plastic bag, combine the lemon juice, oil, lemon peel, 2 garlic cloves, oregano, salt and pepper. Add the mahi mahi; seal bag and turn to coat. Refrigerate for up to 30 minutes.

2. In a large bowl, combine the cabbage, onion, red pepper, cheese, 3 tablespoons olives and parsley; set aside.

3. Place the yogurt, cucumber, dill, coriander and remaining garlic and olives in a food processor; cover and process until blended.

4. Drain fish and discard marinade. Moisten a paper towel with cooking oil; using long-handled tongs, lightly coat the grill rack. Grill mahi mahi, covered, over medium heat or broil 4 in. from the heat for 3-4 minutes on each side or until fish flakes easily with a fork.

5. Place a portion of the fish on each tortilla; top with the cabbage mixture and sauce.

SOUTHWESTERN
CATFISH

SOUTHWESTERN CATFISH

I rub catfish fillets with a blend that includes chili powder, cumin, coriander, cayenne and paprika, then top them with homemade salsa. A green salad, garlic bread and baked sweet potatoes round out the meal nicely.

—**BRUCE CRITTENDEN** CLINTON, MS

PREP: 15 MIN. + CHILLING • **BAKE:** 10 MIN.
MAKES: 4 SERVINGS

- 3 medium tomatoes, chopped
- ¼ cup chopped onion
- 2 jalapeno peppers, seeded and finely chopped
- 2 tablespoons white wine vinegar
- 3 teaspoons salt, divided
- 3 teaspoons paprika
- 3 teaspoons chili powder
- 1 to 1½ teaspoons ground cumin
- 1 to 1½ teaspoons ground coriander
- ¾ to 1 teaspoon cayenne pepper
- ½ teaspoon garlic powder
- 4 catfish fillets (6 ounces each)

1. For salsa, in a large bowl, combine the tomatoes, onion, jalapenos, vinegar and 1 teaspoon salt. Cover and refrigerate for at least 30 minutes.
2. Combine the paprika, chili powder, cumin, coriander, cayenne, garlic powder and remaining salt; rub over catfish. Using long-handled tongs, moisten a paper towel with cooking oil and lightly coat the grill rack.
3. Grill fillets, uncovered, over medium heat or broil 4 in. from the heat for 5 minutes on each side or until fish flakes easily with a fork. Serve with salsa.
NOTE *Wear disposable gloves when cutting hot peppers; the oils can burn skin. Avoid touching your face.*

FAST FIX
HAVARTI SHRIMP QUESADILLAS

Apricot preserves add sweetness to the mushrooms, shrimp and cheese in these grilled quesadillas. Or cook the quesadillas in a skillet until lightly browned. Serve with lime wedges, if you'd like.

—**SUSAN MANNING** BURLINGTON, NC

START TO FINISH: 25 MIN.
MAKES: 2 DOZEN

- ½ pound fresh mushrooms, chopped
- 1 tablespoon canola oil
- 1 tablespoon butter
- 6 tablespoons apricot preserves
- 6 flour tortillas (10 inches)
- 6 ounces Havarti cheese, thinly sliced
- ½ pound cooked medium shrimp, peeled and deveined and chopped
- 2 tablespoons butter, melted

1. In a large skillet, saute mushrooms in oil and butter until tender. Spread 1 tablespoon preserves over half of each tortilla; top with cheese, shrimp and mushrooms. Fold tortillas over. Brush both sides with melted butter.
2. Grill quesadillas, uncovered, over medium heat for 1-2 minutes on each side or until golden brown and cheese is melted. Cut each quesadilla into four wedges. Serve warm.

GRILLED SALMON STEAKS

This is a terrific way to fix salmon…and it's easy. The marinade mellows the fish flavor, and the dill sauce is an ideal complement. I once served this dish to 12 people from the Pacific Northwest, who declared it was the best salmon they'd ever eaten!

—**DEB ESSEN** VICTOR, MT

PREP: 10 MIN. + MARINATING • **GRILL:** 15 MIN.
MAKES: 4 SERVINGS

- 2 tablespoons white wine vinegar
- 2 tablespoons sugar
- 1 tablespoon dill weed
- ¾ teaspoon salt
- ⅛ to ¼ teaspoon pepper, optional
- 4 salmon steaks (1-inch thick and 6 ounces each)

MUSTARD DILL SAUCE
- 3 tablespoons mayonnaise
- 3 tablespoons Dijon mustard
- 3 tablespoons dill weed
- 1 tablespoon sugar
- 4 teaspoons white wine vinegar
- ¼ teaspoon pepper, optional

1. In a large resealable plastic bag, combine the first five ingredients. Add salmon; seal bag and turn to coat. Refrigerate for 1 hour, turning occasionally.
2. In a small bowl, combine the sauce ingredients; cover and refrigerate until chilled.
3. Discard marinade. Grill salmon, covered, over medium heat for 6-7 minutes on each side or until fish flakes easily with a fork. Serve with mustard dill sauce.

DOUBLE K GRILLED SALMON

There's a little story behind the name of my favorite salmon recipe: When my husband, Kevin, and I couldn't find a spicy teriyaki-style marinade to our liking, we created one and named it Double K—for Krista and Kevin. Every time we make this flavorful fish, we're asked how we do it.
—**KRISTA FRANK** RHODODENDRON, OR

PREP: 10 MIN. + MARINATING
GRILL: 20 MIN. • **MAKES:** 8 SERVINGS

- ¼ **cup packed brown sugar**
- ¼ **cup soy sauce**
- 3 **tablespoons unsweetened pineapple juice**
- 3 **tablespoons red wine vinegar**
- 3 **garlic cloves, minced**
- 1 **tablespoon lemon juice**
- 1 **teaspoon ground ginger**
- ½ **teaspoon pepper**
- ½ **teaspoon hot pepper sauce**
- 1 **salmon fillet (2 pounds)**

1. In a small bowl, combine the first nine ingredients. Pour ¾ cup into a large resealable plastic bag; add salmon. Seal bag and turn to coat; refrigerate for 1 hour, turning occasionally. Set aside remaining marinade for basting.
2. Drain and discard marinade. Using long-handled tongs, moisten a paper towel with cooking oil and lightly coat the grill rack. Place salmon skin side down on rack. Grill, covered, over medium heat or broil over medium heat for 5 minutes. Brush with reserved marinade. Grill or broil 15-20 minutes longer or until the fish flakes easily with a fork.

GARLIC-HERB TUNA STEAKS

⑤ INGREDIENTS

GARLIC-HERB TUNA STEAKS

After enjoying yellowfin tuna at a restaurant in southwest Florida, I came up with this recipe so I could enjoy the flavor of my favorite fish at home.
—**JAN HUNTINGTON** PAINESVILLE, OH

PREP: 10 MIN. + MARINATING • **GRILL:** 10 MIN.
MAKES: 4 SERVINGS

- 2 **tablespoons lemon juice**
- 1 **tablespoon olive oil**
- 2 **garlic cloves, minced**
- 2 **teaspoons minced fresh thyme or ½ teaspoon dried thyme**
- 4 **tuna steaks (6 ounces each)**
- ¼ **teaspoon salt**
- ¼ **teaspoon pepper**

1. In a large resealable plastic bag, combine the lemon juice, oil, garlic and thyme. Add the tuna; seal bag and turn to coat. Refrigerate for up to 30 minutes, turning occasionally.
2. Remove tuna from bag; sprinkle with salt and pepper. Drain and discard marinade. Moisten a paper towel with cooking oil; using long-handled tongs, lightly coat the grill rack.
3. Grill tuna, covered, over medium-hot heat or broil 4 in. from the heat for 3-4 minutes on each side for medium-rare or until slightly pink in the center.

SMOKED HONEY-PEPPERCORN SALMON

I found this recipe in an Alaska fishing guide. Now it's the only way we do salmon. The brine gives it a sweet caramelized coating, and the hickory wood chips give it a distinct smoky flavor.

—**JUDY ASHBY** JAMESTOWN, TN

PREP: 20 MIN. + MARINATING • **GRILL:** 45 MIN.
MAKES: 4 SERVINGS

- 1 cup packed brown sugar
- 1 cup water
- ⅓ cup salt
- 1 tablespoon minced fresh gingerroot
- 2 bay leaves
- 1 teaspoon ground allspice
- ½ cup cold water
- 1 salmon fillet (1 pound)
- ¼ cup honey
- 1 tablespoon whole peppercorns, crushed
- 2 cups soaked hickory wood chips

1. In a small saucepan, combine the first six ingredients. Bring to a boil. Cook and stir until brown sugar and salt are dissolved. Remove from the heat. Add the cold water to cool the brine to room temperature.

2. Place salmon in a large resealable plastic bag; carefully pour cooled brine into bag. Squeeze out as much air as possible; seal bag and turn to coat. Refrigerate for 4 hours, turning occasionally.

3. Drain and discard brine; rinse salmon and pat dry. Spread honey over fillet; sprinkle with peppercorns.

4. Add wood chips to grill according to manufacturer's directions.

5. Moisten a paper towel with cooking oil; using long-handled tongs, lightly coat the grill rack.

6. Place salmon on grill rack, skin side down. Grill, covered, over indirect medium heat for 45-50 minutes or until fish flakes easily with a fork.

TERIYAKI-LIME SHRIMP

We grill year-round, so I make these seafood skewers often. The side dishes may vary, but these shrimp are always a stellar main event!

—**KAREN TYSON** CLAWSON, MI

PREP: 10 MIN. + MARINATING • **GRILL:** 10 MIN.
MAKES: 2 SERVINGS

- 3 tablespoons lime juice
- 2 tablespoons olive oil
- 2 tablespoons reduced-sodium teriyaki sauce
- 1 tablespoon balsamic vinegar
- 1 tablespoon Dijon mustard
- 1 teaspoon garlic powder
- 6 drops hot pepper sauce
- 6 uncooked jumbo shrimp, peeled and deveined

1. Combine the first seven ingredients in a large resealable plastic bag; add shrimp. Seal bag and turn to coat. Refrigerate for 1 hour, turning occasionally.

2. Drain and discard marinade. Thread shrimp onto two metal or soaked wooden skewers. Using long-handled tongs, moisten a paper towel with cooking oil and lightly coat the grill rack. Grill, covered, over medium heat or broil 4 in. from the heat for 3-4 minutes on each side or until shrimp turn pink.

SMOKED HONEY-PEPPERCORN SALMON

CILANTRO-BASIL GRILLED SHRIMP

With plenty of cilantro and basil in my garden, and a bottle of tequila in the pantry, I knew just what to do with these shrimp. The crushed red pepper gives them an extra kick!

—**TAMI PENUNURI** LEAGUE CITY, TX

PREP: 15 MIN. + MARINATING • **GRILL:** 5 MIN.
MAKES: 4 SERVINGS

- 3 tablespoons orange juice
- 3 tablespoons olive oil
- 2 tablespoons minced fresh cilantro
- 2 tablespoons minced fresh basil
- 2 tablespoons tequila
- ¾ teaspoon salt
- ½ teaspoon crushed red pepper flakes
- ¼ teaspoon pepper
- 1 pound uncooked large shrimp, peeled and deveined

1. In a large resealable plastic bag, combine the first eight ingredients. Add the shrimp; seal bag and turn to coat. Refrigerate for 30 minutes.

2. Drain and discard marinade. Thread shrimp onto four metal or soaked wooden skewers. Moisten a paper towel with cooking oil; using long-handled tongs, lightly coat the grill rack.

3. Grill shrimp, covered, over medium heat or broil 4 in. from the heat for 5-8 minutes or until shrimp turn pink, turning once.

CILANTRO-BASIL GRILLED SHRIMP

(5) INGREDIENTS FAST FIX
BARBECUED TROUT

This delicious recipe came from a friend. The sauce really gives the fish a wonderful flavor. Even those who aren't that fond of fish will like it prepared this way.
—**VIVIAN WOLFRAM** MOUNTAIN HOME, AR

START TO FINISH: 20 MIN.
MAKES: 6 SERVINGS

- ⅔ cup reduced-sodium soy sauce
- ½ cup ketchup
- 2 tablespoons lemon juice
- 2 tablespoons canola oil
- 1 teaspoon dried rosemary, crushed
- 6 pan-dressed trout
  Lemon wedges, optional

1. Combine the soy sauce, ketchup, lemon juice, oil and rosemary; pour two-thirds of marinade into a large resealable plastic bag; add fish. Seal bag and turn to coat; refrigerate bag for 1 hour, turning once. Cover remaining marinade for basting and refrigerate.
2. Drain and discard marinade. Place fish in a single layer in a well-greased hinged wire grill basket. Grill, covered, over medium heat for 8-10 minutes or until fish is browned on the bottom. Turn and baste with reserved marinade; grill 5-7 minutes longer or until fish flakes easily with a fork. Serve with lemon if desired.

MAPLE-GLAZED GRILLED SALMON

When I made up my mind to serve my family more nutritious dishes, I decided to cook fish more often. This maple-glazed delight is everyone's favorite.
—**KATE SELNER** ST. PAUL, MN

PREP: 5 MIN. + MARINATING • **GRILL:** 10 MIN.
MAKES: 8 SERVINGS

- ¾ cup maple syrup
- 2 tablespoons ketchup
- 1 tablespoon brown sugar
- 1 tablespoon cider vinegar
- 1 tablespoon Worcestershire sauce
- ½ teaspoon salt
- ½ teaspoon ground mustard
- ⅛ teaspoon hot pepper sauce
- 1 salmon fillet (2 pounds)

1. In a small bowl, combine the first eight ingredients. Pour ½ cup into a large resealable plastic bag; add the salmon. Seal bag and turn to coat; refrigerate for up to 2 hours. Cover and refrigerate remaining marinade.
2. Drain and discard marinade. Using long-handled tongs, moisten a paper towel with cooking oil and lightly coat the grill rack. Grill salmon skin side down over medium-hot heat for 2-4 minutes.
3. Transfer to a double thickness of heavy-duty foil (about 17x21 in.). Spoon some of the reserved marinade over salmon. Fold foil around fillet and seal tightly. Grill 5-6 minutes longer or until fish flakes easily with a fork. Open slowly to allow steam to escape. Brush with remaining marinade.

FAST FIX
HADDOCK WITH CITRUS SALSA

I prepared the same favorites for 30 years until an emphasis on health-conscious cooking led me to find new recipes, including this mouthwatering entree.
—**SALLY ROBERTS** PORT ST. LUCIE, FL

START TO FINISH: 20 MIN.
MAKES: 4 SERVINGS

- 4 medium navel oranges, peeled and sectioned
- ½ cup chopped red onion
- ¼ cup lime juice
- ¼ cup minced fresh cilantro
- ¼ teaspoon crushed red pepper flakes
- 1 garlic clove, minced
- 1 teaspoon grated orange peel
- ¾ teaspoon salt, divided
- 1⅛ teaspoons pepper, divided
- 2 teaspoons ground coriander
- 2 teaspoons ground cumin
- 1 pound haddock fillets

1. For salsa, in a bowl, combine the oranges, onion, lime juice, cilantro, pepper flakes, garlic, orange peel, ¼ teaspoon salt and ⅛ teaspoon pepper. Cover and chill.
2. Combine coriander, cumin and remaining salt and pepper; rub over both sides of fillets.
3. Grill, covered, over medium-hot heat or broil 4-6 in. from the heat for 5-6 minutes on each side or until fish flakes easily with a fork. Serve with salsa.

LEMON-PEPPER CATFISH

TANGY SHRIMP AND SCALLOPS

The combination of shrimp and scallops makes this a special dish for company. I serve these appealing kabobs over pasta with a green salad and garlic bread.
—**LAUREN LLEWELLYN** RALEIGH, NC

PREP: 15 MIN. + MARINATING • **GRILL:** 10 MIN.
MAKES: 4 SERVINGS

- 28 **uncooked large shrimp (1½ pounds), peeled and deveined**
- 28 **sea scallops (about ½ pound)**
- ½ **cup butter, cubed**
- 7 **tablespoons lemon juice**
- 5 **tablespoons Worcestershire sauce**
- 1 **to 2 teaspoons garlic powder**
- 1 **teaspoon paprika**

1. Place shrimp and scallops in a large resealable plastic bag; set aside.
2. In a microwave-safe bowl, combine the butter, lemon juice, Worcestershire sauce, garlic powder and paprika. Microwave at 50% power for 1 minute or until butter is melted. Stir to blend; set aside ⅓ cup for basting. Pour remaining marinade over shrimp ans scallops. Seal bag and turn to coat; refrigerate for 1 hour, turning occasionally.
3. Drain and discard marinade. Alternately thread shrimp and scallops on metal or soaked wooden skewers. Grill kabobs, covered, over medium heat or broil 4 in. from the heat for 5-8 minutes or until shrimp turn pink and scallops are opaque, turning once and basting with reserved marinade.
NOTE *This recipe was tested in a 1,100-watt microwave.*

LEMON-PEPPER CATFISH

Nothing beats a late supper of grilled catfish after a hard day's work. This light and lively main course is a favorite of our family during the summertime.
—**REGINA ROSENBERRY** GREENCASTLE, PA

PREP: 5 MIN. + MARINATING • **GRILL:** 10 MIN.
MAKES: 4 SERVINGS

- 6 **tablespoons lemon juice**
- ¼ **cup butter, melted**
- 2 **teaspoons Worcestershire sauce**
- 4 **catfish fillets (about 5 ounces each)**
- ½ **teaspoon salt**
- ½ **teaspoon lemon-pepper seasoning**

1. In a large resealable plastic bag, combine the lemon juice, butter and Worcestershire sauce. Add the fish; seal bag and turn to coat. Cover and refrigerate for 30 minutes, turning occasionally.

2. Drain and discard marinade. Sprinkle fish with salt and lemon-pepper. Using long-handled tongs, moisten a paper towel with cooking oil and lightly coat the grill rack. Grill fish, covered, on medium heat or broil 4 in. from heat for 4-6 minutes on each side or until the fish flakes easily.

 **GRILL SKILL**

Lemon is a natural when it comes to flavoring seafood—grilled or not. But other citrus flavors work, too. When making a marinade that calls for lemon juice, try using lime juice instead. Or, mix lemon and lime for a zesty burst of bright flavors.

BARBECUED SALMON

For a beautiful blend of sweet and spicy, try grilled salmon, basted with barbecue sauce perked up with brown sugar, chili garlic sauce, soy sauce and lime.

—*TASTE OF HOME* TEST KITCHEN

START TO FINISH: 20 MIN.
MAKES: 4 SERVINGS

- ⅔ **cup barbecue sauce**
- 2 **tablespoons brown sugar**
- 2 **tablespoons chili garlic sauce**
- 1 **tablespoon rice vinegar**
- 1 **teaspoon lime juice**
- 1 **teaspoon soy sauce**
- 4 **salmon fillets (6 ounces each)**
- 1 **tablespoon minced fresh cilantro**

1. In a small bowl, combine the first six ingredients; set aside ¼ cup for serving.
2. Moisten a paper towel with cooking oil; using long-handled tongs, lightly coat the grill rack. Grill salmon, covered, over hot heat or broil 3-4 in. from the heat for 5-10 minutes or until fish flakes easily with a fork, basting occasionally with the sauce mixture.
3. Top with reserved sauce; sprinkle with the cilantro.

BARBECUED SALMON

SPICY SHRIMP 'N' SCALLOP SKEWERS

FAST FIX

SPICY SHRIMP 'N' SCALLOP SKEWERS

I love shrimp. Throw in some scallops and I'm in heaven. We serve these skewers with some grilled steaks and a garden salad. I'm getting hungry just thinking about it!

—**TRACI WYNNE** DENVER, PA

START TO FINISH: 30 MIN.
MAKES: 6 SERVINGS

  2 **tablespoons butter**
  ½ **teaspoon chili powder**
  ¼ **teaspoon dried oregano**
  ¼ **teaspoon ground cumin**
  ⅛ **teaspoon dried thyme**
  ⅛ **teaspoon each white pepper, cayenne pepper and black pepper**
 18 **uncooked large shrimp (about ¾ pound)**
 12 **sea scallops (1½ pounds)**

1. In a small saucepan, melt butter. Stir in seasonings; set aside and keep warm. Peel and devein shrimp, leaving tails on.
2. On six metal or soaked wooden skewers, alternately thread shrimp and scallops.
3. Using long-handled tongs, moisten a paper towel with cooking oil and lightly coat the grill rack. Grill seafood, covered, over medium heat or broil 4 in. from the heat for 3-5 minutes on each side or until shrimp turn pink and scallops are firm and opaque, basting occasionally with butter mixture.

SNOW CRAB LEGS WITH DIPPING SAUCES

Whenever I prepare crab legs for my family, I'm sure to serve these three dipping sauces on the side. They really enhance the already fabulous crab flavor.

—**SUZY HORVATH** MILWAUKIE, OR

PREP: 25 MIN. • **GRILL:** 10 MIN.
MAKES: 2 SERVINGS

DILL BUTTER SAUCE
- ¼ cup butter, melted
- 1½ teaspoons lemon juice
- ¼ teaspoon dill weed
- ⅛ teaspoon garlic salt
- Dash white pepper

HORSERADISH CHILI SAUCE
- ¼ cup chili sauce
- ½ teaspoon rice vinegar
- ½ teaspoon prepared horseradish

AVOCADO CREAM SAUCE
- ½ medium ripe avocado, peeled and mashed
- ⅓ cup sour cream
- ¼ teaspoon ground cumin
- 1 teaspoon lime juice
- ⅛ teaspoon hot pepper sauce

CRAB LEGS
- 1 pound cooked snow crab legs
- 1 tablespoon olive oil

1. In three separate small bowls, combine the ingredients for the dill butter sauce, horseradish chili sauce and avocado cream sauce; set aside.
2. Brush both sides of crab legs with oil. Grill, covered, over medium heat for 3-4 minutes on each side or until heated through. Serve with dipping sauces.

PACIFIC RIM SALMON

PACIFIC RIM SALMON

I came across this recipe in a local fund-raiser cookbook. I've made some slight adjustments to it over the years, but it remains a favorite summer meal.

—**AMY SAUSER** OMAHA, NE

PREP: 15 MIN. + MARINATING • **GRILL:** 15 MIN.
MAKES: 8 SERVINGS

- ½ cup unsweetened pineapple juice
- ¼ cup reduced-sodium soy sauce
- 2 tablespoons prepared horseradish
- 2 tablespoons minced fresh parsley
- 5 teaspoons sesame oil, divided
- 2 teaspoons honey
- ½ teaspoon coarsely ground pepper
- 8 salmon fillets (6 ounces each)
- 5 green onions, coarsely chopped

1. In a small bowl, combine the pineapple juice, soy sauce, horseradish, parsley, 3 teaspoons sesame oil, honey and pepper. Pour ⅔ cup marinade into a large resealable plastic bag; add salmon and green onions. Seal bag and turn to coat; refrigerate for 1 to 1½ hours, turning occasionally. Combine remaining sesame oil and remaining marinade for basting. Cover and refrigerate until ready to grill.
2. Drain fish and discard its marinade. Moisten a paper towel with cooking oil and lightly coat the grill rack, using tongs. Grill salmon, skin side down, covered, over medium heat or broil 4 in. from the heat for 8-12 minutes or until fish flakes easily with a fork, basting often with reserved marinade mixture.

**CAMPFIRE CINNAMON
TWISTS, PAGE 267**

CAMPFIRE PEACH
COBBLER, PAGE 269

COOKOUT CARAMEL
S'MORES, PAGE 263

HONEY-BALSAMIC
GLAZED FRUIT, PAGE 260

HOT & HEARTY DESSERTS

When your sweet tooth is calling, your grill has the answer with this variety of **summer specialties.** Here, juicy fruits get a **fiery kick** and classic s'mores receive **special treatments** you won't forget. In fact, you may never want to prepare dessert any other way again!

FRUIT GRILLING CHART

Before grilling fruit, wash it under cool, running water, and use a vegetable brush if needed. Remove any blemished areas. Grill fruit until tender. Turn halfway through grilling time. The cooking times below are general guidelines.

TYPE	WEIGHT OR THICKNESS	HEAT	APPROXIMATE COOKING TIME (IN MINUTES)
APPLES	$1/2$-in. slices	medium/direct	4 to 6
APRICOTS	pitted, halved	medium/direct	6 to 8
BANANAS	halved lengthwise	medium/direct	6 to 8
PEACHES	pitted, halved	medium/direct	8 to 10
PEARS	halved	medium/direct	8 to 10
PINEAPPLE	$1/2$-in. rings	medium/direct	7 to 10

 **RED-HOT DESSERT TIPS**

While most cooks turn to the grill for entrees, it can also be used to make a variety of lip-smacking desserts. When the weather is perfect for a barbecue, keep the coals hot and round out menus with a surprising treat. Follow these tips to grill up simply sweet desserts!

• For the best flavor, make sure to clean the grill between the main course and dessert.

• Desserts can easily burn if unattended on the grill. Fruit and other sweet ingredients contain sugars that burn at 265°. Peaches and pears can stay on the grill for a little longer, but remove juicy citrus fruits after a few minutes.

• Aluminum foil is a great way to prevent sticky juices from dripping between the grates. For quick cleanup after grilling, spray the foil with nonstick spray before placing desserts on the grill.

• To speed up dessert, do as much ahead of time as possible. Cut cake, wash and slice fruit, or mix up sauces the day before. Store everything in the refrigerator so things are ready to grill when you are.

FAST FIX

SEARED POUND CAKE WITH WARM AMARETTO BANANAS

Banana, butter and caramel flavors go so well together! Then you add a sweet almond liqueur, such as amaretto, and a little lemon juice to take this grilled dessert to a new level.

—CAROL TRAUPMAN-CARR
BREINIGSVILLE, PA

START TO FINISH: 25 MIN.
MAKES: 4 SERVINGS

- 4 **teaspoons butter, divided**
- 2 **large bananas, cut into ¼-inch slices**
- 2 **tablespoons brown sugar**
- 1 **tablespoon amaretto**
- 1 **teaspoon lemon juice**
- 4 **slices pound cake (about 1 inch thick)**
  Sweetened whipped cream and toasted sliced almonds, optional

1. Melt 2 teaspoons butter; drizzle over a double thickness of heavy-duty foil (about 10 in. square). Place bananas on foil; top with brown sugar, amaretto and lemon juice. Dot with remaining butter. Fold foil around mixture and seal tightly.

2. Grill, covered, over medium heat for 8-10 minutes or until heated through. Grill pound cake for 1-2 minutes on each side or until lightly browned. Open foil packets carefully, allowing steam to escape. Spoon bananas over pound cake; top with whipped cream and almonds if desired.

NOTE *To toast nuts, bake in a shallow pan in a 350° oven for 5-10 minutes or cook in a skillet over low heat until lightly browned, stirring occasionally.*

SEARED POUND CAKE WITH WARM AMARETTO BANANAS

FAST FIX ▶

GRILLED PINEAPPLE DESSERT

This fresh-tasting, fruity dessert is one of my very favorites. Warm, sweet, buttery pineapple topped with cold ice cream—yum! Granola adds a nice crunch, too.
—**KATIE SISSON** VALLEY PARK, MO

START TO FINISH: 20 MIN.
MAKES: 6 SERVINGS

- 1 **can (20 ounces) unsweetened sliced pineapple**
- 1 **tablespoon butter**
- 1 **teaspoon brown sugar**
- ½ **teaspoon vanilla extract**
- ¼ **teaspoon ground cinnamon**
- 3 **cups reduced-fat vanilla ice cream**
- 6 **tablespoons hot caramel ice cream topping**
- 6 **tablespoons granola without raisins**

1. Drain pineapple, reserving ⅓ cup juice and six pineapple slices (save remaining juice and pineapple for another use).
2. In a small microwave-safe bowl, combine the butter, brown sugar, vanilla extract, cinnamon and reserved juice. Microwave, uncovered, on high for 1-2 minutes or until butter is melted. Brush half of the mixture on both sides of pineapple slices.
3. Grill, uncovered, over medium heat or broil 4 in. from the heat for 3-5 minutes or until lightly browned, turning once and basting with remaining butter mixture.
4. Place pineapple in dessert bowls; top with ice cream. Drizzle with caramel topping; sprinkle with granola.
NOTE *This recipe was tested in a 1,100-watt microwave.*

GRILLED
PEACHES 'N' BERRIES

⑤INGREDIENTS FAST FIX ▶

GRILLED PEACHES 'N' BERRIES

Highlight the natural sweetness of peak summertime fruit with brown sugar, butter and a squeeze of lemon juice. Foil packets make this a go-anywhere dessert.
—**SHARON BICKETT** CHESTER, SC

START TO FINISH: 30 MIN.
MAKES: 3 SERVINGS

- 3 **medium ripe peaches, halved and pitted**
- 1 **cup fresh blueberries**
- 2 **tablespoons brown sugar**
- 2 **tablespoons butter**
- 1 **tablespoon lemon juice**

1. Place two peach halves, cut side up, on each of three double thicknesses of heavy-duty foil (12 in. square). Top with blueberries, brown sugar, butter and lemon juice. Fold foil around mixture and seal tightly.
2. Grill, covered, over medium-low heat for 18-20 minutes or until tender. Open the foil carefully to allow steam to escape.

⑤INGREDIENTS

RED-HOT APPLES

I use Red Hots candies to turn ordinary apples into something cinnamony and sensational. The tender treats bake on the grill during dinner. Then just serve in bowls and top with ice cream.
—**HELEN SHUBERT** HAYS, KS

PREP: 10 MIN. • **GRILL:** 30 MIN.
MAKES: 4 SERVINGS

- 4 **medium tart apples, cored**
- 4 **teaspoons brown sugar**
- ¼ **cup Red Hots**
  Vanilla ice cream, optional

1. Place each apple on a double thickness of heavy-duty foil (12 in. square). Spoon 1 teaspoon sugar and 1 tablespoon Red Hots into the center of each apple. Fold foil around apples and seal tightly.
2. Grill, covered, over medium heat for 25-30 minutes or until tender. Open foil carefully to allow steam to escape. Carefully transfer to dessert dishes. Serve warm with ice cream if desired.

BERRIED TREASURE ANGEL FOOD CAKE

My husband grills anything and everything, even dessert! With his encouragement, I came up with this easy recipe that takes just a few minutes to prepare yet always impresses our dinner guests.

—**ANITA ARCHIBALD** RICHMOND HILL, ON

START TO FINISH: 25 MIN.
MAKES: 4 SERVINGS

- 8 **slices angel food cake (1½ inches thick)**
- ¼ **cup butter, softened**
- ½ **cup heavy whipping cream**
- ¼ **teaspoon almond extract**
- ¼ **cup almond cake and pastry filling**
- ½ **cup fresh blueberries**
- ½ **cup fresh raspberries**
- ½ **cup sliced fresh strawberries**
- ¼ **cup mixed nuts, coarsely chopped**
  Confectioners' sugar

1. Using a 1½-in. round cookie cutter, cut out the centers of half of the cake slices (discard removed cake or save for another use). Spread butter over both sides of cake slices. Grill, covered, over medium heat or broil 4 in. from heat 1-2 minutes on each side or until toasted.

2. In a small bowl, beat cream until it begins to thicken. Add extract; beat until soft peaks form.

3. To serve, stack one solid and one cutout slice of cake on each desert plate, placing the outer edges on opposite sides for a more even thickness. Spoon almond filling into holes; top with whipped cream, berries and nuts. Dust with confectioners' sugar.

BERRIED TREASURE ANGEL FOOD CAKE

HOT PEAR SUNDAES

Who says you can't make dessert on the grill? We whipped up this comforting treat that's sure to turn heads...and keep healthy-eating commitments. Sweetened with cinnamon sugar, the warm and tender pear slices are served alongside a little vanilla ice cream.

—*TASTE OF HOME* TEST KITCHEN

START TO FINISH: 15 MIN.
MAKES: 6 SERVINGS

- 4 **medium ripe pears**
- 1 **tablespoon sugar**
- ¼ **teaspoon ground cinnamon**
  Dash pepper
- 2 **cups reduced-fat no-sugar-added vanilla ice cream**
- 3 **teaspoons honey**

1. Peel, halve and core pears; cut each half lengthwise into six wedges. Mix sugar, cinnamon and pepper; sprinkle over pears.

2. Moisten a paper towel with cooking oil; using long-handled tongs, rub on grill rack to coat lightly. Grill pears, covered, over indirect medium heat 2-3 minutes on each side or until tender.

3. Serve pears with ice cream. Drizzle with honey.

GRILLED APPLE CRISP

The first time I tasted this old-fashioned apple crisp, I couldn't believe it was made on the grill. Topped with a scoop of ice cream, this warm cinnamon dessert will earn you rave reviews.
—**MARGARET RILEY** TALLAHASSEE, FL

PREP: 20 MIN. • **GRILL:** 20 MIN.
MAKES: 6 SERVINGS

- 10 **cups thinly sliced peeled tart apples (about 8 medium)**
- 1 **cup old-fashioned oats**
- 1 **cup packed brown sugar**
- ¼ **cup all-purpose flour**
- 3 **teaspoons ground cinnamon**
- 1 **teaspoon ground nutmeg**
- ¼ **teaspoon ground cloves**
- ¼ **cup cold butter, cubed**
  Vanilla ice cream, optional

1. Place the apple slices on a double thickness of heavy-duty foil (about 24x12 in.). In a small bowl, combine the oats, brown sugar, flour, cinnamon, nutmeg and cloves; cut in cold butter until mixture is crumbly. Sprinkle over apples.

2. Fold foil around apple mixture and seal tightly. Grill, covered, over medium heat for 20-25 minutes or until apples are tender. Open foil carefully to allow steam to escape. Serve warm with ice cream if desired.

FAST FIX
PEACH PIE BUNDLES

With just six ingredients, this recipe is simple yet so satisfying. The sweetness of the peaches makes the perfect follow-up to grilled burgers.
—**JANET BARNARD** TORONTO, ON

START TO FINISH: 15 MIN.
MAKES: 2 SERVINGS

- 2 **cups frozen unsweetened sliced peaches, thawed**
- 4 **teaspoons all-purpose flour**
- 4 **teaspoons sugar**
- ½ **cup graham cracker crumbs**
- ¼ **cup packed brown sugar**
- 4 **teaspoons cold butter**

1. Place the peaches in a bowl. Combine flour and sugar; sprinkle over peaches and toss to coat. In a small bowl, combine cracker crumbs and brown sugar; cut in butter until mixture is crumbly.

2. For each bundle, place half of the peach mixture on a double thickness of heavy-duty foil (about 18x12 in.). Sprinkle crumb mixture over peaches. Fold foil around mixture and seal tightly. Grill, covered, over medium heat for 5-10 minutes or until peaches are tender.

---

⑤ INGREDIENTS FAST FIX
GRILLED ANGEL FOOD CAKE WITH STRAWBERRIES

One night I goofed, accidentally using the balsamic butter I save for grilling chicken on my pound cake. What a delicious mistake that my entire family loved! For a patriotic look, simply add a drizzle of blueberry syrup.
—**MOIRA MCGARRY** PARKMAN, ME

START TO FINISH: 15 MIN.
MAKES: 8 SERVINGS

- 2 **cups sliced fresh strawberries**
- 2 **teaspoons sugar**
- 3 **tablespoons butter, melted**
- 2 **tablespoons balsamic vinegar**
- 8 **slices angel food cake (about 1 ounce each)**
  Reduced-fat vanilla ice cream and blueberry syrup, optional

1. In a small bowl, toss strawberries with sugar. In another bowl, mix butter and balsamic vinegar; brush over cut sides of cake.

2. Moisten a paper towel with cooking oil; using long-handled tongs, rub on grill rack to coat lightly. Grill angel food cake, uncovered, over medium heat 1-2 minutes on each side or until golden brown. Serve cake with strawberries and, if desired, vanilla ice cream and blueberry syrup.

GRILLED APPLE CRISP

✕ JAZZ IT UP

Show off your inner pastry chef and get creative with the recipe for Grilled Angel Food Cake with Strawberries. As if this dessert isn't quick and impressive enough, you can easily put your own mark on it! Garnish the final dish with some chocolate curls or a little caramel drizzle, or top it off with a few sliced bananas or raspberries. Prepare the angel food cake as directed, but swap out the strawberries for cubed cantaloupe and sliced kiwi fruit.

**GRILLED ANGEL FOOD CAKE
WITH STRAWBERRIES**

HONEY-BALSAMIC GLAZED FRUIT

One summer, my mother-in-law made us grilled peaches basted with a sweet and tangy sauce. These are so good, I'm always tempted to eat the whole batch.

—**KRISTIN VAN DYKEN** KENNEWICK, WA

START TO FINISH: 25 MIN.
MAKES: 6 SERVINGS (½ CUP GLAZE)

½ **cup balsamic vinegar**
½ **cup honey**
   Dash salt

6 **medium peaches or nectarines, halved and pitted**
   Vanilla ice cream, optional

1. In a small saucepan, combine vinegar, honey and salt; cook and stir over low heat 2-3 minutes or until blended. Reserve ⅓ cup mixture for brushing peaches.

2. Bring the remaining mixture to a boil over medium heat; cook and stir 4-6 minutes or just until mixture begins to thicken slightly (do not overcook). Remove from heat.

3. Moisten a paper towel with cooking oil; using long-handled tongs, rub on grill rack to coat lightly. Brush the peaches with some of the reserved balsamic mixture.

4. Grill the peaches, covered, over medium heat 6-8 minutes on each side or until caramelized, brushing occasionally with the remaining reserved balsamic mixture.

5. Serve with the glaze and, if desired, the ice cream.

HONEY-BALSAMIC GLAZED FRUIT

⑤ INGREDIENTS FAST FIX

GRILLED BANANAS FOSTER

I worked at a bed-and-breakfast a few years back, and bananas foster was often served as dessert after dinner. This wonderful version can be prepared on your outdoor grill. Once it's grilled, just add ice cream, and you'll have a heavenly treat without heating up your kitchen.

—**KATHLEEN HEDGER** FAIRVIEW HEIGHTS, IL

START TO FINISH: 20 MIN.
MAKES: 4 SERVINGS

- ⅓ cup packed brown sugar
- ¼ cup butter, melted
- 2 tablespoons rum or unsweetened apple juice
- 4 medium bananas
- 2 cups vanilla ice cream

1. In a small bowl, combine the brown sugar, butter and rum. Cut bananas into 1-in. slices; place each banana on a double thickness of heavy-duty foil (about 18 x12 in.). Top with brown sugar mixture. Fold foil around banana mixture; seal packets tightly.

2. Grill, covered, over medium heat for 7-9 minutes or until bananas are tender. Open foil carefully to allow steam to escape. Serve with ice cream.

⑤ INGREDIENTS FAST FIX

GINGER POUND CAKE S'MORES

Kids and adults won't be able to resist this fun spin on campfire s'mores. Pound cake replaces the traditional graham cracker while crystallized ginger can add an unexpected flavor twist.

—**PETER HALFERTY** CORPUS CHRISTI, TX

START TO FINISH: 20 MIN.
MAKES: 8 SERVINGS

- 8 large marshmallows
- 5 ounces bittersweet chocolate candy bars, broken into eight pieces
- 8 teaspoons crystallized ginger
- 16 slices pound cake (¼ inch thick)
- 3 tablespoons butter, softened

1. Cut each marshmallow lengthwise into four slices. Place the chocolate, four marshmallow slices and ginger on each of eight cake slices; top with remaining cake. Spread outsides of cake slices with butter.

2. Grill, covered, over medium heat for 1-2 minutes on each side or until cake is toasted.

FAST FIX

GRILLED PINEAPPLE BUTTERSCOTCH SUNDAES

This sweet treat is a real delight at barbecues. I also like to use bananas for this recipe. Just be careful when grilling them so they don't get too soft.

—**ARLA BOSS** TEMPERANCE, MI

START TO FINISH: 30 MIN.
MAKES: 6 SERVINGS

- 2 fresh pineapples
- 6 tablespoons plus ½ cup butter, divided
- 2 tablespoons sugar
- ¼ teaspoon ground nutmeg
- 1 cup packed brown sugar
- ½ cup heavy whipping cream
- ½ teaspoon vanilla extract
  Dash salt
- 3 cups vanilla ice cream

1. Peel, core and cut each pineapple into six spears. In a small saucepan, melt 6 tablespoons butter with sugar and nutmeg. Brush over pineapple. Grill, covered, over medium heat or broil 4 in. from the heat for 7-10 minutes or until lightly browned, turning occasionally.

2. For sauce, in a small saucepan, melt remaining butter. Stir in brown sugar and cream. Bring to a boil, stirring constantly. Remove from the heat; stir in vanilla and salt. Serve sauce with ice cream and grilled pineapple.

FAST FIX

FRUIT SKEWERS WITH CHOCOLATE SYRUP

With toasted angel food cake and chocolate syrup, this recipe makes fruit seem especially decadent. And it's fun to grill out for dessert!

—**MELISSA PELKEY-HASS** WALESKA, GA

START TO FINISH: 25 MIN.
MAKES: 8 SERVINGS

- 2 cups cubed angel food cake
- 1 cup fresh strawberries
- 1 cup cubed fresh pineapple
- 1 cup cubed cantaloupe
- 1 large banana, cut into 1-inch slices
- 2 medium plums, pitted and quartered
  Butter-flavored cooking spray
- ½ cup packed brown sugar
- 8 teaspoons chocolate syrup

1. On eight metal or soaked wooden skewers, alternately thread cake cubes and fruits. Spritz each skewer with butter-flavored spray and roll in the brown sugar.

2. Place the skewers on a piece of heavy-duty foil. Place foil on grill rack. Grill, covered, over medium heat for 4-5 minutes on each side or until fruits are tender, turning once. Drizzle each skewer with 1 teaspoon chocolate syrup.

 **GRILL SKILL**

Not only does brown sugar sweeten up dishes, it also lends a great color and somewhat caramelized texture to desserts when grilled. You can use light brown and dark brown sugars interchangeably in recipes. The dark brown variety will offer a more intense molasses flavor, however, so plan accordingly.

APPLE PIZZA

3. Grill crust, covered, over medium heat for 1-3 minutes on each side or until lightly browned, rotating halfway through cooking to ensure an evenly browned crust. Remove from the grill. Top with apples and desired topping ingredients.

AMERICANA *Sprinkle with arugula, cooked chopped bacon and shredded cheddar cheese.*

FRUITY AND CREAMY *Sprinkle with dried cranberries; drizzle with cream cheese frosting.*

FRENCH STYLE *Top with sliced Brie cheese and fresh thyme.*

TURTLE DELIGHT *Sprinkle with chopped toasted pecans; drizzle with caramel sauce.*

⑤ INGREDIENTS **FAST FIX**

BANANA BOATS

This recipe, given to me years ago by a good friend, is a favorite with my family when we go camping. It's quick, fun to make and scrumptious!
—**BRENDA LOVELESS** GARLAND, TX

START TO FINISH: 20 MIN.
MAKES: 4 SERVINGS

- 4 **medium unpeeled ripe bananas**
- 4 **teaspoons miniature chocolate chips**
- 4 **tablespoons miniature marshmallows**

1. Cut banana peel lengthwise about ½ in. deep, leaving ½ in. at both ends. Open peel wider to form a pocket. Fill each with 1 teaspoon chocolate chips and 1 tablespoon marshmallows. Crimp and shape four pieces of heavy-duty foil (about 12 in. square) around bananas, forming boats.
2. Grill, covered, over medium heat for 5-10 minutes or until marshmallows melt and are golden brown.

⑤ INGREDIENTS **FAST FIX**

APPLE PIZZA

Mmm! Start with this basic apple pizza, then dress it up any way you like using the ideas at the end of the recipe.
—**R. SANDLIN** PRESCOTT VALLEY, AZ

START TO FINISH: 25 MIN.
MAKES: 2 PIZZAS (4 PIECES EACH)

- 5 **medium tart apples, peeled and sliced**
- 4 **tablespoons butter, divided**
- ½ **cup packed brown sugar**
- 1 **teaspoon ground cinnamon**
- 1 **tube (13.8 ounces) refrigerated pizza crust**

1. In a large skillet, saute the apples in 3 tablespoons butter until crisp-tender. Stir in the brown sugar and cinnamon; keep warm.
2. Unroll the pizza crust and cut lengthwise in half. In a microwave, melt remaining butter; brush onto both sides of crust.

(5)INGREDIENTS FAST FIX

COOKOUT CARAMEL S'MORES

These classic treats make a great finish to an informal meal. And toasting the marshmallows extends our after-dinner time together, giving us something fun to do as a family.

—MARTHA HASEMAN HINCKLEY, IL

START TO FINISH: 10 MIN.
MAKES: 4 SERVINGS

- 8 **large marshmallows**
- 4 **whole reduced-fat graham crackers, halved**
- 2 **teaspoons fat-free chocolate syrup**
- 2 **teaspoons fat-free caramel ice cream topping**

Using a long-handled fork, toast marshmallows 6 in. from medium heat until golden brown, turning occasionally. Place two marshmallows on each of four graham cracker halves. Drizzle with chocolate syrup and caramel topping. Top with the remaining crackers.

 **SPECIAL S'MORES**

Few things tops off a summer meal like s'mores. The recipe for Cookout Caramel S'mores offers a tasty new way to enjoy the campfire staple, but consider other adjustments, too.
• Replace the chocolate bar from traditional s'mores with a peanut butter cup, or spread the inside of the graham crackers with a little German Chocolate Cake frosting.
• Try drizzling honey over the marshmallows, or top them with strawberry or banana slices.
• Want to turn your s'more into a meat lover's must-have? Add a slice of cooked bacon to the sweet treat.

COOKOUT CARAMEL S'MORES

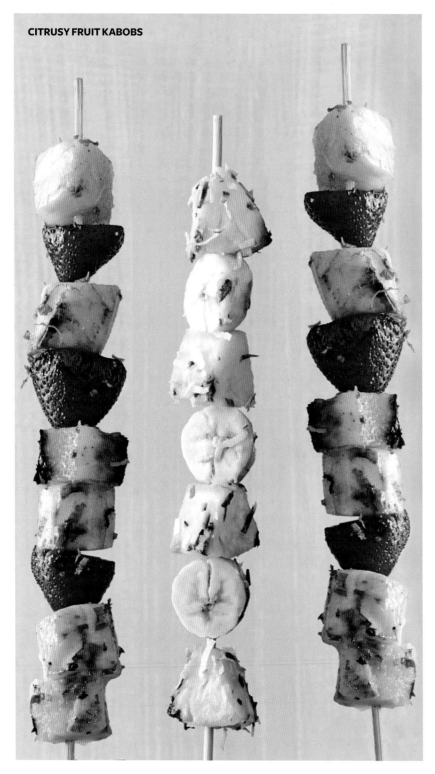

CITRUSY FRUIT KABOBS

FAST FIX

CITRUSY FRUIT KABOBS

Fresh, fruity and lower in sodium and fat than many kabob recipes, this delight on a skewer is perfect when grilling for a crowd.
—**MARY RELYEA** CANASTOTA, NY

START TO FINISH: 20 MIN.
MAKES: 8 KABOBS

⅓ cup orange juice
2 tablespoons lemon juice
4½ teaspoons honey
2 teaspoons cornstarch
1½ teaspoons grated lemon peel
¼ teaspoon ground allspice
24 fresh strawberries
16 cubes fresh pineapple
2 small bananas, cut into 1-inch pieces
2 teaspoons minced fresh mint

1. In a small saucepan, combine the first six ingredients. Bring to a boil; cook and stir for 2 minutes or until thickened. Remove from the heat; cool to room temperature.
2. Thread fruit onto eight metal or soaked wooden skewers. Brush with half of glaze. Moisten a paper towel with cooking oil; using long-handled tongs, lightly coat the grill rack.
3. Grill, covered, over medium heat for 5-7 minutes or until lightly browned, turning occasionally and basting frequently with remaining glaze. Just before serving, sprinkle with mint. Serve warm.

BLUEBERRY-RHUBARB CRUMBLE

A dollop of whipped topping adds a nice finishing touch to this satisfying crumble. Sometimes I like to drizzle a little flavored coffee creamer on top instead.

—NANCY SOUSLEY LAFAYETTE, IN

PREP: 15 MIN. • **BAKE:** 45 MIN. + COOLING
MAKES: 12 SERVINGS

- 6 cups fresh or frozen unsweetened blueberries
- 4 cups diced fresh or frozen rhubarb
- 1 cup sugar
- ¼ cup all-purpose flour

TOPPING

- 1 cup quick-cooking oats
- 1 cup packed brown sugar
- ½ cup all-purpose flour
- ½ teaspoon ground nutmeg
- ½ teaspoon ground cinnamon
- ½ cup cold butter
  Whipped cream, optional

1. In a large bowl, combine blueberries, rhubarb, sugar and flour. Transfer to a disposable foil pan; cover with foil. Grill, covered, over medium heat for 40 minutes or until bubbly.
2. For topping, in a large bowl, combine oats, brown sugar, flour, nutmeg and cinnamon; cut in butter until crumbly.
3. Carefully remove and discard foil, and sprinkle topping over fruit.
4. Close grill cover; grill 15-20 minutes longer or until topping is golden brown. Let cool 10 minutes. Serve warm; dollop with whipped cream if desired.

ROCKY ROAD GRILLED BANANA SPLITS

⑤ INGREDIENTS **FAST FIX**
ROCKY ROAD GRILLED BANANA SPLITS

There's no wrong turn when you travel down this rocky road! Toasty-warm bananas filled with gooey goodness and topped with heaping scoops of creamy perfection are a new cookout must-have.

—LORETTA OUELLETTE POMPANO BEACH, FL

START TO FINISH: 20 MIN.
MAKES: 4 SERVINGS

- 4 medium firm bananas, unpeeled
- 1 dark chocolate candy bar with almonds (3½ ounces)
- ¾ cup miniature marshmallows, divided
- 1 quart rocky road ice cream
  Whipped cream in a can

1. Place each banana on a 12-in. square of foil; crimp and shape foil around bananas so they sit flat.
2. Cut each banana lengthwise about ½ in. deep, leaving ½ in. uncut at both ends. Gently pull each banana peel open, forming a pocket. Finely chop half of the candy bar. Fill pockets with chopped chocolate and ½ cup marshmallows.
3. Grill bananas, covered, over medium heat for 8-10 minutes or until marshmallows are melted and golden brown. Transfer each banana to a serving plate; top with scoops of ice cream. Break remaining chocolate into pieces. Sprinkle chocolate pieces and remaining marshmallows over tops. Garnish with whipped cream.

CAMPFIRE
CINNAMON
TWISTS

⑤ INGREDIENTS FAST FIX ▶
CAMPFIRE CINNAMON TWISTS

Cinnamon rolls get the toasty treatment when wrapped around skewers and warmed over a fire. Brush with butter, then sprinkle with sugar and spice.

—LAUREN KNOELKE MILWAUKEE, WI

START TO FINISH: 25 MIN.
MAKES: 8 SERVINGS

- 2 tablespoons butter, melted
- ¼ cup sugar
- 2 teaspoons ground cinnamon
- 1 tube (12.4 ounces) refrigerated cinnamon rolls with icing

1. Place butter in a shallow bowl. In another shallow bowl, mix sugar and cinnamon. Set aside icing from cinnamon rolls.
2. Separate cinnamon rolls; cut each in half. Roll each half into a 6-in. rope. Tightly wrap one rope around a long metal skewer, starting ½ in. from end; pinch ends to seal. Repeat with remaining cinnamon rolls.
3. Cook over a hot campfire for 4-6 minutes or until golden brown, turning occasionally. Brush with butter; sprinkle with cinnamon sugar. Transfer reserved icing to a resealable plastic bag; cut a small hole in a corner of bag. Drizzle over rolls.

PEACHES WITH RASPBERRY PUREE

This unusual dessert is as pretty as it is delicious. Topped with brown sugar and cinnamon, the peaches come off the grill sweet and spicy. The raspberry sauce adds a refreshing touch.

—NANCY JOHNSON CONNERSVILLE, IN

PREP: 15 MIN. + CHILLING • **GRILL:** 15 MIN.
MAKES: 4 SERVINGS

- ½ of 10-ounce package frozen raspberries in syrup, partially thawed
- 1½ teaspoons lemon juice
- 2 medium peaches, peeled and halved
- 5 teaspoons brown sugar
- ¼ teaspoon ground cinnamon
- ½ teaspoon vanilla extract
- 1 teaspoon butter

In a blender or food processor, process raspberries and lemon juice until pureed. Strain and discard seeds. Cover and chill. Place the peach halves, cut side up, on a large piece of heavy-duty foil (about 18x12 in.). Combine brown sugar and cinnamon; sprinkle into peach centers. Sprinkle with vanilla; dot with butter. Fold foil over peaches and seal. Grill over medium-hot heat for 15 minutes or until heated through. To serve, spoon the raspberry sauce over the peaches.

WARM APPLE TOPPING

FAST FIX ▶
WARM APPLE TOPPING

My husband and I love preparing entire meals on the grill, to the surprise and delight of company. We create this dessert for my mother, who can't eat most grain products. She was thrilled with the sweet fruit topping spooned over vanilla ice cream.

—SHARON MANTON HARRISBURG, PA

START TO FINISH: 30 MIN.
MAKES: 3 CUPS

- 3 medium tart apples, peeled
- ⅓ cup raisins
- 1 tablespoon lemon juice
- ⅓ cup packed brown sugar
- ¼ teaspoon ground cinnamon
- ¼ teaspoon ground cloves
- ⅛ teaspoon salt
- ⅛ teaspoon ground nutmeg
- 2 tablespoons cold butter
- ⅓ cup finely chopped walnuts
  Vanilla ice cream

1. Cut each apple into 16 wedges; place all on an 18-in. square piece of heavy-duty foil. Sprinkle with raisins; drizzle with lemon juice.
2. In a bowl, combine the brown sugar, cinnamon, cloves, salt and nutmeg; cut in the butter until crumbly. Stir in the walnuts. Sprinkle over the apples and raisins.
3. Fold foil around apple mixture and seal tightly. Grill over indirect medium heat for 18-22 minutes or until apples are tender. Serve with ice cream.

GRILL SKILL

Buying fruit to put on the grill? Avoid fruits that are overly ripe. They might be difficult to flip or remove from the grates, and they could fall apart easily. In general, select fruits that have a faint yet sweet aroma. Fruit should gently "bounce back" when lightly pressed with your thumb. Look for fruits that feel heavy for their size, and purchase those without bruises or blemishes for ideal grilled desserts.

DESSERT FROM THE GRILL

I complete grilled meals with this light, refreshing dessert. By the time we're done eating, the coals have cooled to the right temperature. I brush slices of pineapple and pound cake with a yummy sauce, toast them on the grill and top 'em with ice cream and convenient caramel sauce.
—BECKY GILLESPIE BOULDER, CO

PREP: 10 MIN. • **GRILL:** 5 MIN
MAKES: 6 SERVINGS

- 1 **can (20 ounces) sliced pineapple, drained**
- 1 **teaspoon butter**
- ½ **teaspoon brown sugar**
- ¼ **teaspoon vanilla extract**
- ⅛ **teaspoon ground cinnamon**
- ⅛ **teaspoon ground nutmeg**
- 6 **slices pound cake**
  Vanilla ice cream
  Caramel ice cream topping

1. Drain pineapple, reserving ⅓ cup juice and six pineapple rings (save remaining juice and pineapple for another use).

2. In a microwave-safe dish, combine the butter, brown sugar, vanilla, cinnamon, nutmeg and reserved pineapple juice. Microwave, uncovered, on high for 1-2 minutes or until bubbly. Brush half of the mixture on both sides of pineapple rings and cake slices.

3. Grill, uncovered, over medium heat, cook pineapple and cake for 1-2 minutes on each side or until golden brown, brushing occasionally with remaining pineapple juice mixture.

4. Top each slice of cake with a pineapple ring and scoop of ice cream; drizzle with caramel topping. Serve immediately.

CHILI-LIME GRILLED PINEAPPLE

(5) INGREDIENTS **FAST FIX**

CHILI-LIME GRILLED PINEAPPLE

I love grilled pineapple. This recipe combines the fruit's natural sweetness with the tart and spicy flavors of lime and chili powder. It's great for dessert and even as a side dish to ham or pork chops.
—GERALDINE SAUCIER ALBUQUERQUE, NM

START TO FINISH: 15 MIN.
MAKES: 6 SERVINGS

- 1 **fresh pineapple**
- 3 **tablespoons brown sugar**
- 1 **tablespoon lime juice**
- 1 **tablespoon olive oil**
- 1 **tablespoon honey or agave nectar**
- 1½ **teaspoons chili powder**
  Dash salt

1. Peel pineapple, removing any eyes from fruit. Cut lengthwise into six wedges; remove core. In a small bowl, mix remaining ingredients until blended. Brush pineapple with half of the glaze; reserve remaining mixture for basting.

2. Grill the pineapple, covered, over medium heat or broil 4 in. from heat for 2-4 minutes on each side or until lightly browned, basting occasionally with the reserved glaze.

CAMPFIRE PEACH COBBLER

Peach cobbler has been a family classic for 60 years. We prefer peaches, but fresh cherries and berries are fun, too. Almost any fruit would work. Mix and match!
—**JACKIE WILSON** WELLSVILLE, UT

PREP: 25 MIN. • **COOK:** 30 MIN. + STANDING
MAKES: 8 SERVINGS

- 2 cups all-purpose flour
- 1 cup sugar
- 4 teaspoons baking powder
- ½ teaspoon salt
- 1 cup 2% milk
- ½ cup butter, melted

FILLING
- 2 cans (15¼ ounces each) sliced peaches
- ¼ cup sugar
- ½ teaspoon ground cinnamon, optional

1. Prepare campfire or grill for low heat, using 32-40 charcoal briquettes or large wood chips.

2. Line a 10-in. Dutch oven with heavy-duty foil. In a large bowl, combine flour, sugar, baking powder and salt. Stir in milk and butter just until moistened. Transfer to prepared Dutch oven.

3. Drain peaches, reserving 1 cup syrup. Spoon peaches over batter; sprinkle with sugar and, if desired, cinnamon. Pour the reserved syrup over fruit.

4. Cover Dutch oven. When briquettes or wood chips are covered with white ash, place the Dutch oven directly on top of 16-20 briquettes. Using long-handled tongs, place 16-20 briquettes on pan cover.

5. Cook 30-40 minutes or until set and filling is bubbly. To check for doneness, use the tongs to carefully lift the cover. If necessary, cook 5 minutes longer. Let stand, uncovered, 15 minutes before serving.

(5) INGREDIENTS FAST FIX
SUMMER FRUIT KABOBS

Fire up the grill and get out of the kitchen to make these juicy, tasty kabobs. Whether served over pound cake or a scoop of vanilla ice cream, you'll be glad that grilling isn't just for meat and veggies.
—**TRISHA KRUSE** EAGLE, ID

START TO FINISH: 20 MIN.
MAKES: 2 KABOBS

- 1 medium peach, cut into wedges
- 1 medium nectarine, cut into wedges
- 1 medium plum, cut into wedges
- ¼ cup peach preserves
- 2 tablespoons butter, cubed
  Pound cake and whipped topping, optional

1. On two metal or soaked wooden skewers, alternately thread fruits. In a small saucepan, heat preserves and butter over medium heat until butter is melted; set aside ¼ cup for dipping.

2. Using long-handled tongs, moisten a paper towel with cooking oil and lightly coat the grill rack. Grill the kabobs, covered, over medium heat or broil 4 in. from the heat for 8-10 minutes or until fruit is tender, turning and basting with remaining preserves mixture.

3. Serve with cake and whipped topping if desired and reserved sauce.

CAMPFIRE PEACH COBBLER

OLD-FASHIONED
CONEY HOT DOG
SAUCE, PAGE 283

DR PEPPER BBQ
SAUCE, PAGE 275

APPLE & SWEET
PEPPER RELISH, PAGE 282

OLD-FASHIONED
CORN RELISH, PAGE 273

SAVORY SAUCES
& SEASONINGS

Great grilling is all about the seasonings, and you'll be a pro with the **31 finger-licking** sauces, relishes, rubs and other **flavor boosters** in this chapter. Slather on a savory BBQ sauce or get creative with a colorful fruit salsa, and serve up a **taste of summer** whenever the craving strikes.

SWEET & SPICY BARBECUE SAUCE

SWEET & SPICY BARBECUE SAUCE

I've never cared that much for store-bought barbecue sauce. I like to make things from scratch, including this spicy, deep red-brown sauce. You'll find it clings well when you slather it on grilled meat.

—**HELENA GEORGETTE MANN**
SACRAMENTO, CA

PREP: 30 MIN. • **COOK:** 35 MIN.
MAKES: 1½ CUPS

- 1   medium onion, chopped
- 1   tablespoon canola oil
- 1   garlic clove, minced
- 1   to 3 teaspoons chili powder
- ¼   teaspoon cayenne pepper
- ¼   teaspoon coarsely ground pepper
- 1   cup ketchup
- ⅓   cup molasses
- 2   tablespoons cider vinegar
- 2   tablespoons Worcestershire sauce
- 2   tablespoons spicy brown mustard
- ½   teaspoon hot pepper sauce

1. In a large saucepan, saute chopped onion in oil until tender. Add garlic clove; cook 1 minute. Stir in the chili powder, cayenne and pepper; cook 1 minute longer.

2. Stir in the ketchup, molasses, vinegar, Worcestershire sauce, mustard and pepper sauce. Bring to a boil. Reduce heat; simmer, uncovered, for 30-40 minutes or until sauce reaches desired consistency. Cool 15 minutes.

3. Strain sauce through a fine mesh strainer over a large bowl, discarding vegetables and seasonings. Store in an airtight container in the refrigerator for up to 1 month. Use as a basting sauce for grilled meats.

OLD-FASHIONED
CORN RELISH

FAST FIX ▶
ITALIAN SEASONING

Who needs salt when you can give barbecued meats an Italian flair with this distinctive, slightly spicy herb blend? Try it on breads and pasta and stir it into spaghetti sauces and soups as well.
—**TASTE OF HOME** TEST KITCHEN

START TO FINISH: 5 MIN.
MAKES: 7 TABLESPOONS

- 3 **tablespoons each dried basil, oregano and parsley flakes**
- 1 **tablespoon garlic powder**
- 1 **teaspoon dried thyme**
- 1 **teaspoon dried rosemary, crushed**
- ¼ **teaspoon pepper**
- ¼ **teaspoon crushed red pepper flakes**

Place all ingredients, in batches if necessary, in a spice grinder or small bowl. Grind or crush with the back of a spoon until mixture becomes a coarse powder. Store in an airtight container for up to 6 months.

⑤INGREDIENTS FAST FIX ▶
BLAZING MUSTARD

This is a great condiment for Asian entrees, but don't stop there! Try it on grilled hot dogs and hamburgers, too. I even like it on submarine sandwiches and anything that you'd normally jazz up with a little mustard.
—**HARRY GOESCHKO** WAUKESHA, WI

START TO FINISH: 5 MIN.
MAKES: ½ CUP

- ½ **cup ground mustard**
- 1½ **teaspoons sugar**
- ½ **teaspoon salt**
- 3 **tablespoons water**
- 2 **tablespoons white vinegar**

Combine mustard, sugar and salt in a small bowl; stir in water and vinegar until smooth. Refrigerate until serving.

FAST FIX ▶
OLD-FASHIONED CORN RELISH

This was the first country recipe I received after moving away from the city. A neighbor shared it. I've made a few additions to it and gotten quite a few compliments. It's wonderful made with garden-fresh ingredients. Serve it with your favorite meats.
—**JEAN PETERSON** MULLIKEN, MI

START TO FINISH: 30 MIN.
MAKES: 6½ CUPS

- 2 **cups fresh or frozen corn**
- 2 **cups chopped onions**
- 2 **cups chopped seeded cucumbers**
- 2 **cups chopped tomatoes**
- 1 **large green pepper, chopped**
- 1 **cup sugar**
- 1 **cup cider vinegar**
- 1½ **teaspoons celery seed**
- 1½ **teaspoons mustard seed**
- 1 **teaspoon salt**
- ½ **teaspoon ground turmeric**

In a large saucepan, combine all of the ingredients. Bring to a boil. Reduce heat; simmer, uncovered, for 20-30 minutes or until thickened. Store in the refrigerator.

FAST FIX ▶
MOLASSES BARBECUE SAUCE

This delicious and thick sauce has a bold molasses flavor with a hint of citrus. Anyone who gets a taste will be asking for their very own bottle.
—**SANDI PICHON** MEMPHIS, TN

START TO FINISH: 30 MIN.
MAKES: 3½ CUPS

- 1 **can (10¾ ounces) condensed tomato soup, undiluted**
- 1 **can (8 ounces) tomato sauce**
- 1 **cup molasses**
- ½ **cup cider vinegar**
- ¼ **cup vegetable oil**
- 1 **tablespoon dried minced onion**
- 1 **tablespoon grated orange peel**
- 1 **tablespoon Worcestershire sauce**
- 2 **teaspoons ground mustard**
- 1½ **teaspoons paprika**
- 1 **teaspoon seasoned salt**
- ½ **teaspoon pepper**
- ¼ **teaspoon garlic powder**

In a large saucepan, combine all of the ingredients. Bring to a boil. Reduce heat; simmer, uncovered, for 20 minutes. Store in refrigerator.

DR PEPPER
BBQ SAUCE

DR PEPPER BBQ SAUCE

We're stationed in Italy with my husband, who is a lieutenant. He grew up in Tennessee and I'm from Texas, so the dish that spells "home" for us is a good ol' barbecue. I have my own recipe for barbecue sauce that we like to pour all over sliced brisket. Eating it reminds us of weekend barbecues back home.

—**TINA BLACKMAN** NAPLES, ITALY

PREP: 5 MIN. • **COOK:** 35 MIN.
MAKES: 1 CUP

- 1 **can (12 ounces) Dr Pepper**
- 1 **cup crushed tomatoes**
- ¼ **cup packed brown sugar**
- 2 **tablespoons spicy brown mustard**
- 1 **tablespoon orange juice**
- 1 **tablespoon Worcestershire sauce**
- 1 **garlic clove, minced**
- ¼ **teaspoon salt**
- ⅛ **teaspoon pepper**

In a small saucepan, combine all of the ingredients; bring to a boil. Reduce heat; simmer, uncovered, 30-35 minutes or until slightly thickened, stirring occasionally. Refrigerate leftovers.

⑤INGREDIENTS FAST FIX
SWEET-AND-SOUR SAUCE

You won't want to buy bottled sweet-and-sour sauce from the store after sampling this tongue-tingling recipe. I love to serve it alongside chicken.

—**FLO WEISS** SEASIDE, OR

START TO FINISH: 5 MIN.
MAKES: ⅔ CUP

- ½ **cup orange marmalade**
- 2 **tablespoons white vinegar**
- 1 **tablespoon diced pimientos**
- ⅛ **teaspoon paprika**
  Dash salt

Combine all ingredients in a small bowl; cover and refrigerate until serving.

SOUTH LIBERTY HALL RELISH

⑤INGREDIENTS
SOUTH LIBERTY HALL RELISH

My grandparents created this recipe years ago, and our family has treasured it for four generations. It's named after a dance hall my grandparents ran in rural Iowa. Whenever I bite into a hot dog or hamburger dressed up with this tasty relish, I think of them and their delicious country cooking.

—**MELINDA WINCHELL** LAS VEGAS, NV

PREP: 10 MIN. + CHILLING
MAKES: 2 CUPS

- 1 **jar (16 ounces) whole dill pickles, drained**
- ¼ **cup chopped onion**
- 2 **to 3 tablespoons sugar**
- ½ **cup yellow mustard**

Place the pickles and onion in a food processor; cover and process until finely chopped. Transfer to a bowl; stir in sugar and mustard. Store in an airtight container in the refrigerator up to 1 week.

FAST FIX
FINNEGAN HOUSE DRY RUB

I came across this recipe for a dry rub, and I tweaked it to make it my own. The rub is full of flavor and is especially delicious on ribs, but it also goes great on beef and pork chops. For extra punch, you can add a tablespoon or two of cayenne pepper.

—**LISA FINNEGAN** FORKED RIVER, NJ

START TO FINISH: 10 MIN.
MAKES: 1⅓ CUPS

- ½ **cup paprika**
- ⅓ **cup pepper**
- ¼ **cup kosher salt**
- ¼ **cup packed brown sugar**
- ¼ **cup ground cumin**
- ¼ **cup chili powder**
- 3 **tablespoons sugar**

In a small bowl, combine all ingredients. Store in an airtight container in a cool dry place for up to 6 months. Rub over meat or poultry before grilling or broiling.

YELLOW SUMMER SQUASH RELISH

My friends can barely wait for the growing season to arrive so I can prepare this incredible relish. The color really dresses up a hot dog and other grilled staples.

—RUTH HAWKINS JACKSON, MS

PREP: 1 HOUR + MARINATING
PROCESS: 15 MIN. • **MAKES:** 6 PINTS

- 10 **cups shredded yellow summer squash (about 4 pounds)**
- 2 **large onions, chopped**
- 1 **large green pepper, chopped**
- 6 **tablespoons canning salt**
- 4 **cups sugar**
- 3 **cups cider vinegar**
- 1 **tablespoon each celery seed, ground mustard and ground turmeric**
- ½ **teaspoon ground nutmeg**
- ½ **teaspoon pepper**

1. In a large container, combine squash, onions, green pepper and salt. Cover and refrigerate overnight. Drain; rinse and drain again.

2. In a Dutch oven, combine sugar, vinegar and seasonings; bring to a boil. Add squash mixture; return to a boil. Reduce heat; simmer 15 minutes. Remove from heat.

3. Carefully ladle hot mixture into six hot 1-pint jars, leaving ½-in. headspace. Remove the air bubbles and adjust the headspace, if necessary, by adding hot mixture. Wipe rims. Center lids on jars; screw on bands until fingertip tight.

4. Place jars into canner with simmering water, ensuring that they are completely covered with water. Bring to a boil; process for 15 minutes. Remove jars and cool. Refrigerate remaining relish for up to 1 week.

NOTE *The processing time listed is for altitudes of 1,000 feet or less. For altitudes up to 3,000 feet, add 5 minutes; 6,000 feet, add 10 minutes; 8,000 feet, add 15 minutes; 10,000 feet, add 20 minutes.*

PEACH CHUTNEY

PEACH CHUTNEY

Golden chunks of sweet peaches are a wonderful part of this tangy chutney. We enjoy this and many other peach delicacies year-round.

—JULIE ANN MORGAN COLUMBIA, SC

PREP: 20 MIN. • **COOK:** 45 MIN.
MAKES: ABOUT 3 CUPS

- 2 **large onions, chopped**
- 1 **tablespoon vegetable oil**
- 3 **large peaches, peeled and cubed**
- ½ **cup packed brown sugar**
- ¼ **cup sugar**
- ¼ **cup raisins**
- 1 **tablespoon molasses**
- 1 **teaspoon salt**
- ½ **teaspoon pepper**
- ¼ **teaspoon ground allspice**
- 8 **tablespoons vinegar, divided**
- 2 **tablespoons lemon juice**

In a large skillet, saute onions in oil until tender. Add peaches; cook and stir for 3 minutes. Add sugars, raisins, molasses, salt, pepper, allspice and 5 tablespoons of vinegar; bring to a boil. Reduce heat; simmer, uncovered, for 45 minutes, stirring occasionally. Remove from the heat; stir in lemon juice and remaining vinegar. Serve at room temperature with ham, pork or poultry. Store in the refrigerator for up to 3 weeks.

FAST FIX
PAPRIKA DRY RUB

A friend gave me the recipe for this delicious dry rub. I love the punch it gives turkey.
—**JACKIE KOHN** DULUTH, MN

START TO FINISH: 10 MIN.
MAKES: ABOUT 1¾ CUPS

- ½ cup sugar
- ⅓ cup kosher salt
- ⅓ cup garlic salt
- ⅓ cup packed brown sugar
- ⅓ cup paprika
- 1 teaspoon dried oregano
- 1 teaspoon ground cumin
- 1 teaspoon coarsely ground pepper
- 1 teaspoon cayenne pepper

In a small bowl, combine all of the ingredients. Store in an airtight container in a cool dry place up to 1 year. Use as a rub for turkey or chicken.

FAST FIX
NORTH CAROLINA-STYLE BBQ SAUCE

Blending two vinegars helps recreate the BBQ sauce we love from my mother's North Carolina roots.
—**GLORIA MCKINLEY** LAKELAND, FL

START TO FINISH: 25 MIN.
MAKES: 1⅔ CUPS

- ⅔ cup white vinegar
- ⅔ cup cider vinegar
- ½ cup ketchup
- 3 tablespoons packed brown sugar
- ½ teaspoon hot pepper sauce
- ¼ teaspoon salt
- ¼ teaspoon crushed red pepper flakes
- ⅛ teaspoon pepper

In a small saucepan, combine all ingredients; bring to a boil. Reduce heat; simmer, uncovered, 15-20 minutes or until flavors are blended.

5 INGREDIENTS FAST FIX
BARBECUE GRILLING SAUCE

This slightly sweet basting sauce is great on chicken, but don't stop there. Try it on grilled veggies, too!
—**KATHRYN DUNN** AXTON, VA

START TO FINISH: 5 MIN.
MAKES: 2½ CUPS

- 1 bottle (12 ounces) chili sauce
- 1 jar (10 ounces) orange marmalade
- ¼ cup cider vinegar
- 1 tablespoon Worcestershire sauce
- 1½ teaspoons celery seed

In a small bowl, combine all of the ingredients. Store in an airtight container in the refrigerator for up to 1 month. Use as a basting sauce for grilled meats.

FAST FIX
SOUTHWESTERN SEASONING MIX

I like to experiment with spice, and this is one of my favorite creations. There are so many different ways to put it to use. You can even mix it with a cup of sour cream and chill it for a bit. You'll have a great dip for potato chips or veggies.
—**CHERYL MILLER** FORT COLLINS, CO

START TO FINISH: 5 MIN.
MAKES: 1 CUP

- ¼ cup chili powder
- ¼ cup onion powder
- 2 tablespoons ground cumin
- 2 tablespoons ground coriander
- 2 tablespoons dried oregano
- 2 tablespoons dried basil
- 1 tablespoon dried thyme
- 1 tablespoon garlic powder

Combine all ingredients. Store in an airtight container. Use as a seasoning for grilled vegetables or meats.

PAPRIKA DRY RUB

⑤ INGREDIENTS

ALABAMA WHITE BBQ SAUCE

When my boys spent their summers with their grandmother in Alabama, she would treat them to a restaurant that served chicken with white barbecue sauce. Making this now reminds me of those nice times. The white sauce should be applied at the very end of the grilling time.

—SABRINA EVERETT THOMASVILLE, GA

PREP: 5 MIN. + CHILLING
MAKES: 3 CUPS

- 2 cups mayonnaise
- 1 cup cider vinegar
- 2 tablespoons pepper
- 2 tablespoons lemon juice
- 1 teaspoon salt
- ½ teaspoon cayenne pepper

In a small bowl, whisk all ingredients. Refrigerate for at least 8 hours. Brush sauce over meats during the last few minutes of grilling. Serve remaining sauce on the side for dipping.

TANGY BARBECUE SAUCE

My mother-in-law created this recipe, and we just can't get enough of the delectable sauce! I always keep a little out of the basting dish prior to using it on the grill so we have some to serve at the table. It tastes terrific on any grilled meat.

—MARY KAYE RACKOWITZ MARYSVILLE, WA

PREP: 5 MIN. • **COOK:** 35 MIN.
MAKES: 1½ CUPS

- 1 cup ketchup
- 2 tablespoons lemon juice
- 2 tablespoons cider vinegar
- ¼ cup packed brown sugar
- 2 teaspoons prepared mustard
- 1 teaspoon salt
- ½ to 1 teaspoon hot pepper sauce
- 1 bay leaf
- 1 garlic clove, minced
- ½ cup water
- 2 teaspoons Worcestershire sauce

1. Combine all of the ingredients in a small saucepan; bring to a boil, stirring occasionally. Reduce heat; cover and simmer for 30 minutes.
2. Discard bay leaf. Use as a basting sauce when grilling chicken, pork or beef.

FAST FIX

SALT-FREE SEAFOOD SEASONING

Why buy seafood seasoning when you can easily assemble this tasty blend? Use it in all of your favorite seafood recipes, like grilled salmon and shrimp kabobs.

—AVIDCOOK
TASTE OF HOME ONLINE COMMUNITY

START TO FINISH: 10 MIN.
MAKES: 2 TABLESPOONS

- 5 cardamom pods
- 6 bay leaves
- 4 whole cloves
- 1 tablespoon celery seed
- 1 tablespoon whole peppercorns
- 1 teaspoon paprika
- ½ teaspoon mustard seed
- ¼ teaspoon ground mace

Remove seeds from cardamom pods; place in a blender. Add all of the remaining ingredients; cover and process 1-2 minutes or until crushed. Store in an airtight container in a cool dry place up to 1 year.

RHUBARB RELISH

My family likes creating new sauces and relishes to use for our meals. We especially like this zippy relish on roasts.

—MINA DYCK BOISSEVAIN, MB

PREP: 10 MIN. • **COOK:** 30 MIN.
MAKES: 3⅓ CUPS

- 2 cups finely chopped fresh or frozen rhubarb
- 2 cups finely chopped onion
- 2½ cups packed brown sugar
- 1 cup vinegar
- 1 teaspoon salt
- ½ teaspoon ground cinnamon

- ½ teaspoon ground allspice
- ¼ teaspoon ground cloves
- ¼ teaspoon pepper

In a saucepan, combine all of the ingredients. Cook over medium heat for 30 minutes or until thickened, stirring occasionally. Cool; store in the refrigerator. Relish is a nice condiment for poultry, pork or beef.

ZUCCHINI CHUTNEY

There always seems to be more zucchini than I can use, so I've spent lots of time looking for different ways to use it. One day I decided to add zucchini to my homemade chutney. Now we serve it with almost anything—hot dogs, roast beef and chicken—you name it!

—MARILOU ROBINSON PORTLAND, OR

PREP: 20 MIN. + CHILLING
COOK: 45 MIN. + COOLING
MAKES: ABOUT 3½ CUPS

- 2 pounds small zucchini
- 1 tart apple, peeled
- 1 medium onion
- 1 green pepper
- 1 garlic clove, minced
- 1½ cups packed brown sugar
- 1 cup vinegar
- 1 jar (2 ounces) chopped pimientos, drained
- 1 tablespoon fresh gingerroot
- 1 tablespoon Dijon mustard
- ¼ to ½ teaspoon crushed red pepper flakes
- ½ teaspoon salt

1. Peel zucchini and discard any large seeds; chop into small pieces (about 5 cups). Finely chop apple, onion and green pepper; place in a Dutch oven along with zucchini and remaining ingredients.
2. Bring to a boil. Reduce heat and simmer, uncovered, over medium heat until thick, about 45-55 minutes, stirring often. Cool. Ladle into jars; cover and refrigerate.

END-OF-SUMMER RELISH

My family loves this relish and wants it on the table for every meal. My garden can barely keep up with demand! Try it with grilled sausages.

—VIVIAN CONNER SEBRING, FL

PREP: 45 MIN. • **COOK:** 1 HOUR + CHILLING
MAKES: 12 CUPS

- 4 each medium green, sweet red and yellow peppers, cut into 1-inch pieces
- 4 medium onions, quartered
- 4 medium carrots, cut into 2-inch pieces
- 2 medium cucumbers, peeled and cut into 2-inch pieces
- 1 small head cabbage, cut into wedges
- 2¾ cups white vinegar
- 1 cup sugar
- ¾ cup water
- 3 tablespoons salt
- 1 tablespoon mustard seed
- 1 tablespoon celery seed
  Cooked sausage or meat of your choice

1. In a food processor, cover and process the vegetables in batches until finely chopped. Drain vegetables and discard liquid.

2. In a stockpot, bring vinegar, sugar, water, salt, mustard seed and celery seed to a boil. Add vegetables; return to a boil. Reduce heat; simmer, uncovered, 1 hour or until thickened. Store in airtight containers in the refrigerator up to 1 week. Serve with sausage or other meat.

END-OF-SUMMER RELISH

RAISIN PEAR CHUTNEY

RAISIN PEAR CHUTNEY

We have so much fruit in the area that I just can't help making recipes that use it. This hearty chutney is delicious with any flame-broiled meat.

—RUTH ANDREWSON LEAVENWORTH, WA

PREP: 2¼ HOURS • **PROCESS:** 15 MIN.
MAKES: 2 PINTS

- 2 **cups cider vinegar**
- 1¼ **cups packed brown sugar**
- 3 **pounds unpeeled ripe pears, diced**
- 1 **medium onion, chopped**
- 1 **cup raisins**
- 2 **teaspoons ground cinnamon**
- 1 **teaspoon ground cloves**
- 1 **garlic clove, minced**
- ½ **to 1 teaspoon cayenne pepper**

1. In a large saucepan, bring vinegar and brown sugar to a boil. Stir in the remaining ingredients. Return to a boil. Reduce heat; simmer, uncovered, for 2-2½ hours or until chutney reaches desired consistency.

2. Carefully ladle hot mixture into hot pint jars, leaving ¼-in. headspace. Remove air bubbles, wipe rims and adjust lids. Process for 15 minutes in a boiling-water canner.

NOTE *The processing time listed is for altitudes of 1,000 feet or less. Add 1 minute to the processing time for each 1,000 feet of additional altitude.*

GRILL SKILL

When grilling with a sauce, be sure your grill is at the proper temperature before placing food on the grill rack. Only baste with a sauce after you've flipped the food once. This will prevent the brush from coming into contact with uncooked foods and contaminating the batch of sauce. If using a particularly thick or sweet sauce, baste during the last 10 minutes of cooking.

FAST FIX

LEMON-PEPPER THYME RUB

This recipe makes any cut of beef simply delectable. Everyone will want to know the secret ingredient!

—CHARLIE AND RUTHIE KNOTE CAPE GIRARDEAU, MO

START TO FINISH: 10 MIN.
MAKES: ¾ CUP

- 6 **tablespoons lemon-pepper seasoning**
- 2 **tablespoons ground thyme**
- 2 **tablespoons paprika**
- 2 **teaspoons granular garlic**
- 1 **teaspoon sugar**
- ½ **teaspoon salt**
- ¼ **teaspoon ground coriander**
- ⅛ **teaspoon ground cumin**
- ⅛ **teaspoon cayenne pepper**

Combine all of the ingredients; mix well. Apply generously to steaks or hamburgers. Store unused portion in a covered glass container.

FAST FIX

DIXIE HERB RUB

My husband loves it when I season chicken with this flavorful blend, but it's also good with beef and pork. We like to slice the leftover meat for sandwiches the next day.

—TRACI WYNNE DENVER, PA

START TO FINISH: 5 MIN.
MAKES: ⅓ CUP

- 1 **tablespoon each dried basil, thyme and rosemary, crushed**
- 1½ **teaspoons sugar**
- 1½ **teaspoons dried oregano**
- 1½ **teaspoons dried marjoram**
- 1 **teaspoon salt**
- ¾ **teaspoon garlic powder**
- ½ **teaspoon pepper**
- ¼ **teaspoon onion powder**
- ¼ **teaspoon cayenne pepper**

In a small bowl, combine all ingredients. Store in a covered container. Rub over poultry or meat before grilling, baking or broiling.

VIDALIA ONION RELISH

Brats and burgers get star treatment with this sweet onion topping. Bourbon adds a lovely caramel note, and the crushed pepper flakes turn up the heat.

—JANET ROTH TEMPE, AZ

PREP: 1 HOUR • **COOK:** 15 MIN.
MAKES: 3 CUPS

- 4 large sweet onions, chopped
- 2 tablespoons canola oil
- 3 garlic cloves, minced
- ⅓ cup bourbon
- 4 plum tomatoes, peeled, seeded and chopped
- ½ cup golden raisins
- ¼ cup sugar
- ¼ cup packed dark brown sugar
- ¼ cup cider vinegar
- 1 teaspoon mustard seed
- ½ teaspoon salt
- ½ teaspoon ground turmeric
- ½ teaspoon ground mustard
- ½ teaspoon crushed red pepper flakes
- ¼ teaspoon pepper
  Cooked sausage or meat of your choice

1. In a large saucepan, cook onions in oil over medium heat 40-45 minutes or until the onions are golden brown, stirring occasionally. Add garlic; cook 1 minute longer. Remove from heat. Add bourbon, stirring to loosen browned bits from pan.

2. Stir in remaining ingredients; bring to a boil. Reduce heat; simmer, uncovered, 15-20 minutes or until thickened. Store in airtight containers in the refrigerator up to 1 week. Serve with sausage or other meat.

VIDALIA ONION RELISH

APPLE & SWEET
PEPPER RELISH

APPLE & SWEET PEPPER RELISH

Before you turn apples into cobbler or pie, consider making this relish. Alongside grilled pork or even over hot dogs, it will be a game changer at your next cookout.
—**JANETTE SCHULZ** MCDONOUGH, GA

PREP: 10 MIN. • **COOK:** 20 MIN. + CHILLING
MAKES: ABOUT 7 CUPS

- 2 **cups cider vinegar**
- 2 **cups sugar**
- ¾ **teaspoon salt**
- 4 **cups chopped peeled Braeburn or other apples (about 4 medium)**
- 2 **large onions, chopped**
- 1 **medium sweet red pepper, chopped**
- 1 **medium green pepper, chopped**

1. In a nonreactive Dutch oven, combine all ingredients; bring to a boil. Reduce heat; simmer, uncovered, 10-15 minutes or until onions are crisp-tender, stirring occasionally. Transfer to a large bowl; cool to room temperature.
2. Refrigerate, covered, for at least 6-8 hours before serving. May refrigerate up to 2 weeks.

⑤INGREDIENTS FAST FIX

SWEET AND TANGY BARBECUE SAUCE

This sweet and tangy basting sauce came from my husband's family. With just four ingredients, it's simple to stir up. A speedy alternative to bottled sauce, it can be brushed on ribs or even turkey.
—**JENINE SCHMIDT** STOUGHTON, WI

START TO FINISH: 5 MIN.
MAKES: 1⅓ CUPS

- 1 **cup ketchup**
- ⅔ **cup packed brown sugar**
- 2 **teaspoons prepared mustard**
- ½ **teaspoon ground nutmeg**

In a bowl, whisk all ingredients. Use as a basting sauce for grilled meat.

FAST FIX ▶
ZIPPY DRY RUB

Bottles of this spicy blend are fun to share with family and friends. It's a mixture with broad appeal since the rub can be used on all meats or even added to rice while it's cooking for a boost of flavor.

—GAYNELLE FRITSCH WELCHES, OR

PREP: 5 MIN.
MAKES: ABOUT 2½ TABLESPOONS

- 1 **tablespoon salt**
- 1 **teaspoon mustard seed**
- 1 **teaspoon pepper**
- 1 **teaspoon chili powder**
- 1 **teaspoon paprika**
- ½ **teaspoon ground cumin**
- ½ **teaspoon dried coriander**
- ¼ **teaspoon garlic powder**

In a small bowl, combine all ingredients. Store in an airtight container. Rub desired amount onto the surface of uncooked meat. Cover meat and refrigerate for at least 4 hours before grilling.

FAST FIX ▶
SPICY PAPRIKA HERB RUB

Rub this mixture on chicken or roasts to add a nice spicy flavor. It'll turn the meat golden brown, and it tastes marvelous!

—MARIAN PLATT SEQUIM, WA

START TO FINISH: 5 MIN.
MAKES: ½ CUP

- 1 **tablespoon garlic powder**
- 1 **tablespoon brown sugar**
- 1 **tablespoon ground mustard**
- 1 **tablespoon paprika**
- 1 **teaspoon onion salt**
- 1 **teaspoon dried rosemary, crushed**
- 1 **teaspoon ground cumin**
- 1 **teaspoon dried thyme**
- 1 **teaspoon pepper**
- ½ **teaspoon cayenne pepper**

In a small bowl, combine all ingredients; store in a covered container. Rub over meat or poultry before grilling or broiling.

OLD-FASHIONED CONEY HOT DOG SAUCE

OLD-FASHIONED CONEY HOT DOG SAUCE

Camping and hot dogs go hand in hand. Roast some up over the fire, then top with this irresistible one-pot sauce.

—LORIANN CARGILL BUSTOS PHOENIX, AZ

PREP: 10 MIN. • **COOK:** 30 MIN.
MAKES: 2 CUPS

- 1 **pound lean ground beef (90% lean)**
- 1 **cup beef stock**
- 2 **tablespoons tomato paste**
- 1 **tablespoon chili powder**
- 1 **tablespoon Worcestershire sauce**
- ½ **teaspoon salt**
- ½ **teaspoon onion powder**
- ½ **teaspoon garlic powder**
- ½ **teaspoon celery salt**
- ½ **teaspoon ground cumin**
- ¼ **teaspoon pepper**

Prepare campfire or grill for medium-high heat. In a Dutch oven, cook beef over campfire 8-10 minutes or until no longer pink, breaking into crumbles. Stir in remaining ingredients; bring to a boil. Move Dutch oven to indirect heat.

Cook, uncovered, 20-25 minutes or until thickened, stirring occasionally.

FREEZE OPTION *Freeze cooled meat mixture in freezer containers. To use, partially thaw in refrigerator overnight. Heat through in a saucepan, adding a little water if necessary.*

⑤ INGREDIENTS FAST FIX ▶
LEMON & ROSEMARY STEAK RUB

This is a great rub for any cut of beef. It really highlights the meat's flavor.

— BEEF BOARD AND BEEF INDUSTRY COUNCIL

START TO FINISH: 5 MIN.
MAKES: ENOUGH TO SEASON 2 POUNDS OF BEEF

- 1½ **teaspoons grated lemon peel**
- 1 **teaspoon dried rosemary, crushed**
- ¼ **teaspoon dried thyme**
- ¼ **teaspoon coarsely ground pepper**
- 2 **large garlic cloves, minced**

Combine all ingredients. Rub over beef before grilling or broiling.

**WALKING TACOS,
PAGE 297**

ROOT BEER PULLED PORK SANDWICHES, PAGE 300

PREGAME PASTA SALAD IN A JAR, PAGE 286

SPICY TOUCHDOWN CHILI, PAGE 298

BONUS: TAILGATE FAVORITES

It's easy to cheer on your favorite team when you gather pregame with an assortment of hefty **handheld classics.** This bonus section is your go-to destination for tasty **tailgate bites** that promise to get the **party started** even before the first ball is thrown.

**PREGAME PASTA SALAD
IN A JAR**

FAST FIX

PREGAME PASTA SALAD IN A JAR

If you're planning a picnic, make this pasta a day ahead. For my husband's lunch at work, I tie a plastic fork on the jar.
—**PAT NEIHEISEL** LEETONIA, OH

START TO FINISH: 30 MIN.
MAKES: 16 SERVINGS (1 CUP EACH)

- 8 ounces each uncooked bow tie pasta, medium pasta shells and wagon wheel pasta
- 2 cups Greek vinaigrette
- 3 cups cherry tomatoes, halved
- 1 medium red onion, finely chopped
- 1 jar (12 ounces) marinated quartered artichoke hearts, drained and coarsely chopped
- 1 jar (12 ounces) roasted sweet red peppers, drained and chopped
- 1 cup chopped fresh basil
- 1 cup grated Parmesan cheese
- 1 package (3½ ounces) sliced pepperoni
- 1 can (2¼ ounces) sliced ripe olives, drained

1. Cook the pasta according to package directions for al dente. Drain pasta; rinse with cold water and drain well. Transfer to a large bowl.
2. Add vinaigrette to pasta; toss to coat. Add vegetables, basil, cheese, pepperoni and olives; toss to combine. If desired, transfer to covered jars. Refrigerate until serving.

SANDWICH FOR A CROWD

My husband and I live on a 21-acre horse ranch and are pleased to invite friends to enjoy it with us. When entertaining, I rely on make-ahead entrees like this satisfying sandwich. It's perfect for a crowd and it travels well, making it ideal for tailgates and picnics or simply watching a parade or summer fireworks.

—HELEN HOUGLAND SPRING HILL, KS

PREP: 10 MIN. + CHILLING
MAKES: 12-14 SERVINGS

- 2 loaves (1 pound each) unsliced Italian bread
- 1 package (8 ounces) cream cheese, softened
- 1 cup (4 ounces) shredded cheddar cheese
- ¾ cup sliced green onions
- ¼ cup mayonnaise
- 1 tablespoon Worcestershire sauce
- 1 pound thinly sliced fully cooked ham
- 1 pound thinly sliced roast beef
- 12 to 14 thin slices dill pickle

1. Cut the bread in half lengthwise. Hollow out top and bottom of loaves, leaving a ½-in. shell (discard removed bread or save for another use).
2. In a large bowl, combine the cream cheese, cheddar cheese, onions, mayonnaise and Worcestershire sauce; spread over cut sides of bread.
3. Layer with ham and roast beef on bottom and top halves; place pickles on bottom halves. Gently press the halves together.
4. Wrap in plastic wrap and refrigerate for at least 2 hours. Cut into 1½-in. slices before serving.

NACHO POPCORN

FAST FIX ▶
NACHO POPCORN

My husband and I like to munch on this. The nacho flavoring is a zesty alternative to butter and salt.

—LINDA BOEHME FAIRMONT, MN

START TO FINISH: 10 MIN.
MAKES: 5 QUARTS

- 5 quarts popped popcorn
- ½ cup butter, melted
- 2 tablespoons grated Parmesan cheese
- 2 tablespoons dried parsley flakes
- 1 teaspoon garlic salt
- 1 teaspoon chili powder
- 4 to 6 drops hot pepper sauce

Place popcorn in a large bowl. Combine remaining ingredients; drizzle over popcorn and toss until well coated.

⑤ INGREDIENTS
SLOW-COOKED SMOKIES

I like to include these little sausages smothered in barbecue sauce on all my picnic menus. They're popular with both children and adults.

—SUNDRA HAUCK BOGALUSA, LA

PREP: 5 MIN. ● **COOK:** 6 HOURS
MAKES: 8 SERVINGS

- 1 package (1 pound) miniature smoked sausages
- 1 bottle (28 ounces) barbecue sauce
- 1¼ cups water
- 3 tablespoons Worcestershire sauce
- 3 tablespoons steak sauce
- ½ teaspoon pepper

In a 3-qt. slow cooker, combine all ingredients. Cover and cook on low for 5-6 hours or until heated through. Serve with a slotted spoon.

SWEET & SALTY
PARTY MIX

BARBECUE BRATS
& PEPPERS

SWEET & SALTY PARTY MIX

My husband doesn't like traditional party mixes because he thinks they're too salty or sweet. He calls this one his favorite—it's just right.

—JACKIE BURNS KETTLE FALLS, WA

PREP: 20 MIN. • **COOK:** 1 HOUR
MAKES: 16 SERVINGS (¾ CUP EACH)

- 3 cups each Corn Chex, Rice Chex and Wheat Chex
- 3 cups miniature pretzels
- 1 cup dried cranberries
- 1 cup sliced almonds
- ½ cup butter, cubed
- 1 cup packed brown sugar
- ¼ cup corn syrup
- ¼ teaspoon baking soda

1. Place cereal, pretzels, cranberries and almonds in a greased 6-qt. slow cooker; toss to combine. In a small saucepan, melt butter over medium heat; stir in the brown sugar and corn syrup. Bring to a boil; cook and stir for 5 minutes. Remove from heat; stir in baking soda. Drizzle over the cereal mixture and toss to coat.

2. Cook, covered, on low 1 hour, stirring halfway. Spread onto waxed paper; cool completely. Store in airtight containers.

BARBECUE BRATS & PEPPERS

We live in brat country, and this barbecue-style recipe feeds a crowd. The sauce gives it a welcome change from the same old grilled brat.

—MARIA ZRUCKY KRONENWETTER, WI

PREP: 15 MIN. • **COOK:** 6 HOURS
MAKES: 10 SERVINGS

- 2 bottles (12 ounces each) beer or nonalcoholic beer
- 1 bottle (18 ounces) barbecue sauce
- ½ cup ketchup
- 1 large sweet onion, halved and sliced
- 1 large sweet yellow pepper, cut into strips
- 1 large sweet orange pepper, cut into strips
- 1 jalapeno pepper, thinly sliced
- 1 serrano pepper, thinly sliced
- 10 uncooked bratwurst links
- 10 brat or hot dog buns, split

1. Place the first eight ingredients in a 5-qt. slow cooker; stir to combine. In a large skillet, brown bratwurst on all sides over medium-high heat; transfer to slow cooker.

2. Cook, covered, on low 6-8 hours or until sausages are cooked through and the vegetables are tender. Using tongs, serve bratwurst and pepper mixture on buns.

PEPPERED RIBEYE STEAKS

A true Southerner to the core, I love to cook—especially on the grill. I concocted this seasoning rub using pantry staples. Nothing beats the summery taste of these steaks.

—SHARON BICKETT CHESTER, SC

PREP: 10 MIN. + CHILLING • **GRILL:** 15 MIN.
MAKES: 8 SERVINGS

- 4 beef ribeye steaks (1½-inch thick)
- 1 tablespoon olive oil
- 1 tablespoon garlic powder
- 1 tablespoon paprika
- 2 teaspoons dried ground thyme
- 2 teaspoons dried ground oregano
- 1½ teaspoons pepper
- 1 teaspoon salt
- 1 teaspoon lemon-pepper seasoning
- 1 teaspoon cayenne pepper
- 1 teaspoon crushed red pepper flakes

1. Brush steaks lightly with oil. In a small bowl, combine all seasonings. Sprinkle seasonings over steaks and press into both sides. Cover and chill for 1 hour.

2. Grill, covered, over medium heat or broil 4 in. from the heat for 7-8 minutes on each side or until meat reaches desired doneness (for medium-rare, a thermometer should read 145°; medium, 160°; well-done, 170°).

3. Let stand 5 minutes before slicing. Place on a warm serving platter; cut across the grain into thick slices.

JALAPENO POPPER & SAUSAGE DIP

My workplace had an appetizer contest, and I won it with my jalapeno and cheese dip. Wherever I take it, folks quickly gobble it up!

—BEV SLABIK DILWORTH, MN

PREP: 15 MIN. • **COOK:** 3 HOURS
MAKES: 24 SERVINGS (¼ CUP EACH)

- 1 pound bulk spicy pork sausage
- 2 packages (8 ounces each) cream cheese, cubed
- 4 cups shredded Parmesan cheese (about 12 ounces)
- 1 cup (8 ounces) sour cream
- 1 can (4 ounces) chopped green chilies
- 1 can (4 ounces) diced jalapeno peppers
  Assorted fresh vegetables

1. In a large skillet, cook sausage over medium heat 6-8 minutes or until no longer pink, breaking into crumbles. Using a slotted spoon, transfer sausage to a 3-qt. slow cooker.

2. Stir in cream cheese, Parmesan cheese, sour cream, chilies and peppers. Cook, covered, on low 3-3½ hours or until heated through. Stir before serving. Serve with vegetables.

JALAPENO POPPER & SAUSAGE DIP

SWEET & TANGY CHICKEN WINGS

Here's a festive recipe that's perfect for tailgates. Put the wings in before you prepare for the party, and in a few hours, you'll have wonderful appetizers!

—IDA TUEY SOUTH LYON, MI

PREP: 20 MIN. • **COOK:** 3¼ HOURS
MAKES: ABOUT 2½ DOZEN

- 3 **pounds chicken wingettes (about 30)**
- ½ **teaspoon salt, divided**
  Dash pepper
- 1½ **cups ketchup**
- ¼ **cup packed brown sugar**
- ¼ **cup red wine vinegar**
- 2 **tablespoons Worcestershire sauce**
- 1 **tablespoon Dijon mustard**
- 1 **teaspoon minced garlic**
- 1 **teaspoon liquid smoke, optional**
  Sesame seeds, optional

1. Sprinkle chicken with a dash of salt and pepper. Broil 4-6 in. from the heat for 5-10 minutes on each side or until golden brown. Transfer to a greased 5-qt. slow cooker.

2. Combine the ketchup, brown sugar, vinegar, Worcestershire sauce, mustard, garlic, liquid smoke if desired and remaining salt; pour over wings. Toss to coat.

3. Cover and cook on low for 3¼-3¾ hours or until chicken juices run clear. Sprinkle with sesame seeds if desired.

FREEZE OPTION *Freeze cooled fully cooked wings in freezer containers. To use, partially thaw in the refrigerator overnight. Reheat wings in a foil-lined 15x10x1-in. baking pan in a preheated 325° oven until heated through, covering if necessary to prevent browning. Serve as directed.*

SLOW COOKER CHOCOLATE LAVA CAKE

SLOW COOKER CHOCOLATE LAVA CAKE

Everyone who tries this dessert falls in love with it. Using a slow cooker liner makes cleanup a breeze.

—LATONA DWYER PALM BEACH GARDENS, FL

PREP: 15 MIN. • **COOK:** 3 HOURS
MAKES: 12 SERVINGS

- 1 **package devil's food cake mix (regular size)**
- 1⅔ **cups water**
- 3 **large eggs**
- ⅓ **cup canola oil**
- 2 **cups cold 2% milk**
- 1 **package (3.9 ounces) instant chocolate pudding mix**
- 2 **cups (12 ounces) semisweet chocolate chips**

1. In a large bowl, combine the cake mix, water, eggs and oil; beat on low speed for 30 seconds. Beat on medium for 2 minutes. Transfer to a greased 4-qt. slow cooker.

2. In another bowl, whisk milk and pudding mix for 2 minutes. Let stand for 2 minutes or until soft-set. Spoon over cake batter; sprinkle with the chocolate chips. Cover and cook on high for 3-4 hours or until a toothpick inserted in cake portion comes out with moist crumbs. Serve warm.

BIG JOHN'S CHILI-RUBBED RIBS

When my family thinks of summer grilling, it's ribs all the way. Our Asian-inspired recipe is a welcome change from the usual barbecue-sauce versions.
—**GINGER SULLIVAN** CUTLER BAY, FL

PREP: 20 MIN. + CHILLING • **GRILL:** 1½ HOURS
MAKES: 10 SERVINGS

- 3 **tablespoons packed brown sugar**
- 2 **tablespoons paprika**
- 2 **tablespoons chili powder**
- 3 **teaspoons ground cumin**
- 2 **teaspoons garlic powder**
- 1 **teaspoon salt**
- 6 **pounds pork baby back ribs**

GLAZE

- 1 **cup reduced-sodium soy sauce**
- 1 **cup packed brown sugar**
- ⅔ **cup ketchup**
- ⅓ **cup lemon juice**
- 1½ **teaspoons minced fresh gingerroot**

1. Mix the first six ingredients; rub over ribs. Refrigerate, covered, for 30 minutes.
2. Wrap rib racks in large pieces of heavy-duty foil; seal tightly. Grill, covered, over indirect medium heat 1-1½ hours or until tender.
3. In a large saucepan, combine glaze ingredients; cook, uncovered, over medium heat for 6-8 minutes or until heated through and sugar is dissolved, stirring occasionally.
4. Carefully remove ribs from the foil. Place ribs over direct heat; brush with some of the glaze.
5. Grill, covered, over medium heat 25-30 minutes or until browned, turning and brushing ribs occasionally with remaining glaze.

RACE DAY BURGERS

My garden produced a bumper crop of basil one year and I needed ways to use it all. I added it to these burgers, and now it is one of our family's cookout foods.
—**VIRGINIA KOCHIS** SPRINGFIELD, VA

PREP: 25 MIN. • **GRILL:** 10 MIN.
MAKES: 8 SERVINGS

- 4 **sun-dried tomatoes (not packed in oil)**
- 1 **cup boiling water**
- 1 **cup mayonnaise**
- 4 **pieces string cheese**
- ½ **cup minced fresh basil**
- 4 **teaspoons Worcestershire sauce**
- 4 **teaspoons Italian seasoning**
- 4 **garlic cloves, minced**
- 1 **teaspoon salt**
- 1 **teaspoon pepper**
- 3 **pounds ground beef**
- 2 **loaves (14 ounces each) ciabatta bread, halved lengthwise**
- 4 **slices part-skim mozzarella cheese**
  Fresh basil leaves

1. Place tomatoes and water in a small bowl; let stand for 5 minutes. Drain well; place tomatoes in a food processor. Add mayonnaise; cover and process until blended. Transfer to a bowl; cover and refrigerate until serving.
2. Cut each piece of string cheese in half lengthwise and widthwise; set aside. In a large bowl, combine the minced basil, Worcestershire sauce, Italian seasoning, garlic, salt and pepper. Crumble beef over mixture and mix well. Shape into 16 thin patties. Place two pieces of string cheese on eight patties; top with remaining patties. Press edges firmly to seal.
3. Grill patties, covered, over medium heat for 5-7 minutes on each side or until meat is no longer pink. Place four burgers on the bottom of each loaf of bread; top with mozzarella cheese, basil leaves and tomato mayonnaise. Replace the bread tops. Cut each loaf into four servings.

BIG JOHN'S CHILI-RUBBED RIBS

PLAY BALL
CAKE

PLAY BALL CAKE

You won't need fancy pans to make this sporting dessert. Our kids and their cousins all wanted pieces that had the red licorice lacing! Fresh, pliable licorice works the best for forming the laces on the curved ball cake.
—SUE GRONHOLZ BEAVER DAM, WI

PREP: 30 MIN. • **BAKE:** 40 MIN. + COOLING
MAKES: 8-10 SERVINGS

- ½ cup shortening
- 1½ cups sugar
- 2 large eggs
- 1 teaspoon vanilla extract
- 2½ cups cake flour
- 2 teaspoons baking powder
- ½ teaspoon salt
- 1 cup milk

FROSTING
- ½ cup shortening
- ½ cup butter, softened
- 3 cups confectioners' sugar
- 4 tablespoons milk, divided
- ½ teaspoon vanilla extract
- ¼ teaspoon almond extract
  Dash salt
- ¼ cup baking cocoa
  Shoestring red licorice

1. In a large bowl, cream shortening and sugar until light and fluffy. Add the eggs, one at a time, beating well after each. Beat in vanilla. Combine the flour, baking powder and salt; add alternately with milk to creamed mixture, beating well after each addition. Pour 1½ cups

batter into a greased and floured 3-cup ovenproof bowl.
2. Pour remaining batter into a greased and floured 9-in. round baking pan. Bake cakes at 325° for 40-45 minutes or until a toothpick inserted near the center comes out clean. Cool cakes for 10 minutes before removing to wire racks to cool completely.
3. For the frosting, in a large bowl, beat the shortening, butter and confectioners' sugar until smooth. Beat in 3 tablespoons milk, extracts and salt until smooth. Set aside 1 cup frosting.
4. Beat cocoa and 1 tablespoon milk into remaining frosting. Cut a 3x1-in. oval from an edge of the 9-in. cake for the thumb of the mitt. Place cake on an 11-in. covered board; frost with the chocolate frosting.
5. With pieces of licorice, form crosses over thumb opening for laces in mitt. Frost the rounded cake with white frosting. Use licorice pieces to form laces of ball. Place on mitt cake opposite the thumb opening.

⑤ INGREDIENTS **FAST FIX**
GAME DAY SKEWERS
These kabobs are fun, different and delicious, particularly for morning tailgates and pregame get-togethers.
—BOBI RAAB ST. PAUL, MN

START TO FINISH: 20 MIN.
MAKES: 5 SERVINGS

- 1 package (7 ounces) frozen fully cooked breakfast sausage links, thawed
- 1 can (20 ounces) pineapple chunks, drained
- 10 medium fresh mushrooms
- 2 tablespoons butter, melted
  Maple syrup

1. Cut sausages in half; on five metal or soaked wooden skewers, alternately thread the sausages, pineapple and mushrooms. Brush with the butter and syrup.
2. Grill, uncovered, over medium heat,

turning and basting with syrup, for 8 minutes or until sausages are lightly browned and fruit is heated through.

TAILGATE SAUSAGES
Try these grilled sausages for a crowd-pleasing casual meal. Make the tomato sauce loaded with green peppers, then keep it hot in a foil pan on the grill and let your friends serve themselves.
—MIKE YAEGER BROOKINGS, SD

PREP: 30 MIN. • **GRILL:** 10 MIN.
MAKES: 20 SERVINGS

- 4 large green peppers, thinly sliced
- ½ cup chopped onion
- 2 tablespoons olive oil
- 4 garlic cloves, minced
- 1 can (15 ounces) tomato sauce
- 1 can (12 ounces) tomato paste
- 1 cup water
- 1 tablespoon sugar
- 2 teaspoons dried basil
- 1 teaspoon salt
- 1 teaspoon dried oregano
- 20 uncooked Italian sausage links
- 20 sandwich buns
  Shredded part-skim mozzarella cheese, optional

1. In a large saucepan, saute peppers and onion in oil until crisp-tender. Add garlic; cook 1 minute longer. Drain. Stir in the tomato sauce, tomato paste, water, sugar, basil, salt and oregano. Bring to a boil. Reduce heat; cover and simmer for 30 minutes or until heated through.
2. Meanwhile, grill sausages, covered, over medium heat for 10-16 minutes or until a thermometer reads 160°, turning occasionally. Serve on buns with sauce and cheese if desired.

ITALIAN MEATBALL BURGERS

I just love these burgers! They're a big hit with kids and adults. I serve them with sliced green peppers, tomatoes and onions and a jar of crushed red pepper flakes on the side.

—PRISCILLA GILBERT
INDIAN HARBOUR BEACH, FL

PREP: 25 MIN. • **GRILL:** 15 MIN.
MAKES: 8 SERVINGS

- 1 large egg, lightly beaten
- ⅓ cup seasoned bread crumbs
- 3 garlic cloves, minced
- 1 teaspoon dried oregano
- 1 teaspoon dried basil
- ¼ teaspoon salt
- ¼ teaspoon dried thyme
- 1½ pounds lean ground beef (90% lean)
- ½ pound Italian turkey sausage links, casings removed
- ¾ cup shredded part-skim mozzarella cheese
- 8 kaiser rolls, split
- 1 cup roasted garlic Parmesan spaghetti sauce, warmed

1. In a large bowl, combine the first seven ingredients. Crumble beef and sausage over mixture and mix well. Shape into eight burgers.

2. Moisten a paper towel with cooking oil; using long-handled tongs, rub it on grill rack to coat lightly. Grill burgers, covered, over medium heat or broil 4 in. from the heat for 5-7 minutes on each side or until a thermometer reads 165° and juices run clear.

3. Sprinkle burgers with cheese; cook 2-3 minutes longer or until cheese is melted. Remove and keep warm.

4. Grill or broil rolls for 1-2 minutes or until toasted. Serve burgers on rolls with spaghetti sauce.

ITALIAN MEATBALL
BURGERS

GRILLED CHEESE LOAF

FAST FIX ▶

GRILLED CHEESE LOAF

What a fun change of pace! I often serve buttery grilled bread with steak and a salad. This is so quick to make, and it's easy to heat alongside anything else you have on the grill.

—**DEBBI BAKER** GREEN SPRINGS, OH

START TO FINISH: 30 MIN.
MAKES: 10-12 SERVINGS

- 3 ounces cream cheese, softened
- 2 tablespoons butter, softened
- 1 cup (4 ounces) shredded mozzarella cheese
- ¼ cup chopped green onions
- ½ teaspoon garlic salt
- 1 loaf (1 pound) French bread, sliced

1. In a small bowl, beat cream cheese and butter. Add the cheese, onions and garlic salt; mix well. Cut bread, leaving slices attached at the bottom; spread slices with cream cheese mixture.
2. Wrap loaf in a large piece of heavy-duty foil (about 28x18 in.); seal tightly. Grill, covered, over medium heat for 8-10 minutes, turning once. Carefully open foil; grill bread 5 minutes longer.

✕ GRILL SKILL

Going to grill at the tailgate? Place the grill on a solid surface, away from any activities so no one bumps into it. Don't set the grill near shrubs, grass, overhangs or fences. Keep any coolers away from the grill. Set the cooler out of direct sunlight and replenish the ice if possible. Keep foods refrigerated before packing them into coolers and heading out for the tailgate.

FORGOTTEN JAMBALAYA

During chilly months, I fix this jambalaya at least once a month. It's so easy—just chop the vegetables, dump everything into the slow cooker and forget it! Even my sons, who are picky about spicy things, like this comforting dish.

—CINDI COSS COPPELL, TX

PREP: 35 MIN. • **COOK:** 4¼ HOURS
MAKES: 11 SERVINGS

- 1 can (14½ ounces) diced tomatoes, undrained
- 1 can (14½ ounces) beef or chicken broth
- 1 can (6 ounces) tomato paste
- 3 celery ribs, chopped
- 2 medium green peppers, chopped
- 1 medium onion, chopped
- 5 garlic cloves, minced
- 3 teaspoons dried parsley flakes
- 2 teaspoons dried basil
- 1½ teaspoons dried oregano
- 1¼ teaspoons salt
- ½ teaspoon cayenne pepper
- ½ teaspoon hot pepper sauce
- 1 pound boneless skinless chicken breasts, cut into 1-inch cubes
- 1 pound smoked sausage, halved and cut into ¼-inch slices
- ½ pound uncooked medium shrimp, peeled and deveined
  Hot cooked rice

1. In a 5-qt. slow cooker, combine the tomatoes, broth and tomato paste. Stir in the celery, green peppers, onion, garlic and seasonings. Stir in chicken and sausage.

2. Cover and cook on low for 4-6 hours or until chicken is no longer pink. Stir in shrimp. Cover and cook 15-30 minutes longer or until shrimp turn pink. Serve with rice.

FREEZE OPTION *Place individual portions of cooled jambalaya in freezer containers and freeze. To use, partially thaw in the refrigerator overnight. Heat through in a saucepan, stirring occasionally and adding a little water if necessary.*

JALAPENO POPPER CORN CUPCAKES

JALAPENO POPPER CORN CUPCAKES

Sweet cornmeal cupcakes and jalapenos may seem like an unusual dessert, but we guarantee these treats will please.

—TASTE OF HOME TEST KITCHEN

PREP: 40 MIN. • **BAKE:** 25 MIN. + COOLING
MAKES: 1 DOZEN

- 1¼ cups all-purpose flour
- 1 cup sugar
- ½ cup cornmeal
- 2 teaspoons baking powder
- ¼ teaspoon salt
- 2 large eggs
- ½ cup 2% milk
- ½ cup olive oil
- ½ teaspoon vanilla extract
- ¾ cup frozen corn, thawed
- 2 tablespoons finely chopped seeded jalapeno pepper

FROSTING
- ¼ cup panko (Japanese) bread crumbs
- 4 ounces cream cheese, softened
- ¼ cup butter, softened
- 1¾ cups confectioners' sugar

- 1 teaspoon vanilla extract
  Sliced jalapeno peppers

1. In a large bowl, combine the flour, sugar, cornmeal, baking powder and salt. In another bowl, combine the eggs, milk, oil and vanilla. Stir into the dry ingredients just until moistened. Fold in corn and jalapeno.

2. Fill greased or paper-lined muffin cups three-fourths full. Bake at 350° for 24-28 minutes or until a toothpick inserted into cupcake comes out clean. Cool for 5 minutes before removing cupcakes from pan to a wire rack to cool completely.

3. Place the bread crumbs on an ungreased baking sheet. Bake at 400° for 2-3 minutes or until toasted. Cool. In a large bowl, beat cream cheese and butter until fluffy. Add confectioners' sugar and vanilla; beat until smooth. Frost cupcakes. Garnish with toasted bread crumbs and jalapeno slices. Store in the refrigerator.

NOTE *Wear disposable gloves when cutting hot peppers; the oils can burn skin. Avoid touching your face.*

HERBED BEER-CAN CHICKEN

FUDGY S'MORES BROWNIES

I combined the perfect simple summer snack with my favorite brownie recipe to get a treat that's sure to wow at your next tailgate or picnic.

—**JUDY CUNNINGHAM** MAX, ND

PREP: 15 MIN. • **BAKE:** 25 MIN. + COOLING
MAKES: 1 DOZEN

- 1⅓ cups butter, softened
- 2⅔ cups sugar
- 4 large eggs
- 1 tablespoon vanilla extract
- 2 cups all-purpose flour
- 1 cup baking cocoa
- ½ teaspoon salt
- 1 cup Golden Grahams, coarsely crushed
- 1¾ cups miniature marshmallows
- 4 ounces milk chocolate, chopped

1. Preheat oven to 350°. In a large bowl, cream butter and sugar until light and fluffy. Beat in the eggs and vanilla. In a bowl, mix the flour, cocoa and salt; gradually beat into creamed mixture.
2. Spread into a greased 13x9-in. baking pan. Bake 25-30 minutes or until a toothpick inserted into center comes out with moist crumbs (do not overbake).
3. Preheat the broiler. Sprinkle the baked brownies with the cereal and marshmallows; broil 5-6 in. from heat 30-45 seconds or until marshmallows are golden brown. Immediately sprinkle with chopped chocolate. Cover with foil and let stand 5 minutes or until chocolate begins to melt. Remove foil and cool completely in pan on a wire rack. Cut into bars.

HERBED BEER-CAN CHICKEN

Our Fourth of July tradition is to grill chickens that stand up on a can of beer. It might look slightly silly when you are making it, but it's such a fun conversation piece...and you can't beat the tender taste.
—**KAREN BARROS** BRISTOL, RI

PREP: 15 MIN. • **GRILL:** 1¼ HOURS + STANDING
MAKES: 4 SERVINGS

- 2 tablespoons canola oil
- 1 tablespoon minced fresh tarragon or 1 teaspoon dried tarragon
- 1 tablespoon minced fresh basil or 1 teaspoon dried basil
- 2 teaspoons minced fresh parsley
- 1 teaspoon garlic powder
- ½ teaspoon salt
- ¼ teaspoon pepper
- 3 garlic cloves, minced, divided
- 1 broiler/fryer chicken (3 to 4 pounds)
- 1 fresh rosemary sprig
- 1 can (12 ounces) beer

1. In a small bowl, combine the first seven ingredients; stir in half of the minced garlic. Rub mixture over the outside and inside of chicken. Tuck wings under chicken.
2. Prepare grill for indirect heat. Completely cover all sides of an 8- or 9-in. round baking pan with foil. Place a beer-can chicken rack in pan. Remove ⅓ cup beer from can; save for another use. Using a can opener, make additional large holes in top of can. Insert rosemary and remaining garlic into can. Add beer can to rack.
3. Place chicken vertically onto rack. Place pan on grill rack. Grill chicken, covered, over indirect medium heat for 1¼-1½ hours or until a thermometer inserted into thigh reads 180°.
4. Remove pan from grill; tent chicken with foil. Let stand for 15 minutes. Carefully remove chicken from rack.

WALKING TACOS

This chili is perfect on game nights. All the ingredients go right into the chips—no dishes to wash when you get home from the big event!

—BEVERLY MATTHEWS PASCO, WA

PREP: 10 MIN. • **COOK:** 30 MIN.
MAKES: 5 SERVINGS

- 1 **pound ground beef**
- 1 **envelope reduced-sodium chili seasoning mix**
- ¼ **teaspoon pepper**
- 1 **can (10 ounces) diced tomatoes and green chilies**
- 1 **can (15 ounces) Ranch Style beans (pinto beans in seasoned tomato sauce)**
- 5 **packages (1 ounce each) corn chips Toppings: shredded cheddar cheese, sour cream and sliced green onions**

1. In a large skillet, cook the beef over medium heat 6-8 minutes or until no longer pink, breaking into crumbles; drain. Stir in the chili seasoning mix, pepper, tomatoes and beans; bring to a boil. Reduce heat; simmer, uncovered, for 20-25 minutes or until thickened, stirring occasionally.

2. Just before serving, cut open corn chip bags. Add the beef mixture and toppings as desired.

 **CHECK IT TWICE**

Before heading out for the tailgate, make sure you've got the food, the beverages and the following:
- Grilling utensils
- Serving plates or platters
- Plastic wrap or aluminum foil
- Ice
- Trash bags
- Sunblock
- Food thermometer
- Hand sanitizer
- Game tickets

WALKING TACOS

ANTIPASTO PICNIC SALAD

With a tempting blend of meats, veggies and pasta for your tailgate, how can you go wrong? The recipe comes together quickly, serves a crowd and tastes as good at room temperature as it does cold. If you're expecting a smaller group, simply halve the recipe to accommodate the number of guests.

—**MICHELE LARSON** BADEN, PA

PREP: 30 MIN. • **COOK:** 15 MIN.
MAKES: 25 SERVINGS (1 CUP EACH)

- 1 package (16 ounces) medium pasta shells
- 2 jars (16 ounces each) giardiniera
- 1 pound fresh broccoli florets
- ½ pound cubed part-skim mozzarella cheese
- ½ pound hard salami, cubed
- ½ pound deli ham, cubed
- 2 packages (3½ ounces each) sliced pepperoni, halved
- 1 large green pepper, cut into chunks
- 1 can (6 ounces) pitted ripe olives, drained

DRESSING

- ½ cup olive oil
- ¼ cup red wine vinegar
- 2 tablespoons lemon juice
- 1 teaspoon Italian seasoning
- 1 teaspoon coarsely ground pepper
- ½ teaspoon salt

1. Cook pasta according to package directions. Meanwhile, drain the giardiniera, reserving ¾ cup liquid. In a large bowl, combine the giardiniera, broccoli, mozzarella, salami, ham, pepperoni, green pepper and olives. Drain pasta and rinse in cold water; stir into meat mixture.
2. For dressing, in a small bowl, whisk the oil, vinegar, lemon juice, Italian seasoning, pepper, salt and reserved giardiniera liquid. Pour over salad and toss to coat. Refrigerate until serving.
NOTE *Giardiniera, a pickled vegetable mixture, is available in mild and hot varieties and can be found in the Italian or pickle section of your grocery store.*

SPICY TOUCHDOWN CHILI

SPICY TOUCHDOWN CHILI

For me, football, cool weather and chili just seem to go together. Whether I'm cheering on the local team on a Friday night or enjoying a Saturday afternoon of Oklahoma Sooner football with some friends, I enjoy serving this zesty chili on game day.

—**CHRIS NEAL** QUAPAW, OK

PREP: 30 MIN. • **COOK:** 4 HOURS
MAKES: 12 SERVINGS (3 QUARTS)

- 1 pound ground beef
- 1 pound bulk pork sausage
- 2 cans (16 ounces each) kidney beans, rinsed and drained
- 2 cans (15 ounces each) pinto beans, rinsed and drained
- 2 cans (10 ounces each) diced tomatoes with mild green chilies, undrained
- 1 can (14½ ounces) diced tomatoes with onions, undrained
- 1 can (12 ounces) beer
- 6 bacon strips, cooked and crumbled
- 1 small onion, chopped
- ¼ cup chili powder
- ¼ cup chopped pickled jalapeno slices
- 2 teaspoons ground cumin
- 2 garlic cloves, minced
- 1 teaspoon dried basil
- ¾ teaspoon cayenne pepper

1. In a large skillet, cook beef over medium heat 6-8 minutes or until no longer pink, breaking into crumbles; drain. Transfer to a 6-qt. slow cooker. Repeat with sausage.
2. Stir in remaining ingredients. Cook, covered, on low 4-5 hours.

SAUSAGE BREAD SANDWICHES

I make these sandwiches in my spare time and freeze them so they're ready when needed, like when we tailgate before Kansas State football games.

—**DONNA ROBERTS** MANHATTAN, KS

PREP: 30 MIN. • **BAKE:** 20 MIN.
MAKES: 4 SANDWICH LOAVES (3 PIECES EACH)

- 1 **package (16 ounces) hot roll mix**
- 2 **pounds reduced-fat bulk pork sausage**
- 2 **tablespoons dried parsley flakes**
- 2 **teaspoons garlic powder**
- 1 **teaspoon onion powder**
- ½ **teaspoon dried oregano**
- 2 **cups (8 ounces) shredded part-skim mozzarella cheese**
- ½ **cup grated Parmesan cheese**
- 1 **large egg**
- 1 **tablespoon water**

1. Preheat oven to 350°. Prepare the roll mix dough according to package directions.

2. Meanwhile, in a large skillet, cook sausage over medium heat 8-10 minutes or until no longer pink, breaking into crumbles; drain. Stir in seasonings.

3. Divide dough into four portions. On a lightly floured surface, roll each into a 14x8-in. rectangle. Top each with 1¼ cups sausage mixture to within 1 in. of edges; sprinkle with ½ cup mozzarella cheese and 2 tablespoons Parmesan cheese. Roll up jelly-roll style, starting with a long side; pinch seams and ends to seal.

4. Transfer to greased baking sheets, seam side down. In a small bowl, whisk egg with water; brush over loaves. Bake 20-25 minutes or until golden brown and heated through. Cool 5 minutes before slicing.

FREEZE OPTION *Cool cooked sandwiches 1 hour on wire racks. Cut each sandwich into thirds; wrap each securely in foil. Freeze until serving. To reheat in the oven, place wrapped frozen sandwiches on a baking sheet. Heat in a preheated 375° oven for 20-25 minutes or until heated through.*

SAUSAGE BREAD SANDWICHES

FAST FIX
BUFFALO WING MUNCH MIX

I jazz up party mix with spicy hot and cool ranch flavors. Serve this mix tableside with hot wings and celery sticks.

—**KERI THOMPSON** PLEASANT HILL, IA

START TO FINISH: 20 MIN.
MAKES: 3 QUARTS

- 4 **cups Corn Chex**
- 4 **cups Wheat Chex**
- 2 **cups cheddar-flavored snack crackers**
- 2 **cups potato sticks**
- 6 **tablespoons butter, melted**
- 2 **tablespoons hot pepper sauce**
- 1 **tablespoon Worcestershire sauce**
- 1 **envelope ranch salad dressing mix**
- ⅛ **teaspoon cayenne pepper**

1. In a large bowl, combine the cereals, crackers and potato sticks. Combine the butter, hot pepper sauce and Worcestershire sauce. Drizzle over the cereal mixture and toss to coat. Sprinkle with salad dressing mix and cayenne; toss to coat.

2. Microwave half of mixture on high for 2 minutes, stirring once. Spread onto waxed paper to cool. Repeat. Store in an airtight container.
NOTE *This recipe was tested in a 1,100-watt microwave.*

⑤ INGREDIENTS

ROOT BEER PULLED PORK SANDWICHES

My sister shared this incredibly easy recipe with me. My husband is a huge fan of pulled pork sandwiches, and this one works well for potlucks or family picnics.
—**CAROLYN PALM** WALTON, NY

PREP: 20 MIN. • **COOK:** 8½ HOURS
MAKES: 12 SERVINGS

- 1 **boneless pork shoulder butt roast (3 to 4 pounds)**
- 1 **can (12 ounces) root beer or cola**
- 1 **bottle (18 ounces) barbecue sauce**
- 12 **kaiser rolls, split**

1. Place roast in a 4- or 5-qt. slow cooker. Add root beer; cook, covered, on low 8-10 hours or until meat is tender.
2. Remove roast; cool slightly. Discard cooking juices. Shred pork with two forks; return to slow cooker. Stir in barbecue sauce. Cook, covered, until heated through, about 30 minutes. Serve on rolls.

FREEZE OPTION *Freeze cooled meat mixture in freezer containers. To use, partially thaw in refrigerator overnight. Heat through in a saucepan, stirring occasionally and adding a little water if necessary.*

ROOT BEER PULLED PORK SANDWICHES

TEX-MEX CHILI WITH A CINCINNATI TWIST

My husband grew up in Cincinnati, where chili is served over spaghetti, and I grew up in the South. This family-pleaser is a mingling of both worlds...and a great way to make a meal go further.

—STEPHANIE RABBITT-SCHAPP
CINCINNATI, OH

PREP: 35 MIN. • **COOK:** 6 HOURS
MAKES: 7 SERVINGS

- 1 **pound ground beef**
- 1 **cup chopped sweet onion**
- ¼ **cup chili powder**
- 2 **tablespoons ground cumin**
- 2 **teaspoons baking cocoa**
- 1½ **teaspoons ground cinnamon**
- ¾ **teaspoon cayenne pepper**
- ½ **teaspoon salt**
- 1 **can (16 ounces) chili beans, undrained**
- 1 **can (16 ounces) kidney beans, rinsed and drained**
- 1 **can (14½ ounces) diced tomatoes, undrained**
- 1 **can (8 ounces) tomato sauce**
- 1 **medium tomato, chopped**
- 1 **jalapeno pepper, seeded and chopped**
  Hot cooked spaghetti
  Optional toppings: oyster crackers, hot pepper sauce, chopped sweet onion and shredded cheddar cheese

1. In a large skillet, cook the beef and onion over medium heat until meat is no longer pink; drain. Stir in the chili powder, cumin, cocoa, cinnamon, cayenne and salt.
2. Transfer to a 4- or 5-qt. slow cooker. Stir in the chili beans, kidney beans, diced tomatoes, tomato sauce, tomato and jalapeno.
3. Cover and cook on low for 6-8 hours or until heated through. Serve over spaghetti. Garnish with toppings of your choice.
NOTE *Wear disposable gloves when cutting hot peppers; the oils can burn skin. Avoid touching your face.*

CHILI CONEY DOGS

CHILI CONEY DOGS

Everyone in our family, from youngest kids to oldest adults, loves these dogs. They're so easy to throw together and heat up nicely in the slow cooker.

—MICHELE HARRIS VICKSBURG, MI

PREP: 20 MIN. • **COOK:** 4 HOURS
MAKES: 8 SERVINGS

- 1 **pound lean ground beef (90% lean)**
- 1 **can (15 ounces) tomato sauce**
- ½ **cup water**
- 2 **tablespoons Worcestershire sauce**
- 1 **tablespoon dried minced onion**
- ½ **teaspoon garlic powder**
- ½ **teaspoon ground mustard**
- ½ **teaspoon chili powder**
- ½ **teaspoon pepper**
  Dash cayenne pepper
- 8 **hot dogs**
- 8 **hot dog buns, split**
  Optional toppings: shredded cheddar cheese, relish and chopped onion

1. In a large skillet, cook beef over medium heat 6-8 minutes or until no longer pink, breaking into crumbles; drain. Stir in the tomato sauce, water, Worcestershire sauce, onion and seasonings.
2. Place hot dogs in a 3-qt. slow cooker; top with beef mixture. Cook, covered, on low for 4-5 hours or until heated through. Serve on buns with toppings as desired.

⑤INGREDIENTS
THIRST-QUENCHING LIMEADE

Here is a sensational drink to quench the thirst on hot summer days. The combination of lemon and lime is perfect!

—*TASTE OF HOME* TEST KITCHEN

PREP: 20 MIN. + CHILLING
MAKES: 7 SERVINGS (1¾ QUARTS)

- 5½ **cups water, divided**
- 1¼ **cups sugar**
- ¾ **cup lemon juice (about 4 lemons)**
- ¾ **cup lime juice (about 4 limes)**
- 1 **teaspoon grated lemon peel**
- 1 **teaspoon grated lime peel**
  Ice cubes

1. In a large saucepan, bring 1½ cups water and sugar to a boil. Reduce heat; simmer, uncovered, 10 minutes. Cool to room temperature.
2. Transfer to a 2-qt. pitcher. Stir in juices and peels. Cover and refrigerate at least 1 hour. Stir in remaining water. Serve over ice.

HAM-CHEDDAR
CHEESE BALL

BEER DIP

Ranch dressing mix boosts the flavor of this cheesy, fast-to-fix dip. I take it to game-day parties along with a bag of pretzels, and I'm always asked for the recipe. Best of all, it's ready in minutes!
—**MICHELLE LONG** NEW CASTLE, CO

START TO FINISH: 5 MIN.
MAKES: 3½ CUPS

- 2 **packages (8 ounces each) cream cheese, softened**
- ⅓ **cup beer or nonalcoholic beer**
- 1 **envelope ranch salad dressing mix**
- 2 **cups (8 ounces) shredded cheddar cheese**
  Pretzels

In a large bowl, beat the cream cheese, beer and dressing mix until smooth. Stir in cheddar cheese. Serve with pretzels.

⑤ INGREDIENTS **FAST FIX** ▶

CREAMY HOT CHOCOLATE

You need just a few basic ingredients to stir up this spirit-warming sipper. The comforting beverage is smooth and not too sweet, making it just right for chilly autumn days.
—**FLO SNODDERLY** NORTH VERNON, IN

START TO FINISH: 15 MIN.
MAKES: 8 SERVINGS

- ½ **cup baking cocoa**
- 1 **can (14 ounces) sweetened condensed milk**
- ⅛ **teaspoon salt**
- 6½ **cups water**
- 1½ **teaspoons vanilla extract**
  Miniature marshmallows, optional

In a large saucepan, combine the cocoa, milk and salt. Cook and stir over medium heat. Gradually add water; cook and stir until heated through. Stir in the vanilla. Top each serving with marshmallows if desired.

HAM-CHEDDAR CHEESE BALL

This ham and cheese ball studded with pecans is a year-round favorite at our house and always gets rave reviews. Present it with assorted crackers.
—**MICHELE MOORE** MOORESVILLE, IN

PREP: 15 MIN. + CHILLING
MAKES: 4 CUPS

- ½ **pound thinly sliced deli ham**
- ½ **medium onion, cut into wedges**
- 2 **cups (8 ounces) finely shredded cheddar cheese**
- 2 **packages (8 ounces each) cream cheese, cubed**
- 1 **cup chopped pecans**
- 1 **slice Swiss cheese**
  Assorted crackers

1. Place the ham and onion in a food processor; pulse until finely chopped. Add the cheddar cheese; pulse until blended. Add the cream cheese; process until smooth.

2. Shape the cheese mixture into a football; press pecans into cheese mixture. Wrap ball in plastic wrap; refrigerate at least 1 hour.

3. Cut Swiss cheese into strips; arrange over top for laces. Serve with crackers.

CARAMEL NUT BARS

No one can resist these chewy caramel and chocolate bars with a delightful oat crust and topping. They make a tempting dessert or a special snack anytime. These rich bars are perfect for a tailgate, since a little goes a long way and they travel well.

—PATRICIA HILLS SOUTH DAYTON, NY

PREP: 20 MIN. + CHILLING
BAKE: 20 MIN. • **MAKES:** 3 DOZEN

- 1 **cup quick-cooking oats**
- 1 **cup packed brown sugar**
- 1 **cup all-purpose flour**
- ¾ **cup butter, melted**
- ½ **teaspoon baking soda**
- ¼ **teaspoon salt**
- 1 **package (14 ounces) caramels**
- ⅓ **cup milk**
- 1 **cup (6 ounces) semisweet chocolate chips**
- ½ **cup chopped walnuts**

1. In a large bowl, combine the first six ingredients until crumbly; sprinkle 1 cup into a greased 13x9-in. baking pan (do not press).

2. Bake at 350° for 10 minutes. In a small heavy saucepan, cook and stir caramels and milk until the caramels are melted.

3. Pour over crust. Top with chocolate chips and nuts. Sprinkle with the remaining oat mixture. Bake at 350° for 10 minutes. Cool on a wire rack. Refrigerate until set.

CARAMEL
NUT BARS

⑤ INGREDIENTS
DUTCH OVEN
BACON & EGGS

Have an early morning get-together?
Try this hearty meal-in-one! The heat
concentrated on the bottom of the
Dutch oven turns the potatoes into a nice
brown, crispy crust. Folks can just help
themselves right from the grill!
—**MARY BURRIS** OKEECHOBEE, FL

PREP: 40 MIN. • **COOK:** 25 MIN.
MAKES: 8 SERVINGS

- 1 **pound bacon strips, chopped**
- 1 **package (20 ounces) refrigerated
  O'Brien hash brown potatoes**
- 8 **large eggs**
- ½ **cup half-and-half cream**
- ½ **to 1 teaspoon hot pepper sauce,
  optional**
- 2 **cups (8 ounces) shredded cheddar-
  Monterey Jack cheese**

1. Prepare a grill for medium-high
heat, using 32-36 charcoal briquettes or
large wood chips.
2. In a 10-in. Dutch oven, cook bacon
over the grill until crisp, stirring
occasionally. Remove with a slotted
spoon; drain on paper towels. Discard
drippings, reserving 2 tablespoons
in pan.
3. Carefully press potatoes onto
bottom and 1 in. up sides of Dutch oven.
In a small bowl, whisk eggs, cream and,
if desired, pepper sauce until blended.
Pour over potatoes; sprinkle with the
cooked bacon and cheese.
4. Cover Dutch oven. When briquettes
or wood chips are covered with white
ash, place Dutch oven directly on top of
16-18 briquettes. Using long-handled
tongs, place 16-18 briquettes on top of
the cover.
5. Cook 20-25 minutes or until eggs are
completely set and cheese is melted. To
check for doneness, use tongs to lift
cover carefully. If necessary, cook
5 minutes longer.

STEAK AND SHRIMP
KABOBS

You'll make any get-together special with
these attractive kabobs. Cubes of
marinated steak are skewered with
shrimp, mushrooms, tomatoes, green
peppers and onions, then grilled. For
tailgates, I assemble the kabobs at home
and carry them in a large container.
—**KAREN MERGENER** ST. CROIX, MN

PREP: 20 MIN. + MARINATING • **GRILL:** 15 MIN.
MAKES: 6-8 SERVINGS

- 1 **cup teriyaki sauce**
- 1 **can (6 ounces) pineapple juice**
- ½ **cup packed brown sugar**
- 6 **garlic cloves, minced**
- ¼ **teaspoon Worcestershire sauce**
- ⅛ **teaspoon pepper**
- 1 **pound beef top sirloin steak, cut
  into 1-inch cubes**
- 1 **pound uncooked large shrimp,
  peeled and deveined**
- 1 **pound whole fresh mushrooms**
- 2 **large green peppers, cut into 1-inch
  pieces**
- 2 **medium onions, halved and
  quartered**
- 1 **pint cherry tomatoes**
- 1½ **teaspoons cornstarch**

1. In a large bowl, combine the first six
ingredients. Pour half of the marinade
into a large resealable plastic bag; add
the beef. Seal bag and turn to coat;
refrigerate for 8 hours or overnight,
turning occasionally. Cover and
refrigerate remaining marinade.
2. Drain and discard marinade in bag.
On metal or soaked wooden skewers,
alternately thread the beef, shrimp,
mushrooms, green peppers, onions and
tomatoes; set aside. In a small saucepan,
combine cornstarch and reserved
marinade until smooth. Bring to a boil;
cook and stir for 1-2 minutes or until
sauce is thickened.
3. Moisten a paper towel with cooking
oil; using long-handled tongs, rub it on
the grill rack to coat lightly. Prepare
grill for indirect heat, using a drip pan.

STEAK AND SHRIMP KABOBS

Place kabobs over drip pan and grill,
covered, over indirect medium heat for
6 minutes, turning once. Baste with
sauce. Continue turning and basting for
8-10 minutes or until shrimp turn pink
and beef reaches desired doneness.

⚔ GRILL SKILL

We use a grill basket over the open
fire to grill kabobs with slices of
hot dog, ham, mushrooms and
pineapple. Then we slide the food off
the skewer and onto a bun. Topped
with warm cheese sauce, this makes
a tasty filling for simple sandwiches.
They're perfect when tailgating.
RENEE S. NEWMANSTOWN, PA

SUMMERTIME TEA

1 tablespoon finely chopped onion
1 teaspoon prepared mustard
8 slices American cheese
8 hot dog buns, split
8 hot dogs

In a small bowl, combine the first four ingredients. Place a slice of cheese on the bottom half of each bun. Slice hot dogs in half lengthwise; place two halves on each bun. Spoon 1 tablespoon of sauce over each hot dog. Replace top of bun and wrap each sandwich in foil. Grill, uncovered, over medium heat, turning often, for 10-15 minutes.

⑤INGREDIENTS

SPIKED LEMONADE

Rum gives tropical flair to this tasty adult lemonade. For a variation, substitute vodka for the rum.
—*TASTE OF HOME* TEST KITCHEN

PREP: 15 MIN. + CHILLING
MAKES: 8 SERVINGS (ABOUT 2 QUARTS)

2¼ cups sugar
5 cups water, divided
1 tablespoon grated lemon peel
1¾ cups lemon juice
1 cup light rum or vodka
6 to 8 cups ice cubes
GARNISH
Lemon slices

1. In a large saucepan, combine the sugar, 1 cup water and lemon peel. Cook and stir over medium heat until sugar is dissolved, about 4 minutes. Remove from the heat. Stir in lemon juice and the remaining water. Pour into a 2-qt. pitcher; refrigerate until chilled.
2. Stir in rum. For each serving, place ¾ to 1 cup ice in a Collins or highball glass. Pour lemonade mixture into glass. Garnish with lemon slices as desired.

SUMMERTIME TEA

You can't have a summer gathering around here without this sweet tea to cool you down. It's wonderful for sipping while basking by the pool.
—**ANGELA LIVELY** CONROE, TX

PREP: 15 MIN. + CHILLING
MAKES: 18 SERVINGS (¾ CUP EACH)

14 cups water, divided
6 black tea bags
1½ cups sugar
¾ cup thawed orange juice concentrate
¾ cup thawed lemonade concentrate
1 cup tequila, optional
Fresh mint leaves and lemon or lime slices, optional

1. In a large saucepan, bring 4 cups water to a boil. Remove from the heat; add tea bags. Cover and steep for 3-5 minutes. Discard tea bags.
2. Stir in the sugar, concentrates and remaining water. Add tequila if desired. Refrigerate until chilled. Garnish with mint and lemon if desired.

FAST FIX

CARRY-ALONG HOT DOGS

These versatile dogs travel well and grill up in minutes!
—**LORRAINE PRIEBE** NOONAN, ND

START TO FINISH: 20 MIN.
MAKES: 8 SERVINGS

⅓ cup ketchup
2 tablespoons sweet pickle relish

⑤ INGREDIENTS FAST FIX ▶

PEANUT BUTTER CEREAL TREATS

Kids will love these colorful, crunchy bars! They're a fun twist on the traditional marshmallow crispy treats, and because the recipe is so easy, older kids can whip up a batch on their own. The snacks travel and keep well, too.
—**CHRISTIE PORTER** SHIPSHEWANA, IN

START TO FINISH: 30 MIN.
MAKES: 2 DOZEN

- 30 **large marshmallows**
- 3 **tablespoons butter**
- 1 **tablespoon peanut butter**
- 6 **cups Peanut Butter Cap'n Crunch**
- 1½ **cups milk chocolate M&M's**

1. In a large saucepan, combine the marshmallows, butter and peanut butter. Cook and stir over medium-low heat until melted. Remove from the heat. Stir in the cereal and M&M's.
2. Pat into a 13x9-in. pan coated with cooking spray. Cool. Cut into bars.

⑤ INGREDIENTS FAST FIX ▶

BEER MARGARITAS

There's nothing more refreshing than this cool combination of two popular drinks: beer and lime margaritas.
—*TASTE OF HOME* TEST KITCHEN

START TO FINISH: 10 MIN.
MAKES: 4 SERVINGS

- ¾ **cup thawed limeade concentrate**
- 1 **bottle (12 ounces) beer, chilled**
- ¾ **cup vodka**
- ¾ **cup water**
  Ice cubes, optional
GARNISH
  Lime slices

In a pitcher, combine the limeade concentrate, beer, vodka and water. Serve over ice if desired in pilsner or highball glasses. Garnish as desired.
NOTE *This recipe was tested with Corona beer.*

BUFFALO CHICKEN DEVILED EGGS

BUFFALO CHICKEN DEVILED EGGS

My daughter Sara loves spicy Buffalo chicken and deviled eggs, so I combined the two. Make and chill a day before the tailgate so the flavors mingle.
—**ROBIN SPIRES** TAMPA, FL

PREP: 25 MIN. + CHILLING
MAKES: 2 DOZEN

- 12 **hard-cooked large eggs**
- ½ **cup crumbled blue cheese, divided**
- 2 **celery ribs, finely chopped**
- ½ **cup mayonnaise**
- ¼ **cup finely chopped cooked chicken breast**
- 3 **tablespoons minced fresh parsley**
- 1 **tablespoon Buffalo wing sauce or 1 teaspoon hot pepper sauce**
- ⅛ **teaspoon pepper**
  Additional Buffalo wing or hot pepper sauce, optional

1. Cut eggs lengthwise in half. Remove yolks, reserving whites. In a bowl, mash yolks and ¼ cup cheese. Stir in celery, mayonnaise, chicken, parsley, wing sauce and pepper.
2. Spoon into egg whites. Refrigerate, covered, at least 1 hour before serving. To serve, sprinkle tops with remaining cheese and, if desired, drizzle with additional wing sauce.

GENERAL RECIPE INDEX

This handy index lists recipes by category and major ingredient so you can easily find the grilled greats that suit your needs.

DESSERTS (also see Cobblers & Crisps)

DIPS & SPREADS

EGGPLANT

FAST FIX ENTREES
BURGERS, BRATS & HOT DOGS

MAIN DISHES

FISH (also see Seafood)
BURGERS

MAIN DISHES

ALPHABETICAL RECIPE INDEX